24 HOURS IN CHARLOTTESVILLE

24 HOURS IN CHARLOTTESVILLE

AN
ORAL HISTORY
OF
THE STAND AGAINST
WHITE
SUPREMACY

NORA NEUS

BEACON PRESS, BOSTON

BEACON PRESS
Boston, Massachusetts
www.beacon.org

Beacon Press books
are published under the auspices of
the Unitarian Universalist Association of Congregations.

Printed in the United States of America
26 25 24 23   8 7 6 5 4 3 2 1

This book is printed on acid-free paper that meets the uncoated paper
ANSI/NISO specifications for permanence as revised in 1992.
Text design by BookMatters

All maps © Nat Case, INCase, LLC.
Detailed maps are derived from those in Spencer, Hawes, *Summer of Hate:
Charlottesville, USA* © 2018 by the Rector and Visitors of the University
of Virginia. Reprinted by permission of the University of Virginia Press.

Library of Congress Cataloguing-in-Publication Data is available for
this title.

Hardcover ISBN: 978-0-8070-1192-8
E-book ISBN: 978-0-8070-1194-2
Audiobook ISBN: 978-0-8070-1289-5

For Heather Heyer

"If you're not outraged, you're not paying attention."
  —*Heather Heyer's Facebook post*

"If you are neutral in situations of injustice,
you have chosen the side of the oppressor."
  —*Desmond Tutu*

CONTENT WARNING

This book includes graphic descriptions of white supremacist violence, including blood, injury, and death. It also includes incidents of racism, antisemitism, homophobia, transphobia, and Nazi imagery and language.

CONTENTS

MAPS OF CHARLOTTESVILLE

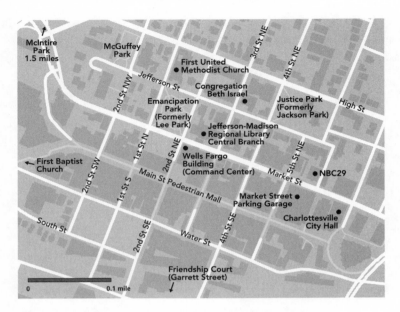

Downtown Charlottesville, Virginia, as of Summer 2017

© 2022 Nat Case. Based on maps in *Summer of Hate* by Hawes Spencer
(University of Virginia Press, 2018).

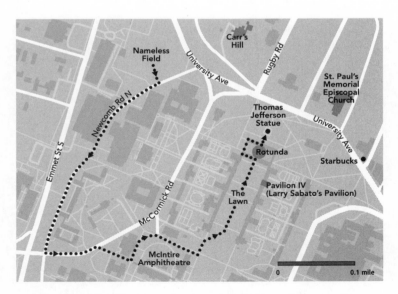

**Torch march path at the University of Virginia and surrounding
areas, August 11, 2017**

© 2022 Nat Case. Based on maps in *Summer of Hate* by Hawes Spencer
(University of Virginia Press, 2018).

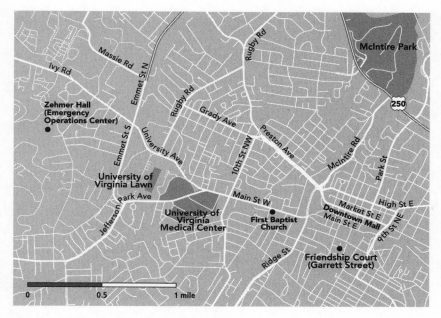

Charlottesville, Virginia, as of Summer 2017
© 2022 Nat Case.

AUTHOR'S NOTE

It was standard hotel fare: lukewarm eggs made from powder, tiny boxes of sugary cereal, and a dirty waffle maker dripping batter onto a Styrofoam plate underneath.

I wasn't hungry but I knew I had to eat. That was the first piece of advice I'd been given when starting as a producer at CNN: During breaking news, eat when you can because you don't know when you'll next have access to food. So before 8 a.m. on August 13, 2017, I swung by the breakfast nook at the Hampton Inn in Charlottesville, Virginia, before embarking on what I knew would be a 15-hour-plus day producing breaking news for Anderson Cooper.

It was the morning after the Unite the Right rally that had taken place in downtown Charlottesville. Hundreds of white supremacists and neo-Nazis had rioted, killing one woman and gravely injuring scores more. Many of the demonstrators were members of avowed white nationalist groups, including Vanguard America (an antecedent of Patriot Front), the Traditionalist Worker Party, the League of the South, and the Ku Klux Klan. They had come in from 35 states and from Canada. That morning, the local community woke up in what felt like a stunned silence, the reality of what had happened crashing back into our collective consciousness. I'd been a part of this community for years and had just moved to New York one month earlier, leaving my job as a local news reporter and fill-in anchor for a new gig at CNN. I had happened to return to Charlottesville that weekend, coincidentally, to pick up the last of my boxes from my old apartment. Now, I was in a war zone.

It was the waffle maker that caught my eye: Standing there were two white men, politely discussing who would pour their batter first. Probably in their thirties, both clean-shaven with close-cropped haircuts, they each respectfully deferred to the other.

One was a uniformed Virginia State Police officer; the other appeared to be a white nationalist, down to the khaki pants and white polo shirt, even balancing a homemade plastic shield on top of his rolling suitcase—the exact type of shield the nation had watched demonstrators use to pummel counterprotesters the day before.

And they were polite. Gracious, even. To each other, that is.

They made their waffles, I grabbed a yogurt cup, and then about 10 minutes later the three of us each made our way to the parking lot just as the sun was coming up. The state trooper got into his squad car and drove away. The other man heaved his bag and shield over the open back of his red Jeep and then hopped inside. By the time I'd started my rental car and looked back, he was gone too.

I thought a lot about those men in the weeks, and then months, and then years that followed. Their blasé interaction belied the deep trauma that a horrified community was just beginning to come to terms with. I watched, shell-shocked and nauseous, while they acted as if the previous day had never happened.

I have since wondered if this was one of the white nationalists later arrested by police. Could his arrest have even been at the hands of that officer at the waffle maker? Or, more likely, did he just melt seamlessly back into his life with few to no consequences?

Then, last year, I had a new question: Could that man have stormed the Capitol on January 6, 2021?

By the time we found ourselves together in that Hampton Inn breakfast nook, a woman had already been killed by a white nationalist. Two Virginia State Police officers were dead. Scores of people had already been injured; some were waking up in the hospital. The damage was all around us. But that police officer and that white nationalist peacefully shared the waffle maker and then went their separate ways. And the stage was set for the continued trauma to come.

History often has a sense of inevitability. We tell stories of the past with the benefit of hindsight; we already know what is going to happen. However, history-in-the-making takes us by surprise. In the cloud of adrenaline and in-the-moment myopia, it can be hard to tell what is about to happen next.

That was not the case in Charlottesville. Many knew what was coming—people of color, especially.

Activists, progressive clergy, and private citizens repeatedly warned local lawmakers, police, and University of Virginia leadership that extreme violence would break out when the neo-Nazis and white nationalists came to town that August. They were largely ignored.

The cost of this refusal to listen, and the resulting lack of police response, was human life. And yet we have seen this same stonewalling, whether willful or unwitting, play out over and over again in the years since, as the white supremacist threat only increased in America.

The story of August 11 and 12, 2017, in Charlottesville is the story of activists explicitly sounding the alarm on a specific, credible threat and the failure of city leadership and law enforcement to protect their citizens.

Much ink has been spilled in trying to make sense of what happened in Charlottesville during those 24 hours, from about 7 p.m. on Friday, August 11, until about 7 p.m. on Saturday, August 12. But the harrowing, traumatic events of that day have also been largely overshadowed by what came next: President Donald Trump declaring that there were "very fine people on both sides," and a rise—or at least an increase in visibility—of white supremacy in the United States.

The voices leading our national conversation about what happened on August 11 and 12 have largely been outsiders: people who were not in Charlottesville that day, who were not the ones "staring Satan in the eyes," in the words of Don Gathers, a cofounder of Charlottesville Black Lives Matter.

This book is different.

This book tells the story of those 24 hours in Charlottesville in the voices of the survivors, activists, politicians, and journalists who were actually there. The bulk of the words you're about to read were collected in dozens of individual, original interviews conducted specifically for this project and totaling over 150 hours of audio recordings. I granted anonymity for those who feared violent retaliation for speaking out, identifying them by initials only. Best practice in oral history work is to compensate the "narrators," or folks being interviewed, both for their time and for the emotional labor of telling their stories. Too often, projects like these rely on unpaid labor from local activists—especially Black women—for their success. For this project, every survivor and activist was offered compensation for their time; some chose to donate that money to charities. Politicians were not compensated. (I should note that while compensation is best practice in oral history interviews, it is *not* standard in journalism and I have never offered compensation for an interview or information in my role as a CNN producer.) Not everyone I approached for this project agreed to be interviewed; some declined to comment or did not respond to repeated interview requests. However, I did request an interview with any public figure mentioned by name in this book. Other sources quoted in this book include court testimony, government reports, and contemporaneous news coverage and social media posts.

One category of voices is very intentionally missing: those of white nationalists and neo-Nazis. I have actively chosen not to interview any Unite the Right participants or sympathizers. They, unfortunately, already have a platform. In some places, I have included words spoken by the rioters that day as recorded in audio or video, or as remembered by witnesses, in order to provide deeper clarity about what happened. In those cases, I contextualize the comments and provide rebuttals on the page.

A further note on language: Many descriptors exist for the participants of Unite the Right. They include, but are not limited to, *white nationalist, white supremacist, neo-Nazi, alt-right supporter*, and *white rights activist*. Many scholars and activists have dedicated extensive time to studying the importance of accurate language to describe these abhorrent individuals—a critical discussion but one beyond the scope of this work. In most cases, I have kept the language that each individual used themselves.

The quotes you'll find in this book have been condensed and edited for clarity and flow. I've taken out many *ums, likes,* and *you knows,* and in some cases corrected location names for accuracy. (For example, there are many parks involved in this story. More than one person mixed up the names of parks, but after I queried, they clarified which park they meant.) One additional note on park names: As part of the reconciliation efforts in spring 2017, Lee Park was renamed Emancipation Park and Jackson Park was renamed Justice Park. I have used the official reconciliation names that were current on August 11 and 12, 2017. Those names were later changed again in 2018 to Market Street Park and Court Square Park, which stand currently. For ease of reading and historical accuracy, I have at times edited quotations to correct verb tenses or make clearer to what the subject is referring. Finally, the names, titles, and occupations of the interviewees are recorded as they were on August 12, 2017.

This project also benefited from the labor of an incredibly talented oral historian, Noor Alzamami, who conducted nine interviews. Research assistant Arya Royal also contributed heavily to the project. Any mistakes that remain, of course, are my own responsibility.

These are the voices of Charlottesville, telling their own story.

CAST OF CHARACTERS

Note: Names and titles reflect those as of August 12, 2017.

Activists

Chelsea Alvarado, counterprotester

Wednesday Bowie, counterprotester

Bill Burke, counterprotester

Kristin Clarens, lawyer and activist

Lisa Draine, local activist

I.B.F., local activist

Jeff Fogel, lawyer and activist

Don Gathers, cofounder, Charlottesville Black Lives Matter

Brennan Gilmore, counterprotester and former US Foreign Service
Officer

Emily Gorcenski, local activist

DeAndre Harris, counterprotester

S.L., counterprotester

Corey Long, counterprotester

Sabr Lyon, counterprotester

Marcus Martin, counterprotester

Rosia Parker, local activist

Tom Perriello, counterprotester and former US congressman

Star Peterson, local activist and street medic

L.Q., counterprotester and car attack survivor

Elizabeth Shillue, Quaker activist

David Straughn, local activist and car attack survivor
Katrina Turner, local activist and car attack survivor
Melissa Wender, street medic
Constance Paige Young, counterprotester

People of Faith

Rev. Brenda Brown-Grooms, pastor, New Beginnings Christian
  Community
Brittany "Smash" Caine-Conley, cofounder, Congregate C'ville
Michael Cheuk, secretary, Charlottesville Clergy Collective
David Garth, retired pastor
Rabbi Tom Gutherz, Congregation Beth Israel
Rev. Dr. Cornel West, civil rights leader, pastor, and writer
Rev. Seth Wispelwey, pastor and cofounder, Congregate C'ville
Rev. Phil Woodson, associate pastor, First United Methodist Church
Alan Zimmerman, president, Congregation Beth Israel

Journalists

David Foky, news director, NBC29
Henry Graff, anchor and reporter, NBC29
Nicole Hemmer, journalist
Kasey Hott, anchor, NBC29
Ryan Kelly, photojournalist
Chuck Modiano, reporter
Zach Roberts, photojournalist
Chris Suarez, reporter, Charlottesville *Daily Progress*
A. C. Thompson, journalist
Zack Wajsgras, freelance photographer
Allison Wrabel, reporter, Charlottesville *Daily Progress*

University of Virginia Faculty

Emily Blout, UVa professor and Mayor Mike Signer's wife
Aniko Bodroghkozy, UVa professor and Congregation Beth Israel member
Allen Groves, UVa dean of students
Walt Heinecke, UVa professor and activist

Willis Jenkins, UVa professor

Larry Sabato, UVa professor, political pundit, and pavilion resident on the Lawn

Jalane Schmidt, UVa professor and cofounder, Charlottesville Black Lives Matter

Teresa Sullivan, UVa president

Lisa Woolfork, UVa professor and member of Charlottesville Black Lives Matter

Students

Diane D'Costa, fourth-year UVa student and Lawn resident

Tim Dodson, managing editor, *Cavalier Daily* (student newspaper)

Alexis Gravely, senior associate news editor, *Cavalier Daily*

Kendall King, third-year UVa student

Natalie Romero, second-year UVa student

Elizabeth Sines, UVa law student

Malcolm Stewart, fourth-year UVa student and senior resident on the Lawn

Devin Willis, second-year UVa student

Government Leaders

Andrew Baxter, Charlottesville fire chief

Wes Bellamy, Charlottesville vice mayor

Terry McAuliffe, Virginia governor

Brian Moran, secretary, Virginia Public Safety and Homeland Security

Mike Signer, Charlottesville mayor

Kristin Szakos, Charlottesville city councilor

Government Documents

Independent Review of the 2017 Protest Events in Charlottesville, Virginia, compiled by attorney Timothy J. Heaphy, known colloquially as the "Heaphy report"

"Virginia's Response to the Unite the Right Rally: After-Action Review," by International Association of Chiefs of Police

Healthcare Workers

Tom Berry, director of emergency management, UVa Medical Center

Beth Mehring, emergency services nurse manager, UVa Medical Center

Alex McGee, chaplain, Sentara Martha Jefferson Hospital

Jane Muir, emergency room nurse, UVa Medical Center

Jody Reyes, incident commander, UVa Medical Center

Community Members

Susan Bro, Heather Heyer's mother

Dr. Andrea Douglas, executive director, Jefferson School African American Heritage Center

Yolunda Harrell, CEO, New Hill Development Corp.

Micah Washington, car attack survivor

Tadrint Washington, car attack survivor

PART 1

WARNING FLARES

CHAPTER 1

"This isn't just a bunch of weird LARPers on some dark corner of the internet."

FRIDAY, AUGUST 11, 2017
CHARLOTTESVILLE, VIRGINIA

CHRIS SUAREZ, REPORTER, CHARLOTTESVILLE *DAILY PROGRESS*: It was like waiting for a natural disaster, like a storm, something you had seen the forecast for days ahead.

ELIZABETH SHILLUE, QUAKER ACTIVIST: We knew this thing was coming, like a tsunami headed our way, and it was hard to think about anything else.

REV. BRENDA BROWN-GROOMS, PASTOR, NEW BEGINNINGS CHRISTIAN COMMUNITY: The air just crackled.

MIKE SIGNER, CHARLOTTESVILLE MAYOR: There were some flyers from the alt-right that were being put on people's windshields, and maybe even people's doors, in the North Downtown neighborhood. And I remember getting a message that said, "They're here."

FLYER: Diversity is a code word for white genocide.

#whitegenocide[1]

CHRIS SUAREZ: It'd been a weird few months before that, going on in May and June.

ALAN ZIMMERMAN, PRESIDENT, CONGREGATION BETH ISRAEL: Through the spring of 2017, there was definitely something happening here in Charlottesville. And as Jews, we knew it involved us, but it wasn't completely clear yet.

INDEPENDENT REVIEW OF THE 2017 PROTEST EVENTS IN CHARLOTTESVILLE, VIRGINIA, compiled by attorney Timothy J. Heaphy, known colloquially as the "Heaphy report": The racially charged events that roiled Charlottesville in the summer of 2017 did not occur in a vacuum. These demonstrations have deep roots in our community and stem from events that occurred much earlier... [and are] rather particularly sad chapters in a lengthy record of social and racial discord in Charlottesville.

Charlottesville is famously the home of America's third president, Thomas Jefferson, his house, Monticello, and the university he designed, the University of Virginia.

TIM DODSON, MANAGING EDITOR, *CAVALIER DAILY*: We see a very white-washed version of American history living here in Virginia and of Thomas Jefferson in particular. We live in the shadow of Monticello. We grow up in the Charlottesville-Albemarle area, learning about Thomas Jefferson as this amazing founder: He is an inventor and he's a president, he's an author and a writer and a scientist. You learn all this stuff about him, but in elementary school we don't talk about Sally Hemings. We don't talk about the horrors of slavery or the repercussions of that, like with the University of Virginia. Yes. It was built by Jefferson, like it was designed by him, but was he the person who actually laid the bricks? No.

Enslaved laborers were the ones who laid those bricks.

STAR PETERSON, LOCAL ACTIVIST AND STREET MEDIC: It is a very small, little university town, obsessed with Thomas Jefferson and not really seeing, *Oh, but remember he was a slave owner?*

WALT HEINECKE, UVA PROFESSOR AND ACTIVIST: Thomas Jefferson was the popularizer of the ideology of white supremacy in the United States as the country formulated.

THOMAS JEFFERSON, in *Notes on the State of Virginia*: ...the blacks, whether originally a distinct race, or made distinct by time and circumstances, are inferior to the whites in the endowments both of body and mind.2

DR. ANDREA DOUGLAS, EXECUTIVE DIRECTOR, JEFFERSON SCHOOL AFRICAN AMERICAN HERITAGE CENTER: Charlottesville is a hugely racist city. It's a Confederate city. When the Articles of Secession occurred, the university raised a Confederate flag—the students did. The Lost Cause Narrative is essentially written in this area, in this community. So as a city, this is as South as you can get. It may not be the deep, Deep South, and so maybe some of the *violent* acts that occur in the Deep South don't occur. The ways in which white supremacy is maintained here, it's not through violence, physical violence. It is maintained through a kind of legal violence. Anytime that you can have an educational system, for instance, where Black children remain in the lower 30 percent of scores over time—that's racism. So anybody who wants to say that Charlottesville is not a racist space doesn't understand what racism actually looks like in its broadest sense. They just believe that if you are racist, you must be violent.

STAR PETERSON: Lots of liberals, great place to eat, lots of really fun, locally owned restaurants. Beautiful, just drop-dead gorgeous, easily the most beautiful place I've ever lived. But then also, yeah, a lot of division, right? A lot of people who are very wealthy, and then people who are getting paid next to nothing to work at the University of Virginia in the cafeterias or cleaning the floors. A lot of the hourly staff refer to the University of Virginia as "the plantation."

REV. BRENDA BROWN-GROOMS: Charlottesville is a very beautiful, ugly city. It's a very beautiful place, physically, with a very ugly underside, of poverty, inequality. And the policies don't line up with who we say we are.

DR. ANDREA DOUGLAS: Charlottesville is a place that is largely based on having a good time: going out into the mountains and enjoying yourself there, or learning a little history and having a little wine. We live in a city where most of the people who *maintain* the city don't even live here. The police don't live here. The fire people don't live here. Schoolteachers don't live here. So it's a very lopsided place in that way, especially when you have so much concentration on someone else's good time.

Marcus Martin, who is Black, lived in nearby Nelson County, but worked and socialized in Charlottesville.

MARCUS MARTIN, COUNTERPROTESTOR: I am the image when they think of a thug. I have that image. I have a beard, I have tattoos. I have a deep raspy voice. I might wear the latest Jordans. I might wear a jersey or white T-shirt. That's what you consider a thug. But I have a gigantic heart—I wouldn't say it's a gold heart, but I have a good heart.

And when you come down there, even if you show a lot of people respect—like as you walk past, *How you doing today, ma'am?* or *How you doing today, sir?*—a lot of people don't even give you a response. Or if it's me holding the door for somebody, don't look at me like I'm *supposed* to hold it for you.

YOLUNDA HARRELL, CEO, NEW HILL DEVELOPMENT CORP.: We can't say that we're this great, award-winning city when it doesn't work for everyone and people that live here are living in two different cities.

For almost 100 years, downtown Charlottesville had centrally featured two statues of Confederate leaders: General Robert E. Lee and General Thomas "Stonewall" Jackson. Discussions about removing the statues had been ongoing for many years, led by city councilors Holly Edwards and Kristin Szakos, but gained new traction in 2016 when high school student Zyahna Bryant started a petition to have the statues removed. The cause was then taken up by Vice Mayor Wes Bellamy, who is Black.

HEAPHY REPORT: This conflict played out in a public discussion facilitated by a Blue Ribbon Commission on Race, Memorials, and Public Spaces, a group convened by City leaders to evaluate the future of the iconic statues.

UVA'S CARTER G. WOODSON CENTER: Like other localities across the nation, Charlottesville erected its Confederate monuments during a period of peak activity from the Ku Klux Klan. In May 1924, Charlottesville unveiled its statue of Robert E. Lee. Leading up to and in the months following the fanfare, the Klan burned crosses and set off explosions in Charlottesville and the surrounding areas. Months later, Charlottesville would unveil its statue to Thomas "Stonewall" Jackson to ever more throngs of expectant guests.[3]

I.B.F., LOCAL ACTIVIST: They were built in the 1920s when there was a growing Black middle class in this area. They are Confederate statues because the subject matter is Confederate, but they weren't from the time. They were really using history to intimidate and subjugate.

JALANE SCHMIDT, UVA PROFESSOR AND COFOUNDER, CHARLOTTESVILLE BLACK LIVES MATTER: During those Blue Ribbon Commission meetings, whenever I would go up to speak, I would just hammer on: *Over half the population was enslaved at the time of the Civil War. Fifty-two percent. Therefore, these statues have been lying to us from the moment they were put in, because we know that Union support was strong here in Charlottesville.* Think about it. Rather than statues telling us that there was some sort of a consensus that these Confederates were heroes, like, no—actually *most* people were glad about Union victory. Most people who lived here were relieved.

HEAPHY REPORT: After receiving recommendations from the Commission, the City Council voted to remove one of them from the park where it stood for years.

Many members of our community embraced the effort to remove the statues, believing them symbols of white supremacy. They began talking not just about the statues, but more systemic issues like race, immigration, and economic opportunity.

The election of President Trump further motivated progressives in Charlottesville. City leaders encouraged this liberal activism. Newly elected Mayor Mike Signer declared Charlottesville the "capital of the resistance" to oppressive policies and systemic inequality.

KRISTIN CLARENS, LAWYER AND ACTIVIST: As soon as we declared our-selves the center of the resistance or whatever, there were some people who wanted to fight against that. When we were talking about becoming a sanctuary city or really signaling to the world that we were this progressive bastion, I think it just invited attention.

TERRY MCAULIFFE, VIRGINIA GOVERNOR: You know, I'd worked hard to rebuild the Virginia economy. And I don't want our cities to be the center of resistance. I'd rather have our cities [be] the center of innovation.

KRISTIN SZAKOS, CHARLOTTESVILLE CITY COUNCILOR: We had declared ourselves a welcoming city. We were committed to our refugees. We were talking a lot about racial justice. We had Vice Mayor Wes Bellamy, who had joined us on council not too long before, who was certainly outspoken and was pulling no punches and talking about the need for racial justice in this town, for a reckoning for the centuries of a lack of racial justice here.

WES BELLAMY, CHARLOTTESVILLE VICE MAYOR: Challenging the status quo or even demanding that Black people be treated as equals was seen as an im-mediate threat. Yes, our community may vote blue and we believed that we were progressive, but our values were deeply rooted in traditional Southern beliefs. Beliefs that meant people of color, specifically Black people, were seen as inferior. I knew that I couldn't stand idle.[4]

KRISTIN SZAKOS: And I think those things, these folks found very threaten-ing and they wanted to stamp it out—or at least frighten it, make it go away.

| **One of those people was a local man named Jason Kessler.**

CHRIS SUAREZ, REPORTER, CHARLOTTESVILLE *DAILY PROGRESS*: Jason, I mean, I talked to him a lot through that year. He was just some local townie, just this random guy, unassuming person. We figured out pretty fast that this guy was a UVa graduate, someone who was in his mid-thirties. It seemed like he didn't have a lot going on for himself. We came to find out that he had self-published some books, like poetry, on Amazon. He just seemed like this local weirdo. He had this sort of political agenda, very strong feelings about what was going on with the Lee statue and upsetting the status quo. A lot of what he was doing was sort of inspired and informed by that very nascent alt-right movement online.

And it was still kind of all under this pretext of *Oh, this is just about the Confederate statues*. But I had picked up on very, very quickly that these are actual neo-Nazi groups and actual white supremacists. And this is actually kind of terrifying.

Kessler began attracting followers.

REV. SETH WISPELWEY, PASTOR AND COFOUNDER, CONGREGATE C'VILLE: The statue was just an excuse. At the same time, the statue represents a lot, and it's very telling that the threat of removing a Jim Crow–era white supremacist participation trophy from a college town that prides itself on being blue was all it took to generate the largest neo-Nazi rally in God knows how many years.

MAY 13, 2017
FESTIVAL OF CULTURES
CHARLOTTESVILLE, VIRGINIA

KRISTIN CLARENS, LAWYER AND ACTIVIST: They came for Mother's Day, that year.

KRISTIN SZAKOS, CHARLOTTESVILLE CITY COUNCILOR: The first thing that made us realize that we were on this national agenda for these white supremacist folks was in May at the multicultural festival, which is this incredible festival that Charlottesville's had for years. All of the immigrants and people of all races and nationalities and languages and colors and sizes—all come together and there's Sufi dancing and African drumming and all the different things that make this community rich and so complex being celebrated in a beautiful way.

EMAIL FROM CITIZEN TO CITY OFFICIALS, 12:49 P.M.: Reports from Festival of the Culture that White Nationalists are converging...Reports are that there are currently over 50. They are holding signs and protesting the imposition of minority stress on whites.

KRISTIN SZAKOS: We were part way through it and we realized that these khaki guys were in the park and they started marching toward us.

The group included white nationalist leader Richard Spencer.

KRISTIN SZAKOS: I hadn't known that they were coming, but folks with the multicultural festival had known. They were ready and they had done some training and they just created this human cordon as those guys were coming down the street. And they just blocked the entrance to the park and said, *You're not coming in.* And they were very nonconfrontational. They were very calm and just held their ground.

Next, the white nationalists marched on then-named Jackson Park. There, a small group of antiracist activists confronted them, attempting to disrupt their speeches and force the demonstration to end. The activists say they asked the general community for help shutting down the demonstration but were left largely unsupported. The activists point to this as an early example of feeling left on their own to confront the white nationalist threat against their city that summer.

Then, night fell.

ALLISON WRABEL, REPORTER, CHARLOTTESVILLE *DAILY PROGRESS*: I was at my boyfriend's house in North Downtown. He worked at the *Daily Progress* with me and lived with other news people. We were going to get some beers and some dinner. We started walking. I distinctly remember not really noticing anything at first, but somebody on the road passes on a bike, and he looked up and he said, *Oh my God.* We looked up, and there was a long line of people with the tiki torches and they were starting to light them.

I remember this feeling, almost like when your stomach drops on a roller coaster. *What is this? Are they going to come attack me for standing here? Are they going to run with these torches and try to light something on fire?*

I remember someone saying, *Is this like a UVa graduation ritual thing or what?*

I was like, *I don't think so.*

HEAPHY REPORT: [They] marched in two single-file lines...carrying lit tiki torches. The group formed into ranks five lines deep in front of the statue of Robert E. Lee, and chanted "blood and soil," "you will not replace us," and "Russia is our friend."

ALLISON WRABEL: I had tweeted something like, *Oh, I've heard it might be Richard Spencer, but we're still working to confirm that*, and he replied with a picture of himself holding a torch.

It really all kind of ended pretty quickly, but everyone was like, *What the heck was this? What the heck just happened?*

WES BELLAMY, CHARLOTTESVILLE VICE MAYOR: Jason Kessler and his minions were not there to defend the statue; they were there to defend their whiteness.[5]

YOLUNDA HARRELL, CEO, NEW HILL DEVELOPMENT CORP.: It was definitely something that spread through the community pretty quickly. When I was a little girl, I was with my stepmother in Montgomery, Alabama, and we accidentally found ourselves in the middle of a KKK march. She turned down the wrong street and I remember her telling us to get down on the floor of the car and we was suddenly surrounded by people in white sheets. I will never ever forget that as a kid and just the fear in her voice. And so for me, it was a flashback to that moment as a kid and thinking how scared we was in that moment. And then thinking, *Wow, like this is what our community is about*. And wondering how much more was going to show itself before it was all said and done.

KRISTIN CLARENS, LAWYER AND ACTIVIST: This isn't just a bunch of weird LARPers on some dark corner of the internet. They have such firmly held convictions and they want violence. And they will show up and they want to scare us. And we've got an environment that's making them feel comfortable doing that here.

TWEET FROM AN ALT-RIGHT MARCHER: This is just the beginning. #saveJacksonAndLee #Charlottesville[6]

FACEBOOK POST FROM A CITIZEN: Where is the loving and nonviolent counter protest?[7]

EMAIL FROM LOCAL LAWYER TO FRIENDS: What do you do when White Supremacists/White Nationalists come to town?

My answer starts with I have no idea. For those in Charlottesville, yes, it did happen.[8]

KRISTIN CLARENS: People had a lot of different reactions. *Did we invite this or are we the victims? Whose fault is this and why? And what do we need to do? And how significant are those changes we need to make?* And people were starting to argue. And it was starting to get tense.

One of those voices was activist Emily Gorcenski. She had been living in Charlottesville with her wife for the past 10 years, but it had never really felt like home.

EMILY GORCENSKI, LOCAL ACTIVIST: I was in Berlin when Richard Spencer came the first time with the torches. And I think that's the moment that Charlottesville became home. It became home when it became a place that I was willing to fight for. It became something I was willing to stand up for and I felt bad that I wasn't there.

ALAN ZIMMERMAN, PRESIDENT, CONGREGATION BETH ISRAEL: Right after that, the Ku Klux Klan announced that they were coming and having a march at the Stonewall Jackson statue.

The Ku Klux Klan march would occur July 8.

EMILY GORCENSKI: And so with that, I was like, *Well, what's my place?* I'm not going to go up and fist-fight a Nazi, because I'll get my ass kicked. I'm not as good a fighter in real life as I am in my head. And so, I realized that the weapons that I had were my words, and my platform, and my ability to shape relationships with media and to have connections with media. I know how this is going to go down in today's media ecosystem. And so that's when I decided that's what I wanted to put my energy into.

When I transitioned, I made a conscious choice to do things under my real name, under my real identity, because I wanted to show...I really believed in being that kind of trans person that I didn't have as a role model. And so I think that it definitely informs every bit of my activism. Because in everything that I fight for, I can see very clearly how queer people are oppressed and get the short end of the stick in all of these conversations. The white supremacist movement is about whiteness, but whiteness is not just about skin color. It's about patriarchy. It's about heteronormativity, cisnormativity. Trans people are one of the most targeted groups by the current white supremacist movement. So I think that being trans informs what I do and that having lived a life of not speaking under my real voice, I know what the power of speaking under my real voice is.

It made me a target, but I also made myself a target. I became a lightning rod on purpose. And the purpose of this was to divert the attention away from the people who were on the ground, doing that organizing, to give them free space and just make it look like Emily Gorcenski is this huge Antifa bigwig or whatever, when really all I'm doing is just shit-posting on Twitter.

Her plan worked. While the white nationalists largely focused on her, groups of activists in Charlottesville organized secretly.

Activists including Rev. Seth Wispelwey and Brittany "Smash" Caine-Conley started a progressive faith group later called Congregate C'ville. They organized counterprotesting trainings with civil rights activist Rev. Osagyefo Sekou.

REV. SETH WISPELWEY, PASTOR AND COFOUNDER, CONGREGATE C'VILLE: I put out the call to friends and clergy we knew and everything: We're bringing in a well-regarded, well-known organizer who's been arrested in Ferguson. Sekou is going to come down and do one of his little workshops. This was top secret because Kessler was trying to dox people. We're like, *This is on the DL. No one's to know that Sekou's in town.*

We had this big open floor plan and piano and he played some music and he did a little theological spiel. We ended up doing our first "ass in the grass" simulations in our backyard. It was like a trial run.

Other activists in Charlottesville were also training within their own organizations. That included Katrina Turner and Rosia Parker, both citizen leaders in Charlottesville's Black community.

KATRINA TURNER, LOCAL ACTIVIST: When we found out the Ku Klux Klan, the KKK, was coming to Charlottesville? We started training immediately. Yes.

ROSIA PARKER, LOCAL ACTIVIST: We don't do nothing without each other.

DAVID STRAUGHN, LOCAL ACTIVIST: Katrina and Rosia are town matriarchs.

ROSIA PARKER: We met at a rally and we've just been connected ever since, and we're both grandmothers and 'splain about our babies. When we got together, it was unstoppable.

You know, a lot of people call us Double Trouble.

So that summer we would go to church, we wouldn't even come home. We would be even training in our church clothes, high heels, shoes, dresses, purse. Myself, Katrina, and her son, Timmy. We trained and we trained and we trained.

Two or three months, we have already trained through to the KKK rally.

JALANE SCHMIDT, UVA PROFESSOR AND COFOUNDER, CHARLOTTESVILLE BLACK LIVES MATTER: There was immense social pressure to not counterprotest. *It's the leftists that are gonna be the problem.* That was the mood all summer. So you really, as an activist, felt like you had to defend your position to counterprotest.

HEAPHY REPORT: The City made a concerted and unified effort to discourage attendance at the Klan event and to schedule alternative events. Chief [of Police Al] Thomas's approach to public communications was "don't take the bait," which he repeated to multiple audiences as a means of encouraging people to stay away from the Klan event. . . .

YOLUNDA HARRELL, CEO, NEW HILL DEVELOPMENT CORP.: I remember [Police] Chief Thomas coming to our church to talk about the KKK coming and asking us to please stay at home. *Don't give them an audience. The best thing we can do is for you all to let us do our job and to not put us in a position where we gotta try to figure out how to protect you while also—unfortunately they have the right to hold this rally.*

So my husband and I talked about it and we're like, *Yeah, we're not gonna go. We're not gonna give them an audience.*

HEAPHY REPORT: The City's attempts to discourage counter-protests at the Klan rally alienated some members of this community.

JALANE SCHMIDT: There just wasn't institutional support for the resistance to this stuff. And in fact, in the lead-up to the Klan rally and stuff, I call it the Phalanx of the Four P's—by which I mean, the politicians, the police, the preachers, and the professors—they're all in lockstep saying, *Don't protest, don't counterprotest, you'll just encourage them, you'll just add fuel to the fire, better to just ignore them.* It's like, *Oh yeah, that worked so well for the good people of Weimar, Germany, didn't it?* You don't ignore fascists when they're coalescing and mobilizing and organizing and coming in public, you don't just let that go.

We were like the hand-waving alarmists and we kept saying, *This is dangerous and it's leading places that are dangerous and it's not just something you can ignore.*

LISA WOOLFORK, UVA PROFESSOR AND MEMBER OF CHARLOTTESVILLE BLACK LIVES MATTER: What you often find when someone is advising you to respond to something that is harmful to you with civility, is that person is not equally harmed or even harmed at all.

I think that one of the reasons that civility gets used is because it's a way to control people's behavior, but in a way that doesn't seem as autocratic as it really is. Civility itself is a kind of a smoke screen.

REV. SETH WISPELWEY: In terms of my own worldview, that I think is also objectively verifiable, white supremacy is a governing and violent ethos for this entire country that informs policies, politics, procedures, the privileges, the power, and wealth of white people, not just in general but over and against people of color.

If white supremacy is the governing and prevailing order, and white supremacists threaten violence and do violence and are looking for violence, you can't ignore it because it is the oxygen we breathe.

When the KKK finally came to town on July 8, the counterprotesters were ready.

HEAPHY REPORT: Eyewitnesses estimated that the Klan had 40 to 60 members while the crowd contained 1,500 to 2,000 counterprotesters.

KASEY HOTT, ANCHOR, NBC29: They ended up being drowned out by so many people, so many counterprotesters, which was wonderful.

JEFF FOGEL, LAWYER AND ACTIVIST: It was like a joke. They were more pathetic than dangerous.

LISA DRAINE, LOCAL ACTIVIST: It was kind of clownish really. It was a small crowd, but they were in their full regalia, the hoods and the insignia and all. It was really very bizarre, but there was nothing frightening about it.

ALAN ZIMMERMAN, PRESIDENT, CONGREGATION BETH ISRAEL: There was nothing scary about it, really. I thought the feeling in the air was triumphant, almost: *Oh, the big, bad Ku Klux Klan came to Charlottesville and we shouted them down, a thousand to one.*

Despite the relative triumph, many people were still extremely disturbed.

DEVIN WILLIS, SECOND-YEAR UVA STUDENT: I was really optimistic and outgoing at 18, and I think the KKK rally burst my bubble for sure. It grossed me out. If a Black counterprotester or whatever got too close, they would do monkey noise or monkey motions in their direction.

ALAN ZIMMERMAN: What surprised us in our congregation and in our temple leadership was the signs that the Klan brought with them were steeped in antisemitism. And we were not ready for that. Like a lot of Americans, we thought of the Klan as being against people of color. We didn't think of them as an antisemitic organization. I mean, we knew it, but we didn't think that was their focus.

HEAPHY REPORT: At approximately 4:25 p.m., the Klan left Justice Park.

That's when the tenor of the day changed.

HEAPHY REPORT: Police lined up the Klan and told them to move quickly. Police formed a wall to separate the Klan from counterprotesters.

KRISTIN CLARENS, LAWYER AND ACTIVIST: When the Klan guys were leaving, [the Klan members'] cars were at the very end in the underground parking lot by one of the police stations downtown. And that felt really infuriating. When the people in the crowd were like, *Wait, what do you mean? You've got their cars there. You're giving them a police escort?*

HEAPHY REPORT: Photographer Patrick Morrissey said that police made repeated demands over bullhorns to disperse and threatened to use tear gas if counterprotesters did not leave the area. Reverend Seth Wispelwey recalled seeing troopers put on gas masks but did not hear any warning regarding the impending tear gas deployment. Alan Zimmerman, president of Congregation Beth Israel, similarly observed law enforcement donning gas masks but did not recall any warnings from police before the release of tear gas.

Then, Virginia State Police officers released tear gas directly into the crowd.

HEAPHY REPORT: Emily Gorcenski told us that at the time the gas was deployed, a line of counterprotesters stood about 15 feet in front of the VSP Field Force, though they were not obstructing or blocking the street. Gorcenski heard screams of pain in the crowd when VSP deployed the first tear gas canister. She was also affected by the tear gas and was forced to flush her eyes. Less than a minute later, Gorcenski heard a second tear gas canister fired by police. Reverend Seth Wispelwey remembered seeing people in the crowd washing their eyes out due to tear gas exposure while police escorted arrestees away for processing. Ann Marie Smith saw people struggling after exposure—crowd members laid down on the ground and received treatment from street medics using milk and water.

TERRY MCAULIFFE, VIRGINIA GOVERNOR: The state police...were able to get the KKK safely out of the garage. Nobody injured or anything, but tear gas. And I guess down in Charlottesville...they didn't like the idea of any police doing anything or tear gas or anything like that. But I mean, they got 'em out and nobody injured.

ZACK WAJSGRAS, FREELANCE PHOTOGRAPHER: It felt very much like just, they were...without *directly* supporting the Klan, they were reacting with violence to one group of people and completely protecting another, so.

COUNTERPROTESTER CHANTS: Cops and Klan go hand in hand! Cops and Klan go hand in hand!

KRISTIN CLARENS: Why is one side getting a police escort and one side getting tear gassed in the street? I understand that the nuances are complicated in terms of providing police protection or security to people and their right to protest. I get that; I'm an attorney. I understand that tension between First Amendment and violence. But I think we had opportunities to provide security and not also provide a welcome mat. And I don't think we got it right. I think history shows we did not get it right.

CHAPTER 2

"Take away the permit,
bad people are coming."

JULY 2017

HEAPHY REPORT: Jason Kessler obtained a permit to convene a rally at the Lee statue [on August 12] at which he planned to bring together a wide array of right-wing and white national-ist groups. This event was called "Unite the Right" and was expected to be a much larger event and more significant public safety challenge than the July 8 Klan rally.

Kessler had filed the permit request on June 13, but it was after the KKK rally on July 8 that fears heightened.

ALLEN GROVES, UVA DEAN OF STUDENTS: By then, the flyers for the Unite the Right rally had started showing up and they had very neo-Nazi imagery, a fascist eagle.

I remember saying to some colleagues at the university, *This is the one I'm worried about. Not these clowns that came up from North Carolina. I'm worried about this one. I think this could attract a lot more people.*

Not all university administrators agreed.

TERESA SULLIVAN, UVA PRESIDENT: In the beginning, it didn't look like it was going to be much. The notion that you needed to *unite* the right suggested they were somehow not united.

That view changed over time. I think it began to look more threatening, though we still had a pretty imperfect idea of who was engaged and how many groups there were, and so on. I was expecting something more or less along the lines of the KKK rally, focused downtown on the park by the statue of Robert Lee.

Some city officials were concerned, however, especially after witnessing what they described as an unorganized and unprepared emergency response to the July 8 KKK rally.

ANDREW BAXTER, CHARLOTTESVILLE FIRE CHIEF: The KKK rally was a dress rehearsal. There were huge red flags.

The city had established a command post to monitor the rally—a central location at which first responders and city leaders would observe events and plan their response. But Chief Baxter remembers it as unorganized and ineffective.

ANDREW BAXTER: You could've walked into the command post on July the 8th and if you'd asked seven people, you would've got at least three different answers about who was in charge. There was a complete lack of clarity based on a complete lack of understanding about what being the incident commander means.

According to US federal government guidance and procedure under the National Incident Management System (NIMS), a single incident commander should head the chain of command and give orders.

ANDREW BAXTER: I hate to be critical of Al, of [Police] Chief Thomas, but he didn't have that understanding.

What should have happened in my view on July the 9th, if not before, was a weekly meeting, if not more frequently, of the president of the university, the city manager, the county executive, and their respective public safety teams.

All right, what do we know, what don't we know, how do we find out what we don't know, who's done this before, who's going to be... You see what I'm saying? Just at a high level, that never happened.... They were doing it like somebody would call Chief Mike Gibson at the university police, and then he would call so-and-so, like there was going to be a football game or something. It was terrifying.

Law enforcement and senior executives and others should have been actively seeking out communications from other communities that had been through this: Portland, Berkeley, there's some of the communities in Kentucky. *Hey, we just had this event and we dodged a bullet, and we had some problems, but this other group has applied for a permit and we're getting intelligence, consistent intelligence that this is going to be a major event. Here's what we've got planned. What are we missing?*

It takes an incredibly mature, confident professional when put under pressure to say, *What am I missing? Does anybody else in this room know anything?* And we did none of that, not a bit.

BRIAN MORAN, SECRETARY, VIRGINIA PUBLIC SAFETY AND HOMELAND SECURITY: We got intel here that this thing could be substantial in size and in nature, of potential violence. And as the date approached, we became very concerned to the point that I started to ask for briefings with Governor [Terry McAuliffe] and the chief of staff, and I would bring in the superintendent of state police. The superintendent shared with me that he was concerned that the city wasn't taking adequate preparations. He specifically expresses, *You know, I'm not sure they're taking this to the level that it should be taken.* And so that's when my involvement became more intense.

At one point I actually went to the governor, I said, *Governor, we continue to be very concerned that this thing could get out of hand.*

TERRY MCAULIFFE: They were very concerned at this point that the city just was not listening to any of the recommendations coming in from the state.

BRIAN MORAN: At that point, we talked about what state resources are available, what state resources we should apply to the situation. And the governor was very receptive, said, *You do whatever you think you need.*

The state government later ended up activating the Virginia National Guard.

TERRY MCAULIFFE: Now we tried to do this secretly. I wanted to make sure we had all the assets down there, but the last thing I wanted was CNN to say, *Terry McAuliffe, the governor of Virginia, has called a state of emergency, is sending the national guard.* Because all that's gonna do is be like Woodstock, everybody [would say], *Ooh, I gotta get to Charlottesville.*

We almost got caught. We didn't *lie* to the press, but we skated it a little bit and said, *Well, we have training exercises going,* which happened to be true. But the truth is we were moving everybody to Charlottesville.

DAILY PROGRESS: While police prepare for protests, local hospitals also are gearing up. Both Sentara Martha Jefferson and the University of Virginia Medical Center are making preparations for the rally by increasing some medical and security staff during the event.[1]

MIKE SIGNER, CHARLOTTESVILLE MAYOR: It was the worst-case scenario that UVa hospital had in mind. I always thought that was interesting, that the public health experts, like just looking at the variables, like in a clear-eyed way, they were like, *There's gonna be mass casualties.*

TOM BERRY, DIRECTOR OF EMERGENCY MANAGEMENT, UVA MEDICAL CENTER: I wasn't getting a lot of intel through law enforcement. They kept it very close and that wasn't surprising to me. And so because of that, I went out and looked for stuff on my own.

Tom Berry had 21 years of experience in the US Army and had participated in the emergency response at the Pentagon on September 11, 2001.

TOM BERRY: It wasn't hard to do through the unclassified network. It was pretty easy to see that people were interested in violence. It wasn't just *likely*; to me, it was more *imminent* based on a lot of the websites that I was looking at. And so from that, I felt it was pretty easy to determine that *something's* going to happen.

BETH MEHRING, EMERGENCY SERVICES NURSE MANAGER, UVA MEDICAL CENTER: I'm very thankful that Tom was as diligent as he was getting intel about what to expect in August because I don't think people would've taken it as seriously had he not done that. I can honestly say if we had had other people in place, we would not have been prepared to the level that we were.

Tom Berry chose Jody Reyes, the medical center's cancer services administrator, to serve as the weekend's incident commander. She too came from an armed services background.

JODY REYES, INCIDENT COMMANDER, UVA MEDICAL CENTER: You have to be able to sit and look forward and say, these are all the different paths that this could take. And one of those would be, you're down on the Downtown Mall, somebody sets off a bomb, you've got a hundred patients. What are you gonna do? Well, you're gonna need to have nurses and doctors available and you need to have beds available. So, how do you do that?

TOM BERRY: I can remember working with UVa health systems executive Dr. Rick Shannon. He was asking me, *Tom, what do you want me to tell the physicians?* Because, I mean, they'll listen to him, a physician, a clinician.

JODY REYES: Some people can see it and they understand, but you're a surgeon and you have had a patient waiting to get their hip replaced for the last six months, and you're supposed to do surgery on them, and a day before, all of a sudden, some leader manager comes to you and says, *You've gotta cancel that surgery 'cause we can't have elective things scheduled because of what* might *happen?*

There's going to be a handful of people who understand and recognize that it's not convenient and the timing stinks, but it's the right thing to do for everybody. And then you're gonna have people who don't understand it at all.

TERESA SULLIVAN, UVA PRESIDENT: We began having meetings every morning, you know, just as a precaution to think about what could happen.

TOM BERRY: Dr. Shannon was taking me to President Sullivan's meetings. He asked me to give an overview to President Sullivan about what we were doing. And I could see shock in her eyes. I think they always thought, it's just Charlottesville, it's never going to happen here. And so that was the approach they took.

And to be honest with you, I felt bad for her because I honestly felt like her staff should be doing more for her. She gave some explanations of some dreams she was having.

TERESA SULLIVAN: There was no question. I was very anxious. The closer we got to the event, the more concerned I became and the more of my daily space it occupied, you know, trying to think about it and plan for it and not really knowing what was coming.

TOM BERRY: After that time where I really explained how we were taking those actionable steps to prepare ourselves, decompressing the hospital in terms of ICU beds, I could tell she really didn't want that to be communicated out. And I think in her mind, she thought that it would make people very fearful. She didn't say those words specifically, but the look I saw in her eyes was that, *Tom, what you just briefed to me, I really don't want that to be our message out because I think it's going to scare people.*

President Sullivan recalls those conversations—and her reaction —differently.

TERESA SULLIVAN: Well, Rick had told me that they were prepared for it, but he also said to me, *We do regular drills for this* and so on. And he seemed quite confident that they were ready to take care of it. But also when he spoke of "mass casualty," I was thinking, you know, more along the lines of things that we would see at football games where you'd have people who had heat exhaustion and stuff like that, the occasional heart attack or stroke. I didn't actually think of it in terms of orchestrated violence.

Five miles down the road at the only other hospital in Charlottesville, Sentara Martha Jefferson Hospital, leaders were having similar conversations.

ALEX MCGEE, CHAPLAIN, SENTARA MARTHA JEFFERSON HOSPITAL: Mass casualties. They were preparing for mass casualties.

I was three months into this new job. I had been asked as a chaplain to attend the senior leadership meetings of the hospital. I was hearing them talk about, if they had to get the stable patients out of the hospital to nursing homes, what routes would be accessible and how were those routing instructions going to be given to ambulance drivers. What surgical materials were likely to be needed ahead of time and how were those gonna be obtained? There were conversations about if people had tear gas on them and they needed to be hosed down how would that occur? Where outside the emergency room were those curtains and hoses or water going to be set up? There was very, very thorough thinking ahead.

I think I was standing there stunned like, *Oh my gosh, these people are so on the ball and these people are here to save lives and to heal people. They're not joking around.*

Charlottesville Fire Department Chief Andrew Baxter was also coordinating his firefighters, paramedics, and staff for the weekend.

ANDREW BAXTER: Our big concern was a Las Vegas shooting style event and, quite frankly, open combat on the streets of the city with high powered weapons, with rifles. So we were trying to prepare for multiple, what we would call red patients, priority one traumas. We had plans in place with the National Guard to land Blackhawks on the football field at Charlottesville High School. That's the level of contingency planning we had done. Because if we needed to evacuate, if we had that many people with gunshot wounds, some of them were going to Richmond, some of them were going to Fairfax, some of them were going to Roanoke. We can't take care of all them.

What really made me nervous was the physical safety of our firefighters and EMTs and paramedics. They're hearing from a lot of the CPD [Charlottesville Police Department] folks—excuse my language—really scary shit. Really, like officers telling their wives, *Honey, this may be it.*

A number of us had been trying to get City Manager Maurice Jones to declare a state of emergency.

HEAPHY REPORT: The executive power for the City Government is vested in a City Manager. Selected by City Council, the City Manager is the "chief executive and administrative officer" for the City Government and thus responsible for enforcing

the laws of the City and ensuring that City employees faith-
fully perform their administrative responsibilities. The City
Manager is also explicitly named as the "director of public
safety" and given general powers of supervision over the
Charlottesville Fire Department (CFD) and the Charlottesville
Police Department (CPD).

ANDREW BAXTER: He wouldn't do it. He didn't want to. Even if it was just declare a state of emergency because we're going to be shutting down traffic on so many streets, likely increased response times...

We didn't want to alarm people. Well, sorry. The only person who's not alarmed is you.

KRISTIN CLARENS, LAWYER AND ACTIVIST: We get more information about a snowstorm or something than we did about this.

JALANE SCHMIDT, UVA PROFESSOR AND COFOUNDER, CHARLOTTESVILLE BLACK LIVES MATTER: The week before, there was a little baby bear that was loose near the children's hospital. You know, wandering wildlife. And the university sent out a campuswide alert: *Stay away from the hospital! There's wildlife! The fish and game people are handling it. You stay!* And then by comparison, the next week, 300 Nazis with torches? Nothing, no warning.

CONGREGATION BETH ISRAEL
DOWNTOWN CHARLOTTESVILLE
EARLY AUGUST 2017

ALAN ZIMMERMAN, PRESIDENT, CONGREGATION BETH ISRAEL: As the Unite the Right rally drew closer, we started to look at some of the online postings, just on websites, Twitter, stuff like that, and we became really concerned: 95 percent of that stuff was about Jews and was sophomoric humor about the Holocaust, jokes about ovens and exterminating Jews. And we started to see this and just become more and more concerned. We really didn't know what to expect that day.

EMILY BLOUT, UVA PROFESSOR AND MAYOR MIKE SIGNER'S WIFE: The Jewish community in Charlottesville is about 400 families, and the synagogue is the only synagogue in all central Virginia.

Congregation Beth Israel is one block from Emancipation Park, where Kessler had applied to hold his rally.

ALAN ZIMMERMAN: We have services on Saturday morning and we thought about canceling services, but we ultimately decided not to.

MICHAEL CHEUK, SECRETARY, CHARLOTTESVILLE CLERGY COLLECTIVE: They decided to have their regular Shabbat service almost as an act of resistance.

ALAN ZIMMERMAN: We started an hour earlier, so if people wanted to get out of downtown before the march officially started at 12 o'clock, they could do so.

We'd hired a security guard the weekend of the Ku Klux Klan march, but we asked him not to come armed. But for the Unite the Right march, we had the security guard come back. He said, *Can I come armed?* And we told him it was OK to do that.

HEAPHY REPORT: Rabbis also removed the synagogue's sacred scrolls for safekeeping outside of the downtown area.

RABBI TOM GUTHERZ, CONGREGATION BETH ISRAEL: We said to ourselves, *Is there anything in this building that just can't be replaced?*

And when we thought that through, we realized this Holocaust Torah, which is a special scroll that our synagogue has...I mean, it couldn't be replaced. So a couple days before August 12, we just sort of quietly removed that Torah. A member took it to their home for safekeeping.

We left one Torah there because we wanted to read from it on Saturday morning.

WES BELLAMY, CHARLOTTESVILLE VICE MAYOR: The activist community had been scouring the internet and dark net for a while now, and they were adamant that the people coming here on August 11th and 12th were serious people who wanted to invoke pain, terror, and real violence.[2]

DAVID STRAUGHN, LOCAL ACTIVIST: We had people inside that were also looking at 4chan and 8chan and Discord and all of these websites that white nationalists run through.

DON GATHERS, COFOUNDER, CHARLOTTESVILLE BLACK LIVES MATTER: It was very much clear to us that we could expect for people to die.

REV. SETH WISPELWEY, PASTOR AND COFOUNDER, CONGREGATE C'VILLE: Our trainings became less and less about, *Here's how to not get your shoulder dislocated if the police drag you away,* and more like, *Here's how to go serpentine and crouch through the ground and cover the body of someone in a live-fire situation.*

LISA DRAINE, LOCAL ACTIVIST: The leaders were saying, *If you decide you wanna be on the street and nobody's pressured to do so, you should make sure that you have some training. You don't wanna go into that situation, not knowing what to expect or how to act.*

DAVID STRAUGHN: We trained for bullet fire: Get down in serpentine in case you hear fire. We trained for chemical warfare, we trained for audio warfare 'cause we heard that they might bring sonar guns that would pierce the ears.

REV. SETH WISPELWEY: Our house became kind of a safe zone. Sekou lived with us for six weeks in our basement during the time in training. We had like 60 to 80 people at any given training. We're doing this in a field behind Sojourners United Church of Christ on these hot-ass muggy days. It was just community members, though, doing this on their free time. That was what was so striking about it. We were building an airplane while flying. I was running out buying cases of LaCroix and snacks for the trainings.

What I'm trying to say is we were taking it really fucking seriously.

Congregate C'ville decided to organize an interfaith prayer service the night before Unite the Right. In a planned demonstration of unity, they invited hundreds of clergy from around the country in what they named the #ClergyCall.

REV. SETH WISPELWEY: That idea originated on my back deck one night where Sekou and I got high after a training. And he goes, *This is going to be big, this is going to be so fucked up, holy shit.* We were saying, *There's going to be so many Nazis.* We didn't know how many.

He's like, *You know what we're going to do? We're going to put out a call.*

And he's stoned. And I'm just looking at the moon and being like, *Uh-huh. Yeah.*

And he's like, *We're going to put out a call. We're going to ring that park.*

That is explicitly where the clergy call came from.

The trainings grew in intensity as August 12 approached.

REV. SETH WISPELWEY: By the last training, the white men in the simulation had to play the parts of the cops and the white supremacists. We were having to pretend to be white supremacists! Like, not saying anything, but beating on... It was crazy.

DAVID STRAUGHN: Everything was placed on the down low, 'cause we didn't know when individuals would strike. We didn't know if they would come early and try to take us out during an organizer's meeting or a training like this or what. I can't tell you how much weight I lost, how much I didn't sleep, how much I didn't eat.

REV. SETH WISPELWEY: In other words, just full-time organizing, around the clock. It's hard to believe it was in four and a half weeks.

REV. SETH WISPELWEY: A lot was happening at city council meetings.

I.B.F., LOCAL ACTIVIST: We'd been trying all summer for that permit to be revoked. Don't let people come.

EMILY GORCENSKI, LOCAL ACTIVIST: There was one city council meeting between the July 8th rally and the August 12th rally, because the summer break was there.

The activists thought their best bet to get the city council to listen to their concerns was to put together a physical document detailing the threats.

EMILY GORCENSKI: We had all of this evidence and all of this chatter about the violence that was going to be created. So we put together a document to try to say, *Look, they're planning. They're talking about how many Black people they're going to beat up. They're talking about how they're targeting Wes Bellamy, specifically. Jason Kessler is organizing with a motorcycle gang. We've got militias that are coming here and saying that they're going to kill people.* All of this stuff.

And we're like, *Here you go. Here's all of this evidence of the very intentional violence that these people want to bring into our community.*

EMILY GORCENSKI'S DESCRIPTION OF DOSSIER CONTENTS: One militia man posted on Facebook, "I can assure you there will be beatings at the August event." Of Black Lives Matter activists, he promised that his fellow militia members "will finish them all off." On the neo-Nazi media portal Daily Stormer, user Exterminajudios (Exterminate Jews) posted, "Antifa and [N-words] will be out in force. We need some military guys there to crack skulls."[3]

EMILY GORCENSKI: The purpose of the dossier was multipurpose, a lot of layers to it. This was not merely an effort to say, *Take away the permit, bad people are coming.* One part of it was, yes, you hope that they listen and you hope that they act and that they do something with the information that you give them. But you don't bank on it, you don't depend on it because most of the time, power is going to let you down.

And so, the secondary purpose of this dossier was to put it on record that we told them so. So that when the ship went down, we could then point back at it and say, *We told you that they would be violent. We told you that they were going to be violent and you're incompetent.*

DOSSIER, AS PRESENTED TO CITY COUNCIL ON JULY 17, 2017:

Dear Esteemed Council Members,

With respect to the issue of public safety surrounding the "Unite the Right" rally currently scheduled for 12 August 2017, we present evidence of threats of violence planned to take place during the event...

Part 3.4.5(b) of the Special Event Regulations of the City of Charlottesville states that a "permit may be denied in writing" if "it reasonably appears that the proposed activity will present a danger to public safety or health...." On these

grounds, we submit the following to support the claim that
it reasonably appears that the proposed activity will present a danger to public safety and formally request that the
Event Coordinator revoke the permit for the proposed August 12
event.[4]

MIKE SIGNER, CHARLOTTESVILLE MAYOR: Emily Gorcenski was so furious at us when she brought that dossier, and it included a lot of that open source stuff. And she told me actually in another meeting, she's like, *Yeah, I had other stuff that I can't produce. But what I brought to you, you should have been able to stop it or turn down the permit.*

But I went through everything that had happened legally and what we'd been told. We couldn't legally have stopped the rally.

It's not clear that is true, given the city code allowing for the city to deny permits out of concern for public safety, but multiple city officials say that is what the city lawyers told them at the time.

KRISTIN SZAKOS, CHARLOTTESVILLE CITY COUNCILOR: We kept being told by our advisers, legal kind of advisers, that there was nothing we could do about it. It was just a free speech issue, and we were just going to have to take it.

Soon, city councilors tried a potential middle option.

KRISTIN SZAKOS: We tried to get the rally moved outside of downtown, because we were worried [that with] so many people in such a dense area, it was just going to explode.

The Unite the Right organizers sued to keep the rally at its original location, and the federal court agreed to take the case. Now, more uncertainty around the rally: Where would it even take place?

REV. SETH WISPELWEY: I remember that feeling once the calendar hit August, like, *Oh God, it's here.* Like a hurtling snowball down a mountain.

I remember days feeling long, but of course they were really full. Things were in motion. And we had prepared. We were preparing.

I.B.F., LOCAL ACTIVIST: I wore a hijab at the time and my parents were really, really worried about my safety. They still lived with me. And so, the Thursday before, I moved out of our home. There was this fear that people might follow you and I didn't want to put them in any kind of danger. So I left home, I packed up my things and I stayed with a friend who was also organizing.

Vice Mayor Wes Bellamy says that white nationalists were threatening him with injury and death via email, social media, and even mailed letters, but he still wanted to go to the rally to counterprotest.

WES BELLAMY, CHARLOTTESVILLE VICE MAYOR: A few guys from the barber-shop told me that they wanted to meet...and it was mandatory. I'm normally not one who likes being told what to do, but I sensed the seriousness of the tone in their voices...I walked in, sat down, and knew immediately that this was not going to go well.

These guys, most of whom were from here, who had been here for years and had a strong footprint in the city, were there that night for one reason: to tell me that I wasn't going to the rally on Saturday.

We had a long conversation, and went back and forth about why I felt I needed to be there, how I didn't want to let the community down. I refused to allow this group to come to our city and simply think that they can take over without any kind of pushback. For them, my brothers standing before me in the barber shop—it was more so about safety. They'd been there for the KKK rally and believed, had I been at that one, that things would not have turned out well for me. In their eyes, going to this rally would be even worse.

I was hell-bent on going to Unite the Right, and eventually they realized that the only way to stop me was by them physically knocking me out. We agreed on a compromise.[5]

Wes Bellamy promised that he would go to the counterprogramming events around the city, and not the rally itself. Then, he too left home for the weekend.

WES BELLAMY: I was informed by the police that it wouldn't be a good idea to stay at my house, so I made other arrangements.[6]

REV. SETH WISPELWEY: On our last training, we encouraged people to write a letter to a loved one just acknowledging with informed consent, like, *I'm going to go out. It's going to be dangerous and volatile.*

ROSIA PARKER, LOCAL ACTIVIST: We was prepared because we had intel. We already knew that they was coming here to kill. They wanted to kill us.

PART 2

THE RIOTS

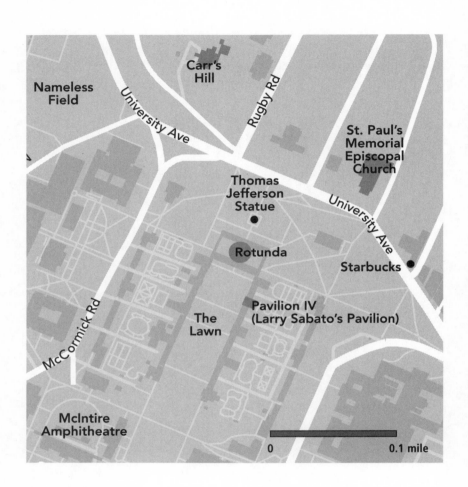

CHAPTER 3

"Is somebody going to respond to this? Because this sounds really bad."

FRIDAY, AUGUST 11

REV. SETH WISPELWEY, PASTOR AND COFOUNDER, CONGREGATE C'VILLE: When I woke up, it was relatively early. It was like, *OK, this is the day. Here's what we're going to do.*

I was having my early coffee and smoke with Sekou on my front porch when we got the message over Signal that the torch-lit rally, which we knew they wanted to replicate, was going to be at UVa.

EMILY GORCENSKI, LOCAL ACTIVIST: When they started organizing this thing, I'm like, *Jason Kessler is an arrogant son of a bitch. He's definitely going to try to pull something the night before, because if I were in his position, that's exactly what I would do.* And there's a handful of places in the city where that can actually be pulled off.

The activists considered several possible locations the white nationalists might hold a torch march Friday night, but soon eliminated most of them for either being too far outside of town or having no symbolism, often important to white supremacists.

EMILY GORCENSKI: We were like, UVa is the only other place that makes sense. So of course, they're going to do it at UVa. That morning we get the confirmation of where and when it would be.

That confirmation included the exact location: the statue of Thomas Jefferson at the UVa Rotunda, across the street from St. Paul's Memorial Church where Congregate C'ville would be holding an interfaith prayer service at the exact same time.

REV. SETH WISPELWEY: Our morning coffee became like, *Well, does that change anything for us?*

We thought that community members and activists would confront it, and that invariably local authorities would step in. Like, this is on UVa's campus. So we were just like, *We're going to stick to what we do, because this will be confronted in some way or another by people. And we'll do our thing and just be vigilant.*

But most people within the local activist groups actually had not decided yet whether they would confront it, and not all activists were making decisions together.

EMILY GORCENSKI: There was a big debate among activists on whether we should counterprotest it or not. Everyone's like, *Are we counterprotesting the torch march?* And I'm like, *Look, I don't care. Just decide, figure it out.*

KRISTIN SZAKOS, CHARLOTTESVILLE CITY COUNCILOR: I started getting calls about maybe noon, one or two o'clock, about the plans for a torchlight march at UVa. I was talking to folks who were monitoring some of the chat on the internet from the folks planning it.

I talked to our police department and talked to the city folks about, *Is somebody going to respond to this? Because this sounds really bad.*

TOM BERRY, DIRECTOR OF EMERGENCY MANAGEMENT, UVA MEDICAL CENTER: I saw it coming at probably 1 or 2 in the afternoon. Everything that I'd read and then anticipated, and we had prepared for, it was becoming real. It was obvious that the ER was probably going to become the center of gravity that evening.

I had the time to go home. I think I changed clothes into something more comfortable. I had something to eat. I got back in my car and I went straight to the ER.

EMILY GORCENSKI: So sometime around 3, [my group of activists] decide not to counterprotest the torch march. I'm like, *Fine, I'll go there. I'm still going to film it.* Everyone else is going to be dealing with the church, whatever. And then I thought about saying, *Well, if we're not going to counterprotest, should we call [the torch march] in to the police?* And I was on the fence about it. And I think it was Jalane who said like, *Oh, I've mentioned this or something like that already.* And so I was like, *All right, it's been handled, it's been gone through official channels. It's fine.*

JALANE SCHMIDT, UVA PROFESSOR AND COFOUNDER, CHARLOTTESVILLE BLACK LIVES MATTER: I really struggled with whether or not to even say anything [to warn University authorities about the torch march]. I'm like, they're not gonna listen to me. I'm like, *Oh we need a living wage, we need affordable housing, it's racist up in here, Nazis are coming.* See? You stopped listening to me three issues ago.

And I'm just like, I cannot be the messenger here. I really want this message to go through. It's not about my ego. The message needs to land.

So Jalane Schmidt found a conduit, someone she thought would be trusted: the mayor's wife.

EMILY BLOUT, UVA PROFESSOR AND MAYOR MIKE SIGNER'S WIFE: It was 2:30. I was doing grocery shopping at Barracks Road, and I get a call from a member of Antifa, which is exceptional unto itself because there's a big cynicism towards government by the far left. So I got a call from that person saying this rally was gonna happen at [UVa's] Nameless Field and that I needed to tell the chief of police and the mayor about it, 'cause it was going to happen and it was gonna happen at night. I remember calling Mike and then him promising to call not only just the chief of police, but the UVa police and the president of UVa at the time about it.

UVa Professor Louis Nelson was also warned about the march on UVa's campus—called "Grounds"—and he in turn called the provost's office. The vice provost then notified university administrators.

3:23 p.m. email to University administrators:

Subject: Possible March tonight on-Grounds

Dear all:

You likely already know this, but if not...Louis Nelson, copied on this message, just received an informal call alerting him to the possibility of an alt-right march on-Grounds this evening, beginning at a Jefferson statue (not sure which one) to St. Paul's Church, coinciding with the prayer service this evening. Just wanted to alert you to this possibility. If you have questions, please contact Louis directly.

Best,

Anda

Vice Provost for Administration and Chief of Staff

Why might UVa administration "likely already know this"? Private emails obtained through a public records request filed by the *Chronicle of Higher Education* show that the university police had received intelligence about the torch march days earlier.

CHRONICLE OF HIGHER EDUCATION: Capt. Donald H. McGee, a university police officer, appears to have heard these concerns as early as August 8, three days before the march on the Lawn. After a meeting that day of the Charlottesville Police Department, Captain McGee warned his superior about a possible "tiki torch march" to be held the night before the big downtown rally. The description proved prescient.

"It was stated that at 9PM there were plans to replicate the tiki torch march they made last month at an undisclosed location," Capt. McGee wrote to Michael A. Gibson, the university's chief of police, and several other officers. "There is concern that the location could be the Rotunda or Lawn area since Mr. Spencer, an alum, will likely be at the Friday event."

Shortly after 5 p.m., Jason Kessler called the university police department directly.

HEAPHY REPORT: Kessler called [UPD Patrol] Lieutenant [Angela] Tabler, then passed the phone to an associate, who informed Tabler that the group planned to assemble at Nameless Field on the University grounds, march to the statue of Thomas Jefferson in front of the Rotunda, and make a short speech. There was no mention of torches.

UVa President Teresa Sullivan says none of this information was escalated to her.

TERESA SULLIVAN: Somebody should have told me, and there were a lot of different people here who could have told me who knew, who didn't tell me.

ST. PAUL'S MEMORIAL EPISCOPAL CHURCH
7 P.M.

DAILY PROGRESS: After an afternoon of sunshine gave way to a brief evening rain shower and an overcast sky, clergy members and people of faith gathered in St. Paul's Memorial Church on University Avenue for a prayer service that was organized in response to the Unite the Right rally on Saturday.[1]

HEAPHY REPORT: Located on University Avenue, St. Paul's sits just across the street from the University of Virginia, a stone's throw away from the iconic Rotunda and the statue of Thomas Jefferson.

REV. SETH WISPELWEY, PASTOR AND COFOUNDER, CONGREGATE C'VILLE: We wanted to have a service that demanded in the name of God and people of conscience that white supremacy must be overcome if America is going to have a successful future.[2]

DON GATHERS, COFOUNDER, CHARLOTTESVILLE BLACK LIVES MATTER: I picked up Dr. Cornel West from the airport and got him positioned and situated.

BRITTANY "SMASH" CAINE-CONLEY, COFOUNDER, CONGREGATE C'VILLE: Like, we knew what to expect, but we had no idea what to expect.

WASHINGTON POST: Doors opened at 7:30 and within minutes some 600 people filled the pews and lined its walls. Many others were turned away.[3]

REV. SETH WISPELWEY: Boy, that church was packed. I mean, we had to turn people away.

Rosia Parker and Katrina Turner arrived together.

ROSIA PARKER, LOCAL ACTIVIST: So we get to the church about maybe 6:30 or so.

KATRINA TURNER, LOCAL ACTIVIST: No, we were late. It was like 7:15–20. We were late.

ROSIA PARKER: No. We first got to the church. Remember? We walked around first before we went to the door. And so by that time it was about 7:15. So then we was told that we couldn't get in the church because the church was packed. So, we end up sitting outside in front of the church.

Another person in attendance: Lisa Draine. Her two daughters, 23-year-old Rebecca and 21-year-old Sophie, had just gotten home from summers abroad only two days earlier, but they wanted to counterprotest on Saturday. So on Friday night, Lisa brought Rebecca with her to the service.

LISA DRAINE, LOCAL ACTIVIST: Sophie had told us that she couldn't go to that service, that she was meeting up with her friends who were planning what they were gonna do the next day. So Rebecca and I went to the service and she didn't come with us.

REV. SETH WISPELWEY: We definitely came close to breaking the fire code. There were about 675 folks packed into St. Paul's.[4]

CHRIS SUAREZ, REPORTER, CHARLOTTESVILLE *DAILY PROGRESS*: The thing that really struck me in all of that was that there was very intense security.

REV. SETH WISPELWEY: We had people within the activist security network sweeping the church for suspicious bags and stuff, making sure that only a couple of doors were open, letting in our VIPs through the back alley.

WILLIS JENKINS, UVA PROFESSOR: I [was] standing guard at the front doors.... A few hours earlier, for reasons that remain unclear, Charlottesville police had pulled back the officers initially promised to the church where the meeting was held, so organizers had scrambled to ask some allies for security help. I was asked to come help, not because I was experienced in security, but because I was nearby and trusted. By then organizers knew (and UVa administrators had been alerted) that there would be a torch-lit rally at the Rotunda, which was across the street from the church. About 10 of us stood on watch outside, all unarmed.[5]

WASHINGTON POST: The church service began at 8 p.m. Sitting in the pews were clergy members from all over the country who had paid their way to come to Charlottesville to support those protesting against the Unite the Right rally.[6]

There were many local residents on hand as well, including long time activists with experience in civil rights rallies and newcomers who wanted to voice their opposition to what they saw as an ugly threat to their city.[7]

REV. SETH WISPELWEY: The spirit was alive, for lack of a better word. The gospel singing, the freedom songs.

I.B.F., LOCAL ACTIVIST: It was like a pep rally, almost. It was like, *We're going to be OK, we're going to be fine there. We are here together in solidarity*, et cetera, et cetera.

REV. DR. CORNEL WEST: We have to take a stand. That's why some of us came to fight and get arrested, if necessary.[8]

MIKE SIGNER, CHARLOTTESVILLE MAYOR: Cornel West had been my professor at Princeton and when I heard that he was coming, I reached out to him.

We had this really nice conversation, but what I had seen from the clergy organizers and from the groups that were leading this was that there was enough confrontationalism in this group. I don't think—it wasn't entirely around that pole at all, but it had enough in it that I didn't think that this was gonna be the event that would somehow calm the whole city down and avoid a conflict.

So I was sitting there with a knot in my stomach during the whole service and during everything that was happening that night, 'cause I was worried about this clash that I feared was gonna come.

SINGING: We shall not, we shall not be moved
Just like a tree that's planted by the water, we shall not
  be moved
We are fighting for our freedom...
Black and white together...
Gay and straight together...
Jewish, Christian, Muslim...
We are fighting for our children...[9]

DON GATHERS: It was like Sunday morning at a Baptist church! It didn't matter about belief or sect or religiosity, it was just a commonality of people coming together to worship and to denounce evil.

RABBI TOM GUTHERZ, CONGREGATION BETH ISRAEL: There was a moment during the service when people came up to us to receive blessings from the clergy and a sense that we were entering into kind of a sacred moment, really. That this was going to be sort of a moment of...I don't want to use strong terms but...of good and evil.

We're going to go into the fray against this terrible ideology and this terrible hatred that had come to our town, and there was something sacred about that.

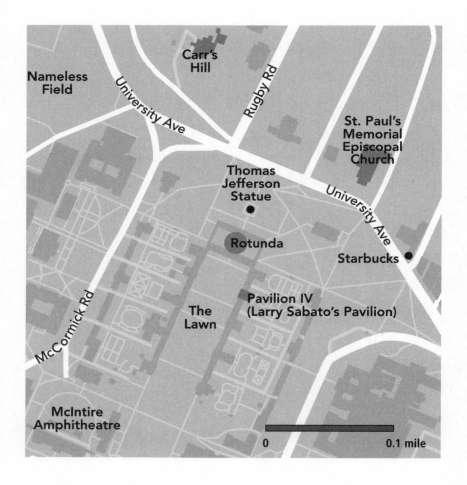

CHAPTER 4

"We have a tip that something is going to happen on Grounds."

> The Lawn is essentially UVa's central quad, designed by Thomas Jefferson himself. It's ringed by small, single dorm rooms that open directly onto the grass. Today, it is an honor for a student to be selected to live in a Lawn room, even though the rooms lack many modern comforts, including bathrooms.

MALCOLM STEWART, FOURTH-YEAR UVA STUDENT AND SENIOR RESIDENT ON THE LAWN: Around 8 that night, there was still a little bit of sunlight out. One of the Lawn residents was like, *Guys, President Sullivan's on the Lawn saying hi to people.* I was like, *Oh, you know what, T-Sully is here, let me go say hello, I haven't seen her since I moved in.*

TERESA SULLIVAN, UVA PRESIDENT: I had walked over to the Lawn after dinner because it was the day the Lawnies could move in and I just went to say hello.

MALCOLM STEWART: So we start chatting and she's like, *I just knew Lawn residents were moving in, and I want to come by and meet people and say hello.* And

I was like, *Cool.* At 7:57 p.m., a GroupMe message came from one of the other senior residents.

TEXT FROM A SENIOR RESIDENT ADVISER, 7:57 P.M.: From one of my
staffers: Heads up that there might be a secret alt right
rally at the rotunda tonight. Stay safe everyone.

MALCOLM STEWART: Immediately following that message, another senior resident sent a link to a website.

IT'S GOING DOWN TWEET, 7:43 P.M.: Multiple sources confirming
neo-Nazis will converge at 9 PM at Jefferson Statue at UVa
campus. #Charlottesville #defendcville #NoNewKKK[1]

IT'S GOING DOWN ARTICLE, TWEETED OUT AT 7:43 P.M.: Local organizers in Charlottesville have now received word from an anonymous source that Unite the Right can't wait for Saturday—they
are planning a repeat surprise torchlit rally on University
of Virginia (UVa) campus tonight. Sounds like Richard Spencer
wants back on his old stomping grounds, right where he and his
white supremacist followers can feel at home.

...As IGD reported today, the right's leaders are documented
calling for armed violence against anyone who crosses them.[2]

MALCOLM STEWART: Immediately following me getting this message at 7:57, I read it, saw it, and I pulled President Sullivan aside. I said, *Hey, President Sullivan, can I borrow you for a second?* I pull her out onto the Lawn and I turn my phone around and I say, *Have you seen this?* As she took my phone, looked at it and saw the time and the location plans, she said, *Well, this is news to me.* Those are her exact words.

And I looked at her, I was like, *OK, so what would you like us to do?*

And she's like, *I need to get in touch with the police chief.*

TERESA SULLIVAN: I went back up to Carr's Hill [the president's residence] and started making some phone calls. And I talked to Marge Sidebottom, who was the emergency operations director. And she came over, and it was Marge who told me there had been a phone call that afternoon to the police department.

And she said that they had said there was gonna be a small number of people who would walk on the sidewalks up University Avenue to the Thomas Jefferson statue, read a speech, and then go home. Both the street and the sidewalks are considered public, so we actually can't control that. And that by itself didn't sound very threatening, but that also turned out not to be true. I mean, first of all, lying to a police officer is a pretty serious matter. You don't do that.

I also understand the call came from Jason Kessler, who was over and over identified as a UVa alumnus. And, you know, I think at UVa, we tend to accord to both our alumni and our students a kind of a generous belief that they're subscribing to the honor code.

At home 20 minutes south of town, Dean of Students Allen Groves was having dinner with his husband, Adam.

ALLEN GROVES, UVA DEAN OF STUDENTS: I'm thinking I need to get a lot of sleep tonight, because it's going to be a really challenging day tomorrow. And the phone rang around 8:20 and it was President Sullivan. And she said, *Allen, I just heard from a student that they're coming to Grounds tonight. They're coming to Grounds.* And I said, *I'll be right there.* So I told Adam, *I got to go back in. They may be coming to UVa.* And he said, *Well, you're not going alone. I'm going with you.*

So our dog Gracie, we piled her in the car and he got in the car and we drove and I got to UVa around nine. There's two guys helping a friend move into a Lawn room and otherwise it looks like a very quiet Friday night before students start to come. So we go to the other side of the Rotunda, the Jefferson statue side. There were those wooden benches and Adam and I sat down with Gracie at a bench and I said to him, *It seems very quiet.*

Meanwhile, the church service continued across the street.

REV. SETH WISPELWEY, PASTOR AND COFOUNDER, CONGREGATE C'VILLE: The first couple of hours flew by.[3]

At about 8:30 p.m., the US District Court issued its order preventing the city from moving the Unite the Right rally out of Emancipation Park. The park would therefore be the location of the rally on August 12.

MIKE SIGNER, CHARLOTTESVILLE MAYOR: We got the news about the court decision and I had to go draft a statement, we had to go work on it. I was sitting there not doing anything. So we left.

At 8:43 p.m., the first 911 call came in.

HEAPHY REPORT: An anonymous male caller claimed to have an AR-15 rifle and threatened to open fire inside the church in five minutes.

One block away, *Daily Progress* reporter Chris Suarez was writing his article in a Starbucks, trying to make his print deadline.

CHRIS SUAREZ, REPORTER, CHARLOTTESVILLE *DAILY PROGRESS*: Someone in our newsroom heard over the police scanner that there had been threats called in to the church. I have a distinct memory of seeing text messages from friends in the newsroom about the threats, telling me this is going on. All kinds of wild stuff, that someone was going to shoot up the church.

Unbeknownst to the organizers of the service or the worshippers inside, four responding police officers searched outside the church for a potential shooter and found none. The service continued. At 8:56, another call came in.

Heaphy report: An unidentified male called the [Emergency Communications Center] and threatened to walk inside St. Paul's and kill a large number of parishioners.

Again, police responded, but found no threat. The service continued.

At the same Starbucks down the street where Chris Suarez was working, a small group of activist street medics was holding an emergency meeting to discuss their plans for that night's torch march. They had only just found out it would take place at UVa.

STAR PETERSON, LOCAL ACTIVIST AND STREET MEDIC: There weren't that many of us, maybe eight, maybe five?

MELISSA WENDER, STREET MEDIC: I had taken on some degree of making sure things were in place and the supplies were in place. *Did we have aspirin? Did we have Gatorade? Did we have bandages? Did we have saline solution?*

STAR PETERSON: I remember us warning the Starbucks employees. We just went and told the people working there, *A bunch of Nazis are coming. I highly recommend you close and you go home now. Don't stay open late.* So, they called their manager and they're like, *We're getting out of here.* I'm glad that we did that.

MELISSA WENDER: My regular medic partner wasn't available, so I was actually partnered that night with Star. And I didn't really know Star in advance of that, but we talked enough and, you know, we go through a series of questions about whether you're willing to be arrested and your degree of medical training and this and that. And we thought we could work well together for that night.

STAR PETERSON: That was my first time running as a marked medic. Basically, if you're a marked medic, you don't protest. You wear the big cross or whatever. You don't participate in any of the actions. You're just there to provide first aid. Medics generally agree not to protest if we're marked, because then the cops will start aiming for us more than they already do.

MELISSA WENDER: Being a medic is a super interesting role because you're both involved and you're staying detached at the same time. So things were gearing up and then we decided to go over by the Rotunda.

In the student newspaper office in the basement of nearby Newcomb Hall, rising junior Tim Dodson was just biting into a takeout order of tacos. As the managing editor of the *Cavalier Daily*, Dodson was waiting for the court decision as to whether the white nationalists would be permitted to rally in the location they'd originally requested, Emancipation Park.

TIM DODSON, MANAGING EDITOR, *CAVALIER DAILY*: I'm just eating dinner and we're waiting for the injunction. Then we got word that there was going to be some sort of gathering of, at the time what we called the alt-right.

It was a really skeleton crew who was in town for *Cav Daily* at that point. The school year hadn't started yet. So I was texting different news writers trying to figure out, *Hey, is anyone able to come to UVa at this moment because this will probably be some sort of news story and we should try to report on it.*

ALEXIS GRAVELY, SENIOR ASSOCIATE NEWS EDITOR, *CAVALIER DAILY*: I was at home and going to start writing a story about the ruling. I was just tip-tapping on my laptop, writing my little story and then Tim texted me and he's like, *We have a tip that something is going to happen on Grounds. I'm not sure what it is. Can you come down?* Because we're short staffed and we're all doing everything, I was like the resident photographer for the weekend. So I just grabbed my camera and I was like, *OK, well, I'll come meet you at the Rotunda and we'll see what's happening.* I was going in kind of naively.

They got to the Rotunda, where more journalists were waiting.

DAVID FOKY, NEWS DIRECTOR, NBC29: We had been hearing this rumor that there was gonna be some sort of march or demonstration or torch thing at the Rotunda. But because we were so unsure if this was gonna happen, I didn't mind going out and hanging out on Grounds, waiting to see if these rumors were true.

There were a couple of journalists just down there sitting on the benches, just keeping an eye out, being real low key sitting around. We were just chatting.

ALEXIS GRAVELY: Tim was already there and he was talking to some other reporters there that I didn't know. Someone was from South America. And I think that was my first indication where I was like, *Whoa, this is kind of a big . . . Someone flew all the way from South America to cover this?*

We were standing there, but it was still very unclear what was happening. And so, we sort of realized that we were in the wrong place because the Rotunda was quiet, comparatively.

DAVID FOKY: We weren't seeing anything. We weren't hearing anything. Like, we were getting ready to leave.

Meanwhile, a group of student activists was gathered at Professor Walt Heinecke's house nearby, eating spaghetti he cooked for them and making protest signs for the next day.

KENDALL KING, THIRD-YEAR UVA STUDENT: Walt Heinecke was a teacher, a friend, a mentor of mine and a couple other of the people who were organizing that summer.

WALT HEINECKE, UVA PROFESSOR AND ACTIVIST: I just really wanted to support the cause and support them personally in the work that they were doing. It's really difficult to be an activist at UVa. The culture is anti-activist, and the small group of activists that come and go in UVa's history get punished a lot and they don't have a lot of resources and they don't get a lot of support. The faculty don't really support them very much.

I considered these students my colleagues. They asked me if they could use my house to organize for August 11th, 12th. I think they felt it was a safe space to organize and it was off the grid and nobody knew about it, like nobody knew where to find them.

So they came on the afternoon of the 11th and I think there was 20, 25 of them at the house and they were getting organized and figuring out where they were gonna sleep. I mean my house isn't that big; it's three bedrooms and a living room and it's not that big. So I told them, if you guys wanna stay...and they did, they wanted to stay over. So people brought sleeping bags. I think they trusted me to create that kind of a space for them.

KENDALL KING: That night we were going through the day's agenda for August 12th and we were saying, *OK, does everybody have a buddy? Does everybody have water? Here's our starting point.*

Professor Heinecke left the students in his house to finish eating while he headed to the church service at St. Paul's.

DEVIN WILLIS, SECOND-YEAR UVA STUDENT: At some point during the dinner, somebody came in—I don't remember who it is anymore—and informed us like, *Hey, we heard that Jason Kessler and some of his people are going to have something and it might be at UVa.*

KENDALL KING: So we were just like, *All right, drop everything. Let's go. Get your buddy.*

DEVIN WILLIS: One of the signs was already finished that we had intended to use for Unite the Right. So they were like, we're going to take this sign and go over there. And it will be like July 8th. They say their part, we say our part, and then everyone goes home.

Devin, Kendall, and other friends drove over to Grounds, parked, and then met up with a few more friends at the Jefferson statue outside the Rotunda. There was only a handful of students there. They didn't see any white supremacists, only the few journalists waiting.

DEVIN WILLIS: We're like, *OK, so we got here first.*[4] Someone decided the plan was that we're going to link arms and we're going to form a circle at the base of the statue.[5]

KENDALL KING: We had no intention of it being any sort of message about protecting the institution or defending Jefferson. A common civil rights tactic is to hold hands and form a blockade.

At the statue, Devin met up with his friend Natalie Romero, also a UVa student.

NATALIE ROMERO, SECOND-YEAR UVA STUDENT: I was wearing flip-flops, a little tank top, some knitted shorts.[6] Like, in no way was I trying to meet protesters. I was just, you know, it's your school. I'm walking distance, really. I just wanted to witness it for my own eyes.[7]

DAVID FOKY, NEWS DIRECTOR, NBC29, AT THE ROTUNDA: All of a sudden, somebody said that there were people gathering at Nameless Field. I'm a townie, I know UVa a little bit, but like I had no idea where Nameless Field was.

CHRIS SUAREZ, REPORTER, CHARLOTTESVILLE *DAILY PROGRESS*: Someone texted, *They're at Nameless Field.* Like that's where they're meeting. And I was like, *What the—is that a made-up name?* Like, what?

Nameless Field is the actual name of a large field at UVa.

DAVID FOKY: So once we figured that out, we went down there.

While the students continued to wait at the Rotunda, the journalists walked to Nameless Field to find the white supremacists.

TIM DODSON, MANAGING EDITOR, *CAVALIER DAILY*: I remember walking down to Nameless Field, and I recognized Jason Kessler, I think because he had been on TV and I was seeing photos of him in the *Daily Progress*.

Emily Gorcenski had also arrived at Nameless Field. She was alone because on Friday afternoon she'd received a call from the FBI asking her about her plans for the weekend.

EMILY GORCENSKI, LOCAL ACTIVIST: The FBI calls me and they're like, *So Emily, we hear you're planning a terror attack at the [Saturday] rally.* And I'm like, *Well, you heard wrong.*

They're like, *Yeah, we got an anonymous tip. These are usually false, but we have to investigate.* Da, da, da, da, da, da.

And so, I know that they're following my Twitter. I know that they're seeing that I'm an antifascist or whatever. And so I don't want to talk to them, but at the same time, I'm just like, *There's no plans for violence. It's been really clear what I've been doing, what I've been organizing. I can document everything if I need to. No, I'm not planning a terror attack, but have you considered the Nazis might be planning a terror attack?*

But because the FBI called me, I was like, *Well, I can't network anymore with the rest of the activists because the Feds are on me.* So then, I had pulled myself out of the network. So I went basically alone that night.

I livestreamed it. I wanted to show how pathetic they were. And they were very pathetic until somehow the 40 people turned into 400 like that. I mean, it was freaky. And then, things got real and then things got serious.

DAVID FOKY: Then we realized in the dark, there were hundreds of people down on that field and it became apparent that something was happening.

CHRIS SUAREZ: I came upon them, like, *Oh my God. This is a ton of people. And that's a lot of torches.*

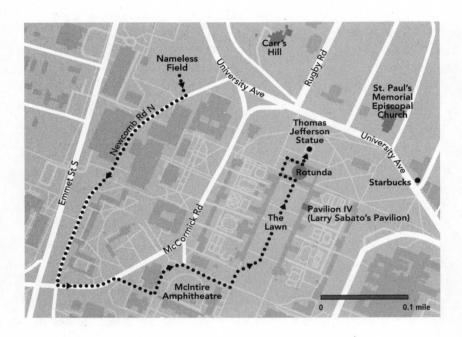

CHAPTER 5

"These are racist people carrying torches."

NAMELESS FIELD

UNIVERSITY OF VIRGINIA

9:45 P.M.

DAVID FOKY, NEWS DIRECTOR, NBC29: There were just scores and scores of people down there and they started handing out the tiki torches.

CHRIS SUAREZ, REPORTER, CHARLOTTESVILLE *DAILY PROGRESS*: I could tell immediately—this might be hyperbole, but this was four to six times, maybe up to ten times, as big as May. That was the first sign of like, *This is gonna be nuts.*

TERESA SULLIVAN, UVA PRESIDENT: I could barely make them out from where I was on Carr's Hill [across the street and up a hill]. And it was really too late to stop it at that point, particularly since at that point, I still thought it was going to be on the public sidewalks and therefore First Amendment protected.

ALEXIS GRAVELY, SENIOR ASSOCIATE NEWS EDITOR, *CAVALIER DAILY*: When we got there, the torches weren't lit yet, so it still wasn't very clear what was happening. And then I turned because Jason Kessler was behind me and there were a lot of people talking to him. So I looked to see what he was talking about. And then I turned back, and then Nameless Field was completely lit up. It just happened so quickly. It was just all very coordinated.

TERESA SULLIVAN: Then I saw the flames light up and I said to Marge [Side-bottom, emergency operations director], *What is going on here?* And Marge said, *I don't know. I don't know about this.* And she got on her cell phone too. So I don't think anybody was prepared for the torches.

I was pretty alarmed about this. First, there were so many more people and I knew we had very few police on Grounds that night because we had every-body on duty the next day. And we had everybody on 12-hour shifts the next day. And so we didn't have very many police. I didn't know if [the marchers] were armed or not. I could tell they were chanting, but I couldn't understand what they were saying. And so the lack of knowledge was scary, I think.

After that, it went really quite quickly. They obviously were quite organized.

TIM DODSON, MANAGING EDITOR, *CAVALIER DAILY*: There were people shouting, *If you're over 190 pounds, you need to get on the side.* I think it's 'cause they wanted larger men to protect the marchers.

EMILY GORCENSKI, LOCAL ACTIVIST: You could really tell that a lot of them were edging for violence. There's some pushing, shoving. I figured as long as I'm around the media, I'm not going to get picked up, because they're not going to beat somebody up on camera. And if they do, then great, we've made our point. Hopefully, the Saturday rally gets shut down.

REV. SETH WISPELWEY, PASTOR AND COFOUNDER, CONGREGATE C'VILLE, AT ST. PAUL'S: The service was running a little long, but we were nearing the end with some of our last singing.

SMASH CAINE-CONLEY, COFOUNDER, CONGREGATE C'VILLE: Seth and I were sitting next to each other and he leaned over and said to me that there was something going on over on UVa Grounds.

REV. SETH WISPELWEY: We were getting texts that there was a lot of white supremacists out, through a group message chain with my fellow clergy colleagues and a couple of people who were out in front of the church.[1]

The first time I heard that the march was approaching the church, we didn't know where it was headed. We actually thought it was approaching the church. We didn't know what we couldn't see, so I went outside on the front steps of St. Paul's.

He couldn't see anything, but checked in with the volunteer security team.

REV. SETH WISPELWEY: And they were like, *Well, we're going to keep eyes, but yeah, keep it going a little bit longer.*

At this point we're closing out with freedom songs, but we're meant to be at the end. And so Sekou is stretching it out more with "This Little Light of Mine" and this and that. And so at that point, the crowd doesn't know.

I.B.F., LOCAL ACTIVIST: Reverend Sekou was looking out and he was singing "This Little Light of Mine," and everybody was singing along as a powerful song.

And I don't know how he knew. I don't know who told him, but he turned around and his face changed. He turned towards the back where most people couldn't see him and his face changed. And I remember in that moment just being like, *Something is wrong.* It's not even like I'd known him so long or so much, but something about that. I felt my whole body buckle and I was like, *Something is very wrong and I don't know what it is.*

ROSIA PARKER, LOCAL ACTIVIST, OUTSIDE ST. PAUL'S: We sat outside maybe 45 minutes, I guess, maybe an hour almost. And then somebody came outside to get us and told us that we needed to go inside because something was getting ready to happen.

KATRINA TURNER, LOCAL ACTIVIST: We started seeing lights coming towards us. And so that's why they hurried us up in the church because they didn't know what was going on.

ROSIA PARKER: We couldn't get into church at first because it was full. And now that the danger is approaching now y'all made space to allow us in church? Y'all knew we were out there. You all knew the intel that they were coming. So even if the church was full, how did y'all make space?

So that kind of makes us feel some type of way, a little bit.

ALLEN GROVES, UVA DEAN OF STUDENTS, ON THE LAWN: I was communicating with President Sullivan and all of a sudden, there's this huge roar in the distance, kind of like a football game in the distance. I texted her. And I said, *Did you hear that?* Because she's at Carr's Hill across the street. And she said, *I did*. And I said, *Do you know where it's coming from?* And she said, *I don't, maybe Nameless Field?* Because it was that direction. And so at this point, I'm like, *Something is happening.* What, I didn't know. Candidly, there was a lack—the president and I didn't know what the university police knew at that moment.

Brian Moran was already in Charlottesville doing a preparatory walk-through of Emancipation Park downtown with Virginia State Police Superintendent Steve Flaherty. He also says he didn't know the torch march was coming.

BRIAN MORAN, SECRETARY, VIRGINIA PUBLIC SAFETY AND HOMELAND SE-CURITY: While I'm walking with Steve, he says, *We just got word that there's a protest on the Grounds.* And it turns out the state police had never been told about the protest, which goes to some of the communication breakdowns. So I said, *Well, where is it?* And he said, *Well, I think that they're going to the Rotunda.* And so I drive over to the Rotunda, try to find it.

And my first thought: *Where are the police?* That's what I was saying: *Where the heck are the police?* There's nobody there.

I said well, if there's a large demonstration, I don't see any police presence. So I was skeptical of the intel, but then I saw the lights.

DAVID FOKY, NEWS DIRECTOR, NBC29, IN NAMELESS FIELD: They all took off marching. And they climbed the hill out of Nameless.

TIM DODSON, MANAGING EDITOR, *CAVALIER DAILY*: It's kind of a steep hill between the parking lot and Nameless Field. I start to follow them.

DAVID FOKY: We ran along with them, our photojournalist Jeremy and I.

ALEXIS GRAVELY, SENIOR ASSOCIATE NEWS EDITOR, *CAVALIER DAILY*: They were chanting, *You will not replace us*. It was just so loud. And we were just following them. And I remember being struck by how coordinated it was. Like, this was not some impromptu thing.

I remember that's when I started getting a little emotional, which I almost felt ashamed by because I feel like journalists are always . . . Like, it's sort of shunned if you get emotional covering things because you're supposed to be neutral.

ALLEN GROVES, AT THE ROTUNDA: I'm trying to figure out what's happening. And now it's getting dark. And I do remember at one point President Sullivan texted me, I think it was one word, *amphitheater,* that she had heard from someone. And so I went around, I told Adam, *Keep Gracie, be safe.* I ran around to the Lawn [to find the white nationalists].

TIM DODSON: The march winds its way onto McCormick Road and they march past the amphitheater.

ALEXIS GRAVELY: The sidewalk is very narrow there. And so we were feeling a little cramped in. And I was like, *I'm a Black woman and these are racist people carrying torches, so maybe we should go elsewhere.* And so we went around and walked up past the Lawn rooms, sort of ahead of them.

TIM DODSON: Then they ended up on the southern part of the Lawn, and that's when it became clear they were going to the Rotunda.

BRIAN MORAN: Sure enough, I see these lights, near the Lawn coming toward the Rotunda. And so I pull over, I walk up to the Rotunda.

LARRY SABATO, UVA PROFESSOR, POLITICAL PUNDIT, AND PAVILION RESIDENT ON THE LAWN: All of a sudden, we heard this chanting and this noise, even before we saw anybody.

WASHINGTON POST: . . . the marchers continued their rapid trek across the university campus, their torches a line of fire as they hurried in formation past the school's iconic buildings. At times running to keep in formation they passed. The campus was almost entirely empty and silent except for the marchers and their threatening chants.[2]

ALLEN GROVES: Larry Sabato was out on the Lawn at this point. And so I see Larry and I go over and I said, *They're coming, apparently.* And he said, *Yeah, I've got some students in my Pavilion basement.*

It's now dark. It's about 10 o'clock and you could see them now coming and turning from where the amphitheater was, up the Lawn.

We were just blown away by both the numbers and all the flaming torches. And there were probably two- to three hundred of them. And as they're coming up, they're probably four to six abreast in a column coming up, and they're chanting, "You will not replace us."

BRIAN MORAN: They walked in unison, like you did when you were in elementary school, walked to the cafeteria.

ALLEN GROVES: And at one point when they come up to that last higher level of the Lawn where the rooms are, they change it to, "Jews will not replace us." And they start laughing.

LARRY SABATO: My jaw hit the floor. It was right out of the 1930s, really. And it *looked* like it was out of the thirties. I'm sure they were modeling it after the old newsreel films of the Nazis in Germany.[3]

WHITE NATIONALISTS: You will not replace us!
Jews will not replace us!
You will not replace us!
Jews will not replace us!

MALCOLM STEWART, FOURTH-YEAR UVA STUDENT AND SENIOR RESIDENT ON THE LAWN: They were escorted by police officers. Anytime someone kind of stepped out of it, some of the officers basically seemed to coax them back in with the crowd to just walk up the Lawn.

In the dark and chaos, it was unclear which department the officers were from.

MALCOLM STEWART: I went and found Larry Sabato and Dean Groves.

ALLEN GROVES: The bigger guys were on the outside. The not-as-big guys were on the inside and some women, not a lot of women, but some women. And I saw a couple of sheathed knives, I did see a couple of handguns as they're coming up.

TIM DODSON, MANAGING EDITOR, *CAVALIER DAILY*: This felt like some really absurd nightmare. It didn't feel like I was at UVa. It felt like I was in some other dimension.

LARRY SABATO: They had the meanest look on their faces, just full of hate. Contorted, really. And they were spoiling for a fight, no question about it, they were spoiling for a fight.

Lawn resident Diane D'Costa had just moved in that day.

DIANE D'COSTA, FOURTH-YEAR UVA STUDENT AND LAWN RESIDENT: I was in my room. As I'm putting sheets on my bed and trying to get my stuff together, 'cause I have like boxes and things all around, that's when I heard them outside of my door.

It was the guttural belly chant of, *Jews will not replace us*. It just sounded like an angry guttural chant of like an angry mob.

I just looked out my peephole. All I could see was just the flames.

At that point I was just kind of in shock. I was just trying to understand what was happening. My body is physically reacting, like in fear. It looked like a river of flames. It was flowing from the south end of the Lawn coming from the amphitheater, up towards the Rotunda. And you could just see this river of flames moving.

My door opened straight onto the Lawn. They were no more than four yards in front of me. Just the sidewalk and then the grass, and they were right on the grass. I was terrified. As a Jewish person, hearing "Jews"...[4] I was scared for my life. My chest started tightening up, and there was ringing in my ears. I was kind of in shock of what was happening and trying to process what was going on, but I was terrified.

WHITE NATIONALISTS: You will not replace us!
Jews will not replace us!
One people, one nation, end immigration.
You will not replace us!
Jews will not replace us!

DIANE D'COSTA: I took off my Hamsa necklace, an upside-down hand with an evil eye for protection, and my Shema ring, with Hebrew letters in a circle just on the ring, and threw it away and grabbed a sweater to leave.[5]

I just tried to hide any part of my Jewish identity. And looking back on it, I was really upset with myself that I did that. But I just didn't want any markers of who I was to cause me to be harmed. So I just did those things instinctually.

When I opened my door to walk out, the person closest to me had a swastika on his arm. I could see the mass of people carrying flames, walking, marching towards the Rotunda. They were still chanting *Jews will not replace us.*

It was the most traumatized I ever felt as a Jewish person. I was scared for my life. I thought that I was going to die if people knew who I was.

UPD TIMELINE: 10:07 p.m. Group begins to go up Rotunda stairs.

ALLEN GROVES, UVA DEAN OF STUDENTS: They're clearly moving around to the Jefferson statue side.

NATALIE ROMERO, SECOND-YEAR UVA STUDENT, AT THE STATUE: We weren't there for long before they arrived. [The students] kind of embraced each other.[6]

DEVIN WILLIS, SECOND-YEAR UVA STUDENT: We didn't have enough people to form the ring around the base of the statue. I could hear them talking about it on the other side: *We don't have enough, we don't have enough, we don't have enough.*[7]

I'm holding hands with Nat. It was just a lot of really loud and deep shouting coming from the other side of the Rotunda.[8]

NATALIE ROMERO: I just heard loudness, almost like thunder, like the earth was growling, essentially.[9] When we heard the roaring, we were like, *What should we do?* We just linked arms and held hands and started to sing.

I looked down, closed my eyes, prayed a little bit. I was terrified.[10] To my right was Devin. And we were just holding hands. We just looked at each other like, *It's OK, we're going to be OK.*[11]

DEVIN WILLIS: You start to see the glow, this mysterious glow on the other side of the Rotunda. And the shouting and growling gets louder, and these people, these lights, start rushing over the steps. I can see the steps from where I'm standing, and this ocean of light and flames just starts spilling over both sides of the steps and washing down.[12]

I was really scared because it looked like a lynch mob. Fire is a very intentional thing and it's a very scary thing.[13]

NATALIE ROMERO: The swarms of people coming down at us, just...the sky was dark with flame, dark and angry. It just felt like war. It literally was like a scene straight out of a movie swarming down towards us.

You wouldn't even understand the magnitude. They were coming from either side, it felt like hundreds of people. Angry, upset, screaming, yelling.[14]

We were singing at first. Then it was like complete silence. Like, what do we—what am I going to sing right now? I'm terrified.

EMILY GORCENSKI, LOCAL ACTIVIST: That's when I realized it was real. That's when I realized that this was no longer...that this was something much more serious than even I had imagined it to be. And when I got to the square around the statue and saw the students, my heart sank.

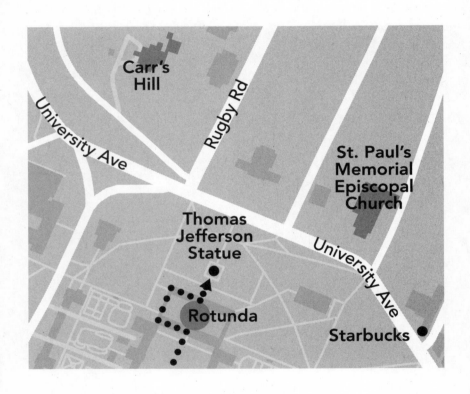

CHAPTER 6

"If they could have killed us all right then, they would have."

DEVIN WILLIS, SECOND-YEAR UVA STUDENT: You start to hear what they're saying.

WHITE NATIONALISTS: Blood and soil!
One people, one nation, end immigration.
You will not replace us!
Jews will not replace us!

DEVIN WILLIS: The vast majority of the men were white, adult-looking. A lot of them had the same haircuts. And almost all of them were wearing some combination of a white dress shirt or polo shirt and khaki pants. I also saw several people who had holstered weapons on the side of their hip.[1] And they basically just rushed the entire area and surrounded all of us in a matter of seconds.[2]

I realized as they were coming, and as it was too late to go anywhere, that I was really wrong about how many people would be there.[3]

The students were vastly outnumbered by the white nationalists, though they were not entirely without allies.

KENDALL KING, THIRD-YEAR UVA STUDENT: I think we felt really safe because Emily was there and there were a couple other community members who we had organized with.

EMILY GORCENSKI, LOCAL ACTIVIST: And at that point, I'm like, *OK, well, I came here to film. I'm going to film.* At that point, my only thought was, *Keep the camera going at all costs. You have a job, you have to do it.*

Because it's one of the few ways that we have as individuals to have a voice greater than what we would normally be able to achieve. It shows what's going on in real time. It uses the power of the networks that we have already built. It gives you a perspective that's nearly a first-person perspective of what's happening. It's unedited, it's uneditable. Then, they completely surrounded us and wouldn't let us out.

COUNTERPROTESTERS: Black lives matter! Black lives matter!

KENDALL KING: I was with my buddy, who was Devin. We just chanted and chanted and chanted, but then it became clear once they surrounded us, it was like, *Oh shit, what have we done?*

The street medics arrived on scene. From the Rotunda, they watched the situation at the statue as the student activists there, along with the handful of community activists and Emily Gorcenski, were surrounded by white nationalists.

STAR PETERSON, LOCAL ACTIVIST AND STREET MEDIC: I wanted so badly to jump in with my friends who were around the statue. My medic buddy was like, *Nope, you are a marked medic. You stay out until they need you to come in and fix somebody.* I was like, *Well, fuck this. I will never be a marked medic again.* Yeah, so I had to stand there and watch this hoard surround some of the people I love most in the world.

MELISSA WENDER, STREET MEDIC: They were saying, *Jews will not replace us.* And I'm Jewish myself.

ELIZABETH SINES, UVA LAW STUDENT: Through the chaos, there were students at the base holding a sign: *VA Students Act Against White Supremacy.*[4]

That was the sign completed at Professor Heinecke's spaghetti dinner.

NATALIE ROMERO, SECOND-YEAR UVA STUDENT: Once they started to sur-round us, they kind of directly came at Devin and I. And they were saying very specific things to us:

Go back to where you came from.

Stupid bitch.

Stuff like that. Monkey noises.[5]

DEVIN WILLIS: I've really tried to drive these comments out of my mind, but I know that the monkey noises were happening again.[6] And it's extremely hot because of all the flame.[7]

NATALIE ROMERO: Devin and I were the only people of color on that side. And it was very, very obvious and very apparent. They were screaming at *us.*[8] I tried to jump up onto the statue, but there's literally no little platform or anything. And I'm wearing sandals. So I'm like, I'm going to get tram-pled. For reference, I'm 4'10" and a half. I'm tiny. And everyone is just giant, screaming.[9]

Across the street, the prayer service was still ongoing.

WALT HEINECKE, UVA PROFESSOR AND ACTIVIST: I'm on that grassy area in front of St. Paul's chatting with SURJ [Showing up for Racial Justice] secu-rity folks and this activist from the anarchists of color group came up to me. And she looks up and sees me and says, *Hey, Walt, your students are surrounded by neo-Nazis at the Rotunda.* And for a minute, I didn't quite—it didn't quite process, but she came back and she said, *Hey, Walt, man, these, these kids are surrounded and it's not pretty.*

So I ran over there and lo and behold, I saw these 150, 200 neo-Nazis with torches. The students were in a circle, locked arms around the statue. And I looked around and I didn't see any police presence.

The unidentified police who had been walking alongside the march-ers earlier were no longer visible, according to scores of witnesses. It's not clear where they went.

ALLEN GROVES, UVA DEAN OF STUDENTS: Walt comes running up to me and says, *Allen, where are the police?* I said, *I don't know.*

And so he said, *The students are surrounded.* And I said, *What do you mean the students are surrounded?* And he said, *There's a group of students who've locked arms around the statue. They're in the middle there.* And I said, *We've got to get them out.*

KENDALL KING, AT THE STATUE: I have no clue what's set off anything, but I remember immediately just like a lot of jostling, a lot of brawling, like a lot of fist fighting.

CHRIS SUAREZ, REPORTER, CHARLOTTESVILLE *DAILY PROGRESS*: I was at the top of the Rotunda looking down when I saw, suddenly, flames being flung at people. They were screaming. Obviously something very bad was happening.

CHRIS SUAREZ TWEET, 10:15 P.M.: White lives matter chant drowning out black lives matter chant. Fighting breaking out now.[10]

DEVIN WILLIS: Tiki torches, still on fire, were being thrown in our direction. They're also being wielded as weapons. They're being swung at the crowd. You're just trying to make yourself as small as possible so you get hit by as few things as possible.[11]

BRIAN MORAN, SECRETARY, VIRGINIA PUBLIC SAFETY AND HOMELAND SECU-RITY: It broke out into absolute chaos there for, I don't know, it seemed like a long time, but it probably was a few minutes.

DEVIN WILLIS: So at about that moment is when Dean Groves appears. Dean Groves was the dean of students at UVa at the time. He was somebody, I think, whose job it was to know everybody.

ALLEN GROVES: I remembered Devin. We had met his first year. I had asked a student, a fourth-year who was in charge of this group called Black Male Initiative, which was a conversation group, and I said, *Would you mind if I attended one of these? And I promise, I won't say anything, but I'd love to ... it would help me grow as a person to hear this perspective.* And he said, *Absolutely, Dean Groves.* So I came and kind of sat off to the side and Devin was a brand new first-year. You could tell he was so gifted and so bright and so thoughtful in the points that he made that evening. And so he and I ended up having a couple of lunches and stayed in touch with each other. And so, yes, I recognized him that night. He was the one person, the one student I recognized.

It didn't surprise me he was there because he was a person of strong values and strong beliefs and he wanted to take a stand against this. But Devin is not a large guy. And I had seen the guys that were surrounding him and I was very worried about violence.

So I just pushed through the crowd and Walt, to his credit, was right behind me. And I don't remember a lot of calculated analysis. I just felt like, *I'm the dean, these are my students. And I've got to protect them.*

I leaned in to Devin and I said, *It's Dean Groves. It's Dean Groves.* I'd taken my hat off so they could see this [white] hair, which is kind of part of my brand, and so I said, *It's Dean Groves. This is terribly unsafe. I've got to get you out of here.*

And I still remember, I never saw it coming: One of the torches comes flying in and hits me. It was thrown as a spear and it hit me kind of in the chest and arm. And I cut my arm and I remember yelling an expletive and kicking the little canister away, the flaming canister away on the ground.

And then just all hell broke loose. They started beating the students and the community members that are around the statue with their torches. There was Mace everywhere. And so I was grabbing students and pulling them out of the way and coming back in and trying to get them out of the mob. I got Maced in the face. I remember doubling over and trying to catch my breath and clear my face.

LARRY SABATO, UVA PROFESSOR: He was right in the middle of it and really tried to get those people away from the students. They were vicious to him and everyone else. I don't know if they knew he was dean of students or not, I'm not sure it mattered one way or the other.

I felt kinda guilty for standing on the steps.

WALT HEINECKE: Within seconds after that, I noticed that one of those leaders of the neo-Confederates was punching one of the lead student organizers in the face. And then seconds after that, the neo-Nazis and the neo-Confederates started Macing us or pepper spraying us. I got hit in the lip and on the leg, I was wearing shorts. And it just turned into a melee.

DAVID FOKY, NEWS DIRECTOR, NBC29: It was like when you see the movies of foot soldiers clashing with hand-to-hand combat.

EMILY GORCENSKI: A fight broke out to my right. They recognized me. They knew who I was, they knew I was trans. They were directing hate at me. They were saying things like, *Oh there's only two genders.* One person was like, *Have you cut off your part, like what kind of sicko are you?* I found out later looking at the Discords, they were stalking me. They were following me that night.

I got punched. I got kicked. I remember getting hit in the head. I thought it was with a torch. I stepped forward at one point and I got shoved back. I thought I was going to die.[12]

DEVIN WILLIS: There's a lot of pepper spray in the air. It's like there's no fresh air left to breathe. All you can do is just try to get lower.[13]

KENDALL KING: I got pepper sprayed in the eye, so I stopped being able to understand what was going on around me, which was also terrifying. .

DEVIN WILLIS: I remember that someone from the direction of the mob threw some mysterious fluid. It looked like it came out of somebody's tiki torch canister, and they threw it at the direction of our feet. It seemed like it might be some type of lighter fluid or something like that, and I thought that their strategy was going to be to burn us alive.

It got on and near my shoes, which was really scary. So I tried to break the trail. And so I tried to stand further on the marble of the statue and off of the brick that was now doused. I thought I had made a very terrible mistake and that I might die that night.

NATALIE ROMERO, SECOND-YEAR UVA STUDENT: I felt like a mouse, trapped, like a Salem Witch Trial type, like I'm about to be burned at the stake.[14] It felt like forever.[15]

WHITE NATIONALISTS: White lives matter! White lives matter! White lives matter! White lives matter!

EMILY GORCENSKI'S LIVESTREAM: We are penned in. We are surrounded on all sides by hundreds of Nazis. We have no way out.[16]

EMILY GORCENSKI: The thing that really sticks out in my head is how happy the Nazis were to be doing the violence. They were angry, they were rageful, they were violent. But when they had us surrounded, they were euphoric. There was almost a sexual happiness that they had. There was nothing that they wanted to be doing more than being there, outnumbering a bunch of students, 10 to 1, 20 to 1, and committing massive amounts of violence. If they could have killed us all right then, they would have. If they had guns and if the cops weren't watching, they would have. This was their pogrom; this was their Kristallnacht.

DAVID STRAUGHN, LOCAL ACTIVIST: You couldn't believe how happy they were, shirtless, dancing around. I said, *Oh my God, these are the imps of Satan!* This is what I imagine hell to look like: just crazy fucks dancing around in fire while other people suffer and die.

TIM DODSON, MANAGING EDITOR, *CAVALIER DAILY*: At this point I'm at the part of the Rotunda steps that overlooks the statue. I don't remember seeing any police. Nobody had intervened to break this thing up.

WALT HEINECKE: At 10:04 or something, I called the police, I called 911.

What's the nature of your emergency?

I'm like, *Well, there's 150 neo-Nazis and they're beating people up here and there's no police!*

BRIAN MORAN, SECRETARY, VIRGINIA PUBLIC SAFETY AND HOMELAND SECURITY: Finally, some police arrived.

Both university police and City of Charlottesville police eventually responded.

LARRY SABATO, UVA PROFESSOR: You had a long line of police on the steps of the Rotunda, but they weren't, they weren't interjecting themselves.

ALEXIS GRAVELY, SENIOR ASSOCIATE NEWS EDITOR, *CAVALIER DAILY*: I was on the steps and the police officers were *above* me on the steps. And I'm like, *Why? Why are you up here and not down there?* Like, there's something wrong here. They were just watching. I just remember thinking, like, *They do not seem to be here to stop any of this.*

DAVID FOKY: I have no recollection of police officers, certainly in uniform, being in the middle of that melee trying to stop it.

LARRY SABATO: We were all looking to this line of police, like *What are you going to do?*[17]

At home, Mayor Mike Signer found out what was happening from social media posts.

MIKE SIGNER: I called Pat Hogan, UVa's chief operations officer, and told him what I was watching.[18] He said he was on vacation; it sounded like there were kids in the background. And he said, *I'm not in town right now.* And then—and I'm paraphrasing, but he said, *From what I hear, everything is fine.*

Everything was happening so fast, but it was dumbfounding that he didn't know about it, while it was happening in real time. I was relaying something that I was watching on social media to him. This is real fog of war stuff. It was kind of crazy that I just had to say, *Look at this website,* and then he looked at it and then he said, *I gotta call our chief of police.* And then he was off the line.[19]

REV. SETH WISPELWEY, PASTOR AND COFOUNDER, CONGREGATE C'VILLE, AT ST. PAUL'S: I go back out front within a few minutes and that's when you could see all the fire, all the torches from the steps of the church.

WILLIS JENKINS, UVA PROFESSOR: As the torches came into view at the Rotunda, someone sprinted across the street with an urgent message: Students were holding their ground at the Jefferson statue at the bottom of the Rotunda steps with no one to defend them. She pleaded with us to go assist them.[20]

SMASH CAINE-CONLEY, COFOUNDER, CONGREGATE C'VILLE: I remember saying like, *We're gonna go figure it out right now.* And a few of us went to a room to try to talk about how to respond. I think individually I really shrank away in that moment. I think I allowed other people to make decisions 'cause I was scared and didn't know what to do.

WILLIS JENKINS: The lead organizer instructed us to remain at our posts, for there were hundreds of people in the church and no police in sight; our duty was to protect the assembly. The messenger cursed us in frustration and ran back.[21]

I am haunted by that moment. Of course we should not have relayed to the crowd of untrained people inside the building, many already fearful of the situation outside, an invitation to confront an armed mob, and of course all of us standing guard could not have abandoned our post. But I am a faculty member, and those were our students.[22]

SMASH CAINE-CONLEY: I know why decisions were made to protect people in the church and I don't necessarily disagree with those. I think for me it's more about how I responded individually. I really regretted not directly going to help them. It wasn't random people asking me for help—the folks that were asking for help and some of the students that were at the statue were people I *know*.

I definitely didn't know any of the details of what was happening, I was just being told, *There are Nazis here surrounding the statue. There are people in danger.* And I think that that should have been enough.

I.B.F., LOCAL ACTIVIST: There was a church full of people, if we had just walked across... if we had just gone out the front door and been like, *What are you doing?* Maybe it would have changed things? It almost holds greater trauma because it was just a few folks against hundreds of people with fire, and I was right there and I didn't do anything. I know rationally that there were reasons that everyone made the choices that they did and that it was based on the information we had at the time, and it was the best that we could do. But still I can't help but feel really guilty about it.

REV. SETH WISPELWEY, INSIDE THE CHURCH: [Sekou] made the announcement to the church. *It's come to our attention...* like we're trying not to start a panic. We had them sit down. We really didn't want to create a panic. It was full. We had people of all ages and backgrounds there. And he said, *We've got a situation outside. We're going to keep singing. And this is—it's all right, but we're going to—no one go out the front doors right now.* That was the initial announcement.[23]

DON GATHERS, COFOUNDER, CHARLOTTESVILLE BLACK LIVES MATTER: The service continued, with a heightened awareness of the immediate surroundings. We had people posted at every possible entrance, both inside and out, folks who had literally put their bodies on the line in case it came to that.

No one was coming out. No one was going in.

False rumors spread that the white nationalists were, in fact, marching on the church.

JALANE SCHMIDT, UVA PROFESSOR AND COFOUNDER, CHARLOTTESVILLE BLACK LIVES MATTER: It was like a fog of war kind of thing. There's pandemonium. *The Nazis are marching toward the church.* That's what we heard.

JALANE SCHMIDT TWEET, 10:07 P.M.: Trapped, w 100s, inside St. Paul's church after #defendcville prayer service. Alt-right gathered outside.[24]

REV. TRACI BLACKMON TWEET: They are coming for the church! Police all around. They won't let us go outside. Y'all these KKK are marching with torches!

ROSIA PARKER, LOCAL ACTIVIST: I felt like the four little girls in the Birmingham Church, the girls that got burnt at Martin Luther King's church. You kind of like, this can't be real? It's just like a movie or something playing in your head.

Due to her public activism, Jalane Schmidt had already been tagged as a high-profile target for the white supremacists. She had her own activist security detail that weekend.

JALANE SCHMIDT: We were just like, *Oh hell no, I'm getting outta here.*

I'd been mentioned by name in these forums, these chat rooms and whatnot. So I was warned to really take care and not stay in my house during all this. I didn't stay in my house for eight days.

So we were busting toward a side door to get out.

We went down an alleyway and then hopped into [my security's] car and took back streets out of there.[25]

LISA DRAINE, LOCAL ACTIVIST: [My daughter] Rebecca and I, instead of leaving at that point, we went out the back and came around to the front of

St. Paul's and we're standing on the steps. And from there, we could see this squiggly line of fire. We were like, we should go and see what's happening. So we actually walked down University Avenue until we were directly across from the Rotunda. And then at some moment we heard the chant, *Black lives matter, Black lives matter.*

And I turned to Rebecca and I said, *I bet you Sophie's there.*

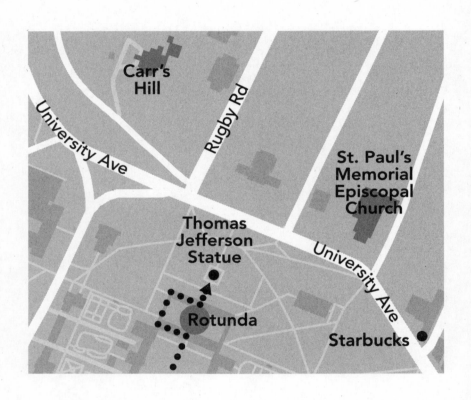

CHAPTER 7

"Does this change what we're going to do tomorrow?"

10:15 P.M.

LISA DRAINE, LOCAL ACTIVIST: So we ran across University Avenue and scampered up through the bushes and we arrived on this scene of total chaos.

DEVIN WILLIS, SECOND-YEAR UVA STUDENT, AT THE JEFFERSON STATUE: It got to a point where I was just so horrified and I was so afraid and I felt like I had a lot to live for. I wanted to leave. I was like, *I'm ready to go.*[1]

NATALIE ROMERO, SECOND-YEAR UVA STUDENT: I was just like, *Which way? How do we get out of here?* You couldn't really see an exit.[2]

DEVIN WILLIS: Eventually we were able to communicate amongst ourselves that we were going to try to escape, but that would require, of course, letting our hands go and collapsing and forming a group so that we could get out. And that was as dangerous as it sounded.

So the plan was that because me and Nat were being targeted and that because we are very obviously people of color—I'm a Black man; she's a Latina woman—that we were in the most danger. And the fight was happening on our side. So our friends formed a circle around us and tried their best to escort us off of the statue, but the minute that we let go of our hands, of course, the white nationalists basically pummeled us. They took advantage of the chaos. And so all the friends were thankfully very quick in collapsing around me and forming a circle around me and Nat. The white nationalists are beating, badly, my friends who are standing between us and them. And so I'm watching—as me and Nat are basically crawling off the statue—I'm watching the people who are standing above me, my friends, take pepper sprays at point-blank range directly into their eyes. I'm watching them take punches and kicks to their backs and the backs of their heads as they're just trying to escort us off the statue.[3]

NATALIE ROMERO: I don't know how they did it.[4]

DEVIN WILLIS: We hobble over to a group of benches and we try to rally ourselves. We try to lick our wounds. People were doing first aid. So I'm watching close friends of mine get milk poured on their eyes. Everyone is coughing, crying, getting themselves together.[5]

I felt like I had just been attacked and driven off of the statue, and that that was, in my 18-year-old imagination, somehow embarrassing.[6]

WHITE NATIONALISTS: Torches out!

ELIZABETH SINES, UVA LAW STUDENT: The torches went out in a wave.

LISA DRAINE: You could see torches going out and people running in all directions, people fighting—like on the ground fighting and then people on the ground. There was some chemical agent in the air. We were like, *Oh my God.*

And we found Sophie and her friends all huddled there and kind of shell-shocked. And it was like, *Oh my God, Sophie, come home with us.* And she was like, *No, no, I need to debrief with my friends and I'll be home later.*

The dinner with friends Sophie had told her mother about was the gathering at Walt Heinecke's house. She had been there with Devin Willis, Kendall King, and the other students.

LISA DRAINE: And, of course, we didn't know what had happened at the time. But if you look at the photos, you'll see a big white banner that says, "VA students against white supremacy." Sophie was one of the people holding that banner.

KENDALL KING, THIRD-YEAR UVA STUDENT: I remember I couldn't find one of my friends and that freaked me out a lot. And I was really scared that they had essentially taken her.

Kendall later tracked down her friend.

Other counterprotesters ran over to St. Paul's to get help. At that point, many of them had been Maced and pepper sprayed at point-blank range.

REV. SETH WISPELWEY, PASTOR AND COFOUNDER, CONGREGATE C'VILLE AT ST. PAUL'S: I remember a young Black woman just screaming, *We need help. We need water.* So I'm running back to the kitchen of this church with them like, *Come back, we're filling up these old milk jugs with water.* Then we were looking for milk, which is the better thing.

STAR PETERSON, LOCAL ACTIVIST AND STREET MEDIC, AT THE STATUE: I ended up going to the eye wash station.

KENDALL KING: Street medics came and washed our eyes out.

NATALIE ROMERO: By then I had already been Maced. There was somebody in a wheelchair. It was a student. They were getting their eyes washed out.

ALLEN GROVES, UVA DEAN OF STUDENTS: They had Maced a young woman in a wheelchair! I'm like, *Honest to God . . .*

NATALIE ROMERO: And then there was a couple of other people on the floor getting their eyes washed out, including me.[7]

STAR PETERSON: Even after you rinse out their eyes, there's not a lot you can do. Right? Except sit there and suffer.

So, there was someone, I had no idea who they were, but I just said, *Hey, do you want to hold my hands?* So, I just sat there, and again, they couldn't even open their eyes, and just held their hands while they went through the worst of the pain.

ALEXIS GRAVELY, SENIOR ASSOCIATE NEWS EDITOR, *CAVALIER DAILY*: The police were there afterwards, but by then it was too late.

ALLEN GROVES: I was trying to talk to the police because they didn't know who the bad guys were and I was trying to yell at them, no, no, no. The people who were still there were students and a couple of townspeople who had been Maced.

WALT HEINECKE, UVA PROFESSOR AND ACTIVIST: The police showed up and were basically saying, *This is an illegal assembly and we're gonna arrest you.* They were gonna arrest the students.

NATALIE ROMERO: There were police that lined up and then started to tell people that they had to leave—including us. They were like, *Everyone has to go.*[8]

WALT HEINECKE: So I told the students, I said, *It's time to go. You guys gotta get outta here.* So, they went off, they all kind of scurried out the back way.

MALCOLM STEWART'S GROUP TEXT, 10:24 P.M.: It's dying down. Interviews are happening. I met Dean Grove's dog. She's a good dog.

ALLEN GROVES: Once people had cleared out, we were there, and Gracie was comforting several people. And we're fortunate that's just her personality.

She was what's called a flat coat retriever, so, imagine a black golden retriever. We had adopted her from the Charlottesville SPCA. We wanted to save an older dog, and so she was eight years old. She had been pretty badly abused. She couldn't be a more chill, easygoing, sweet dog.

I didn't realize I was bleeding until after I pulled my shirt up after it was all done and realized that, yeah, it [the thrown torch] had cut me and there was blood on my shirt and on my arm. Remarkably, not as bad as it could have been—if the flaming gel from the canister and stuff had hit me dead in my chest and that had caught fire, that might have been pretty dicey.

TOM BERRY, DIRECTOR OF EMERGENCY MANAGEMENT, UVA MEDICAL CENTER: We started receiving ambulances and pickup trucks. Some people were throwing their buddy into vehicles and showing up right there at the ER bay. That's when it became real.

TERESA SULLIVAN, UVA PRESIDENT: You know, we had a police officer who went to the hospital that night. He had a knee injury.

As the torch march dispersed and students nursed their wounds, people in the church finally breathed a sigh of relief. It looked like they

weren't being targeted, for now. Organizers at the church officially lifted the lockdown with a closing prayer and a coordinated exit.

CHURCH LEADER, TO THE CROWD: I think it's a good time for a prayer for our enemies. God called us to the hard work of loving our enemies. Lead them and lead us from prejudice to truth. Deliver them and deliver us from hatred, cruelty, and revenge.[9]

DON GATHERS, COFOUNDER, CHARLOTTESVILLE BLACK LIVES MATTER: We then slowly began to allow people to exit the church. No one left on their own.

REV. SETH WISPELWEY: We started evacuating people out the back of the church, through the kitchen, as I recall, and then the side and the back alleys down Chancellor Street. For folks who might not have had someone we insisted on a buddy system, that they meet their new best friend, because we really wanted to make sure people got to their cars safely. But there were so many people, we had people go out in groups.[10]

I.B.F., LOCAL ACTIVIST: We had to evacuate the church. And I remember taking off my hijab, it was white and sea green stripes, and putting on a hat—it was Smash's hat because I didn't have a hat—and then leaving out the back door, and running to the car, and the car driving back to [our activist] headquarters [at an apartment].

REV. SETH WISPELWEY: After the service we were going to use one of their big gathering fellowship rooms to do, as best we could, some of that tactile bodily awareness training for people. We never got to do it.

KATRINA TURNER, LOCAL ACTIVIST: I had called my sons and I told them, *Look, we're locked in the church. They just tried to surround this church with tiki torches. Please come up here and get us. You have to come up here now!* That was just all I had to say. *Please come up here and get us. We need help.* And they came. So both my sons came to the church and started helping people get back to their cars.

REV. SETH WISPELWEY: I don't think the church was fully empty of attendees until maybe 11:30.

DON GATHERS: We had just had a wonderful evening. No one was going to take that from us. That was what their intent was, and we weren't going to allow that to happen.

A valiant goal, but the trauma seeped in. Rev. Wispelwey's seven-year-old daughter, a person of color, was at the service with him.

REV. SETH WISPELWEY: We wanted to be upfront with her and also recognize the tender age.

She was old enough to know what her parents were about and doing, knew it was serious, knew that it was hateful, knew that it was a threat to her, and she freaked out, for lack of a better word. I can only describe it as a panic attack. She was crying uncontrollably.[11]

There was a lot of comforting and she didn't want to leave me because she knew I was part of the response to these people. So just being like, *We're OK. Daddy's gonna be OK and Mommy's gonna look after you.* But like, *These men are dangerous.* These were hard conversations to navigate with a seven-year-old.

After the service, the clergy activists headed to a nearby hotel called The Graduate, where Don Gathers worked his day job.

REV. SETH WISPELWEY: We're waiting for other people to get to the hotel to talk through like, *Does this change what we're going to do tomorrow?* Because by then, word is starting to come, like some bad shit went down at the statue, worse than we already saw.

DON GATHERS: As we got Dr. [Cornel] West down to the hotel, there actually were several of the Nazis gathered outside on the sidewalk. The hotel is right there. So, I mean, it was not a surprise that some of them were actually staying there.

REV. SETH WISPELWEY: And someone looks outside the lobby windows and is like, *That looks like Augustus Invictus.*

Invictus is a well-known white supremacist who was scheduled to speak at Unite the Right the next morning.

REV. SETH WISPELWEY: We're like, *Shit, this is supposed to be the safe space.*

I still have my clergy collar on at this point. A friend of ours, a fellow white man, went out to confirm it was Invictus and document his vehicle. I wanted to make sure he was OK, and hold space by the door, and pulled out my own phone to take pictures, which set Invictus off.

Augustus Invictus starts coming at me. He's, like, backing me up into the lobby. The activists still back in the lobby were not tall, straight, white men like me. They're spooked and crouching behind couches, everything, because these are folks of different marginalized identities and so on. And he's like threatening me and being like, *What church do you go to?* And everything. And I'm just standing there, like, *You'll find out tomorrow.* And he is like, *Well y'all are going down tomorrow.* I stood my ground there in the lobby because I could tell, like, this isn't good. And eventually they back off. They drove off.

But later I got called on this kind of chauvinistic impulse [to confront Invictus]. It was a good learning moment for me too that just because you're doing the "right thing" on paper, I hadn't thought like I'm also bringing risk into this place where these other comrades are.

So eventually, I'd say at least midnight, we went up to the spare room. It's a big room, two queens, and someone had gotten some pizza and we stayed up 'til like 3 a.m. talking through, learning what had happened.

I was listening and everything and we're like, *Do we continue with what we're planning to do?*

SMASH CAINE-CONLEY, COFOUNDER, CONGREGATE C'VILLE: We took in everything that had already happened and tried to process with one another what the rest of the weekend was going to go like. That in and of itself I think was a really hard space to be in because of what had already happened. And then we were trying to figure out how to do the next day.

REV. SETH WISPELWEY: In the end we decided that our presence and the story we hoped to bring should continue.[12]

Across Charlottesville, shell-shocked activists and witnesses headed toward an uneasy sleep.

DIANE D'COSTA, FOURTH-YEAR UVA STUDENT AND LAWN RESIDENT: I didn't want to be anywhere near the Lawn that night. My friend, who lives in

Charlottesville, texted me. And he said, you can stay at my parents' house in Charlottesville, and I gladly took him up on that offer.

He pulled up in the alleyway right next to Pavilion Ten, and I ran out the back of the Pavilion straight to his car. It was like I was fleeing my house and it was wild because I have memories of my family telling me stories of my great-grandmother fleeing Poland. And it felt like fleeing my home from Nazis, but on the Lawn.[13]

Then we drove down and there were still people [including white nationalists] walking, and that was like pretty scary. I just remember crying, thinking that people would see me.

MELISSA WENDER, STREET MEDIC: I don't remember what time I left. I don't remember whether I walked home by myself or with someone else. I don't know what time I got home. Don't know a thing about it.

KENDALL KING, THIRD-YEAR UVA STUDENT: The group of us, which was maybe like 25, 30, found everybody, checked in, walked to the end of the Lawn, sat on the stairs of Cabell Hall and sort of assessed our wounds. And basically we were like, *Is everyone OK? What did we learn about tomorrow? Are we still OK to go out tomorrow? And unanimously: Yes. Yes. Yes.* Everyone was like, *That was horrible. We are traumatized, but we will absolutely be there tomorrow at 6 a.m.* That was a really moving, amazing moment.

NATALIE ROMERO, SECOND-YEAR UVA STUDENT: I didn't know what the effect of the spray was. So I didn't know that you shouldn't shower. I got in the shower to cry. I kind of sat there, and as the water is hitting me, it's just like reliving it all again, because it started to go back into my eye. It spread through my body, my entire body. And, yeah, I sat there in pain from the stinging of it. And I—once I realized I was making it worse, I just kind of sat in the tub trying to make sense of what I had just witnessed.[14]

ALLEN GROVES, UVA DEAN OF STUDENTS, AT HOME: So I get home probably around 1 a.m. I remember going in the shower at my home and turning on the shower and putting my head under it. And my eyes just exploded because the dried Mace on my face was activated by the water. And so the worst impact of the Mace was actually in my shower at home.

KATRINA TURNER, LOCAL ACTIVIST: After church, I just went home, cried a little and went to sleep. That's all I could do. I mean, we knew that we had another day coming. Just had to get my rest, and get ready.

ROSIA PARKER, LOCAL ACTIVIST: And for me, I had to come home and get my community prepared because I live in a low-income neighborhood where the white supremacists have already been. So trying to prepare my community for what was to come: talking to different people and basically trying to be around my children for a time.

I was just praying and going into worship, reading my Bible, doing what I had to do. I knew that I might not make it back home. I was mentally prepared to die that day.

EMILY BLOUT, UVA PROFESSOR AND MAYOR MIKE SIGNER'S WIFE: We were advised by the FBI at that time to not be in our house for the weekend. We were getting a steady stream of white supremacist threats, mostly threats based on my husband's religion, Judaism. I think the ones that were most powerful and scary came through the mail, 'cause they figured out where we lived, and were targeting us in a consistent way. And so we bundled up our little babies, three-year-olds, and we took them to a different location and we stayed in a different place.

MAYOR MIKE SIGNER JOURNAL ENTRY, 1:15 A.M.: There is going to be an unlawful assembly after about 20 minutes tomorrow. And there will be some mayhem. And then there will be a day of *brush fires* around the city, just as Baxter predicted. I do wonder if there will be rioting or some form of it. I'm glad we have our crisis communications guy with us, but this is going to be bad and will be a rough stomach-turning day. These guys tonight were like ISIS, spectacular propaganda and striking where it was least expected and will make the most impact. Spencer is smart that way, this plays right in his strike zone. And the whole weekend is now teed up for maximum impact and maximum fear among the "cucks" as they called them.

TERRY MCAULIFFE, VIRGINIA GOVERNOR: It became clear to me, when Brian [Moran] briefed me and said they literally were throwing the torches at people, that these were jackasses and this was going to be very, very serious. And I said to Brian . . . *We better be ready 'cause this is gonna be much worse. These people are here to hurt people.*

BRIAN MORAN, SECRETARY, VIRGINIA PUBLIC SAFETY AND HOMELAND SE-CURITY: I got to the room and called the president of the university, Sullivan. And she called me back around midnight and said that somebody had known about this march, but it never got to her. And she said, *I don't know if we're prepared for tomorrow.* Here it is midnight, you know.

TERESA SULLIVAN, UVA PRESIDENT: There was more going on in terms of encoded messages and so on that we just weren't aware of. We just didn't have a sophisticated enough intelligence operation, you know? And in part, I think that's because university police, they're still trained with respect to the Vietnam War–era protests, when the objective is to preserve everybody's rights, but the protest is usually a reasonably peaceful protest, maybe some angry words said, but not much more than that. This was not that. And you know, despite our many days of preparation, we weren't ready for what this was.

I.B.F., LOCAL ACTIVIST: I came back to headquarters and my best friends from the grad programs were there and one of them, she held me and she was like, *Oh my God, you're shaking.* And I didn't, I hadn't realized that.

I think I was more angry because we *knew* that they were going to come. We knew the route they were going to take because they've been tweeting about it and they've been chatting it in Discord. People in front of me had shared it with UVa leadership, with the UVa security to just be like, *just so you know.* And nothing. They faced no resistance, they faced nothing. And so I think I was more pissed that no one had listened.

EMILY GORCENSKI, LOCAL ACTIVIST: What has me jaded about the antifascist community is we talk about *we keep us safe,* but I was fucking there and they weren't.

It was a huge colossal fuck-up. It was a catastrophic mistake. Because you don't leave people undefended. You don't leave people vulnerable, people without protection. The students, the community members, the people of the church. You just don't do that. It was a huge failure.

My wife was watching from home on my livestream, at my house, which had been doxed. My phone died because I was livestreaming the whole thing. Phone died, found a friend, called her, told her I was OK, I'd be on the way home, pack a bag, get something to eat. We're going.

I came home and I was waiting for my other partner to come up from Roanoke, Virginia. And so we put together some bags and I brought Christine, my wife, to one of her friends' places. Yeah, I think before the torch march, I even taught her how to use my nine-millimeter. And basically said, *If anyone that you don't know tries to come through that door, this is what you do.*

I brought her over to her friend's place where I knew that there would be no way of tracing her or finding her. And then my other partner and I went, and we were going to stay home that night, but we couldn't. And so we went to an Airbnb and crashed there, and I packed up my guns and found a safe house. I was just scrolling Twitter, seeing all of the harassment that was being thrown at me.

[The Nazis] walked away and they got away with it. They're coming in here the next day ready to do more. I thought like, *Here we go. Yeah, here we go.*[15]

ALEXIS GRAVELY, SENIOR ASSOCIATE NEWS EDITOR, *CAVALIER DAILY*, ON GROUNDS: As fast as everything happened, it was just gone. I just walked back to the *Cav Daily*'s office in Newcomb, and we started debriefing with Tim and Daniel, and writing, and that was that. I think I left like 2:30.

My grandmother's generation, they lived through cross burnings and church burnings and bombings and things like that. But I felt like that was our generation's first really visual representation of racism.

And so I understand why people would say we never could've believed this would happen because it was so overt versus—the sort of racism that we'd been dealing with up until Trump was systemic and microaggressions and things like that. And so unless you were Black or were a person of color, those were sorts of things that you probably wouldn't be familiar with.

But no I wasn't like, *Oh my God, my dear UVa. Like, the bastion of equality. Like, how could this happen*? Like, no. I'm like, *OK. Yeah, this checks out for a place that was built by slaves.*

Videos of the torch march and the ensuing violence spread rapidly around town. One person watching the videos that night was 32-year-old Heather Heyer. She'd already known the alt-right rally would be happening in downtown Charlottesville the next day, and while she was a vehement supporter of justice, she'd originally decided not to go to counterprotest, fearing violence.

SUSAN BRO, HEATHER HEYER'S MOTHER: She had planned on not going. But when she saw videos from Friday night, she'd said, *I have to go.*

Heather was feisty. Mouthy at times. No nonsense. She was a true Gemini with a heart of gold and yet she could be just as obstinate and stubborn as you'd ever wanna see. But she cared deeply for others and she cared deeply, deeply, deeply for the rights of others. Always did. Always everything had to be explained to her from early childhood in terms of is this fair or not fair. And so I'd have to resort to the, *'Cause I said so and that's the end of it. I don't care if you think it's fair or not.*

She definitely had rough teen years and made life pretty miserable for both of us for a while. But she had moved out finally by age 26, and was then 32 and was getting her life together. She had a career, she was a certified paralegal, she worked at a bankruptcy firm and she helped clients not become clients by offering them some quick suggestions as a way to avoid bankruptcy. She worked very hard to teach her mother to be an antiracist.[16]

I think everybody's aware that Black people don't get a fair shake. I think that we're lying to ourselves if we say otherwise. But it never really brought it home so intensely to me as when her boyfriend was living with us, who was Black, and we would go to dinner, we'd get the dirty looks, we'd get the snide remarks from time to time. I began to realize just how much, day to day, the struggle can be just to be alive and to be Black in America.[17]

She was one of my first teachers.

I think ultimately that's what made her decide that she had to take a stand when she saw them chanting in Charlottesville on the university campus the night before.[18]

She said, *OK, this is beyond what I thought it would be.* She had been going to stay away with her best friend, who was gay—they were staying away for his safety—and she said *I'm gonna do this.*[19]

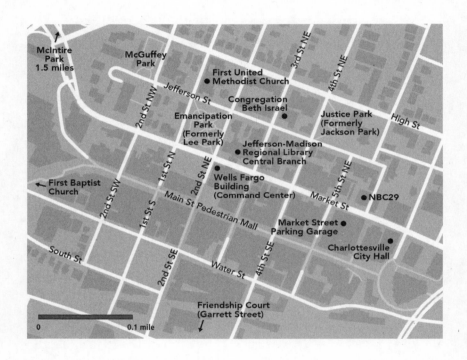

McIntire
Park
1.5 miles

McGuffey
Park

First United
● Methodist Church

3rd St NE

4th St NE

Jefferson St

Congregation
Beth Israel
●

Justice Park
(Formerly
Jackson Park)

High St

2nd St NW

Emancipation
Park
(Formerly
Lee Park)

Jefferson-Madison
● Regional Library
Central Branch

1st St N

2nd St NE

5th St NE

← First Baptist
Church

Wells Fargo
Building
(Command Center)

Market St

● NBC29

2nd St SW

1st St S

Main St Pedestrian Mall

Market Street ●
Parking Garage

South St

2nd St SE

4th St SE

Water St

Charlottesville
City Hall

Friendship Court
(Garrett Street)
↓

0   0.1 mile

CHAPTER 8

"We need to go confront literal Nazis."

The night of August 11 seemed to bleed into the early morning hours of August 12.

SMASH CAINE-CONLEY, COFOUNDER, CONGREGATE C'VILLE: I got home and tried to sleep for like two hours, which didn't really happen obviously.

TOM BERRY, DIRECTOR OF EMERGENCY MANAGEMENT, UVA MEDICAL CENTER: I didn't feel comfortable going home that night. I kept a cot in my office for whatever—snowstorms, Ebola responses, the floods that occur a lot in the hospital with old pipes that are breaking. So I just went back to my office, set up the cot, got some light sleep.

WEDNESDAY BOWIE, COUNTERPROTESTER: Everybody else was like, *Let's get our rest.* And I was like, *I cannot sleep.* So I stayed up literally all night. I was just anxiety-ridden and reading as much as I could about any articles I could find, anything about what to expect the next day.

DON GATHERS, COFOUNDER, CHARLOTTESVILLE BLACK LIVES MATTER: I'm not certain that I went to sleep. If I did, I'd have to say I was back up by 4:30?

REV. SETH WISPELWEY, PASTOR AND COFOUNDER, CONGREGATE C'VILLE: I got up early, 5:30 a.m., ate a banana with peanut butter, and got in the car.

CHRIS SUAREZ, REPORTER, CHARLOTTESVILLE *DAILY PROGRESS*: I was up pretty quickly, probably 6, 6:30. I really don't even remember making coffee or having breakfast or anything. I just got up, put on clothes, and was out the door. I remember riding my bike up to First Baptist on Main Street.

DON GATHERS: I had organized a 6 o'clock sunrise service at First Baptist Church for that Saturday morning in preparation for what we had to go out and face that afternoon, not knowing what to expect, but knowing that we needed to come together and pray about it as a community.

First Baptist Church was founded during the Civil War, in 1864, as the Charlottesville African Church.

DON GATHERS: I headed to the church to make sure everything was set and ready. And I'll tell you, when I got there, there were already people there—folks who had volunteered to serve as security. There were also plainclothes CPD as well as some in uniform. Eyes and ears all over the church.

REV. SETH WISPELWEY: The band had already gotten set up and everything. People were starting to come. We filled it pretty well. There were a few hundred people.

WES BELLAMY, CHARLOTTESVILLE VICE MAYOR: I drove to First Baptist in silence. No Jeezy, no Chance the Rapper, no R&B, no nothing. Just silence. The sun had yet to come out. Few cars were on the road. It was a surreal moment. Upon arrival, I embraced my brother Deacon Don Gathers, and his energy was one of a warrior prepared for battle.[1]

DON GATHERS: It may well have been one of the most incredible Saturday mornings of my entire life. Just seeing that many people flowing into the building for worship service on a Saturday at six o'clock, 6:30 in the morning, and seeing the sea of people. God, we must've had another 350 to 400 people packed into that church in the morning.

REV. SETH WISPELWEY: It was a waking up. A pump-up-and-go.[2]

SINGER: I need you today!

SPEAKER: Come on, put your hands together!

CROWD: Cheers

SPEAKER: Praise God, praise God, praise God. If you haven't been moved yet this morning, check to make sure you have a pulse.[3]

CROWD: *Laughter*

SMASH CAINE-CONLEY: It was much smaller than the night before. And it was primarily folks who were wanting to engage that day in some way, shape, or form.

It definitely had a different feel too. There was more of an ominous feeling in the air for sure. We were preparing ourselves to leave and to engage something pretty scary.

SPEAKER: It is indeed one of the great honors and moments of my life to be able to stand before you to introduce today's speaker. We have with us today our beloved brother Dr. Cornel West.[4]

The crowd cheered and then stood, one by one, to welcome Dr. West with a standing ovation as he took the stage. Then, just before he even began to speak, another standing ovation.

REV. DR. CORNEL WEST: Are we ready to be a hope this morning in the face of what we understand structures of evil to be? We not here to hate anybody; we here to love. And we're lovin' in such a way that we hate the structures of evil. That's what it's all about. And that's why when they see us with a smile, they gonn' say, "Who are these strange folk of all colors and sexual orientations and religious tradition? Don't they realize that they could get hurt? Don't they realize that some of them might get hit? Some of us might even get shot." That's all right. We are willing to pay the cost of truth, of justice, of beauty.[5]

SMASH CAINE-CONLEY: Cornel West always has really incredible things to say and, I think, a way to get people's spirits in a place where they're ready to engage things that are scary.

REV. DR. CORNEL WEST: This is the time for action. This is not a
moment for sunshine soldiers.

When we march this morning, when we hold hands and lock in
this morning, when we sing this morning, when we get arrested
this morning, when we go to jail this morning, let's try to
remember those—the best of those came before—who sacrificed
so much for us. Who paid a greater cost than we gonn' pay
today.[6]

REV. SETH WISPELWEY: So, I missed some of West's talk actually because
I was part of a group kind of having these little huddles in the basement.
We're sending kind of "runners" to Market Street to get reports on what
the situation was. You know, *Kind of still quiet. Militia's there. They're armed.*

SMASH CAINE-CONLEY: After the service ended, that's when things started
to get a little dicey.

DON GATHERS: It was my intention as I was putting this thing together, to
cut it off at a point where, OK, those who want to leave and go home safely
before the beast is released, so to speak, would have time to do so.

Rev. Sekou stepped forward.

DAVID GARTH, RETIRED PASTOR: He announced that we would divide up
in two groups and if we had had nonviolence training and we were willing
to be arrested, that we would march to [the site of the rally] Emancipation
Park, with the statue of Lee. Those of us who had not had nonviolent
resistance training, we would be in a different march downtown, but not at
the same location.

MICHAEL CHEUK, SECRETARY, CHARLOTTESVILLE CLERGY COLLECTIVE: I remember Sekou just being really, really frank and clear with the participants
there, saying, *OK, it's gonna be dangerous. We could get hurt. We may even get
killed. There's no shame if you decide to participate and counterprotest in a different
way, but want to be very clear about that.*

SMASH CAINE-CONLEY: We started to get some pushback from some folks.
Not any local folks, but some people that had come to be with us. We were
kind of being accused of putting people in a dangerous situation.

REV. SETH WISPELWEY: There were accusations being thrown around of being a martyr. And just not knowing the weeks of training that we had.

MICHAEL CHEUK: There was kind of a standoff.

SMASH CAINE-CONLEY: I was just really confounded. I was like, *I can't believe this is happening,* because we were extremely clear with people leading up to this weekend of what we expected. We expected it to be violent, we expected it to be dangerous. And we particularly called for white folks, and I was hoping for white male Christian pastors, to come and put their bodies on the line. So I think getting that pushback from folks about the choices we were making—to be in solidarity with our community and with activists in our community—was really disappointing.

Like, we literally need to leave now to go confront literal Nazis. Now is not the time for me to explain to you why we are doing this and how we've built relationships in our community and how local people of color have asked us to do this work. So that was really challenging.

REV. SETH WISPELWEY: And also, the maxim is, *Listen to local leaders, follow local organizers.* Well, we *were* that. This is our hometown, we were listening to *our* local organizers and activists and our local Black women. Like, me, I'm accountable to Brenda Brown-Grooms and Yolonda Jones and Jalane Schmidt and Lisa Woolfolk and others who we were all consulting this whole time.

Cornel just sat quietly. He was just like, *I follow local leadership.* And he was like, *I'm going with these people. I trust Sekou. We've made our peace with the cross, we know who we're accountable to.*

Most of the out-of-town clergy, many of whom were white, chose not to directly confront the white nationalists. The group that ended up marching to Emancipation Park was much smaller than expected. Even without the strength in numbers they'd anticipated, they continued on.

SMASH CAINE-CONLEY: We went and lined up in front of the church kind of two by two and had a prayer. And we started marching.

Across the city, secular activists were also preparing, coming to terms with what the day had in store.

SABR LYON, COUNTERPROTESTER: Waking up that morning, it's the regular anxiety of the day. I was trying to...because my mom came with us, I was trying to give her a realistic expectation. My wife who was then my fiancée, they had both done antiwar rallies and things, and my mom is one of the people who walked out of her high school so they could wear pants when it was wintertime or whatever. So, she had done protests and things, but she had never been to one where it was going to be a war zone.

I knew there was a chance somebody was going to die. I hadn't spoken to my dad for more than six months at that point, but I called him that morning and I said, *In case I die today, I need you to know that I may not be able to be in contact with you, but I love you. I just want to let you know we are going to war. What they're going to say on Fox News that you're going to watch is all going to be lies. Know that when they're telling lies, they're telling lies about me*, and I hung up the phone.

Star Peterson woke up at home with her houseguests she'd met the night before: two medics who had offered to sleep over and keep an eye out for Nazis.

STAR PETERSON, LOCAL ACTIVIST AND STREET MEDIC: I made coffee and cinnamon rolls for them or something. I was so nervous and so ready for it to get over with. I mean, I was very aware that I might die that day.

CONSTANCE PAIGE YOUNG, COUNTERPROTESTER: We all knew what had happened the night before, and so the fear, at least for me, was coming from, *Are there explosive devices out on the street? Am I going to be shot today? Will I be shot at? Will I be physically assaulted?* You kind of go through your head and you ask yourself, *What am I capable of? What am I capable of? How can I protect myself here? I'm unarmed.*

EMILY GORCENSKI, LOCAL ACTIVIST: My wife was like, *You need to promise me after last night that you don't go to the front lines.* And I was like, *I promise you that. I've seen enough action.*

LISA WOOLFORK, UVA PROFESSOR AND MEMBER OF CHARLOTTESVILLE BLACK LIVES MATTER: I remember very early that morning, texting one of my good friends and I said, [*My spouse*] *Ben and I are going to this rally. And if anything should happen to us, I want the boys, our kids, to live with my sister-in-law Molly in New York. And I'm telling you this not because I don't love my sisters, but my sisters live in the South. They live in Texas and they live in Florida. And I believe that the boys will be better served in school by living in Manhattan and going to schools in New York City.*

DAVID STRAUGHN, LOCAL ACTIVIST: We wrote bail support phone numbers on each other's arms and legs with Sharpies. We packed our bags full of water, fruit, and a change of clothes for the impending tear gas. We were ready.[7]

MARCUS MARTIN, COUNTERPROTESTER: My fiancée at the time, Marissa, wanted to go. I couldn't allow her to go alone and her mind was made up. So I was like, *I gotta go.*

We met at the McDonald's downtown. We parked our cars over there and then we started to walk, and that's when a big group [of white nationalists] walked right past us. Like, that's when we first got there. Wow. They walked right past us and that's when Marissa looked at me and grabbed my hand and was like, *I don't want, I don't think we should be, I don't think we should do this.* And then I told her, I was like, *Babe, just hold my hand and don't let it go.*

| **Many activists came in from out of town.**

BILL BURKE, COUNTERPROTESTER: That was my first trip to Charlottesville. I heard about the Unite the Right in Chicago at a socialist conference. It was my birthday weekend, August 13th. So I was like, I'll just go yell at some Klansmen for my birthday.

I had to work Friday and I was planning on leaving really early Saturday morning. So I got up, probably left the house about four, five o'clock in the morning for Charlottesville. It was about a six-hour drive.

CONSTANCE PAIGE YOUNG, COUNTERPROTESTER: I was there once before and I remember I bought a dress from a vintage shop. It's a 1960s–style dress, I think, with a high collar and it's made of raw silk, it's blue, it's very pretty. I went to a couple of wineries out there. Yeah, so that was my only experience with Charlottesville before.

A friend of mine had been arrested in July. Another friend of mine was medic-ing. They told me about it—it sounded horrifying. And it sounded unacceptable. If there's a screaming, abandoned baby, you go and tend to it, you don't ask questions about it. It seemed like this was a situation that should be addressed. So, I didn't contemplate the decision. The decision made itself to just go ahead and go.

WEDNESDAY BOWIE, COUNTERPROTESTER: We got up pretty early. And we went to Bodo's and got bagels. That's a big Charlottesville thing. If you go to Charlottesville, you got to get Bodo's Bagels.

One of the people that came with us was a street medic. And so, my plan for the day was stick with her and just bodyguard her and anybody she needs to take care of.

I went into that situation knowing that it was going to be violent and knowing that it was going to be dangerous and my purpose with it was like, *I'm a large person. I'm six feet tall. I'm no lightweight.* My expectation was, *I'm going to need to physically put myself between people in order to be a protector.*

While activists streamed into Charlottesville from elsewhere, many local Black families chose to leave town entirely.

WES BELLAMY, CHARLOTTESVILLE VICE MAYOR: You see, for a lot of Black people, this issue wasn't necessarily ours to fight.[8]

A large majority of Black people that I spoke with were clear that they weren't going downtown that day. Several encouraged me to not attend. Many people of color believed that it wasn't our fight and that the white supremacists' minds were not going to be changed by Black people confronting them. That instead, they would be more prone to listen to other white people, and as people of color, their time would be better served protecting their own communities, their own peace of mind, and their own bodies.[9]

YOLUNDA HARRELL, CEO, NEW HILL DEVELOPMENT CORP.: There's a very big difference between the Black person and the white person in that situation. For the Black person—like you got several things to think about. I've got a real thought of, *I could lose my life just simply be being Black.* I don't have to say anything. I don't have to do anything. It could just be because someone is so hate-filled. For me, as a Black person, what would I accomplish by being there? Because they're here to demonstrate their hate. Me being there is not gonna change that.

And so the idea that you could actually be out—not even involved in that, in what was going on—and come across a group who is now amped up and feeling like they can do something to you? Now you become a prisoner in your own community.

My husband and I made a decision. We're not even staying in town for that. Like, we're just gonna leave. We're gonna go outta town. Because that just has the potential to just get out of control and we are a little town. What's gonna happen if it gets outta control? And do we wanna find ourselves in a situation where we're fighting for our lives?

DR. ANDREA DOUGLAS, EXECUTIVE DIRECTOR, JEFFERSON SCHOOL AFRICAN AMERICAN HERITAGE CENTER: There are multiple reasons why you would say, yes, there were not many Black people on the streets.

Many people say, *We have bigger problems than this. Those statues don't bother us. We don't occupy those places anyway. So it doesn't matter to us. What matters to us is putting food on the table.* They're working as hard as they can to make ends meet in a service industry. And so that also speaks to the fact that—the African American population in Charlottesville, 39 percent of it is impoverished, right? So 39 percent of 8,000 [Black] people [living in Charlottesville] are impoverished. That's a big number. And of that 39 percent, a good number of those people are young people. So, when you look out and you say, *Where are the Black people?* Well, you know, you're not sending your kids out there. You're not sending your older population out there. And then the numbers become very small, really.

And at the same time, you also have to go defend your home because they were headed towards Garrett Square. And the young men there were like, *You're not passing these gates.*

So that's a real space too, you know: making sure that the alt-right were turned back from these Black spaces was also what some of the Black men, the young men were engaged in.

WES BELLAMY: With this in mind, I would say that less than 20 percent of the people who were counterprotesting were Black.[10]

| **Also gearing up: Charlottesville's reporters.**

HENRY GRAFF, ANCHOR AND REPORTER, NBC29: My mom called me and she was like, *I don't want you to go to work today*. And I'm like, *Well, I have to go to work.*

But did you see what happened on the TV last night?

And I was like, *Yes, I saw. I watched it. I'm very sad.*

And I think it did—yeah, it stacked the deck. If you were holding on hope that it was going to be peaceful, I think by watching the events unfold the night before, that little hope went away.

But we had a meeting, we got our assignments. We were given special [health] insurance cards with IDs because nobody knew what was gonna happen.

TIM DODSON, MANAGING EDITOR, *CAVALIER DAILY*: My car was outta commission for whatever reason. So I was driving my mom's minivan, a Honda Odyssey.

ZACK WAJSGRAS, FREELANCE PHOTOGRAPHER: Being someone who was really obsessed with photojournalism and had encountered a lot of war photography, I had always wondered if I would report on something like that. And what the role of doing that was, with clear danger present.

And just hearing lots of reports of people bringing guns. I was like, *Oh my God, is this something we're going to experience today?* I think literally from the time that we got in the car, my heart basically just started racing from then.

HENRY GRAFF: There were people you knew. Small town, you know, there's Joe Blow from down the street or Carrie you see at the bar sometimes.

It's quiet. I can see police officers, I'm like, *Hey, how are you, be safe today. Please remember me, if you need to pull me out of something, I'm a good guy, please!*

I mean, these are cops you know. I remember walking down Market Street and hugging Tammy Shiflett—she was the officer who parked at 4th Street—being like *I hope you have a safe day*. 'Cause I have interviewed her 100 other times on other random bullshit topics that we cover for the normal news every day. And here I'm like, *I hope you survive*. That kind of stuff where it's like, *God, what are we doing here?*

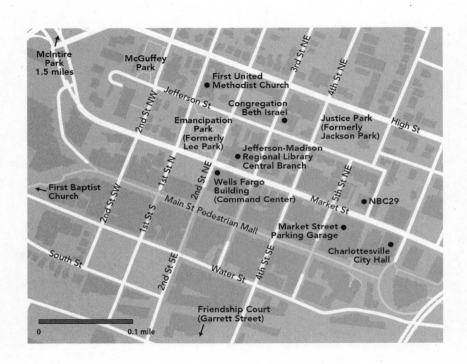

McIntire
Park
1.5 miles

McGuffey
Park

First United
● Methodist Church

Congregation
Beth Israel
●

3rd St NE

4th St NE

Jefferson St

2nd St NW

Justice Park
(Formerly
Jackson Park)

High St

Emancipation
Park
(Formerly
Lee Park)

Jefferson-Madison
● Regional Library
Central Branch

1st St N

2nd St NE

5th St NE

First Baptist
Church

Wells Fargo
Building
(Command Center)

Market St

● NBC29

Main St Pedestrian Mall

1st St S

Market Street ●
Parking Garage

2nd St SW

4th St SE

Charlottesville
City Hall

South St

2nd St SE

Water St

Friendship Court
(Garrett Street)

0   0.1 mile

CHAPTER 9

"This is fucked up as a football bat."

Meanwhile, the second group of protesters—those who would not engage in direct action—marched downtown.

DAVID GARTH, RETIRED PASTOR: It was a sunny day. We left maybe sometime around between 7 and 8 and started to walk. It was a casual crowd. I noticed that our state senator was there, and I think there were some other people who were my age. I was 74.

KRISTIN SZAKOS, CHARLOTTESVILLE CITY COUNCILOR: I was walking with Don Gathers. It's a pretty short distance. I think we were walking fast. I think everybody was amped up a little bit, but it was quiet, as I remember. We were chanting things and carrying banners and signs, and more of a sense of real determination, girding ourselves for the day.

DON GATHERS, COFOUNDER, CHARLOTTESVILLE BLACK LIVES MATTER: We marched in unison into McGuffey Art Park. There was a separate vigil being held there.

MEDIA ADVISORY FOR MCGUFFEY PARK EVENT: There will be information, teach-ins, and speakers in addition to prayer and meditations, music and art, and an opportunity for respite.

This event was known as the PARJ, the People's Action for Racial Justice, organized by Professor Walt Heinecke. The idea had started a few weeks before, when he had met with Jalane Schmidt and her partner, Mimi Arbeit.

WALT HEINECKE, UVA PROFESSOR AND ACTIVIST: I met with Jalane and Mimi downtown somewhere, and we were just sort of chitchatting about what was going on and how to respond. And they had told me that one of their SURJ members, a young woman who I actually know who was in [one of my] classes, a little bit of a hippieish woman, had gone down and tried to get permits to do some kind of art protest in McGuffey Park. And the city had rejected them. I kind of got the sense that the city kind of just thought she was a lefty kind of crazy person, [and] young. And so they didn't give her a permit. So Jalane and Mimi just said, *Hey, can you help? Can you help us get permits for counterprotests?* And I said, sure.

So the next day I put on a suit and tie—you know, the UVa blue blazer and the khakis—and went down to the Parks Department and filled out a permit for the People's Action on Racial Justice, and they gave me the permit.

And I don't know if they were just being discriminatory against the young woman, or what was going on, but they gave *me* the permits.

Now, part of my motivation for doing that was going back to July 8th—the way that the police treated the progressive protesters. They tend to shut down free speech and assembly pretty quickly on them with no reason. And that whole thing made me think, *Well, if the city's gonna be kind of fascistic about counterprotesters protesting, I want a place for free speech and I want a protected place for free speech and free assembly, so that Antifa and progressive protesters and activists in Charlottesville could come and have a safe space.*

So, I put together a group. I put out a call to the activist networks and I asked for people who wanted to volunteer. And I got a really solid group of diverse folks to sign up. Devin was on that steering committee.

DEVIN WILLIS, SECOND-YEAR UVA STUDENT: I got up early because I promised that I would be at McGuffey Park bright and early so that I could help set up the park.[1] I had already given my word that I would come and help out with like water bottles, set up folding tables, that kind of thing. One, you don't want to, like, quit halfway through the job; and two, I think, based off of how that small, tiny rally went the night before, I was like, OK, these guys are dangerous. They're violent. And what we're doing at the PARJ is more important now than ever. There needs to be a safe space. And yeah, I had responsibilities. I had to go.[2]

When I got to the park that morning, I did my job. I helped with logistical things: unfolding tables, helping point out where porta potties should be, putting down the water bottles.[3]

WALT HEINECKE: We started setting up the medic tents. We set up the rain tents and the PA system. And then security came. We had walkie-talkies and I handed out the walkie-talkies to kind of circulate in the near area and give us intelligence about where these neo-Nazis were marching and where they were coming.

DON GATHERS: There was already a huge vast number of people there waiting. It had been marked a safe space, a safe haven for people who wanted to come and be out with the community. The Care Bears, if you will, and the nursing staff and first aid people were assembled there.

MICHAEL CHEUK, SECRETARY, CHARLOTTESVILLE CLERGY COLLECTIVE: They're called Care Bears. They have little wagons that they actually pull in out in the streets to give people water or Band-Aids or whatever they may need and so forth.

REV. SETH WISPELWEY, PASTOR AND COFOUNDER, CONGREGATE C'VILLE: It's humid as hell. It's August and we're robed up. Like we would have passed out if someone hadn't been shoving water bottles in our hands.

BRENNAN GILMORE, COUNTERPROTESTER AND FORMER US FOREIGN SERVICE OFFICER: People were writing lawyers' numbers on their arms, doing this traditional protection stuff before a big rally, and then handing out leaflets with legal advice.

WEDNESDAY BOWIE, COUNTERPROTESTER: I remember we followed a trail of glitter down the sidewalk to get to the park. And that was nice. It was like, *Oh, I wonder who did this?* It was a nice distraction.

DON GATHERS: Various speakers took the mic. We had clergy from everywhere.

DAVID GARTH, RETIRED PASTOR: There was a band there and people were playing. There was music, recorded music, and there were some stands or tables had been set up and there were balloons and it was basically a kind of a fair. A festival sort of mood intended, I guess, for people who might have gone to the Lee statue but wanted someplace else where the danger would not be evident at all.

KRISTIN SZAKOS, CHARLOTTESVILLE CITY COUNCILOR, AT PARJ: I was going through the motions in a way on the ground as myself, worrying about the bigger picture that I couldn't see. And I was getting texts every now and then from the city manager, the police chief. It was surreal to be on these two planes: both being part of the establishment that was supposed to protect the city and then myself, as a human being. One reason that I chose not to go to the rally itself, the big one, was that I knew because of my work on the statues since what, 2012, that some of the [alt-right] folks organizing this rally knew who I was and that I would trigger it. I would trigger violence and I didn't want that to happen.

It wasn't that I was afraid. I just didn't want to provoke them personally. I had been under a lot of personal scrutiny and ire for almost a year before that from the right, from white supremacists. My home phone number was put on Aryan Nation websites, so people were calling me all the time. And people were telling me what time I went to bed last night, calling to just show me that they were watching my house and threatening horrible things to me and my kids. So, I had been living with that going into that summer.

I just felt if I had been an anonymous person, I probably would've been there, but I felt like it would just make it worse if I went. It would be about me, and that seemed to distract from what people were trying to achieve there.

ACTIVISTS AT PARJ, SINGING:
Over my head I see peace in the air.
Over my head I see peace in the air.
Over my head I see peace in the air;
There must be a God somewhere![4]

KRISTIN SZAKOS: I spent quite a lot of the time on the corners of the park that face downtown—because we started about, oh, maybe 8:30—to see these roving bands of white nationalists coming toward the park. Just trying to, I think, freak us out or something, or I don't know what their intent was. But the first ones looked like they were trying to look like Vikings, and they had these big flags and these Norse avenger fantasy characters. And they were shouting something indecipherable and they were marching toward the park.

DAVID GARTH: I could see alt-right folks coming and going to the Lee statue park. And they had helmets and they were carrying sticks and weapons of some kind. I was genuinely afraid. And for me, that just confirmed that I was in the right place. To go to a safe space.

KRISTIN SZAKOS: And some of the folks who were doing security at the park—just citizen security, not police—were starting to engage with them, shouting at them and throwing things at them. And I remember I went and talked to them and asked if they could try to move that away from McGuffey, because I felt like that was really drawing them in, and they did. They were great.

But I was also texting the police department and saying, *These guys are coming to McGuffey Park right now. The rally's supposed to start at noon, but it's 8:30 and they're already out here. Can you get some folks around this park?* Because they weren't. There was one down on Market Street, one police officer alone or maybe two. And there were a couple more over on High Street, but I had not seen a police presence around the park and I thought it might be a good idea.

They didn't come. I don't know why. The two policemen who ended up on Market Street did come, but there was never any kind of protective cordon or anything at McGuffey Park. So, we really relied on prayer and hope and these few citizen security people who were watching the edges.

CONSTANCE PAIGE YOUNG, COUNTERPROTESTER: I just had this feeling something was going to happen. I had on long sleeves...I was trying to protect my body. And I did see people there who were not ready, who looked very, very green. This was not green stuff. There's nothing about this that would scream fun protests down at the National Mall in DC, where the cops are used to protesters. I think I even saw a couple of minors, and I'm thinking to myself, *Why are you here?*

You can't reconcile flip-flops and Klansmen. There's nothing that's about safety there. There ain't no safety there.

HEAPHY REPORT: Some who marched to McGuffey walked over to the First United Methodist Church [FUMC], where prayer services happened inside while medical tents and counterprotester support organized in the back parking lot.

MICHAEL CHEUK, SECRETARY, CHARLOTTESVILLE CLERGY COLLECTIVE: There were people out in the parking lot. They had set up kind of a security station there.

REV. BRENDA BROWN-GROOMS, PASTOR, NEW BEGINNINGS CHRISTIAN COMMUNITY: I'm a stroke survivor, so I wasn't gonna do well in the street. So I was among those who were deployed to First United Methodist Church. The praying vigil were there. There was also the welcoming station and where people could come in for medical aid.

HEAPHY REPORT: Deborah Porras, a minister who traveled to Charlottesville to support counter-protest efforts, told us that FUMC had installed metal detectors and required white males to have a "sponsor" to enter the building.

REV. PHIL WOODSON, ASSOCIATE PASTOR, FIRST UNITED METHODIST CHURCH: No weapons of any sort would be allowed inside the church. Everyone who sought access to our church's safe space would be subjected to having our volunteers review their identification and submit to being scanned by a metal detector. Unless there was an emergency as determined by the members of the leadership team, armed police officers would also have to adhere to our zero-tolerance rule for weapons in the church. But in the event of an emergency, anyone and everyone who needed sanctuary would be provided with it. This included fire department, emergency response personnel, and armed officers if they were stationed around our churches. If somebody started shooting shit up or blowing shit up, the church was going to open its doors to everybody. That's what we agreed upon.

That morning I spoke with each of those groups—firemen, police officers—early in the morning, and then in no uncertain terms made clear that if a bomb went off or a gunman went rogue, that they were absolutely allowed to come inside for safety.

Using the church's facilities to pee and needing sanctuary are two distinctly different needs. And so there were many times throughout the day when First UMC volunteers had to prioritize the physical and mental care that people were receiving inside and unfortunately had to turn a number of simple "bathrooms seekers" away. If those cops wanted to hand me their guns while they walked inside to pee, we would've had a different conversation.

The rules inside said, *No one calls the cops. If you're inside this church, you do not call the police. That's up to those of us on the outside. Or those of us in leadership positions. Notify one of us that had our pictures up there on the board. These are the people you talk to before you call 911.*

Just two blocks away, Jewish worshippers congregated for Saturday services in Charlottesville's only synagogue.

ALAN ZIMMERMAN, PRESIDENT, CONGREGATION BETH ISRAEL: So my very first memory of when I got downtown was—and this is just a very Charlottesville thing—was, *Hmm, that was easy finding a parking spot.*

And I went to the synagogue. The guard was there. We had maybe, I don't know, 30 people. Yeah, pretty normal size of people that come to services, although the mixture was a little bit different. A lot of the elderly people that regularly came were not there, but then there was some people that I normally don't see at services that came and they were like, *I wanted to be here because I don't want to be chased away from services.*

RABBI TOM GUTHERZ, CONGREGATION BETH ISRAEL: After what happened on Friday night I think we all kind of thought, *All bets are off on this one.* Whatever we were thinking was going to happen—we just really didn't know. Kind of had a very strong feeling about that. We just did not know.

City officials were also preparing for the day.

ANDREW BAXTER, CHARLOTTESVILLE FIRE CHIEF: So I get up Saturday. I check Twitter and probably NBC29 and CBS19. And I went to Ridge Street to the firehouse, to check with the off-going shift commander. We've essentially got 80 percent of the fire department working that day, plus all these mutual aid resources coming in.

City officials monitored events from two main command centers: Unified Command, located in the Wells Fargo building overlooking Emancipation Park and staffed by top decisionmakers, and the Emergency Operations Center, 2.5 miles away at Zehmer Hall on UVa's Grounds.

Baxter had been planning on spending the day at Unified Command (also called the command post or command center), but says city leaders told him he was not on the list.

ANDREW BAXTER: They said, *We don't need you in the command post.* I think part of that was some hubris on their part. And I think part of it was at that point, [City Manager] Maurice [Jones] and [Chief of Police] Al [Thomas] had started to see me as a nag. And they didn't want me in the room. Hubris is a really...I'm careful using that word, but I think it fits.

INTERNATIONAL ASSOCIATION OF CHIEFS OF POLICE AFTER-ACTION RE-
VIEW: ...not all key personnel were operating from the site
designated by the city as Unified Command at the Wells Fargo
Building overlooking the demonstration site. Several satellite
posts, including the Fire Branch, were working in support of
the event but apart from the Unified Command.[5]

Also denied entry to the city's command post: Mayor Mike Signer.

MIKE SIGNER, CHARLOTTESVILLE MAYOR: I had asked Maurice Jones if I could go be at the command center, which is at the Wells Fargo building. And he said, *There isn't space for you here.* I had not been—this is really important—I had not been given anything to do.

City Manager Maurice Jones was within his authority to deny Mayor Signer access to the command center due to Charlottesville's system of government, in which the mayor holds a largely ceremonial role. Instead, Mayor Signer considered attending the actual protest.

MIKE SIGNER: I talked to my wife, Emily, about it, and she said, *I won't, I won't allow you. I don't want you to be out there unless you have somebody from the police with you.* And that seemed prudent based on the conversations we had with the FBI and the ADL.

And Al Thomas, earlier that week, had denied me that request. He said, *I'm sorry, we just don't have anybody.* And I was like, *OK, well.*

So, I just went over to City Hall to my office there. I had to walk through the Downtown Mall to get there. And it gives me chills to think about it because I walked through the Downtown Mall. There were hundreds of officers everywhere.

I probably got over to City Hall at like eight o'clock, maybe. It was so weird because it was . . . There was nobody there. I mean, the entire staff was cleared out.

He sat in his office with two outside crisis communications professionals he had hired for the weekend, whom he says were also not invited into the command center.

MIKE SIGNER: It's just us three, like tapping away. Me getting a zillion emails and texts. It's eerily quiet.

Fire Chief Baxter headed instead to the Emergency Operations Center (EOC). When he arrived with his friend and colleague Dan Eggleston, fire chief for Albemarle County (the county surrounding Charlottesville), he was shocked by the limited number of people there—and their relatively low seniority.

ANDREW BAXTER: There's a vice president from the university, a lieutenant from CPD, a sergeant from VSP [Virginia State Police], Deputy County Executive Doug Walker, and a number of other people. Dan and I are both looking at each other like, *This is fucked up as a football bat.* But our responsibility's to make this as good as it can be.

So we had to create, essentially from scratch, a regional emergency oper-ations center with the people that were in that room. And we did. We did an hourly briefing. We tried desperately to get information from the command post, but here's how bad that was: We have a CPD lieutenant sitting in the regional emergency operations center, and the only way she's getting infor-mation about what's happening on the ground is by listening to her radio, to one channel on the radio. And we're monitoring Facebook Live and Periscope. And our job is to have situational awareness of everything that's happening, so we can pre-position resources and anticipate what the inci-dent commander on the ground is going to need. Zero communications. It was horrible, absolutely horrible.

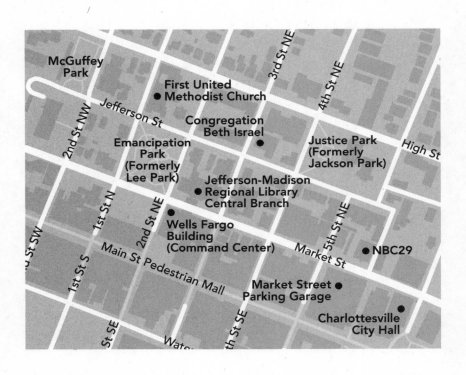

CHAPTER 10

"I remember thinking, *Somebody is going to die today."*

ABOUT 8 A.M.

SMASH CAINE-CONLEY, COFOUNDER, CONGREGATE C'VILLE, MARCHING TO EMANCIPATION PARK: That morning it didn't feel extraordinarily hot yet. It was overcast a bit. I think it was pretty, in my mind. But it was eerily quiet. I had never seen Charlottesville so quiet before. There was hardly anyone around on the streets anywhere.

CHRIS SUAREZ, REPORTER, CHARLOTTESVILLE *DAILY PROGRESS*: I was just riding along and watching the clergy start marching to Emancipation Park. They weren't chanting or anything. It was just kind of a very solemn thing.

REV. SETH WISPELWEY, PASTOR AND COFOUNDER, CONGREGATE C'VILLE: You could almost smell and feel dread.

Once we turned onto Market Street, we pulled out into a single-file line in front of the sidewalk facing the park.

WEDNESDAY BOWIE, COUNTERPROTESTER: It was early. There weren't any Nazis around yet.

CHRIS SUAREZ: By the time we got close to the Lee statue, that's when I saw all the militia guys. I could pick up on the fact that this isn't law enforcement.

REV. SETH WISPELWEY: It looked like you were going into a militarized zone. Big, burly militia members, big guns, camo.

WASHINGTON POST: The Southern Poverty Law Center, a nonprofit watchdog group that monitors extremist organizations, classifies 276 militias in the country as "antigovernment groups," meaning they generally "define themselves as opposed to the 'New World Order,' engage in groundless conspiracy theorizing, or advocate or adhere to extreme antigovernment doctrines."

REV. SETH WISPELWEY: I remember explicitly, the guy right in front of me. He had a patch that had the Stars and Bars on it. These guys were not neutral peacekeepers, of course.

Other militia members, however, did not wear Nazi or white nationalist insignia. Law enforcement from different agencies, including the National Guard, were also posted in and around Emancipation Park. In many cases, the two groups were virtually indistinguishable.

RABBI THOMAS GUTHERZ, CONGREGATION BETH ISRAEL: Nobody quite knew who was who.[1]

TOM PERRIELLO, COUNTERPROTESTER AND FORMER US CONGRESSMAN: You could not tell who was National Guard and who was white supremacist. They were in full camo. They had earpieces in. They were moving in formations. They had open long guns. They were, in every meaningful way, exactly how National Guard would be out in the streets. And they saw themselves that way.

STAR PETERSON, LOCAL ACTIVIST AND STREET MEDIC: I just remember being like, *Who are those people? I'd really like to know which side they're on because they make me very nervous.* They're in full-on fucking military gear.

HEAPHY REPORT: They carried long guns and wore body armor.

SMASH CAINE-CONLEY: I know that they think they were there to keep the peace, but it's really disconcerting walking towards people with semiautomatic guns and army fatigues. If I see a white man with a large gun, I'm not really gonna be like, *Oh, are you my friend or not?* I'm probably gonna be like, *I don't wanna be near you right now.* It's hard to distinguish.

VSP TROOPER, TO A COLLEAGUE: What are they, like military? They're more armed than we are.

BRENNAN GILMORE, COUNTERPROTESTER AND FORMER US FOREIGN SERVICE OFFICER: I remember thinking that I've had more clarity in civil unrest in war-torn countries in sub-Saharan Africa because there's a cleaner delineation of who the armed combatants are. As soon as I walked to the main area of the park I saw all the guns, and I couldn't tell who was legitimate security, state police, National Guard, or who was militia. And I just looked around and saw weapons everywhere.

JEFF FOGEL, LAWYER AND ACTIVIST: I went over to one of them and I said hello. He seemed very stern and very serious. He didn't want to answer me. And I said, *Well, what are you doing here?* Blah, blah, blah. He eventually said, *Well, we're here to protect people's rights.*

It certainly wasn't clear to me how he was doing that, standing in the middle of Market Street with an AK-47.

BRIAN MORAN, SECRETARY, VIRGINIA PUBLIC SAFETY AND HOMELAND SECURITY: I started sending pics to the governor of these folks with their long arms, long rifles assembling.

TERRY MCAULIFFE, VIRGINIA GOVERNOR: And I was really astounded because these people have better weapons than our people have. And they're marching in military procession, they are pretending to be real military, with outfits like they're real military. They have semiautomatics, they've got their pistols all strapped to their sides, to their calves, to their ankles.

And so I called Brian and said, *This is not something else we needed added in!*

And so I said, *Well, Brian, go talk, find out who the hell they are.* And he's got the phone open and I can hear 'em.

BRIAN MORAN: One of the militiamen said to me, *You gotta talk to my CO, sir, you gotta talk to my CO.* It's like, they're obviously an organized militia. They had a commanding officer.

TERRY MCAULIFFE: Now we've got all these folks that don't answer to any of us with a lot of guns. So that was very disconcerting to me.

BRIAN MORAN: One point I walked over to see if the farmer's market's open. And son of a—it is! The farmer's market, which is, what, three blocks away? Is open! They're going about their business. I think to myself, *Do you have any idea that there are people two blocks away carrying long rifles and there's about to be a thousand white nationalists two blocks away from you and how many counterprotesters?* And they're going about their business at the farmer's market!

So I got a cup of coffee, walked back. I tell the superintendent, I said, *I just got coffee! They have a farmer's market down there, you know?* And then there was a woman jogging with her dog and her baby stroller. It was like business as usual.

BRENNAN GILMORE: I remember thinking, *Somebody is going to die today. This is going to be bloody.*

REV. SETH WISPELWEY, AT EMANCIPATION PARK: And then, we flagged out into a single file line, basically face-to-face with the militia that were on the sidewalks.

HEAPHY REPORT: There was no barrier between them and the armed militia, who stood just a few feet away.

SMASH CAINE-CONLEY: We spread out and linked arms.

WEDNESDAY BOWIE: Cornel West was out there and a bunch of other people in vestments. And they were holding hands and forming a barrier around the park.

REV. SETH WISPELWEY: There's a weird mix of being so real and yet... What, we're in our full clergy drag in the city that I grew up in? That I went to this library on these same streets where I was 5 and 6 and 7 that I now bring my daughter to at age 5, 6, and 7? It doesn't compute.

And yet that was the clearest call I'd ever experienced that summer. I don't know. It's hard to explain the mix of peace and trepidation—that's why you train that way. It's tactile. It's the training paying off. All I have to do is pass the whisper down the line. *OK, now walk. OK, now we're standing out here, now we're spreading out here. OK, we're gonna kneel.* That was what we worked on.

SMASH CAINE-CONLEY: We didn't carry any sort of weapons, but we also wanted to be really clear that nonviolence isn't just about whether or not you carry a weapon: that nonviolence is about the systems that do harm particular folks in our society.

So we lined up in front of the park and began to sing.

SINGING: Ain't gonna let nobody
Turn me 'round
Turn me 'round
Ain't gonna let nobody
Turn me 'round
I'm gonna keep on walkin'
Keep on talkin'
Marchin' into freedom land.[2]

SMASH CAINE-CONLEY: Some of the militia joined in our hymn singing, which I have to admit was pretty disconcerting to me.

SINGING: This little light of mine,
I'm gonna let it shine.

HENRY GRAFF, ANCHOR AND REPORTER, NBC29: This little light of mine! I started bawling that morning. They were singing and urging for peace.

STAR PETERSON, LOCAL ACTIVIST AND STREET MEDIC: Clergy were singing so I was like, *Well, medic duty.* So I handed out cough drops and they were like, *Thank you,* and I was like, *I know protest. This is what people need. We need cough drops. Hope nobody needs anything more than cough drops today.*

WEDNESDAY BOWIE: The whole street was filled with people from our side.

STAR PETERSON: They already had the cops around the wall of the park. We noticed they were facing out. They faced who they think the threat is. They're facing us.

LISA DRAINE, LOCAL ACTIVIST: Sophie and Rebecca left earlier and met up with students, so I was not with them at the time. I headed on up to

McGuffey and I was trying to hook up with a couple of my friends from Congregate and couldn't find them, it was pretty crowded. So I was like, *I'm just here by myself. I don't really wanna be by myself. I'd rather actually be with my girls.* I was texting Rebecca and said like, *What are you guys doing?* So I walked over [to where they were gathering with their friends] and I show up and the girls were like, *Moooommm!!! What are YOU doing here? Why are you here?*

And I said, *Well I was by myself and I didn't wanna be by myself.* But you know, I could tell they were kind of embarrassed.

So anyway, people, they were getting ready, gathering noisemakers and planning what they were gonna chant and that sort of thing. One of the people that were leading them said, *Everyone needs to make sure you have a buddy.* And of course I turned to my girls and they're like, *No, the two of us are buddies. You're gonna have to find someone else.* So I'm looking around and somebody said, *Who doesn't have a buddy?* And it was like me and a few others. And I ended up being buddies with Devin Willis! We had never met each other. He knew I was Sophie's mom and he was like, *Sure, why not?* So the two of us were together as the whole group walked down Market Street.

SMASH CAINE-CONLEY: It wasn't too long after we got to the park that the white supremacist groups started to march in.

DAVID FOKY, NEWS DIRECTOR, NBC29: These alt-right guys, these Nazi sympathizer guys, that mishmash of people started coming towards the park. They were coming from all points. They were walking down the street, coming in groups in a defensive mode where they march together in tight groups with shields and helmets.

WEDNESDAY BOWIE: It was really very surreal. They would have banners and stuff, and they'd just march down the street.

SMASH CAINE-CONLEY: The streets were getting really full. These white supremacist groups would march past us, oftentimes bumping into us or trying to insult us whatever way they could.

REV. SETH WISPELWEY: They were yelling homophobic, misogynistic slurs. *Is this every lesbian clergy in America?* And *Jesus hates you, God hates you.* They would start chanting, *Fuck you, faggots*, and *White lives matter* and this kind of stuff.

COUNTERPROTESTERS: We're here, we're gay, we fight the KKK!
We're here, we're gay, we fight the KKK![3]

REV. PHIL WOODSON, ASSOCIATE PASTOR, FIRST UNITED METHODIST CHURCH:
A lot of the people who turned up to resist these Nazis were members of the LGBTQ community. White supremacy takes out everything that is not of itself. And so any person of color was in danger, anything that was not white male cis-hetero Christian was in danger.

COUNTERPROTESTERS: Fuck you fascists, fuck you fascists![4]

REV. SETH WISPELWEY: You have people always that are like, *Oh, it's racist and Islamophobic.* When you get really face-to-face with it, a lot of our experiences, it's really homophobic and really antisemitic.

SMASH CAINE-CONLEY: This very loud crowd was forming of antifascist activists, activists of every stripe, like any type of activist that resists white supremacist violence—everyone was there. So we knew the time was now to do an action.

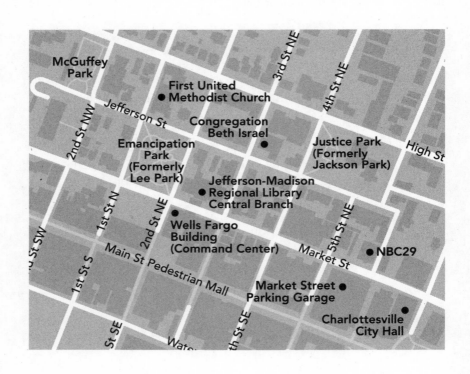

CHAPTER 11

"It seemed like war in downtown Charlottesville."

SMASH CAINE-CONLEY, COFOUNDER, CONGREGATE C'VILLE: We decided that we were going to form a blockade on the stairs that go up to the park.

CHARLOTTESVILLE POLICE DEPARTMENT SERGEANT: That's OK—they keep people out of that area, I'm fine with that.

SMASH CAINE-CONLEY: We were intending to block the stairs even if a group tried to get through. A group did indeed start marching toward us, and Seth and I were on the end of the line that was facing the park.

HEAPHY REPORT: [The white nationalists] marched up the stairs, shields first, and pushed through the line of clergy.

SMASH CAINE-CONLEY: They started marching toward our group, started pushing the front of our blockade with their shields and batons and trying to ram through us.

REV. SETH WISPELWEY, PASTOR AND COFOUNDER, CONGREGATE C'VILLE: I heard yelling—I don't really want to say it, but I heard yelling, *Kill the faggot priests.* I also heard, *Move the fuck aside, clergy*, while they were pushing through.

And then the next thing I knew I was pushed, along with colleagues, into the bushes.

When I stood up and got my bearing again, a large man was just kind of standing over me and yelling, *Fuck you, faggot* over and over in my face.

SMASH CAINE-CONLEY: Somebody in our front line broke the line and let them through! I honestly couldn't believe it. I was so stunned.

REV. SETH WISPELWEY: Part of the reason it caught us by surprise is there's 30 state police officers *right* there.

INTERNATIONAL ASSOCIATION OF CHIEFS OF POLICE AFTER-ACTION RE-VIEW: The Virginia State Police (VSP) dedicated approximately 600 sworn members to the event, the largest deployment in decades.[1]

REV. SETH WISPELWEY: And I'm standing next to Dr. West and he's like, *Oh my God, no one's getting arrested today.*[2]

SMASH CAINE-CONLEY: I was so pissed off. I didn't wanna lose my cool and start cursing at my own folks while the white supremacists were there. So I waited 'til the white supremacists went through. The folks with us started trying to sing "This Little Light of Mine," which was just really embarrassing to me. We've just been run over by group of white supremacists! They're insulting us, calling us names, and you're singing a child's hymn? I was like, this is unreal to me.

After they kind of streamed through, I turned around and I yelled like, *Why the fuck did that happen? How did we let them through? Why did we let them through?*

And I pretty much said, *If you're not here to keep the discipline, then get off the line. Like if we're gonna be here, we're going to do what we said we came to do.*

I think I was enraged for a few reasons. I think I was still feeling my regret from the night before and not showing up the way that I wanted to show up. And we've been training for months and here we're doing our direct action and it failed and, in my mind, it failed miserably.

REV. SETH WISPELWEY: And so I and some of the other leaders of Congregate decided it was still worth making a presence, recognizing that this was an intense situation, but put us as the leaders out in front and lower on the steps.[3]

And then, some of the protesters we had also talked with, they're like, *Well, if you're down with that, we'll stand here with you and hold.* And we're like, *All right, just so we're clear, we're going to hold space, but we're committed to not hitting back if hit.* And they're like, *We're down with that. We'll protect you.* So, that's what I mean when I say Antifa saved our lives.

DAVID STRAUGHN, LOCAL ACTIVIST: If it wasn't for Congregate and if it wasn't for Antifa, much more people would have died that day. Antifa does not get the credit that they deserve for preserving life and for steadfast alliance in the face of just straight-up evil.

SMASH CAINE-CONLEY: After I had my little tirade yelling session at folks, I think people were ready to not let another group through.

HEAPHY REPORT: The clergy reformed their line.

REV. SETH WISPELWEY: And then that's when we saw another large group coming up the street.[4] A huge group of men were walking with shields, flags, different insignias.[5]

DEVIN WILLIS, SECOND-YEAR UVA STUDENT: You couldn't even see into the park because all along the perimeter of the park, these guys are just hanging out on the edges and heckling all the passersby and all the counterprotesters. They seemed more interested in what was happening in the street than what was happening inside their rally.

REV. SETH WISPELWEY: There's this concept of holy foolery. Part of the idea is we're all in our clergy drag. The robes and the stoles and the what-have-you, which is already meant to be this striking *otherness*. It's part of the theater of it, to take attention away.

If there was one do-over, I wish we had waded into the middle of that, right there, that intersection and just started doing the Funky Chicken, in terms of thinking about what could you take the tension away with.

DEVIN WILLIS: The vast majority of [the white nationalists] had some combination of white top, white dress shirt with khaki or navy bottoms, whatever, kind of like a school uniform. But then you also saw a lot of people in riot gear, tactical armor, these militia fake-fatigue kind of getups. You had people wearing helmets, carrying massive Nazi flags, or Third Reich flags, whatever you want to call them. There was a lot more paraphernalia.

It looked like a costume party or something. It was weird.[6]

NATALIE ROMERO, SECOND-YEAR UVA STUDENT: There were multiple people with Hitler on T-shirts, swastikas, lots of that. Lots of that.

MELISSA WENDER, STREET MEDIC: There is an industry in Hitler T-shirts. The fact that someone needed to make them and design them and print them and advertise them—and people ordered them and there was more than one and it wasn't hand drawn.

BRIAN MORAN, SECRETARY, VIRGINIA PUBLIC SAFETY AND HOMELAND SE-CURITY: They were almost like clans of white nationalists, with different banners, different insignia on their banners.

TOM PERRIELLO, COUNTERPROTESTER AND FORMER US CONGRESSMAN: Now keep in mind, there were like six or seven different tribes. They were wearing literally different outfits. You had the preppy boys all in the khakis and the white shirts and the MAGA hats. You had the people in full-on militia gear. You had the people dressed in sort of medieval cosplay.

HEAPHY REPORT: As the groups marched to the southwest entrance of Emancipation Park, the counterprotesters swelled around that area. Market Street was quickly filling up.

LISA DRAINE, LOCAL ACTIVIST: We were right in the middle of where you saw the whole thing kind of devolving. They started fighting each other, throwing things—like you could see bottles, like just flying through the air. It became just this chaotic scene and all, but I was trying to just concentrate on Devin. I was like, *I'm sticking with Devin, I've got his back* and it was that thought of, *I'm a white woman, I can protect this young Black student, I've got you Devin.*

CONSTANCE PAIGE YOUNG, COUNTERPROTESTER: At one point I was standing shoulder-to-shoulder in a sea of Black people. Dozens of Black people. These fascists are walking by and they're screaming at us, into a sea of dozens of Black people, that Jewish privilege exists. And I'm just like, *Why are y'all telling us this?*

This one guy is uncomfortably close to me. And when I think back about it, it's sort of like—this short white man is screaming at this taller Black woman. He's not screaming racist slurs about Black people to me. He's talking about Jewish people to me. And all of this is just ridiculous. It's just absurd and violent.

And I remember just thinking like, *What the hell? What the hell, why are you doing this?* I spent a lot of time trying to really understand these people. Ain't nothing to understand. It's just hateful.

So this was the first time that I really experienced the sheer hatred for Jewish people. And my boyfriend at the time—my ex-boyfriend is a Jewish guy, and I was dating him when all this happened. And so we had some conversations about this afterwards, and I started getting a better understanding. It felt like, as a Black woman, they would just want me dead. They don't want me around. But the feeling that I got that they had about Jewish people was that they were pissed. They were angry, like they had something to prove there. So it was a different kind of hate. And it was the first time that I was learning this. Actually feeling it.

TWEET FROM CHRIS SUAREZ, REPORTER, CHARLOTTESVILLE *DAILY PROGRESS*, 9:46 A.M.: Another column of #unitetheright protesters have arrived.

ZACK WAJSGRAS, FREELANCE PHOTOGRAPHER: A big group of counterprotesters locked arms and formed this huge wall. I turned around and saw [protesters and counterprotesters] walking at each other, and it wasn't a full-on run, but they just collided at one point. People were throwing hands and things were just swinging around and it was very chaotic very quickly after that.

I took a step back and this woman, right in front of me, charged right into the center of the white supremacists. And I got some of the very first, very crisp pictures of the day of them basically grabbing her by her ponytail, slamming her onto the ground, getting right up towards her face and just punching her. These two or three guys just whaled on this woman for a second. And she just got up and kept fighting.

MARCUS MARTIN, COUNTERPROTESTER: I was with [my fiancée] Marissa, Courtney Commander, and Heather Heyer. And then at the same time, I was on probation. I mean, you expected clashes, you expected fights. So every time we got near a neo-Nazi or something like that, we got away from him. Because if I get into a fight, I'm with nothing but women. That's putting them in a bad spot. I couldn't put 'em in danger, or put myself in the line of it and get myself in trouble. So we got away from it.

NATALIE ROMERO, SECOND-YEAR UVA STUDENT: There's a set of steps. And so a lot of [the alt-right] were up there throwing things into the crowd, throwing liquids, canisters, yelling, spitting on people—doing all kinds of stuff. And they had their shields, their signs, their flags, their poles, et cetera.[7] I saw someone, for example, with a hammer—just, walking around with a hammer on their shoulders.[8]

At this intersection, there was a white police car right there blocking the street. There was a group of women alongside the cop car, not covering the whole street, just alongside the police officer's car. When I saw the group of women—there was white women, some older, younger—and I decided to join them at the very end of the line. It was a small line.

When the protesters saw us they're like, *These bitches,* et cetera. They were saying just really rude, ugly things about women.

And they're like, *We don't care,* like, *Run through them.* Like, *It doesn't matter.* Like, *These bitches are in the way.* Other things like that.

Honestly, I'm in this line thinking, *I'm OK. We're a small group of women. They're not going to do anything. Why would they be violent to a group of women that are literally doing nothing?* And especially because I'm in a group of white women. And I'm thinking, I'm a light-skinned Latina. I'm like, *Maybe they won't notice.*

I just didn't—I didn't see a reason why me being in that line would trigger them. But no, they came directly at me and spit on my face and called me really mean things and asked me what the hell I was doing there. And I should go back to where I came from. I'm from this country. I was born here, you know.

And then they pushed me and they threw me against the cop car and they walked past me. They had no reason. No reason at all to even interact with a line of women, because there was plenty of space all around us. There was sidewalk. There was everything. You had so much space to go around. But no, no. I'm spit on. I got spit on by people who hate me and think that I should not be alive and that I threaten their existence.

I'm just trying to go to school, man. I'm just trying to get out of poverty. They were so happy that they ran through women like that for no fucking reason—I'm so sorry for my language, but—and they went around us. I was just in shock.[9]

DON GATHERS, COFOUNDER, CHARLOTTESVILLE BLACK LIVES MATTER: It seemed like every five, six, seven, eight feet, fights were breaking out. It was like a battle scene from a war. Chaotic. It was just unrelenting chaos.

At any moment, at any second, you were aware that gunshots could erupt. At any moment, you didn't know if a grenade was going to be thrown out at your feet, because they had them. You literally didn't know what to expect. But you knew to expect the worst.

CHRIS SUAREZ, REPORTER, CHARLOTTESVILLE *DAILY PROGRESS*: It just was really chaotic. I saw someone throwing the C'ville newspaper stand. I remember seeing guys burning Confederate flags. I remember hearing people talk about like, *Fire the first shot of the race war,* like hearing that phrase.

DEVIN WILLIS, SECOND-YEAR UVA STUDENT: At that point, one of those militia brigade things pulls up. I just remember seeing a bunch of older, bearded men. And I don't remember much about the color of their uniforms, but they were marching in this quasi-military formation, and they're marching directly for our chain, because why go around us, right? And then they charge into the middle of it and we stand pretty strong, but they are grown men and eventually knock everybody down. So I get knocked to the ground. After that, I'm a nonviolent person, so I fled.[10]

SABR LYON, COUNTERPROTESTER: The stuff that people don't talk about that day are the inch-deep neck wounds from sharpened flagpoles and the guy that had the fricking Taser that almost got my friend. One of the people with a neck wound that I saw refused treatment because they didn't want their name to be [recorded] . . . just wild shit.

BRENNAN GILMORE, COUNTERPROTESTER AND FORMER US FOREIGN SER-
VICE OFFICER: My worst-case scenario that flashed before my eyes was:
Somebody opens fire, and then it just triggers a free-for-all and people start
drawing weapons and no one knows who they're shooting at, no one knows
who's "legitimate" or not.

WHITE NATIONALIST: I'll shoot you. If you want to play that way,
I'll play.[11]

TOM PERRIELLO, COUNTERPROTESTER AND FORMER US CONGRESSMAN: I did
interview a bunch of these [white nationalists]. They were there to start a
war. They were not subtle about it. They were like, *Yeah, we are ready to die.*
Several of 'em said, *We're ready to kill.*

They were looking for a fight. For very legitimate reasons, people—
including myself—were not gonna concede this space to them.

I think it easily could have been a hundred dead that day.

ANDREW BAXTER, CHARLOTTESVILLE FIRE CHIEF: What I think is just incredible is the fact that nobody got shot. I mean, you had fully armed militias
wandering around the city from different political persuasions with AR-15s,
and SKSs, the civilian version of the AK-47, and everything else under the
sun. And there was only one round of fire, and it didn't hit anybody.

This hasn't been said publicly because I'm sure people are afraid to
say it. But some of the restraint that particularly CPD showed—it is not
unreasonable to say that had they engaged, that there would've been a
blood bath.

I know, from talking to individual officers that were there that day, that
they were afraid that if they engaged—I'm not talking about what they were
ordered to do or not ordered to do, but from a moral perspective and an
ethical perspective, they were confronted with a choice. *If I engage with this
guy, and he pulls out his club, I'm pulling out my Taser. And if he pulls out a Taser,
I'm pulling out my sidearm. And if he pulls out a pistol, I'm pulling out my rifle....*
I mean, that's going to happen, right? And the fact that they didn't begin
that forced continuum process probably saved lives. Again, it's a what-if, but
I'm still amazed to this day that nobody got shot.

You're a police officer, you've had the minimum training at the Virginia Training Center in the Shenandoah Valley. You've been on the job what, 18 months? Two years? And you're in a command-and-control system that from day one was broken, and you still make good decisions? That's amazing.

HENRY GRAFF, ANCHOR AND REPORTER, NBC29: I had a conversation with a cop the next day and he was like, *Yeah, Henry, I mean we probably would have shot a lot of people, so there's this balance of when the cops get involved.*

Most local activists didn't see it that way.

DON GATHERS, COFOUNDER, CHARLOTTESVILLE BLACK LIVES MATTER: I just remember, I continuously was muttering, *My God, my God.* And then I became aware of the positioning and the posture of the police. And the fact that they were standing idly by, arms folded, watching all this happen right in front of them. And was taking no action whatsoever. I was thinking, *This is what anarchy looks like. This is the wild, wild West.* It was hard for me to fathom: seeing them doing absolutely nothing. As all this was happening right in front of them.

SABR LYON, COUNTERPROTESTER: There were [police] snipers on the roof all day. Snipers, watching them fuck with us.

ZACK WAJSGRAS, FREELANCE PHOTOGRAPHER: I had the thought of just, *How is this? How were the police on July 8th ready to shut down everything at the first sign of frustration from counterprotesters? And now there's armed people in this park straight up attacking people. People getting mashed up right in front of each other.*

During this street fighting, with no separation between the protesters and counterprotesters, the police stood behind layers of barricades.

HEAPHY REPORT: Charlottesville resident Tanesha Hudson approached police officers standing at the barricade in Zone 2, just above where the clergy and militia were facing each other . . . she wanted to know why there were no law enforcement officers on the outside of the barricades. Gibson replied, "We got everyone we can out here to keep people safe. . . . They've gone through weeks and weeks of planning to do the best they

can. There's no one in the middle this second. When things
happen, we'll respond."

Hudson was taken aback. "When they happen?" she asked in disbelief. "You're supposed to prevent it from happening."

ZACK WAJSGRAS: And the police are just behind three layers deep in fences,
just watching it happen. And people—including journalists on that little
pod on the side, right between the park and the library—were yelling at the
police and being like, *What are y'all doing? When are you going to stop this?*

HEAPHY REPORT: Lieutenant Hatter...ordered his men to back
up from the barricades as tensions rose. In a conversation
recorded by his body camera, Sergeant Larry Jones explained
to officers that extra space would create a "reaction gap" in
case someone came over the barricade.

As Sergeant Jones stood behind the barricades...he remarked
to other officers that the groups should "save their energy,"
as it was not yet 10:00 a.m.

JEFF FOGEL, LAWYER AND ACTIVIST: Some of us started screaming at them,
like, *Do something. You can't just stand there and watch, you gotta do something!*
    I remember seeing a bottle come flying, looked like it was gonna hit one
of the troopers and I'm thinking to myself, *Oh great.* Now *they'll react.* It
didn't hit the trooper. And they didn't react.

A. C. THOMPSON, JOURNALIST: At 10:15 a melee erupted. A group of white
supremacists, some with their hands taped up like boxers, punched, kicked,
and choked people who tried to block their path, leaving them bloodied on
the pavement.[12]

DEVIN WILLIS, SECOND-YEAR UVA STUDENT: They're picking fights with
anybody who they can get to. And they are throwing water bottles that are
filled with urine.[13]

MELISSA WENDER, STREET MEDIC: Some people were throwing urine. There
were urine bombs.

DAVID STRAUGHN, LOCAL ACTIVIST: People were asking me like, *Yo, I heard
Antifa was acting the fool and throwing all this shit at people.* It's like, actually that

was the complete opposite. White nationalists threw bags of feces and urine and bottles at *them*. It's really shameful how Antifa was turned into this great big boogeyman through all of this.

HENRY GRAFF, ANCHOR AND REPORTER, NBC29: My boss [David Foky] came down in the middle of it all, because it was getting very unruly and very dangerous, to protect us. He's a 6'5" guy, he's a big dude, a linebacker build.

DAVID FOKY, NEWS DIRECTOR, NBC29: My thinking was that if I was gonna have crews out in the field in the middle of all this, I needed to be out there as well to try and keep an eye on the situation, to try and make sure that they were OK. This wasn't something to try and manage sitting back in an office.

HENRY GRAFF: So he was covering me and shielding me and I was shielding the photographer, who I had a hand on his backpack because stuff was being hurled. I mean, eggs, everything you can think of. They were throwing bottles of piss. What else were they throwing? It was concrete which they would put in a can, is what state police told me at the time. I don't know who started it. It was concrete and you would put it in a Coke can and that was being hurled back and forth too, so hard projectiles coming at ya.

I've never been involved in war. Don't ever wanna be. I hope that's not a representation of what it was, but it seemed like war in downtown Charlottesville.

JEFF FOGEL: I mean, [the white nationalists] just had lost control of their emotions. They'd lost control of some of their physical capacities. That there were people like this in the country, and obviously there were more than just the people that showed up that day, was a very frightening notion.

BRENNAN GILMORE, COUNTERPROTESTER AND FORMER US FOREIGN SERVICE OFFICER: I had been working in conflict areas for about 10 years at that point, in Tanzania, on the Congo conflict. I have been detained by child soldiers at gunpoint before, and had been in areas where there's border shelling. And I would trade anything for not being in mob violence.

DAVID FOKY: If you had said to me, *You're gonna have dozens of people fighting each other with sticks and poles and bottles of water being thrown, and the cops would watch it and do nothing?* Inconceivable, beforehand. Inconceivable in the moment!

I can remember looking at a Charlottesville police officer who was standing there watching all this. And I remember looking at him and going, *What are you guys doing?* And he looked back at me and he just sort of shrugged like they were just as astounded that they were sitting there watching it as we were, and seeing their inaction.

HENRY GRAFF: David and I, we went up to cops and were like, *What are you all doing? These people are beating the crap out of each other!* And they're just looking at you and they can't respond to you for one, because they know I'm the news guy but, two, they're just waiting for orders.

LEGAL OBSERVER TO POLICE, CAPTURED ON BODY CAMERA FOOTAGE: You tear-gassed us last time, what are you doing?[14]

I.B.F., LOCAL ACTIVIST: It almost felt like they were being really vindictive. That was the feeling at that time like, *Oh, you didn't want us to be involved. You thought we were too involved? Now let us just step back and let whatever the hell happen. We're not going to get involved.*

WEDNESDAY BOWIE, COUNTERPROTESTER: It did not feel like just general ill-preparedness, because they had been pretty prepared and very present during the KKK rally [in July]. There was an air of like, *Fuck you guys. You're on your own.*

TOM PERRIELLO, COUNTERPROTESTER AND FORMER US CONGRESSMAN: Look, there's a hockey fight approach sometimes, which is like, you wait for the fight to happen and then you let them let off steam, and then you pull them apart. They weren't doing any of that. I mean, *I* broke up five fights that day. I was using restraining force many times. I am not a particularly big guy. It was mainly just people like me and Brennan Gilmore and others who were just stepping in and having to break up fights and stuff.

REV. SETH WISPELWEY, PASTOR AND COFOUNDER, CONGREGATE C'VILLE: I remember seeing and recognizing—because I mean, I had supported his first run for Congress—Tom Perriello's out there trying to break up fights.

He has a polo shirt on, he's like, *Hey, Hey.* His polo shirt is getting ripped. That stands out to me.

HENRY GRAFF: I remember looking at my boss one time and I was like, *David, how much longer can we do this? I mean, how much longer can this keep happening before . . .*

Somebody's gotta step in and do something at some point. You know? Like this is getting out of hand. This is getting dangerous. People are bleeding everywhere right now. There's pepper spray everywhere. I'm tired of being Maced, pepper-sprayed.

It's just like, *What are we doing here?*

CHAPTER 12

"It turned into an all-out battle."

CONGREGATION BETH ISRAEL

9 A.M.

ALAN ZIMMERMAN, PRESIDENT, CONGREGATION BETH ISRAEL: You could just hear the commotion a block away, and there were all kinds of just people milling about on the street in front of CBI. Some of them were Antifa people wearing homemade protective gear. Some of them—there were quite a bunch of yuppy-looking guys, who I later learned were neo-Nazis.

So services started and I was pretty nervous and I was standing out in front of the temple with the guard. Forty congregants were inside.

ANIKO BODROGHKOZY, UVA PROFESSOR AND CONGREGATION BETH ISRAEL MEMBER: We had a rather lightly attended regular service. The stained-glass windows of our 1882-built sanctuary obscured any view of the outside.

For me, going to services seemed the absolutely right thing to do on that day. I'd never felt more Jewish. I had planned to join the antiracist/antifascist counter-demonstrations following services. Even though I'd done nonviolent direct action training the day before and had participated in other sessions that emphasized the threats we would be facing just being downtown, I can't say I felt frightened or imperiled. I don't think I could quite comprehend what was going to happen that day and what a target our synagogue could be.

ALAN ZIMMERMAN: At one point, there were three guys in camouflage gear carrying long rifles standing in front of the synagogue that were making me very nervous. Had they tried to enter, I don't know what I could have done to stop them, but I couldn't take my eyes off them, either. Perhaps the presence of our armed guard deterred them. Perhaps their presence was just a coincidence, and I'm paranoid. I don't know.

Several times, parades of Nazis passed our building, shouting, *There's the synagogue!* followed by chants of *Sieg Heil* and other antisemitic language. Some carried flags with swastikas and other Nazi symbols.

A guy in a white polo shirt walked by the synagogue a few times, arousing suspicion. Was he casing the building, or trying to build up courage to commit a crime? We didn't know. Later, I noticed that the man accused in the automobile terror attack wore the same polo shirt as the man who kept walking by our synagogue; apparently it's the uniform of a white supremacist group. Even now, that gives me a chill.[1]

MIKE SIGNER, CHARLOTTESVILLE MAYOR: People felt like they were being terrorized there, in front of the synagogue.

WEDNESDAY BOWIE, COUNTERPROTESTER: I saw one, exactly one, cop at the synagogue, which…hah…why would you want more than one police officer on scene at a synagogue that has services on the day of a white supremacist rally?

ALAN ZIMMERMAN: A frail, elderly woman approached me Saturday morning as I stood on the steps in front of our sanctuary, crying, to tell me that while she was Roman Catholic, she wanted to stay and watch over the synagogue with us. At one point, she asked, *Why do they hate you?* I had no answer to the question we've been asking ourselves for thousands of years. At least a dozen complete strangers stopped by as we stood in front of the synagogue Saturday to ask if we wanted them to stand with us.[2]

Then I started getting texts. My wife, Nancy, was home and she was texting me going, *Are you okay? Are you all right? It's on the news. It's on CNN. There's fighting going on.* Other people from outside Charlottesville were texting me, going, *What's going on there? Are you all right?*

I went back into the synagogue to make closing announcements at services. I remember it was getting really hot outside. The synagogue was nice and cool. It seemed much more peaceful in there.

ANIKO BODROGHKOZY: Following services, we moved to the modern part of the building for blessings and a bit of challah. The assembly room on the second floor, O'Mansky Hall, has large ceiling-to-floor windows overlooking the street in front of our building's front entrance. I wandered over to look down at the street.

I saw a large contingent of neo-Nazis with poles and flags marching past. One happened to look up. The first thought that went through my mind: *I hope he thinks this is a church.* Our Gothic-revival building has spires topped with fleur-de-lis decoration. From the ground they sort of look like crosses.

RABBI TOM GUTHERZ, CONGREGATION BETH ISRAEL: I did say to people, *Look, you might not want to go out the front door. You might want to go out the back.* Later on, this got construed as Jews sneaking out of their synagogue. We were not sneaking out of our synagogue. It was more of a case of. . . It's an unstable situation out there. Many people left the synagogue by the front door. I mean, not everybody left by the side door. And the side door was not a back door, it opens onto 3rd Street. It just seemed less conspicuous, and it was uncertain what was going on out in the street.

ANIKO BODROGHKOZY: Rabbi Tom instructed us to exit the building by the back doors and go in groups. I left with my buddy Cora, but we weren't going home. These two middle-aged Jewish ladies were heading out to stand up against the neo-Nazis outside. I kept my Star of David pendant on for the rest of that awful day.

EMILY BLOUT, UVA PROFESSOR AND MAYOR MIKE SIGNER'S WIFE, AT THE EMERGENCY OPERATIONS CENTER AT UVA: I remember being kind of glued to my phone [later in the day] and then getting a text—*We are looking at social media and there's talk about surrounding the synagogue*—that was just horrifying and giving that information to a local police officer. The police officer said, *Where is a synagogue?*

She was surprised that even the synagogue existed and had no idea where it was. And the synagogue was on one of the side roads adjacent to Emancipation Park right there. And that a police officer in the small little city did not know where the synagogue is was just extraordinary, extraordinary by the fact of the ignorance and is really, really concerning. How can they protect us if they don't even know where the synagogue is?

MICHAEL CHEUK, SECRETARY, CHARLOTTESVILLE CLERGY COLLECTIVE: A little bit later I happened to run into Rabbi Tom, who is the lead rabbi at the synagogue, and he said something to the effect of, *Yes. Yes. There is an absolute threat that the synagogue might be damaged or vandalized, burned, whatever. However, we made sure that our people are safe. That's not like slinking away because some members are actually on the streets with the counterprotesters too. So we are not victims.*

TOM BERRY, DIRECTOR OF EMERGENCY MANAGEMENT, UVA MEDICAL CENTER: We were constantly going through a process of getting updates from the ER, from the ICUs, from the operating rooms because it's not like we closed the hospital. I remember that there were stories of patients arriving who were in labor.

JANE MUIR, EMERGENCY ROOM NURSE, UVA MEDICAL CENTER: I remember I didn't have to go to work until 11, which was nice.

I lived very close, but there were so many barricades to get to the hospital that I remember thinking, *Thank God I can walk to work because I have no idea how I would've gotten to work with all of the redirection.*

I had just graduated. I remember being nervous. I mean, every day you were kind of terrified. What kind of mess, what very scary situation am I gonna be dealing with?

But the hospital had also prepared us very well in terms of email correspondence, saying, *Here's what you can expect and here's our plan.* So that kind of alleviated some of my anxiety.

I just remember like every surgeon in this health system was in our emergency room. But at that point it was quiet. There was a lot of people rolling their ankles on the way, walking downtown, people who got in an altercation with somebody, earlier stages of what was unraveling that day. And they were all being cared for in our express care area. So I was bopping around, jumping in and taking care of people who rolled their ankles, and getting them discharged quickly. 'Cause we were told, *You need to get people out immediately. We are discharging everyone from the hospital. You need to get everybody out of this hospital because you need to make beds available.* I remember patients were distressed because we were being very intense with like, *You need to get out, you need to leave, you need to go home.*

Some of the patients were white nationalists.

JANE MUIR: We were trying to be strategic with where we placed certain people. You can't stick someone who is being really rowdy in a hallway next to someone, you know . . . like this isn't gonna end well for physical and political reasons. So there was some of that happening.

And I remember having conversations with them about where they came from. And I just remember being amazed at all over the country where these people came from.

ANTI-DEFAMATION LEAGUE: Unite the Right drew white supremacists from at least 35 states.[3]

JANE MUIR: I think every clinician has moments where their ethics are challenged as a provider, as a clinician. You're reminded that your job is really to do what's right for them, and that is helping them heal and helping them get the care that they are [entitled] to. And I think that was one of the first instances where I was fighting some of the anger I had about what was happening in our town, what was happening to groups that have been marginalized. And you have that loyalty to your home, to your community. And that was the first kind of taste of that for me, that challenge against my role as a clinician.

JODY REYES, INCIDENT COMMANDER, UVA MEDICAL CENTER: That's where your Hippocratic oath to do no harm, you have to rise above that. And you have to realize that, *I'm not here to make a judgment on it and I'm not here to take sides. I am here to do a job and that is to provide care to anybody who needs it.*

And we talked about that a lot, because I started off the morning when we kicked off and I said, *This is a raw subject for a lot of people and you all likely have visceral feelings about what's happening today, but I implore you, you have to put those aside. We will care for whatever comes in our door and we will care for them as if it was our family member. We'll sort out all the rest later.*

MAYOR MIKE SIGNER, IN HIS CITY HALL OFFICE: City Manager Maurice Jones is sending out these occasional updates to [City] Council on what's happening. Keep in mind, at that point, I can't see from my window what is happening four blocks down, because my office didn't overlook the street. And so I'm kind of absorbing everything through text and through everything I'm watching online. But it was just really disjointed reality. And then he's sending these texts every 20 minutes to Council.

It was clear that there were riots breaking out in the street. I had no idea until later how bad the policing was because I couldn't observe it and there wasn't coverage in the moment. The crisis communications people I was with said, *You need to be over there* [in the command center] *because the whole country is watching this and the city.*

Mayor Signer texted City Manager Maurice Jones to ask again if he could come to the command center.

MIKE SIGNER: And then I said, *I need to be over there.* And then he said, *You can't be over there. There's not room. You can sit in the conference room.* And then I just said, *I'm going to go over there.*

And I marched over there with the two people from Powell Tate [the crisis communications firm] because I thought it was a crisis and that you needed the government. I sent Maurice these very explicit texts where I'm like, *We need to be unified. We need to be on the same page.* And he said, *There's no disunity. There's no problem.*

And then we had this really awkward confrontation at the Wells Fargo building. I walked in past these Virginia State Police. And then I couldn't get in. [Maurice] denied me entry.

EMILY BLOUT, UVA PROFESSOR AND MAYOR MIKE SIGNER'S WIFE: [Mike] and I tried to get in. It was on the eighth floor of this office building and I was just outraged that they would not let us. The city manager said, *You cannot come in.*

MIKE SIGNER: And it was then we had this altercation. I mean, it was very brief. And then I just left and I went over to the other center, the Emergency Operations Center [EOC], which is where the fire chief was, which is where the university president was and some of these other functionaries. Then that was where I was the rest of the afternoon.

ANDREW BAXTER, CHARLOTTESVILLE FIRE CHIEF, AT THE EOC: I can laugh about it now, but at some point, we've got the vice president of the University of Virginia and the president of the University of Virginia walking into that EOC looking at me and [county fire] Chief Dan Eggleston, and saying, *Can you give us an update?* And I'm like, *Hah, absolutely. But don't you think it's odd that the fire chief from the City of Charlottesville is the person who's giving you the update?* I think it's odd! It was messed up.

HENRY GRAFF, ANCHOR AND REPORTER, NBC29, AT EMANCIPATION PARK: It was just a melee for a while. People were beating the crap out of each other in front of you.

DON GATHERS, COFOUNDER, CHARLOTTESVILLE BLACK LIVES MATTER: Everyone had to do any- and everything that they possibly could to defend themselves. We were on our own. There wasn't anything that the city was going to do or going to be able to do to protect us at that point.

EMILY GORCENSKI, LOCAL ACTIVIST: I was like, *OK, this is a fucking shit show.*

ZACK WAJSGRAS, FREELANCE PHOTOGRAPHER: There became this no-man's-land, basically, in the crossroads of the streets near the library. And the white supremacists were on the corner of the park and everybody else was around the side and people were throwing things at each other and then they would get closer at different points and clash.

I found myself up in the bushes on the edge of the actual park in between the fence line where all the rally people were and where all the counterprotesters were. And then people started throwing things. And that was when I got hit with a water bottle filled with someone's urine on my arm. And it just splashed all over me and it smelled disgusting and it was just...But I just didn't really stop and think about it because it was just like, *Well, OK, this is the type of environment we're in right now.*

Zack Wajsgras had only just graduated from college that May. Two days before the rally, he had interviewed for a staff photographer position at the *Daily Progress*.

ZACK WAJSGRAS: And so, that was another huge reason why I decided to come to the rally too. At one point, I was watching these other photographers. I happened to notice this really famous *National Geographic* photographer was there, and I honestly was trying to look to whoever seemed to be the calmest in the situation. He kept running in and he would jump in and then jump out. And I was trying to keep moving like that. And so, I would jump in when they got really close to each other to try to get where the actual point of clash was. And so, I think at one point I just got a little bit too close and someone's metal pipe just bonked me on the top of the head. And I remember just being really stunned by it.

This woman, right in front of me, I saw pass by me. And a man just popped her right in the face. And she just immediately fell down and was just yelling by how much pain she was in.

It turned into an all-out battle multiple times.

TOM PERRIELLO, COUNTERPROTESTER AND FORMER US CONGRESSMAN: I mean, to me, the shocking thing was not that it started that way, but that this went on for like three hours and the police still hadn't moved in.

CIVILIAN SHOUTING AT POLICE BEHIND THE BARRICADE, CAPTURED ON BODY CAMERA FOOTAGE: This is shameful! I am a teacher, I am a community member, take care of your people! What the fuck are you doing?[4]

WEDNESDAY BOWIE, COUNTERPROTESTER: Basically, the cops were hiding behind the Nazis.

HEAPHY REPORT: Chief Thomas's response to the increasing violence on Market Street was disappointingly passive.

Captain Lewis and Chief Thomas's personal assistant Emily
Lantz both told us that upon the first signs of open violence
on Market Street, Chief Thomas said "let them fight, it will
make it easier to declare an unlawful assembly." Thomas did
not recall making that statement, though he did confirm that
he waited to "see how things played out" before declaring the
unlawful assembly.

Regardless of what he said, Chief Thomas's slow-footed response to violence put the safety of all at risk and created
indelible images of this chaotic event.

BRIAN MORAN, SECRETARY, VIRGINIA PUBLIC SAFETY AND HOMELAND SE-
CURITY, AT THE COMMAND CENTER: I'm watching this out the sixth-floor
window, command center's down the other end of the hall. I'm watching
this thing, going back and forth, walking back and forth saying, saying what's
going on and what, what, what are we gonna do? And this thing is escalating.

HEAPHY REPORT: At 10:59 a.m., Captain Shifflett relayed to the
Command Center that 2nd and Market Street were once again
"getting ready to erupt any second now." A moment later, he
reported another fight of "about forty people going at it,
they're using sticks." He again radioed, "Weapons are being
used on Market and 2nd Street." He added, "Recommend unlawful
assembly."

BRIAN MORAN: The last thing people need is some politician in the room
making decisions, but I'm watching it live. And I'm on the phone with the
governor. And I started seeing what appeared to be Molotov cocktails tossed
in the air.

TERRY MCAULIFFE, VIRGINIA GOVERNOR: He really, at this point, is feeling
that the fighting is getting out of control. That literally someone is gonna
pull out a gun. Someone's gonna get killed. It got to a tipping point.

BRIAN MORAN: And I said, *Governor, this has to stop. You gotta call the state of
emergency. This is it. This is, this is way out of control.*

And he said, *Call it, do what you need to do. Call the state emergency.*

CHAPTER 13

"Call the state of emergency."

BRIAN MORAN, SECRETARY, VIRGINIA PUBLIC SAFETY AND HOMELAND SE-CURITY: I ran down the other end of the hall, grabbed the superintendent. I said, the governor's called the state of emergency. It's gotta stop. And then we got the police out there [into the streets]. The directions to the police was call the state of emergency.

HENRY GRAFF, ANCHOR AND REPORTER, NBC29: They're on the bullhorn saying it's an unlawful assembly.

DEVIN WILLIS, SECOND-YEAR UVA STUDENT: The police began using megaphones to tell everyone that it was time to leave.[1] When I heard that, I complied. I was ready to go. So I found my friends, and we started heading along Market Street to leave the city.[2]

HENRY GRAFF: As the news trickles out through the crowd everybody's hearing it, understanding it, digesting it.

ALEXIS GRAVELY, SENIOR ASSOCIATE NEWS EDITOR, *CAVALIER DAILY*: We could hear it on the loudspeakers, but people weren't really dispersing.

HEAPHY REPORT: At almost the exact moment the unlawful assembly order went out, a smoke grenade was deployed by someone at the southeast corner of the Park. The crowd scattered. Overhead,

the VSP helicopter footage showed the smoke tail of the grenade trailing back and forth as demonstrators and counterprotesters picked it up and threw it back at each other. Out of
the pure happenstance of that smoke grenade, much of the crowd
dissipated—for a moment.

ALEXIS GRAVELY: That was the moment where I was like, *Oh my God, I'm
going to get seriously injured here because the crowd just moved.* And I was like, *Am
I going to get trampled by this crowd moving back?*

NICOLE HEMMER, JOURNALIST: Police eventually did move, starting at the
back of the park. They pushed the white nationalists out into the streets,
right into the crowd of antiracist protesters.[3]

DAVID FOKY, NEWS DIRECTOR, NBC29: And now you're like, wait a minute.
You're gonna push this crowd out of Emancipation Park, out into all the
people that they've been fighting with? You have 'em sort of contained in
that park. And now you're telling them they've gotta leave the park?

HEAPHY REPORT: ...the [Virginia State Police] mobile field
force units pushed the Unite the Right protesters right back
onto Market Street, where a larger group of counterprotesters
were waiting for them.

DON GATHERS, COFOUNDER, CHARLOTTESVILLE BLACK LIVES MATTER: You
gotta know what's going to happen when you do that. And we're not split-
ting atoms here or doing stem cell research. You gotta already know what's
going to happen.

BRENNAN GILMORE, COUNTERPROTESTER AND FORMER US FOREIGN SERVICE
OFFICER: It was like kicking this hive of bees.

HEAPHY REPORT: Lieutenant Hatter described the dispersal of
Emancipation Park on August 12 as the "most messed up thing
I ever saw." Hatter noted that the alt-right demonstrators
were screaming at the VSP and CPD officers as the [VSP] mobile field force pushed from the rear of Emancipation Park,
commenting that "you are pushing us right into the crowd."

Hatter agreed with this assessment, noting that the effort was "causing confrontations and pushing [the alt-right] right into their enemies."

BRIAN MORAN: Now you have these thousand white nationalists and counterprotesters roaming the streets. How do you patrol that? How do you enforce safety?

CHRIS SUAREZ, REPORTER, CHARLOTTESVILLE *DAILY PROGRESS*: [The white nationalists] were being all funneled through the corner of the park and it did—I kind of hate to repeat the characterization that the white nationalists used—but they kind of put them through a gauntlet. That is true.

DON GATHERS: Now you got a plethora of nasty fights breaking out. There are those sticks, flagpoles and bats, and anything that you can imagine.

STAR PETERSON, LOCAL ACTIVIST AND STREET MEDIC: A person went up to an officer and said, *The Nazi pulled a gun on me.* And the officer said, *I don't do guns.* I don't know if they were a fucking school cop or some shit or a fucking parking ticket cop. I don't remember who it was, but I just remember someone being told by a cop, *I don't do guns.* Like working at Subway and saying, *I don't do sandwiches.*

I remember looking over one of the barricades down past the library and I saw this white, masc-presenting cop with this red face. And he's just grinning at us. He's just watching people get hurt and fight and doing nothing but grinning. That's the big thing that stuck out to me from that.

HEAPHY REPORT: Lieutenant Jim Mooney related to us how frustrated he and other CPD officers were, having been removed from their zones almost an hour earlier. "We were sitting there with our thumbs up our asses," he told us.

Lieutenant Hatter lamented the fact that there were "people getting hurt, and I'm standing around behind a steel fence." Rather than breaking up fights, he was "guarding an empty parking lot." Hatter commented that CPD should have been in the street, rather than standing around twiddling their thumbs in a secure area of Emancipation Park.

[CPD] Detective Mark Frazier was more critical. He told us that CPD "failed this community" on August 12.

ZACK WAJSGRAS, FREELANCE PHOTOGRAPHER: The line of state troopers marched in or national guardsman or whatever, and dropped a bunch of colored tear gas and things like that. And just told everybody to disperse and leave the park immediately.

DON GATHERS: Tear gas is going off. And let me tell you, that's some nasty stuff. That stays with you for a while. Literally every part of your body burns. And if it hits your eyes and you touch your eyes trying to clear it, that just makes it worse. It cuts off your breath—your pores literally feel like they're on fire. The recommendation is to get milk for your eyes and face. Water over the rest of your body. It is the most unnerving thing which you can imagine happening to you because you literally feel like you're on fire from the inside out. You're choking, you're gasping for air. It's as though, if you can imagine, your body is on fire underwater. You're burning and you're trying to breathe at the same time and none of it is working.

BRENNAN GILMORE: The heat of the day rises, people are more violent when things get hot.

EMILY BLOUT, UVA PROFESSOR AND MAYOR MIKE SIGNER'S WIFE: It's terribly, sweltering hot in Charlottesville in August. It was oppressive heat, oppressive heat.

TOM PERRIELLO, COUNTERPROTESTER AND FORMER US CONGRESSMAN: It was like a hundred degrees out.

ZACK WAJSGRAS: It was blisteringly hot.

BRENNAN GILMORE: It was a hot day.

JODY REYES, INCIDENT COMMANDER, UVA MEDICAL CENTER: It was hot, but it was a beautiful day.

CHRIS SUAREZ: It was very hot, and it was a very clear day too. There weren't any clouds or anything. You can just kind of imagine that mid-August hot day, right around noon.

REV. SETH WISPELWEY, PASTOR AND COFOUNDER, CONGREGATE C'VILLE: The hot sun baking down.

KRISTIN SZAKOS, CHARLOTTESVILLE CITY COUNCILOR: I grew up in Mississippi. I wouldn't notice.

CHRIS SUAREZ TWEET, 12:05 P.M.: Police have taken over Emancipation Park. Seems like reports of a declared unlawful assembly are accurate.[4]

CHRIS SUAREZ: It was just so chaotic. I had no idea what was going to happen next, 'cause it was like—this was still before the thing was supposed to start at noon. So I was like, *Well, I guess it's over?* Like, *What's going to happen next?*

TERRY MCAULIFFE, VIRGINIA GOVERNOR: We cleared the park and then, I'll never forget it, feeling actually, OK, great! This is done. And this melee did not happen.

Of course, a melee did happen. But the governor says he didn't know, based on what he saw on TV.

I.B.F., LOCAL ACTIVIST: It feels like from national news, the rally is over. And I was very resentful because I was like, *That wasn't like—you think it's done? Like the threat is gone? It's not. I don't.*

MARCUS MARTIN, COUNTERPROTESTER: You couldn't just leave. You couldn't just walk away from it. I may not live down here, but I know people that's a part of this community. I work down here. This is how I provide for myself. So it's like, *I'm part of the community too.* So it's like, *You can't allow that to happen. You can't allow people to come up there and just be bullies.* It was like, *Are y'all serious? Like y'all really feel like this? Over a fucking statue?* It's just like, *You're not even* part *of here.*

LISA DRAINE, LOCAL ACTIVIST: I lost sight of the girls, 'cause I was keeping my eye on Devin. And I get this call from Rebecca, who's like, *Where are you?* And I'm like, *I'm still at, I'm here on Market Street. Where are* you? And they're like, *Oh no, you gotta get out of there. You're gonna get arrested, Mom!*

ELIZABETH SHILLUE, QUAKER ACTIVIST: We were able to get into First United Methodist Church and immediately went out to the back of the church so we could look out. It was incredible. It had turned into a war zone.

REV. PHIL WOODSON, ASSOCIATE PASTOR, FIRST UNITED METHODIST CHURCH: We had rabbis and other people out on the front porch, praying and singing. We had systems and ways to announce lockdowns in the church. And so we pull all people who were outside, we're saying, *The church is locking down. There's a chance. Get inside.* We pull people in, close the doors, we lock it.

REV. BRENDA BROWN-GROOMS, PASTOR, NEW BEGINNINGS CHRISTIAN COMMUNITY: Somebody let loose a canister of, what's that stuff...tear gas, mm-hmm. And then we closed the church's door, but the gas got into the church and everybody was gasping.

MICHAEL CHEUK, SECRETARY, CHARLOTTESVILLE CLERGY COLLECTIVE: I was a little afraid because if somebody came in, we had no escape other than if the windows were able to be open, then we could jump out. I knew that I could easily be targeted as one of the groups that is part of the problem, in terms of the "browning" of America. And, and yet, in terms of my personal experience, I haven't felt and experienced the level of trauma that could really trigger me. I grew up in a generation where my main goal was to assimilate. I came to the states when I was seven, so I really don't have a Chinese accent. I was part of that generation that said, *You come to America, we gotta find you an American name.* My full name is Cheuk Koon Hung. My aunt, who sponsored us, she gave me the name Michael because she did not want me to be incessantly teased when I was in the second grade. So my identity, frankly, was just kind of torn in some ways.

So I want to just acknowledge that there's a large part of me that has been kind of Americanized by white America. I didn't fit into that binary of white and Black. And so in so many ways, I have been spared from many of the kind of systemic racism and some of the microaggressions that my Black brothers and sisters experience.

But, however much that I identify internally as kind of more white sometimes, there's no way getting around that, externally, I'm Chinese all the way. And if somebody has something against Asians, then I'm an easy target.

At this point the clergy activists from Congregate left the safe zone where they had regrouped and headed back into the street.

SMASH CAINE-CONLEY, COFOUNDER, CONGREGATE C'VILLE: We had gotten word that these white nationalist groups were causing chaos and destruction as they were leaving the park. So we started marching back toward the park.

REV. SETH WISPELWEY: And then—I'll never forget this, especially after what happened earlier—we just marched down in our robes and everything, and this huge cheer goes up. People clapping, a lot of antifascists.

SMASH CAINE-CONLEY: It was the wildest thing. I think that moment was really incredible to me because I felt like we had failed, right? We had failed several times already. And to know that people were *for* our presence?

No one else was showing up, right? The police weren't showing up. No one else was showing up at that intersection to help protect people as white nationalists were doing violence. So the people were glad to see us.

So once we were there, we tried to help usher the white nationalists along, tried to step in when they were doing bodily harm to people as they were passing and then created a roadblock there so that they could not come back.

I remember watching a police officer watching a fight and just wondering, *What the hell is going on here?* And I also feel a little torn because we also don't want heavy police involvement or violence anywhere we are. So in a way you're like, *Yeah, please stay away.* But then you're pissed off because the only time they stay away is when white supremacists are doing harm to community members.

HEAPHY REPORT: We asked the command staff why no order was given to send a CPD squad in riot gear or another field force out into the streets. . . . They explained their view that, had officers been sent into the crowd, officers would have been put into a deadly force situation. Colonel Flaherty concurred with that assessment. He explained that he feels that only "fools rush in" to a situation in which they are not adequately protected.

MARCUS MARTIN: I recall a moment where everybody was taking a break. We was sitting down outside a parking garage. We was under a tree. So the next thing everybody was like, *Where's Heather, where's Heather?* And we look up and we seen Heather talking to a person with a helmet on, in a uniform. So we thinking Heather knows this person. So when Heather comes back over there, we actually were like, *Yo, you know 'em?* And then Heather was like, *No.* And then it was like, *So why was you talking to 'em?* She was like, *Just trying to understand like, why they're down here.* And then Heather was like, *Yeah, but I pretty much told 'em how fucking dumb they was.*

TWEET FROM ALLISON WRABEL, REPORTER, *DAILY PROGRESS*: More heading down Market Street. Pepper spray is lingering in the air.[5]

Among the white supremacists marching out of Emancipation Park was James Alex Fields, who earlier had been seen wearing a black shield. As they marched out of the park, they chanted "Jews will not replace us" and "You will not replace us."[6]

DAVID STRAUGHN, LOCAL ACTIVIST: We watched all of the white supremacists march down Market Street, away to McIntire Park. Many of them looked despondent and rejected, but I imagine that to always be the face of a white supremacist: wrinkled and sneering, always angry and full of rage. Soon after, we watched Richard Spencer run down the street, surrounded by a security circle of Nazis. The onlookers cheered and screamed as he sped by with his group.[7]

CHUCK MODIANO, REPORTER: Someone on the hill was saying, *Black lives splatter! Black lives splatter! Black lives splatter!* And I'm fumbling for my phone, and by the time I hit the record button, it stopped. And I was like, *Oh, I wish I got that. I wish I got that on video.*

DAVID STRAUGHN: Then the police in riot gear returned, preparing to disperse the crowds still remaining in the street.[8]

SMASH CAINE-CONLEY: That's when the police obviously got really militarized. It very quickly turned from a melee and chaos to feeling like we were under occupation by militarized police.

It's really just a surreal experience to see these militarized police marching in unison in all these lines, but that's all one side of you. And on the other side of you, there's white nationalist groups with their very large guns. And then next to them are a bunch of local activists in like T-shirts and their

Nikes. We stayed there for a while to kind of make sure that it was safe and that no one was gonna be harmed by the police.

Now all these actors are in the same space and it's kind of like a powder keg, right? You don't know who's gonna set it off, but you know it's gonna get set off.

HEAPHY REPORT: Once Emancipation Park was clear, the violent conflicts spread beyond the park. Small groups of people wandered through the streets and engaged in frequent skirmishes unimpeded by police. Violence erupted at the Market Street parking garage, Justice Park, High Street, the Water Street parking area, and on the Downtown Mall. Police attempted to respond to these violent conflicts, but were too far away and too late to intervene. The result was a period of lawlessness and tension that threatened the safety of the entire community.

The most notorious incident from those tense moments involved a homemade flamethrower and a gunshot. As alt-right demonstrators left the park and turned right to move west down Market Street, they passed by counterprotester Corey Long [who is Black]. Video taken by a bystander shows Long igniting the spray from an aerosol canister and pointing the flames at passing demonstrators.

COREY LONG, COUNTERPROTESTER: I went out to voice my opinion. To have my freedom of speech. Just like the racist Nazis who took over my town.[9]

THE ROOT: Long said the only weapon he had was a can of spray paint that a white supremacist threw at him earlier, so he took a lighter to the spray paint and turned it into a flame thrower. And a photographer snapped the photo.

But inside every photograph is an untold story. If you look closely at Long's picture, there's an elderly white man standing in between Long and his friend. The unknown man was part of the counterprotests, too, but was afraid, and Long and his friends were trying to protect him. Even though, Long says, those who were paid to protect the residents of Charlottesville were doing just the opposite.[10]

WEDNESDAY BOWIE, COUNTERPROTESTER: I remember seeing Corey with his flamethrower and just being like, *Holy fucking shit. This is some wild-ass shit, huh?*

Seeing a guy, shirtless, holding off Nazis from attacking an elderly man with a flamethrower—that was one of the most surreal things that I saw all day.

HEAPHY REPORT: Richard Wilson Preston, a Ku Klux Klan leader from Maryland, saw this as he exited the park. He drew his handgun and pointed it at Long while screaming at him to stop. Preston loaded a round into the chamber of his gun then fired a single shot at the ground next to Long.

COREY LONG: At first it was peaceful protest. Until someone pointed a gun at my head. Then the same person pointed it at my foot and shot the ground.[11]

ZACK WAJSGRAS, FREELANCE PHOTOGRAPHER: At one point, we heard the gunshot go off and just, no one even seemed to pause. It just, like, happened. And a few people looked at each other and then people just kept running at each other and the moment moved on.

PASSERBY, CAPTURED ON VIDEO: That was a gunshot![12]

HEAPHY REPORT: [Preston] holstered his gun and walked away. VSP troopers, identified by their neon yellow vests, stood in a line behind two barricades about twenty feet away. None appeared to react.

After this incident, Corey Long walked down Market Street with his friend DeAndre Harris, a 20-year-old high school special-education aide.

ZACK ROBERTS, PHOTOJOURNALIST: I saw a young African American man [DeAndre Harris] chased by a bunch of white protesters—saw one with a red Make America Great Again hat on, a bunch of them in full combat gear, like kind of fake combat gear, wearing helmets and waving batons. They basically chased after him.

HEAPHY REPORT: At about 12:07 p.m., the group [of white suprem-acists] stopped in front of the Market Street garage and a fight broke out.

CHUCK MODIANO, REPORTER: It all happens really, really fast. I'm walking up the street and I hear a bunch of commotion and I hear and I see the white supremacists running back towards the garage. So I immediately turn and run that way. And as I'm running, you know, it's chaotic.

HEAPHY REPORT: From our review of the ample open source video footage of this confrontation, it appears that a counterpro-tester attempted to yank a flag away from a Unite the Right demonstrator who resisted and fought back. During that strug-gle, a second counterprotester named DeAndre Harris rushed in and used a club, possibly a Maglite flashlight, to strike the alt-right demonstrator's head or shoulder. Nearby demonstra-tors rushed over to fight back and deployed pepper spray.

DEANDRE HARRIS, COUNTERPROTESTER: I was here as a counterprotester, but just to voice my opinion about the KKK and white supremacy and things like that. I wasn't out here being violent. I wasn't out here to be violent.[13]

COURT DOCUMENTS: Harris intended to simply attend the counter-protest to show solidarity with those advocating for equality and love over racism and hate.[14]

HEAPHY REPORT: The struggle moved into the parking garage. Harris appears to have tripped or been pushed to the ground, which left him defenseless against a mob of angry alt-right demonstrators that descended upon him with flagsticks, shields, and pieces of wood.

WHITE SUPREMACISTS: "Go, go, go, go, go, go!"[15]

With Long nearby, multiple white supremacists converged on Harris, attacking him with a large wooden plank, a tire thumper, a flagpole, and bare fists.[16]

ZACH ROBERTS: There was probably six to ten people actively trying to attack DeAndre. And he ended up being almost thrown into a parking garage arm and it broke. And then one of the Unite the Right people grab that parking arm and started beating him with it.

DEANDRE HARRIS: I kept falling. I didn't even realize I was being hit at the time. I was just trying to get up and run, but then I fell, then I got up again, then I fell. When your adrenaline is running so high, you don't feel none of it until after the fact.[17]

TWEET FROM CHUCK MODIANO, REPORTER: Fight broke out. Nazis beat black kid w/sticks at end.

COREY LONG: The white supremacists told us to "die, n****r" in the garage.[18]

The fact was that [photographers] just stood around recording everything. The fact that they didn't help us. . . . It was outrageous.[19]

Only one journalist did: Chuck Modiano kicked one of the men who was on Harris.

CHUCK MODIANO TO WHITE SUPREMACISTS, RECORDED ON VIDEO: "Yo! Yo! Get the fuck out of here! Yo, get the fuck out of here!"

CHUCK MODIANO: I tried to do something. I very feebly tried to kick a guy. I thought I kicked him harder than I did, looking at the video. I'm upset I didn't do more, if being quite honest with you.

ZACH ROBERTS: Chuck's a great guy. He was much, much closer than I was. And basically from that moment, they all kinda scattered.

WHITE SUPREMACIST, RECORDED ON VIDEO: "Yo! Let him up, let him up!"

Long helped Harris get into a stairwell to hide.

COREY LONG: The Nazis tried to force their way into the stairway that we were hiding in.[20]

DEANDRE HARRIS: I got hit in the head and I had to get staples in my head to seal it back up. I broke my wrist right here. I busted my lip. I chipped my tooth. I'm on my knees just getting beat with poles and signs and being kicked and hit. It's crazy.[21]

COURT DOCUMENTS: Harris suffered several physical injuries as a result of the assault, including a spinal injury, broken wrist, chipped tooth, concussion, head wound requiring 10 stitches and other internal injuries.[22]

There was only one law enforcement officer in the garage, who eventually tried to render aid and called an ambulance: Sheriff James Brown, who is Black.

HEAPHY REPORT: Charlottesville Sheriff James Brown was standing outside the CPD headquarters, which is located next to the Market Street garage.

Someone stopped him and said that a Unite the Right member had drawn a firearm, but then Brown heard the sound of heavy sticks hitting the pavement. Sheriff Brown turned and saw Harris being beaten, attempt to get up, and then stumble to the stairwell. Brown went to assist Harris. As he walked towards him, he picked up a 36-inch baton that had been carried by a Unite the Right demonstrator.

Sheriff Brown reached Harris and attempted to render aid in the stairwell. Harris's head had been split open and he was bleeding. He described the scene as "surreal." When Brown looked around, he realized he was the only law enforcement officer in the garage.

At 12:08 p.m., a radio call went out.... A few minutes later, the CPD SWAT unit arrived in their Bearcat armored vehicle. Street medics and police officers moved Harris across the street to the alcove in front of NBC29's studio.

WRAL-TV REPORT: Harris said he's alive thanks to a stranger he only knows as Karen.[23]

DEANDRE HARRIS: She talked to me and kept me calm and really kept me awake. I was fading and she woke me up.

HEAPHY REPORT: By 12:28 p.m., paramedics arrived and transported Harris to the triage center at COB McIntire.

ZACH ROBERTS, PHOTOJOURNALIST: I walked down to the street, I saw what I believe is a state trooper, and I was just like, *I just witnessed this* [*assault*]. And I was showing him the photos on the back of my camera and he just shrugged his shoulders and walked away. That was the moment where I'm just like...Here's evidence of a brutal beating by multiple people who are still in the vicinity most likely, 'cause it was like five—maybe not even five minutes afterwards—and the police officer had no interest whatsoever at even looking at the photos!

DEANDRE HARRIS: I was losing so much blood, the people at the hospital told me I was lucky.[24]

TERRY MCAULIFFE, VIRGINIA GOVERNOR: At this point, to be honest with you, it's over. It's done before it started. It had fist fights, but no damage done, no property—nothing set on fire, not a window had broken. Subsequently we did hear a couple of people were hurt. Remember that young Black kid in the parking garage but we, you know, we didn't know that at this point. It's over.

REV. PHIL WOODSON, ASSOCIATE PASTOR, FIRST UNITED METHODIST CHURCH: The police pushed them into the community. And so what we had for hours after that were bands of Nazis roaming through downtown with a lot of north downtown cut off from their access, but a lot of southern downtown, like Friendship Court, where we have a lot of subsidized housing and where a lot of other Black and brown people live and well into Belmont area, it pushed them towards these low-income, predominantly Black neighborhoods and pushed them in that direction.

And so even just the setup of the police was guarding this north downtown, white, single-family housing neighborhood. And so they come this far but no further, but pushed them into the walking mall where people were, and then down towards Friendship Court apartments, and other areas that are predominantly Black and low-income housing in the city.

DAVID STRAUGHN, LOCAL ACTIVIST: This was an attempt to cause harassment and violence at multiple locations. Not just one place in the Downtown Mall. That's another thing where people get it twisted. They thought [the alt-right groups] were all coming to meet together. Oh no. They were coming to catch bodies. They were coming to get one. They were like, *Yo, they beatin' Black ass in Charlottesville in August. You wanna roll? Hell fucking yeah!*

That was the point. It wasn't for free speech. It wasn't to meet underneath the flag and celebrate constitutional rights. No, it was about possibly murdering and beating the shit outta Black people and having the autonomy to do it.

SMASH CAINE-CONLEY, COFOUNDER, CONGREGATE C'VILLE: Then we really just started marching around, particularly downtown as we heard that something was happening in a particular place. We would get some communication that there was a white nationalist group in this spot and they were causing some sort of harm or disruption. And we would march in that direction and then we would hear that there would be somebody somewhere else. So we would march in that direction, and really just try to put our bodies into places where there could be violence and try to support people with our words or our actions.

DAVID FOKY, NEWS DIRECTOR, NBC29: By and large, it was—we thought it was winding down and we could start putting our stuff together for the six o'clock news.

And then one o'clock came.

CHAPTER 14

"It was like the resistance camp at the end of the world."

ABOUT I P.M.

HEAPHY REPORT: Many of [the counterprotesters] regrouped at McGuffey Park, where they waited to determine where they should go next.

REV. SETH WISPELWEY, PASTOR AND COFOUNDER, CONGREGATE C'VILLE: Everyone's like, *OK, the streets feel safe enough*. We're all pulling back.

ELIZABETH SINES, UVA LAW STUDENT: When I look back on what happened, this is what I will choose to hold onto; it was the first time I felt at peace. There were no Nazi groups or white supremacists on site—just counterprotesters. It was like the resistance camp at the end of the world.[1]

There was a soft breeze. Balloon bouquets were everywhere, someone had made a papier-mâché statue of Sally Hemings. There was diversity in age, race, gender, and ability.[2]

SMASH CAINE-CONLEY, COFOUNDER, CONGREGATE C'VILLE: There were protest puppets and there was music and there was free food. It was a space of community, a celebration. That was really beautiful to be in and it was a stark contrast to what we had been doing the rest of the day.

NATALIE ROMERO, SECOND-YEAR UVA STUDENT: We were at the park with swing sets, eating oranges and kind of sitting, hanging out, drinking waters. People were just sitting in circles in groups, getting to know each other.[3]

WEDNESDAY BOWIE, COUNTERPROTESTER: I remember I went and got on the swings, because I hadn't been on swings in a really long time, and realizing that the day was ending and that we'd probably be heading home and being surprised that I was still in one piece.

DAVID STRAUGHN, LOCAL ACTIVIST: I remember positioning my bookbag as a pillow, finding a shady spot below a large tree, and lying underneath it. I basked in the glory of the moment.[4] Shit's over.

I thought the day was won. We all did.[5]

CHELSEA ALVARADO, COUNTERPROTESTER: People were just talking, eating food, because there was snacks and stuff.[6]

REV. SETH WISPELWEY: Someone shoved a peanut butter sandwich in my face. I remember having half.

SMASH CAINE-CONLEY: We had been marching throughout the city all day and standing and hadn't slept for awhile. And it was hot. It was August and we're wearing clergy robes.

STAR PETERSON, LOCAL ACTIVIST AND STREET MEDIC: Somebody was there making vegan burritos. I remember telling my friend like, *Oh gosh, they have vegan food*, and being all excited.

SMASH CAINE-CONLEY: I ate a burrito and that was fantastic.

ELIZABETH SINES: A DJ was playing reggae.[7]

Lisa Draine found her daughters in the crowd and they relaxed a bit together.

LISA DRAINE, LOCAL ACTIVIST: We're sort of like, *Wow, I guess it's over.* So eventually I was like, *I'm just hot and tired.* And then I was like, *I think I'm just gonna go on home.* So I left the girls with their friends.

SMASH CAINE-CONLEY: At some point, the clergy left there and went back to [regroup].

EMILY GORCENSKI, LOCAL ACTIVIST: That's when the call for support came.

NATALIE ROMERO: Someone started to let people know that the white nationalists were near Friendship Court, harassing people in that direction.[8]

WEDNESDAY BOWIE: That didn't really mean anything to me, but it was explained that it's a low-income, predominantly Black neighborhood and that it would be really bad if Nazis started shit there.

Friendship Court, often called "Garrett" after its Garrett Street address, is a Section 8 housing development that is home mostly to people of color. It's across the Downtown Mall from McGuffey Park.

STAR PETERSON: They were like, *We're going to send scouts out.* So I was like, *Well, let's fucking go now.* I used to be a fast walker. So I ended up being at the front of that crowd.

DON GATHERS, COFOUNDER, CHARLOTTESVILLE BLACK LIVES MATTER: Through our intel and then from things that they had left behind, we found that they had maps with targeted areas that they planned on going into to wreak havoc. And there were places on some of those maps that, please forgive me, but this is what they called them: they were n*****hoods and we found out that they were planning to head over to Garrett.

NATALIE ROMERO: We were walking towards Friendship Court.[9]

BILL BURKE, COUNTERPROTESTER: We get down there and there were no Nazis around. But there were people who lived there in the place. So some of our people went over and talked with them.

STAR PETERSON: I remember a lot of people coming out of their homes and looking at us. We're told, *Hey. The threat's gone right now.*

BILL BURKE: They decided that a huge group of us being there would probably draw the Nazis [back] to them. So we decided we'd leave a couple of people in the area so that they could run back up the hill and get us if they needed to or whatever.

STAR PETERSON: I remember coming around the corner near where the parking garage is. We could see the Downtown Mall. I remember seeing another group of people. It was clear that they were on our side. And I just remember it being really joyous and lots of celebrating. And the thing was, the Unite the Right rally was shut down. They didn't get to have any of their hate speech. So I just remember it being really joyful. One group was coming down this way and we came up and then merged with them and then all walked together.

The group swelled to a couple hundred counterprotesters.

KATRINA TURNER, LOCAL ACTIVIST: Once we merged together, we just started celebrating and singing and chanting "Black Lives Matter," and just celebrating at that point, because [the white nationalists] had left Friendship Court and everything.

NATALIE ROMERO: It was two groups of people coming together. People were just kind of happy to see each other. Kind of like, *How are you all? Great to see you all.*

Natalie Romero was marching with a group of friends, including Kendall King and Lisa Draine's daughters, Sophie and Rebecca.

KENDALL KING, THIRD-YEAR UVA STUDENT: I just was like, *Oh my God, this is the best moment of the day.*

ZACK WAJSGRAS, FREELANCE PHOTOGRAPHER: At one point, there was a group of people who were dressed as clowns. I have a picture of five people dressed as clowns, just standing on the corner while I was walking past them.

BILL BURKE: It was the most pure, ecstatic joy.

Counterprotester Marcus Martin joined the crowd with his fiancée, Marissa Blair, and friends Heather Heyer and Courtney Commander.

MARCUS MARTIN, COUNTERPROTESTER: We found that big crowd of happy people: cheers, clowns, people singing kumbaya and shit.

ELIZABETH SINES: It felt like we had won: We had taken back our town and protected our people.[10]

EMILY GORCENSKI: Everyone was celebrating, but my thought is like, *We're on a street that's not closed to traffic. The cops are still out. There's National Guard out, got a helicopter flying over us. And we are in a kettle zone. We're not in a good spot.* So we need to get back to the streets that we're allowed to be on and get back to the parks where we're supposed to be. So I'm like, *OK, let's start walking back up to the park.*

ROSIA PARKER, LOCAL ACTIVIST: So that's when we turned around to come back up to the Downtown Mall.

This one particular officer came from just out of nowhere. It's almost like he was an angel. He looked at me and Katrina and he was like, *Don't go down 4th Street, because I'm warning y'all, everywhere that y'all go, it's going to be considered an unlawful entry. Black Lives Matter, y'all are a danger right now, do not go down 4th Street.* So me and Katrina and her son, we looked at each other. We started talking among ourselves and we was like, *We've got to lead these people and make sure we don't go down 4th Street.*

KATRINA TURNER: We got to a spot and didn't know which way to go. And somebody hollered, *Which way do we go?*

ROSIA PARKER: And we was like, *Don't go down 4th Street. Anywhere but 4th Street.*

KATRINA TURNER: And this is what we were trying to tell one of the members of Black Lives Matter: that we were told, *Don't go down 4th street.* But he was the one in charge of the bullhorn and all that. We know he says, *Go ahead, go left.*

ROSIA PARKER: And that was 4th Street.

NATALIE ROMERO: Someone said: *Turn left.* I don't know who. We started making a left.

BILL BURKE: There's a saying in the leftist world, when you don't know, *Always go left.* So we started chanting, *Always go left,* and that's when we decided to turn left and go over Water Street there.

ELIZABETH SINES: 4th Street is pretty narrow, I would say much narrower than an ordinary street. And it's buildings on both sides, so it adds to the feeling of it being pretty narrow.[11]

It was packed. There were a lot of us all in a line, like a big group. So it was a tight squeeze. We had to converge and kind of like—I don't know how to describe it best—take a big group and put it into something smaller.[12]

ZACK WAJSGRAS: Everybody was packed into there and still cheering and stuff. I was going around the edges, but then I just wedged myself right into the center of the crowd in the intersection. Just smack in the middle.

KATRINA TURNER: My son Timmy and another Black Lives Matter member were right there with Heather, walking with Heather.

SUSAN BRO, HEATHER HEYER'S MOTHER: My daughter Heather was wearing black because she was tending bar that afternoon. She worked two, sometimes three jobs, just to live on her own. And she hated to walk in the heat and here it is an August day and she's dressed in black with her full-length hair in a long thick braid because that keeps it under control. But just the fact that my daughter was out there walking tells me how passionate she was about that.[13]

HEAPHY REPORT: The group of several hundred counterprotesters paused for a moment as they decided where to go. Some within the crowd started to move north up 4th Street SE, back towards Justice Park. They maneuvered around two cars that appeared to be stuck at the intersection after having driven south on 4th Street.

Stuck in one of those cars were sisters Tadrint and Micah Washington, 27 and 23 years old. They had heard about the rally but had no plans to get anywhere near it.

TADRINT WASHINGTON: I was coming from a friend's house in Friendship Court. There were a lot of detours that way, which brought me down to Water Street. All the people was right there. We was at a stop sign behind a van. And we got stuck because of the crowd.

ELIZABETH SINES: That was when the car came.[14]

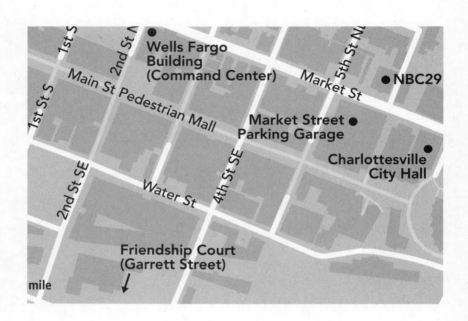

CHAPTER 15

"I heard a car revving."

I:4I P.M.

RYAN KELLY, PHOTOJOURNALIST: I saw the car backing up the hill. I thought nothing of the car. I assumed it was turning around the block to get out of the way and get on wherever he was trying to go. So I started taking some pictures.[1]

MARCUS MARTIN, COUNTERPROTESTER: I was just walking behind Marissa, and I was looking at my phone about to go on live, like let everybody know that *Hey everything's fine. Everything's fine.*

And then I heard the tires screech.

ELIZABETH SINES, UVA LAW STUDENT: You heard it before you saw it.[2]

S.L., COUNTERPROTESTER: I heard a car revving.[3]

BRENNAN GILMORE, COUNTERPROTESTER AND FORMER US FOREIGN SERVICE OFFICER: I heard from behind me, a squeal and acceleration.[4]

WEDNESDAY BOWIE, COUNTERPROTESTER: I was in a space between one parked car and a black pickup truck that was parked, and that was about a car-length's worth. I remember seeing something in the corner of my eye.

BRENNAN GILMORE: When it hit the mall, because there's a big dip there, it slowed for a second. And I remember having this split-second thought, *Oh, he's just . . . This guy's trying to scare this crowd. That's really fucked up.* It was an instant, but then it's no sooner that I had that immediate thought that he then really accelerated and slammed into the crowd.

CONSTANCE PAIGE YOUNG, COUNTERPROTESTER: The only thing that I could think of was, *We're all getting struck. We're about to get struck.* I didn't think, *Jump. Run.* There was nothing there. It was just, *We're about to get struck.*

I remember being consciously aware that this was happening. This was going to happen.

ELIZABETH SINES: In my mind, I can still see it in slow motion. You just see a car fly down the road and hit this large group and crash into a car that had been at the base.[5]

STAR PETERSON, LOCAL ACTIVIST AND STREET MEDIC: I never saw the car coming. So never, ever had a chance to get out of the way.

ELIZABETH SINES: It sounded like if you would take a metal baseball bat and slide it across a wooden fence. Something I'll never forget.[6]

MARCUS MARTIN: I looked up and just see people in the air. So I did what any person would do, I got my loved one out the way. I pushed Marissa out of the way.[7] And then I got hit.

ZACK WAJSGRAS, FREELANCE PHOTOGRAPHER: Just the sound of bodies hitting metal and then very shortly after just piercing screams.

EMILY GORCENSKI, LOCAL ACTIVIST: Thump, thump, thump, thump.

KATRINA TURNER, LOCAL ACTIVIST: Wop, wop, wop, wop.

STAR PETERSON: I just heard three bumps. Two of them were his left tires going over my leg.[8]

DAVID STRAUGHN, LOCAL ACTIVIST: I just see people flying up into the air. People in the air. People on the ground.[9]

KATRINA TURNER: All's we saw was bodies fly. All I saw was people in black. And I didn't know who it was, I didn't know if it could have been my son.

ELIZABETH SINES: I jumped over someone who had been hit who was unconscious on the road.[10]

ROSIA PARKER, LOCAL ACTIVIST: It's a movie. It's a movie, and I'm standing. Right there. And I'm watching how many times when Heather got hit. I'm watching it, looking directly at her, counting how many times that she twirled around in the air and when she hit and rolled off the car, and I'm like, *Oh shit.*

STAR PETERSON: I didn't know Heather Heyer, but I saw this white femme-presenting person flying through the air facing me. Everything slowed down and I remember thinking, *That's what someone's eyes look like when they're dead.*

ROSIA PARKER: Our Care Bears pushed us out the way, so we hit the brick wall.

SABR LYON, COUNTERPROTESTER: There's no time for thought and in the moment I pushed my then-fiancée so hard, I left a hand print on her back. I pushed her hard enough to push my mom out of the street.

TADRINT WASHINGTON, SURVIVOR: Before I know it, my head was in the steering wheel. I remember hitting my head, seeing a lady come over on my windshield.

L.Q., COUNTERPROTESTOR: I did not feel the impact, and I did not feel my legs break as he drove into me. And I was still confused as I flew upside down through the air. Then as he plowed into Tay Washington's car, I heard the cars crashing around me right before I landed on her hood. If she had not been there, I believe I would be dead.[11]

TADRINT WASHINGTON: I'm still in shock. I'm still like, *Am I seeing this or am I not?* Really, to be honest with you, I thought somebody bombed us. My vision wasn't really there because I hit my head so hard.

ZACK WAJSGRAS: Right after it happened, it was just black. My senses were not receiving information.

NATALIE ROMERO, SECOND-YEAR UVA STUDENT: I get hit and the next thing I know is just darkness.

I could hear my heart beating. You know in movies, those war scenes where they were just hit or something, and it's just flashing? I couldn't see too much, but I felt dripping on my face.[12]

KENDALL KING, THIRD-YEAR UVA STUDENT: It smelled terrible, like burning rubber. It was very quiet for one second while everyone figured out what the fuck happened. Then it was absolute, total chaos.

CONSTANCE PAIGE YOUNG: I just remember it felt like there were a thousand pounds tied on my lower body. And I was just grabbing at anybody. Grabbing at anybody to try to...and I remember I had tunnel vision. So, I couldn't see on the sides. I could only see literally what was directly in front of me. And it was almost like I had this vision as if it were in a movie. Nothing, nothing existed. This was just the only thing that my brain was thinking was, *You get the hell out of here. You got to run.*

S.L., COUNTERPROTESTER: The very edge of my thigh made impact with the car and it knocked my feet out from under me, so I landed on my face a few yards from where I had been standing.[13] I knew my face was wet with blood. I was in shock, and I did not know what happened to me. There was a moment I thought I could be dying.

BILL BURKE, COUNTERPROTESTER: Next thing I know I was on the side of the road and there was a girl telling me that my head's bleeding, that I had a cut or a hole in my head, and I was looking at her and the words weren't making any sense. And she took my hand and put it up where my head was bleeding and I tried to stand up and I felt the most excruciating pain I've ever felt before. I mean, instantly took me to my knees and I closed my eyes and I was like, *Oh, man, this is it.*

RYAN KELLY, PHOTOJOURNALIST: I knew immediately that something horrible had happened and I knew it had happened intentionally.[14]

ZACK WAJSGRAS: I was frozen and I took a step back. So, I just was like, *OK, I didn't get hit.*

LISA WOOLFORK, UVA PROFESSOR AND MEMBER OF CHARLOTTESVILLE BLACK LIVES MATTER: I looked up and I saw a shoe, just a shoe floating in the air. And I looked at it and I was like, *What is happening? Is someone throwing shoes? Are people throwing projectiles? What is this?* [Someone] had been hit by the car with such force that his shoe had flown off his body and into the sky about 10 feet.

ELIZABETH SINES, UVA LAW STUDENT: I don't know exactly how we made it over to the side of the road, but we jumped to the right side of the road.[15]

STAR PETERSON, LOCAL ACTIVIST AND STREET MEDIC: The next thing I remember is just being in the street and being like, *OK. I need to get out of the street in case there's more cars coming.* So I tried to move and it was too soon to even feel pain yet. I just registered my right leg doesn't work. So I yelled. Somebody pulled me out of the street and onto the sidewalk.

S.L.: John pulled me up off the street and we ran. Our only choice was pushing up against a brick wall on 4th, John shielding me with his body.[16]

BRENNAN GILMORE, COUNTERPROTESTER AND FORMER US FOREIGN SERVICE OFFICER: I could have reached out and touched his car. I was right next to it. The window was darkly tinted, and I could just see that it was a man with close-cut hair. Couldn't tell much more than that.

The driver was James Alex Fields, the white supremacist seen earlier in Emancipation Park carrying a black shield and chanting "Jews will not replace us" after the unlawful assembly was declared.

WEDNESDAY BOWIE, COUNTERPROTESTER: I just was running towards the car because I could see that there were people on the ground and that people were hurt. I wasn't processing anything. I didn't have any thoughts of like, *This is on purpose.* I just knew that we needed to get to people. And I had a medic. But I got two feet away from the bumper, a foot and a half, two feet away from the bumper, and I saw the reverse lights come on.

S.L.: At that moment Fields slammed his car into reverse.[17]

WEDNESDAY BOWIE: I very clearly remember having the thought, *I'm going to get hit by a car. And I hope this doesn't suck.*

And actually, getting hit by the car did not suck because he was not going very fast when he caught me on his bumper, so that was fine. It was just getting picked up. But I got stuck on his trunk. I was bent in half. I was basically lying on his back windshield with my legs down, and I was like, *Don't go under the wheels. Don't go under the wheels.*

He ended up smashing me into the black truck, into the driver's side door of the black truck, ass first, basically. And because of that, I didn't get run over. But I broke my pelvis.

I'm not sure if it was when I impacted with the truck and my face hit his back windshield or if it was when I impacted with the ground, but at some point, I broke my orbital socket. I think that was the blow that caused me to lose consciousness. I was unconscious when I hit the ground.

SABR LYON, COUNTERPROTESTER: There's this person down with an obvious head wound. My mom goes to grab them out of the road and I see the car starting to back up and I screamed bloody murder. She almost got run over a second time.

ELIZABETH SINES: He started backing over the people that he had hit.[18] That's when the panic really set in for me. It became obvious that he was trying to kill as many people as he could.[19] We started screaming.[20]

DAVID STRAUGHN: That's when everyone starts to scream. I try to scream, but there's no sound that comes outta my mouth.

The car appeared suddenly, right in front of me. A gray Dodge Charger with the windshield smashed, and the bumper torn away from its right side. A man in front of me began whaling on the car with a large stick, bashing out the back window.[21]

S.L.: Despite the confusion, it was clear to both John and I that we were under attack. We felt completely vulnerable and desperately hoped Fields would not veer into us or emerge with a weapon.[22]

TWEETS FROM EMILY GORCENSKI, LOCAL ACTIVIST: After the car hit, I ran through the crowd because I was concerned he might pop out and start shooting. I pulled my weapon—no round was chambered—just in case that happened.[23]

EMILY GORCENSKI: I had done a lot of work mentally to prepare myself for what my limit of violence was and what I would do in those situations. And this was one of those situations where it's like, if there's a possibility of lethal force, I'm going to be willing to defend. So basically, at that point, it was like, *If this guy gets out and tries to shoot somebody, I'm going to try to shoot him.*

BRENNAN GILMORE: So I ran up the street and was shouting, *Go, go get out of this canyon that we're stuck in!*[24]

ELIZABETH SINES: Someone yelled, *Go to the alleys, go to the alleys!*[25]

NATALIE ROMERO, SECOND-YEAR UVA STUDENT: Somebody—I heard someone pull me. I felt someone pull me.[26]

BRENNAN GILMORE: We ducked around the corner.[27]

ELIZABETH SINES: People flocked to the alleys and began climbing ladders and staircases to get to higher ground.[28]

NATALIE ROMERO: I believe that if I hadn't been pulled, he would have run over my legs.[29]

BILL BURKE, COUNTERPROTESTER: I tried to get up and...I was an EMT beforehand. So my first instinct was to kick in and help somebody. And I tried to sit up and I don't even think I made it to my knees, I just went back down and passed out again.

MARCUS MARTIN, COUNTERPROTESTER: I stood up and I stepped on my right leg first and then when I went to go step with my left, like everything just pushed up in my leg and I collapsed and that's when the pain started. My ankle was broken and my tibia was actually really bad: The injury came from my knee, the crack spiraled all the way down my bone.

The medics just start running up to you. And I didn't know where Marissa was. And so when the medic was running up, *Are you OK?* I was just, *Go find her. She's wearing white shirt, blue shorts.* I would say about five, six times they ran up to me, asked me what's wrong. And I told 'em, I gave 'em all the same answer: *Find her.*

And then I heard her voice. Then I laid eyes on her and then that's when I could worry about myself.

KATRINA TURNER, LOCAL ACTIVIST: So after I was pushed out the way of the car, like Rosia said, we got separated. So Rosia was gone. I couldn't find Rosia. I couldn't find my son. And I just get hollering, *Rosia! Timmy? Rosia! Timmy!* I just kept hollering for 'em.

But one of the [activist] security came and said, *We will find Rosia. We will find Timmy, but you have to get to safety right now.* So he took me into an alley and there were other people that had ran into this alley. So he told me, he said, *You'll be safe right here. I'm going to find your son. We're going to get you to him.*

RYAN KELLY, PHOTOJOURNALIST: I actually chased the car, thinking he would get pulled over or get in a wreck or arrested. I thought I would capture that. But none of that happened.[30]

DAVID STRAUGHN, LOCAL ACTIVIST: I chase after the car 'cause I just don't know what to do. It was long out of sight. I ran in futility. I had to do something. I had to do more.[31]

RYAN KELLY: By the time I got up to the cross street, he was long gone. I asked a couple of people who saw what happened, they said he got further than I could have made it.[32]

NATALIE ROMERO: Chaos. Blood. People didn't know what to do. It was terrifying. It was straight out of like—you've seen domestic terrorism before in the news or random places that weren't in my life. That's what that was. That's what it looked like.[33]

TADRINT WASHINGTON, SURVIVOR: I closed my eyes to try to get my vision back because my head was hurting so bad. I just remember kept saying, *What happened, what happened?* And as I'm trying to get my vision back just something struck me: *your little sister. You can't panic.*

MICAH WASHINGTON, SURVIVOR: As soon as I hit the dashboard—for some reason, I always snap into protective mode when crazy things happen. I know she's the older sister, but I'm the one that snaps in protective mode and immediately, I was worried about her. She kept asking, *What happened, what happened?* I'm telling her, *I'm not sure what happened, but we're OK. You're OK. We're OK.*

And at this point I'm not sure what's going on with her because she's laid straight back into her seat, arms by her side and her eyes are closed. She's slightly shaking all over. So at this point I'm really, really scared, but I'm still trying to comfort her saying, *We're OK, it's going to be OK. It's going to be OK.*

TADRINT WASHINGTON: I'm also an EMT. I'd just graduated. We are somehow taught to be prepared for some of these things, but you can't really prepare for these things. So I was trying to remain calm for her, but I don't know how well I did that.

And I just remember when I got myself back together, I started to wiggle my fingers because I wanted to see if my blood was circulating. My finger's moving. I tried to wiggle my toes to make sure my spinal cord wasn't messed up in any way. I still couldn't really see—I had spots in my eyes. So I'm just trying to make sure I'm not bleeding. My extremities are moving.

NATALIE ROMERO, SECOND-YEAR UVA STUDENT: The flashes, the noise. A lot of people are trying to talk to me. A lot of people are trying to keep me awake. I was holding a pole because I—I just wanted to lay down, but I knew if I laid down I would fall asleep. And if I fell asleep, I might not wake up. In trainings we were taught that all the time: *Keep consciousness. Keep your consciousness, because you could die.* So that's what I thought was about to happen. I thought that I was about to die. I was like, *These are my last seconds of breath. I need to call my mom right now.*[34]

CHAPTER 16

"I always wondered: *Was she afraid?*
Did she see him coming?"

REV. SETH WISPELWEY, PASTOR AND COFOUNDER, CONGREGATE C'VILLE:
At that point I was about a block and a half up Water Street. A restaurant owner who liked what Congregate was about at the time was running Escafe. He was a big fan of what we were doing. And so that had been set aside as a safe space for us, for anyone who wanted to just check in and get a bite maybe.

Escafe was the city's only downtown establishment known for a roaring dance floor. As the only gay bar in downtown Charlottesville, it also served as a safe space not only for queer people in town but also for people of color and others who felt they didn't fit in with the majority.

REV. SETH WISPELWEY: I stood out on the outdoor patio for a smoke, just to catch a breath. We're like, *What's going on? We're going to take stock.* I sat down two, three minutes, halfway done with the smoke and was alone on the patio, and this woman runs up red-faced, hyperventilating, distraught.

At first she's like, *Please help, please come.*

And I was like, *What's going on? Take a seat.*

She's like, *No, no, no, no, no, you need to help.* And I stand up. *You guys have to come down. A car hit a bunch of people. There are bodies everywhere. People are hurt.*

I stick my head in like, *Clergy, we need to go. Hey, Congregate, Clergy, where's Smash?* I said that something's happened—a bunch of people are hurt.

SMASH CAINE-CONLEY, COFOUNDER, CONGREGATE C'VILLE: So I was talking to this reporter. I had my clergy robe open. I'm trying to air out and it's like halfway on.

REV. SETH WISPELWEY: And because we were disciplined, I remember asking Smash for permission, *Is it OK with you if I, and some others, run down?*

SMASH CAINE-CONLEY: I told Seth, I was like, *Go, run, I'm right behind you.*

REV. SETH WISPELWEY: We just started sprinting down Water Street.

DON GATHERS, COFOUNDER, CHARLOTTESVILLE BLACK LIVES MATTER: Seth and I were running together, not imagining what it could have been because we had just left from that area. I just knew I had to get there.

SMASH CAINE-CONLEY: I told the reporter, *I'm really sorry, I have to go.*

I just remember running as much as I could, 'cause I was exhausted. My body honestly felt like it wasn't really working. I don't really have my clergy robe on, it's like flapping through the wind.

REV. SETH WISPELWEY: I remember I can hear the fire engine right on my heels the whole time, getting louder and louder, screaming, and I slowed down just as I came up on 4th Street.

DON GATHERS: And we get there. And when I tell you that it literally looked as though a bomb had been dropped in the middle of that intersection... there were bodies scattered literally everywhere. Blood, bruises, broken bones. It's.... there is just no describing the carnage that existed there.

REV. SETH WISPELWEY: There was blood everywhere. There was a young Black woman just writhing on the ground at the corner of the intersection. There's medics everywhere. There's glass, there's blood.

DON GATHERS: We got there before emergency services did. We got there before the police did.

REV. SETH WISPELWEY: There were people performing CPR on a woman. And right next to them, I just kind of yelled in their ears, *What do you need? How can we help?* And they said, *We need space. We need space. Please help clear the street.*

So we turned around, and at that point more of my Congregate colleagues were catching up, and so we helped clear the road.[1]

SMASH CAINE-CONLEY: We were trying to get people onto those sidewalks because ambulances were on their way and the streets were just filled with people. A really striking moment to me is me and a few other clergy folks are trying to get people onto the sidewalks, and these two guys were just standing there talking to each other, having a normal conversation.

I don't know what they were talking about, but they weren't moving. I screamed at them. I was like, *Get on the sidewalk!* We're trying to move them and people are on the ground dying and they're just having a normal conversation. They eventually got on the sidewalk and looked at me like, *Calm down.* And I—I still remember that. Like, *I can't believe that in that moment you told me to calm down.*

STAR PETERSON, LOCAL ACTIVIST AND STREET MEDIC: When I switch into emergency mode, I'm in "we're taking care of this" mode. Sometimes I get bossy. As I'm laying on the ground, I just started ordering around whoever was near me and I was like, OK. *There's a phone in the front pouch. Open the front pouch and go to such and such and tell them that we need an ambulance here.* Because I knew that we needed to alert the core medics so everybody could find out, and obviously we needed EMS. But I wasn't at all, I don't think, aware of—I don't know, the amount of damage or whatever, or that my leg had been crushed. All I knew was my leg didn't work when I tried to get out of the street.

At some point, medics jumped in, got my head in a safe place, had me on my back. And a friend from earlier that day was there just standing over me, looking really concerned. And I was like, *I need to see someone's face. I need you to stay there so I can see your face.*

TADRINT WASHINGTON, SURVIVOR: We were still in the car. I remember my sister just asking me, *Are you OK, we going to be fine?* And what she's seeing and what I'm seeing it's not the same thing because I'm on this side of the car. And basically when I pull myself back together, she was just like, *Tay, they trying to resuscitate some woman over here.*

MICAH WASHINGTON, SURVIVOR: I'm looking outside. It was almost surreal. I would've never expected to see someone coming down my sister's windshield, to look back in the rear and see EMTs fighting as hard as they can to revive someone. I mean, as hard as they can. I could see the intensity, the passion that they had behind trying to bring this woman back.

TADRINT WASHINGTON: I didn't see the woman on the other side, which we later learned was Heather—I didn't see her but Micah did. And she's like, *They're having trouble*, because I guess she can see them really trying to save her. And she's like, *How bad are you hurt? Can you go try to help them?* And me being the person that I am, I was willing...I wanted to go help this lady but my legs was so messed up because I guess I hit the dashboard or whatever, that I couldn't really move.

ROSIA PARKER, LOCAL ACTIVIST: I'm trying to help the lady in the silver car, which her legs went up under the steering wheel. So I went from being a victim to survivor now.

So her legs, I'm trying to get her out of this car and her legs are pinned up under the steering wheel. We're trying to help them get out the car and we can't get them out of the car. There is no police, no nothing out there. So everybody's hollering.

So by this time, I see my daughter out there. And so my daughter looks and she was like, *Oh my God, Heather!* 'Cause my daughter knew Heather. So we start hollering for medics. They tried to do CPR.

BILL BURKE, COUNTERPROTESTER: I was going in and out of consciousness. And one time when I woke up, they were doing CPR on Heather Heyer. I was right on top of her. My head was right on top of her chest. And they were doing CPR on her, and I was trying to count how many repetitions they were doing on her to try to stay awake. And I remember counting 29, and that was the last number and I was out again.

HEAPHY REPORT: Ms. Heyer succumbed to her injuries at the scene. Chief Baxter told us that she had already died when CFD

[Charlottesville Fire Department] arrived, but given the raw emotions of the crowd fire fighters continued to perform CPR on her.

ANDREW BAXTER, CHARLOTTESVILLE FIRE CHIEF: People that are in cardiac arrest when we arrive on the scene, who've died from blunt trauma, don't survive. Heather Heyer's already passed away. In a mass casually incident, the correct thing to do is to write this patient off. That's what triage is: We're going to try and save some other people's lives.

But the first-to officer makes a decision. He read the tenor of the crowd. He said, *We're working this*, meaning we're going to do CPR and whatnot.

I talked to him at length afterwards and I think it really was a conscious decision on his part. And the ability to make that decision and do that, where you've got these street medic folks and law enforcement folks trying to help from various agencies, and the chaos of that scene, that's like PhD level responder stuff right there. Just amazing.

SUSAN BRO, HEATHER HEYER'S MOTHER: I always wondered: *Was she afraid? Did she see him coming?* She was deaf in one ear, so . . .

KENDALL KING, THIRD-YEAR UVA STUDENT: My buddy and I knew, *OK, we have friends who are ahead of us.* We found Sophie, and Sophie's sister Rebecca was like, *I've got her. You get Natalie.* So we picked Natalie up, just 'cause it was like total fucking chaos. At this point I was extremely distraught. I was not well. And my buddy, thank God, had a much more level head and was basically just like, *Kendall, call an ambulance and tell them, tell them to meet us at the Market Street parking garage,* 'cause we had to get out of there. I mean, Heather Heyer was going through CPR right next to us and we were just like, *This is so horrible.* Like we can't have this person who's bleeding a lot and very delirious also be swarmed and stormed by all of these fucking reporters, who just have these big-ass cameras in our face. I was like, this is absolutely absurd. You're in the way of us trying to get out. And I got so angry at the reporters. 'Cause I was like, *This is my friend and she is really badly hurt and she looks horrible. Like she looks like she's gonna die. And if you take another picture of her, I'm gonna kill you.*

But basically as fast as we could—'cause there were so many reporters trying to take pictures of us and literally in our way—my buddy picked up Nat, I called the ambulance.

NATALIE ROMERO, SECOND-YEAR UVA STUDENT: They were like, *We need to take you to the ambulance.* But the ambulance wouldn't be able to make its way towards me. Because there was people on the ground and stuff. And I couldn't walk. So I had both arms on people's shoulders and they took me.

We were walking past people. I could see the ambulance. Once they grabbed me and sat me down, I lost consciousness then.[2]

DON GATHERS, COFOUNDER, CHARLOTTESVILLE BLACK LIVES MATTER: The adrenaline is still pumping through you. You're aware of your surroundings, but it's like you're outside of yourself, looking back at yourself. As weird as that might sound.

It was then that I saw that...I stood right there on the corner where the paramedics were working on Heather. Working as feverishly and as delicately as they can. Or as they could. And I know it sounds over-the-top, but I literally saw the life leave her body. There just wasn't anything that they could do...

I think it was at that point, it was at that moment that I think all the fight left my body. I just didn't have anything left.

WEDNESDAY BOWIE, COUNTERPROTESTER: I was basically in the middle of the street when I landed and I was unconscious, and some people dragged me back so that I was out of the street a little bit. And when they sat me up is when my memory from the day kicks back in.

Because I remember I said, *My legs won't move. Something's broken. My hip's broken.* And I remember seeing the face of one of my friends that I had driven with. One of my friends had also run at the car with me. And so, I was very concerned that they had also been hit by the car. I was screaming for them. And then my other friend was freaking out and she's calling my husband at the time. Thank God she had his number because my phone got smashed.

Oh, also my can of Mace that was in my backpack exploded. I also got Maced while I was getting hit by a car.

REV. SETH WISPELWEY, PASTOR AND COFOUNDER, CONGREGATE C'VILLE: All of a sudden I hear, *Father, this woman needs help*. And he's looking at me and I guess mistakes me for a Catholic priest. And he just pushes this young woman into my arms, who's kind of falling down sobbing and everything. She had just seen Heather Heyer die and everything. I just hold her for a bit.

ELIZABETH SINES, UVA LAW STUDENT: Not long after, a truck pulled up and no one knew if this was another vehicle—if that was part of an organized attack. All we could do was run. It was awful. People were lying in the streets. People were bleeding. People were having panic attacks.[3]

ROSIA PARKER, LOCAL ACTIVIST: It's like a movie, that this shit really—excuse my French but like—this shit really fucking happened. And you're standing there. You don't know if you're pissing, shitting or . . . like you're in complete . . .

KATRINA TURNER, LOCAL ACTIVIST: Shock.

ROSIA PARKER: Yeah, and you might not even call it shock. It was just so much.

ELIZABETH SINES: You saw people trying to shield people receiving medical treatment with their banners.[4]

TWEET FROM ALLISON WRABEL, REPORTER, *DAILY PROGRESS*, 1:46 P.M.: Injured people are limping down Water Street.[5]

ROSIA PARKER: We knew we weren't supposed to go up that street. And to go up that street anyway and everything that took place on that street? It's almost like for me—I feel responsible. I still hold myself accountable for the actions.

BRENNAN GILMORE, COUNTERPROTESTER AND FORMER US FOREIGN SERVICE OFFICER: At that point I thought there were probably a dozen people dead. It had just been bodies, bodies, bodies. And the speed at which—the violence of the incident—I thought there were probably a lot of dead people there.

There's no other explanation for what I just witnessed than an intentional attack on these people. During the summer, as I had dug more into this movement, I had started seeing these memes about Black Lives Splatter, and how to trick out your car to better run over protesters. And this was something that was on social media. Even people I knew, conservative class-mates from high school and folks that I did fishing tournaments with and stuff, were posting these jokes on Facebook based just about running over protestors.

So, I remember at some point right in the aftermath, thinking, *One of these guys has seen these memes and decided to be the one to do it.*

CHAPTER 17

"Where were the cops? How did this happen?"

EMERGENCY OPERATIONS CENTER
UNIVERSITY OF VIRGINIA
1:41 P.M.

MIKE SIGNER, CHARLOTTESVILLE MAYOR: There was a big conference room where they had these tables arranged, sort of like a U. And there were probably 20 people seated with laptops around them, and they had a big monitor, a screen where live feeds were being projected.

ALLEN GROVES, UVA DEAN OF STUDENTS: We were essentially using other people's Facebook and Twitter feeds of what was happening to watch this. We see Heather Heyer and everyone hit by the car.

MIKE SIGNER: I had been working in this separate room across the hall from there. I literally heard somebody scream. And then I came in and somebody said, *There's been a car attack.*

EMILY BLOUT, UVA PROFESSOR AND MAYOR MIKE SIGNER'S WIFE: A man on the phone in this operation center screaming out, *Mass casualty event. We have a mass casualty event.* And everyone just absolutely froze. Everyone there froze. And it was everything that we were worried about.

MIKE SIGNER: And then I sat down and I watched the video wherever it was being played. And it was so horrifying.

My very first instinct was that it had to have been an accident. Somebody like an elderly person, who had fallen asleep or had had a spasm, or…

I looked at the video a few more times. And then it was so clear that it was intentional.

BRIAN MORAN, SECRETARY, VIRGINIA PUBLIC SAFETY AND HOMELAND SECU-
RITY: Then I called the governor.

TERRY MCAULIFFE, VIRGINIA GOVERNOR: He said, *Are you sitting down?* And I said, *Yeah I'm sitting down and watching the TV.*

BRIAN MORAN: I said that the unspeakable has happened—that guy's driven into a crowd. There's gonna be…we don't know the extent of it, but you can…the speed that he drove. I mean, it…it's gonna be bad.

TERRY MCAULIFFE: We did know that a lot of people had been hurt.

ANDREW BAXTER, CHARLOTTESVILLE FIRE CHIEF: One of the things we re-
alized very, very quickly: We need to gain control of the emotional state of this room. Someone had slapped some of the video up onto the big screen in the front of the room. And I went to the IT guy and I said, *Turn that off. Because now we're just watching people's trauma, and we need to be in a position to make decisions, and that's not informing our decision making. It's just trauma for us. So we need to…* And we turned the lights down.

Then I got the group together and said, *OK, this is a horrible event. We plan for this. Folks are executing the plan. Let's contact the people that you're responsible for, make sure they have everything they need. If there's critical information you think we need to know at an executive level, please make sure it gets up.* And then the room kind of calmed down.

NBC29 STATION
DOWNTOWN CHARLOTTESVILLE
I:41 P.M.

DAVID FOKY, NEWS DIRECTOR, NBC29: We heard over the scanners that there had been protesters hit by a car, and it was literally a couple of blocks from the station.

HENRY GRAFF, ANCHOR AND REPORTER, NBC29: We hear on the scanner, *Mass casualty incident*. Myself and a photographer went running out the door.

DAVID FOKY: I didn't run—I have bad knees—but I moved as quickly as I could. I was down there fairly quickly 'cause I remember watching CPR being performed on one of the people that had been hit.

HENRY GRAFF: I watched them do CPR on Heather Heyer, who died. I remember calling work and talked to a boss who was like, *You've never sounded so shook before in my life*.

We were so close. We got down there before a lot of police and medics were able to. It was just—I mean it was a lot of bodies everywhere.

I remember interviewing people and I was asking them, *Are you sure this wasn't some scared senior citizen or someone who just got spooked or someone who just didn't know what was going on?*

And people were like, *No, this was very deliberate. The person, they like backed up, they rammed*, and it was like, *God, how could this happen here?*

TIM DODSON, MANAGING EDITOR, *CAVALIER DAILY*: Suddenly, now that a car attack had happened, police seemed interested in trying to control the situation.

ZACK WAJSGRAS, FREELANCE PHOTOGRAPHER: The first thing that arrived, of course, was a giant armor-clad vehicle with a dude with the big gun hanging out the top of it. So, not the most reassuring thing at first.

SMASH CAINE-CONLEY, COFOUNDER, CONGREGATE C'VILLE: All of a sudden, police roll in with a tank and try to get everyone out of the way. It's just heart wrenching and enraging.

EMILY GORCENSKI, LOCAL ACTIVIST: I was trying to get people off the street, trying to clear the way so that the ambulance could come. And so then what did the police do? They bring a fucking Bearcat.

HEAPHY REPORT: The CPD SWAT team drove the armored Bearcat vehicle down 4th Street to secure the roadway north of the injured counterprotesters.

WEDNESDAY BOWIE, COUNTERPROTESTER: It was just a couple of feet away from me. And I remember there was a guy out the top of that vehicle and he was pointing a freaking gun into the crowd. And I remember just like . . . I was just absolutely flipping my total shit at him. I was screaming. And any cop that came near me, I was just like, *You motherfuckers!* Blocking the closest access for an ambulance to get to me.

EMILY GORCENSKI: I wanted a fucking ambulance. I wanted them to bring everything you've got. Because, I knew that they [the police] had ambulances up there. I knew that they had these little John Deere gators, these four- or six-wheel carts with medical aid. I knew that police should have first responder training. Fucking get people here that could help save lives!

SMASH CAINE-CONLEY: The presence of a tank and the presence of aggressive police officers is not what you need when you've just experienced a horrific crisis. It was really jarring for folks and I think really traumatic for folks, and just added to the layers of trauma that folks were already experiencing.

I guess it was a crime scene, so they're trying to clear it out and preserve it perhaps.

SABR LYON, COUNTERPROTESTER: Guns pointed at us, tanks right behind them. They have a big-ass torpedo-looking motherfucker, pointing at my mother and my fiancée and this head-wound victim.

And my friend who was with us, he's a Black man and he's got a gun pointed at him and he's just emphatically trying to talk to this guy, like, *Why are you pointing this gun at us? Why are you pointing it at us?* and just the obvious reasonable emotional response to this.

So I stand in between the gun, looking this officer in the face and I'm like, *This man behind me is my brother. He is a human being. He is my dear, dear friend. He is just going to talk to you.* I said, *He is not going to put his hands on you. He is just going to talk to you. We are upset. That is a reasonable thing to be in this situation, don't you think?*

And the guy looked a little surprised that I asked his opinion. And I was like, *Don't you think that being upset right now is reasonable?* I repeated myself. This part of the day is the most ingrained in my head.

He kind of looked around and was like, *Yeah.*

I was like, *I understand that you have to come in, so that the ambulance can come in, because you don't know if there are enemy forces here.* I'm talking to him like we're in a battle, because we are, right? I'm like, *I'm aware you have to secure the hospital people, like the true EMS people. I get that, but can you put your gun back up and let this man talk at you?*

And he was like, *OK.*

And I was like, *Fine.*

And I stepped back and I looked at my friend and I was like, *Keep talking at him, he's open now. I connected to this man. I think you can too.*

And that gave me this idea in this moment. It's just chaos. People are screaming, there's crying, and again, in this moment my brain goes into this hyper focus of: What am I able to do now?

Well, the people that are injured are taken care of. So I just start going down the line of these [police officers]. They're taught to stand apart or whatever, and you just go from one to the next to the next and I just connect with them.

I understand that this whole "humanize me" thing doesn't change anything, but it plants a seed. There's this little seed: *I'm human like you.* So one guy I actually got to tear up, which was one of the things I'm proudest of in my life.

MELISSA WENDER, STREET MEDIC: We hear people shouting, *Medic!* There's chaos, there's screaming. And we do not know what's happened. We heard something about a car crash. We come upon this young woman, maybe 20 years old, who something's happened to her leg, she's crying, she's got a friend with her, and we decide to help her. When we start to take out our scissors to cut off her leggings, she's like, *Oh no, don't cut off my leggings.* You know, like she likes those leggings. So we started to try to pull her leggings up and it obviously hurt her a real lot. And she's like, *Cut them.*

Her friend is with her this whole time. And at some point we turn our attention to the friend who's in a sort of panicky way. And she's so worried about her friend and her friend's leg. We're like, *Are you OK? She's like, yeah, I hit my head, but I'm fine.* And then we look at her and she has blood coming from her nose.

Which like, OK, you possibly have a head injury. We talk with her about the unlikely situation that she could have had an internal bleed or something like that. And she decides to go be checked out by the hospital, which I think makes sense.

Then we find out that Star, who I had just run with the night before—her leg was seriously, seriously crushed.

WEDNESDAY BOWIE: I waited quite a while for an ambulance because they were getting other people that were closer to the scene first. I don't know if they even knew I was there for a while. But I was actually ... My femoral artery had been damaged when my pelvis broke, so I was actually bleeding out internally.

I remember, they put me on a stretcher finally, and they rolled me down the street and somebody got a picture of that. And it ended up everywhere, on CNN and stuff. And that's actually how my parents found out I was in Charlottesville. My mom's best friend since kindergarten, her daughter's husband saw that on the news and said, *Amy, call Marjorie.*

TADRINT WASHINGTON, SURVIVOR: And at that point, I think so much time went by I couldn't even tell you exactly the time. But I just know we sitting there a while and I started to get really, really hot. And I'm starting to realize what's going on and I see all these people around me trying to save people. And I still didn't know how we got in the situation, but I just know it's a lot of people everywhere, screaming. It's a lot of people hurt. And I just remember a couple EMTs coming to me and this one Samaritan—I don't know her name, she wasn't from Virginia, but she was an EMT. And she stayed there with me for a while before a Virginia EMT came.

And when they came, they checked me over. I told them I wasn't bleeding or anything. I told them I guess my legs is really screwed. And they helped me out the car into the ambulance.

WEDNESDAY BOWIE: I remember getting put in the ambulance, and they were putting multiple people in at a time. And I remember there was one person in the ambulance who was a man, and I was really worried about him because he kept saying his name.

STAR PETERSON, LOCAL ACTIVIST AND STREET MEDIC: I remember the ambulances being double stacked, which is fucking creepy. Again, I couldn't see much. They put the real neck brace on me. And honestly, the medics saved my ability to walk by having me supported and immobilized there because I found out later I had two broken parts of my back. And about

25 percent of paralysis actually happens after an incident when the broken parts of your spine cut your spinal cord. So very grateful that they had me immobilized until the ambulance got there.

And then they popped me in the ambulance. I can't look anywhere but up, but I remember, I think I asked for something for pain. I remember just spelling out my legal name very—I don't know—robotically maybe, or just clearly.

BILL BURKE, COUNTERPROTESTER: I remember being in the ambulance and there was a young Black kid, a brand new EMT. And the paramedic was telling him what to do and he was hesitant. And he said, *I'm afraid I'm going to hurt him.* And I said, *Bro, everything hurts. Ain't nothing going to hurt me more.* I said, *Just do what you got to do, man. I'm OK.*

HEAPHY REPORT: EMS personnel classified the injuries according to severity and prioritized transport to hospitals accordingly. Seventeen required hospitalization, and all 17 were transported to hospitals...

DAVID FOKY, NEWS DIRECTOR, NBC29: I was seeing a lot of people who had been hurt. I was seeing a lot of angry people. *I'm* angry that this had happened. I was seeing emergency crews responding. And then people wanting to tell us the stories of what they had seen. And, *Where were the cops? Where were the cops? How did this happen?* Just anger and frustration and fear and confusion. All of the things that you can imagine in a situation like that, just on such clear display.

That's when I ran into Don Gathers.

DON GATHERS, COFOUNDER, CHARLOTTESVILLE BLACK LIVES MATTER: I began to walk up Water Street. Just done. Spent. Head bowed, shoulders slumped, tears just streaming out of me. And I remember, very distinctly—and I will never forget this, this stands out in that day as much as anything—someone grabbing me and just holding me and squeezing me. And whispering in my ear, *Don, you can't give up. You can't stop.* And that somebody was my friend David Foky, the news director over at 29.

He just held me and squeezed me and just told me, *You can't give up. You can't.*

DAVID FOKY: I'd known Don for a couple of years and he was so clearly upset that, without asking, I just embraced him. I couldn't think of anything to do that was a better decision in the moment, than to give him a hug and let him know that he wasn't alone in this.

Don is such an important person in this community. That he was talking about he didn't think that he could go on doing this anymore, that would be a tragedy—if he stopped fighting for what he believed in because of this. And we talked about that, just the two of us. There were so many people around, but in that moment, it was just the two of us.

DON GATHERS: And after that, I kind of got myself together. We got reports and calls that some of the Nazis were on the mall and were threatening some of the businesses. So you had to just put your big boy underwear on again and go back to work.

UVA MEDICAL CENTER
1:41 P.M.

JODY REYES, INCIDENT COMMANDER, UVA MEDICAL CENTER, IN THE HOSPITAL COMMAND CENTER: We were all watching these Periscope things. We watched it in real time. We were only a mile away.

JANE MUIR, EMERGENCY ROOM NURSE, UVA MEDICAL CENTER, IN THE ER: I just remember the charge nurse getting the call, like, *OK, now we're having a mass casualty incident. A car ran through the crowd.* She was so calm and then the rest of us being like, *This is gonna be something . . .*

JODY REYES: If you're panicked, people are going to lose faith. They're gonna lose confidence. So, you gotta watch some idiot drive a car into a crowd of people. I don't have time to sit there and think about how horrible that is. You have to say, *OK. And now what, how are we going to react?* We had no idea how many people were hurt. It could have been 15 people dead as fast as he was going.

JANE MUIR: You don't even know how many people are coming. That's the scariest part. And I was newer. So that was very frightening.

Then people started mobilizing and coming up with, *This room is gonna be for this person, that we name this.* All the people who are traumas have a name designation that's a country. So like Bosnia, or whatever. So, they started writing: like, here's the room and here are gonna be these people coming up with a plan.

TOM BERRY, DIRECTOR OF EMERGENCY MANAGEMENT, UVA MEDICAL CEN-TER: We went into our mass casualty protocol. The ER—because it's a teaching hospital, it's just not practicing MDs and RNs. There were also a lot of students all the time. And so that's what really made it so crowded within the ER. But all I remember is the images of trauma teams that were preparing to receive patients into the trauma rooms, within the ER operating rooms. I think just the energy is what I remember most.

JANE MUIR: We all had prepared for which rooms we were gonna be in. They were prepared for so many patients, that there were like four of us in a room [including only two nurses].

Muir was used to more medical professionals responding to a trauma case, especially more nurses.

JANE MUIR: And I remember that being kind of scary, like, *Am I gonna be able to do everything with my other nurse?*

And then you don't know what the injuries are gonna be. So you have to basically pull out all the resources that you have. We have a trauma cart—if you've cracked the cart, that [means] it's potentially gonna be something severe, because the trauma cart is to place arterial lines, give rapid blood, put central lines in, basically get some surgical things started.

I remember in the room, the surgeon at the head of the bed saying, *This is like every other patient we've had, this is no different from any other situation we've had, we're gonna do what we always do. They're gonna come in, we're gonna assess their airway. We're gonna be methodical. We're gonna do good communication. It's no different from how we usually work together.* And I remember that being very grounding and important because it was scary.

HEAPHY REPORT: Those taken to UVa were admitted through the main lobby, where the treatment teams were standing by according to plan. The speed of the response is particularly impressive given the large number of people crowded at the scene of the homicide.

JODY REYES: So again, you gotta think about logistics. You gotta think about how things happen. If you need to have 10 ambulances coming in all at the same time, you're not gonna do that through the emergency department opening, right? The doors are not made for that. So we rerouted all the ambulances to come through the front door.

STAR PETERSON, LOCAL ACTIVIST AND STREET MEDIC: The next memory I have is being in the ER.

MARCUS MARTIN, COUNTERPROTESTER: When we got to the hospital, they wouldn't let Marissa come back there with me. I kind of got a attitude about that, *Like, what? Nah, she's coming with me with like, what the fuck y'all talk about.* And then they wouldn't allow her to come. So they put her in a room.

Then Marissa overheard some cops talking and was like, *One girl died.* And then that's when they told Marissa it was Heather. And then, and then Marissa texted me: Heather died.

STAR PETERSON: Some police officer asked for permission to speak with me and I remember the nurse or whoever just being like, *Two minutes*, and they asked me what the car looked like.

I was like, *I don't know. I just remember seeing a truck when I was down on the ground.*

Marcus Martin says another police officer came into his room and asked to take his clothes as evidence.

MARCUS MARTIN: She was being a dickhead. She literally told me to take off my clothes and I'm looking at her like, *Are you serious right now?* Like, *Will you look at my fucking leg like a bent-up paper clip? And you really want me to take my clothes off right now?* I was like, *Ma'am, can you please just get out? Just leave me alone.*

Marcus Martin says the police officer told him she'd just go get a warrant if he refused to hand over his clothes.

MARCUS MARTIN: And then when she said that, I kind of let her have it. Like, *Look lady, you need to get the fuck outta my face. I just literally got hit by a fucking car.*

STAR PETERSON: I remember asking, *Am I going to be able to walk again? Am I going to be paralyzed?* And I had no idea who was dead or alive at that point. So I remember just thinking, *What can I deal with? I can deal with being in a wheelchair for the rest of my life. I can't deal with my friend being dead.* And that was just what was going through my head.

I remember being very eager for them to get me into surgery because I was in so much pain and I knew that at least I could be unconscious during the surgery, and I wouldn't have to be frightened and in pain for a little while.

WEDNESDAY BOWIE, COUNTERPROTESTER: I remember getting to the hospital, and I remember them putting me in a CT scan. And I remember being examined by trauma doctors. And then, I think that was at that point when the blood loss started to get to me because after the doctors first examined me, I didn't remember anything anymore.

NATALIE ROMERO, SECOND-YEAR UVA STUDENT: I regained consciousness in the hospital. At first I couldn't even remember who I was for a second. I'd say, *What happened to me? What happened?* No one really wanted to tell me. When I woke up, I came in and out multiple times, but some of the upperclassmen folks from my scholarship were there.

I asked them and the nurse that was there, like, *What happened to me?* And they said, *Nat, you were hit by a car.* And then I asked them, *Am I going to be able to walk? Do you know if I have a spinal injury? Is that what this is? Am I paralyzed?*

No one answered me. No one answered. Everyone just stared at me. No one could say yes, no, not the nurse, anyone. So I just sat there crying and fell back asleep.[1]

BILL BURKE, COUNTERPROTESTER: They take me to do the x-rays and CT scans and all that kind of stuff. And by then I was really wigging out because I couldn't get hold of my wife. And one of the x-ray techs let me use her cell phone to call my wife. And I told her what happened. She said, *Yeah,*

I seen it on the news. And the next thing I said, *I think the girl died*. And then that's when she said, *Yes, she did*. My wife told me that I was right on top of her, and that they reported that she was dead.

NATALIE ROMERO: It was maybe the fourth time that I woke up that they said that it was going to be difficult, but they think I was going to be able to walk. And then I found out I had MRIs and all this stuff done to me while I was unconscious.

There was a skull fracture and they, while I was unconscious, stitched it up. I had a tooth fractured. That's a dead tooth in me now. It pushed back, and the impact of the tooth and everything cut open my lip. So I had multiple stitches also done while unconscious. It was ginormous. I couldn't drink water. I could barely eat. There was some leg injury, et cetera. So I had a severe concussion, skull fracture, lip laceration, the shattered root of a tooth, amongst other things.[2]

LISA DRAINE, LOCAL ACTIVIST: I got home and I swear not 20 minutes later, I get a call from my friend who says to me, *You gotta get back down here. Sophie's been hit by a car*. And I was like, what? And in my mind, I'm thinking it's been an accident. I knew there were lots of people in the streets. Most of the streets were shut down, but I was like, somebody sideswiped her, or, you know—I just didn't think at that point that anything bad had happened. So my husband Joel and I jump in the car.

And all this time, I'm trying to call Rebecca 'cause I knew they were together. I knew they were buddies. So I'm calling Rebecca, who's not answering. So I still have no idea what's happening. The ambulances can't get through.

Rebecca finally answered.

LISA DRAINE: And all she could tell us was that Sophie's head was bleeding. Three minutes later she calls and says, *We're now in an ambulance, but they've diverted us to Martha Jefferson*. So we drive all across town and pull up at the emergency room of Martha Jefferson, we jump out of the car and there's Rebecca standing outside the emergency room doors. And she just breaks down when she sees us—she obviously had been holding it together, and she still couldn't really tell us, I mean, imagine, at this point we don't really know what has happened, but she couldn't tell us what has happened. She was just crying. And she was saying, *They wouldn't let me go in with Sophie. They're barring the door.*

So there's a security guard at the door to the emergency room. And he says, *We're not letting anyone except for the patients in. We're in a lockdown situation.* And we were like, *Lockdown?* And he said, *It's a mass casualty situation.* And we're like, *what?!* Again, I'm still thinking she was just, you know, hit by chance. And at the same time there are ambulances arriving. So it's clear that she's not the only one that's injured at this point. And maybe about 20 minutes later, a guy comes back and says, *OK, one of you can go in to be with your daughter.* My husband is a physician. So of course we send Joel in.

Hours later, Sophie was discharged and was able to see her mother for the first time since the car attack.

LISA DRAINE: So she comes out, [they] wheel her out, and her leg was broken, but they couldn't tell how badly 'cause it was really swollen. So we get her home, and that sort of just begins the whole unfolding of figuring out what happened.

Another mother in the Charlottesville area got a similar phone call that afternoon: Susan Bro, the mother of Heather Heyer.

WASHINGTON POST: Bro's trailer home in Ruckersville, Va., is tucked away amid farmland...she spent her spare time knitting, crocheting and designing patterns. She called herself a homebody and enjoyed batch cooking and making cheeses.[3]

On August 12, around the time of the crash, Bro was at her friend Cathy Brinkley's house.

SUSAN BRO, HEATHER HEYER'S MOTHER: I was at my best friend's house and I get a phone call.[4]

My son calls and says that he has called Heather's phone, somebody picked it up and said they don't know what happened to his sister. He saw her—he saw the car attack on TV.[5]

I'm a little frantic because I don't even know anything about a car that's hit somebody.[6]

I was 45 minutes away. My friend is driving [us] in. And I kept calling the hospitals, as my friend was driving.[7]

There's only two hospitals in Charlottesville. We're searching frantically for what hospital she's at. Both hospitals I'm calling are saying, *We don't have a patient by that name. We don't have a patient by that name.* Her ID was apparently not on her; her phone was nowhere to be found. Nobody for sure knew who she was as far as I can tell.[8]

So I finally get a hold of her friend Marissa, who I had only met one time. I found out from her, who found out from one of the girls she was with, who actually located her in the hospital by showing her picture around and saying, *OK, we can't find this person. Can you find them?* And then they, of course they wouldn't tell her anything. They just said, we need the next of kin.

Marissa says come to the far side of UVa from the emergency room. That the emergency room is barricaded. And that's all she will tell me.

So I get there, they search my backpack, I tell Cathy to wait outside for my husband 'cause he was actually out of town that day. And they search my backpack and they don't say anything to me and I don't even know if that was law enforcement or who that was exactly. And they tell me, *Stand over here.*

They hand me a number 20 on a piece of paper that I still have on my refrigerator, and nobody says anything to me, looks at me, talks to me.

And suddenly two strangers that I don't know, two women, grab me on either side and walk me up this ramp. This is the same ramp that I would walk down on my dinner break when I was pregnant with Heather, cause I used to be a switchboard operator in that same building.

And I walk into the room and a gentleman identified himself and he just said, *I'm sorry. Your daughter . . .* I don't remember the words he used now . . . *was pronounced at such and such time* and the full meaning of that hit me and I sat down and this awful wail came out of me.[9] It was something between a scream and a wail.[10]

CHAPTER 18

"Senseless deaths for a rally that should have never happened."

ABOUT 2 P.M.

HEAPHY REPORT: After the car attack, many counterprotesters were on edge. Anger burned.

SMASH CAINE-CONLEY, COFOUNDER, CONGREGATE C'VILLE: I don't think we had any indication that the attack that just happened wouldn't somehow happen again. We didn't know if that was part of a calculated, broader attack. We had no idea who it was or what group they were a part of or anything like that. I don't think it felt like it was over.

That's why we were still marching around downtown for a little while.

CONSTANCE PAIGE YOUNG, COUNTERPROTESTER: We didn't know—bombs could be somewhere. We didn't know what the hell anything was.

CHRIS SUAREZ, REPORTER, CHARLOTTESVILLE *DAILY PROGRESS*: And then it just got even crazier.

TERRY MCAULIFFE, VIRGINIA GOVERNOR: At that point I determined, I gotta get down there. So my helicopter, the one we use for the governor called Trooper One, that helicopter is in Charlottesville, but it's doing surveillance actually. They're the ones that followed James Fields's car. And so the state police get Fairfax One, the helicopter they use here if there's a car accident they land on the highway, to fly me down.

MIKE SIGNER, CHARLOTTESVILLE MAYOR: We got news that the governor was coming to Charlottesville. That was a surprise. And when the governor comes, that's going to be a big deal.

We have a meeting scheduled at probably five o'clock to talk about the press conference that is going to happen with the governor. Like, *What do we say? How are we going to do this? Who's talking when? What the hell are we saying?*

Chief Al Thomas looked down at his phone and he said, *Oh. A helicopter has just gone down.*

DAVID FOKY, NEWS DIRECTOR, NBC29: One of the first things that pops into your head is, *Well if Governor McAuliffe is flying here in a helicopter and a helicopter just crashed, did the governor of Virginia just go down in a helicopter?*

BRIAN MORAN, SECRETARY, VIRGINIA PUBLIC SAFETY AND HOMELAND SECURITY: *Chopper down. Chopper down.*

There were moments there when we didn't know whose helicopter it was. I'm standing next to the superintendent, I'm in the command room and we're just looking at each other.

KASEY HOTT, ANCHOR, NBC29: They thought for sure at the time that it was the governor's helicopter that had gone down. We knew that he was in the air. We just thought that was his. The implications of that . . . it was crazy.

People on the governor's staff started calling and calling the governor. His phone went straight to voicemail.

TERRY MCAULIFFE: I'd been burning my phone up and stupidly, I probably should have had a charger. So I get on the helicopter and my phone dies. It is dead literally two minutes after I get on.

No one was able to reach me for 20 minutes, since my phone was dead, and they were in a panic.[1]

They were actually looking to find out where the lieutenant governor was because they thought I'd gone down on the helicopter.

CHRIS SUAREZ: People were speculating or tweeting, *What? Someone shot down a helicopter?* I'm thinking to myself like, *No, come on, like this* can't *be real. This cannot be real. Like this isn't* Grand Theft Auto, *you know, this isn't someone shooting like a rocket launcher at a helicopter that went down.* This is just so nuts. Like this is unreal.

HENRY GRAFF, ANCHOR AND REPORTER, NBC29: You're just like, *Jesus Christ, what else could happen?*

TIM DODSON, MANAGING EDITOR, *CAVALIER DAILY*: There were rumors that were spreading that maybe these far-right militia members had blown up a police helicopter. Some of these guys were well armed. I think a lot of people were thinking that at the time, which maybe that seems absurd but these people had better weapons than some of the police did.

DON GATHERS, COFOUNDER, CHARLOTTESVILLE BLACK LIVES MATTER: I don't know much about aviation, but it was always my understanding that helicopters are basically... They don't just drop out of the sky. It was a clear sky.

MIKE SIGNER: It sort of strained credulity to think that it could have been brought down, but on the other hand, not crazy. I mean, what if you did have some kind of attack on a helicopter, right? I don't know how that could have been done and why you would have a helicopter attacked in the city of Charlottesville or Albemarle County, but it's not crazy. And, I mean, I had some fear in my mind that it could have been intentional or sabotage or something.

ANDREW BAXTER, CHARLOTTESVILLE FIRE CHIEF: So we were sending units. They tried to make a rescue, but it was too late.

KASEY HOTT: We found out later that it was the VSP helicopter that had gone down and not the governor's.

DAVID FOKY: It wasn't his helicopter that crashed. It was the state police helicopter that had been circling Charlottesville that day with two state police officers on board.

Both Virginia State Police officers were killed: Lieutenant H. Jay Cullen and Trooper Berke M. M. Bates.

MIKE SIGNER: There weren't any indications that it was intentional that I was hearing. Nobody had cited anybody, and nobody had claimed any credit. And so it seemed like it was more just tragic.

DAILY PROGRESS: Authorities have said there is no indication that foul play was a factor in the crash.[2]

ANDREW BAXTER AT THE EMERGENCY OPERATIONS CENTER (EOC): There was a sergeant from VSP in the EOC with us. He's an old salty, VSP guy. He's a smoker too, which is odd. You don't see that in VSP anymore really, and it's probably grandfathered in somehow. I doubt they still let you do that. So he would leave the EOC once every 90 minutes or so to go outside and suck down a cigarette in about 13 seconds and come back in. But I saw him walk outside at some point after we learned what had happened, and I went outside to talk to him. And he was dear, dear close friends with Jay Cullen, the lieutenant who was killed.

And I said, *Man, you take the time you need. If you need to . . .* And he's like, *No, I'm OK.* And five minutes later, he came back in and did his job.

BRIAN MORAN: What was already just a devastating mood through the course of the day just got even worse, if that's fathomable.

ALLEN GROVES, UVA DEAN OF STUDENTS, AT THE EOC: Looking at the faces of some of the state police people when their helicopter goes down and they know these guys . . . there was just so much that day that was so powerful and so overwhelming.

BRIAN MORAN: At that point, the governor came.

TERRY MCAULIFFE: There are moments you never forget and that was one of them. I let out a high sigh and slumped down and stared at the table. I was frozen for a moment, having a hard time believing it really could be true. Jay was my regular pilot and led our State Police Aviation Unit, and Berke, a newly minted pilot, had been on my Executive Protection Unit (EPU), which made him like a member of my family. Berke was definitely a character. He was always larger than life. My thoughts were racing. I thought of both Jay and Berke, all the times we'd joked around together, all the talks we'd had, all the kindness they'd shown my family.[3]

BRIAN MORAN: [The governor] had to call [his wife] to tell her who was in the copter, because Berke was an Executive Protection Unit agent, and the family had become very fond of him, very close. So I remember him calling Dorothy about who died, Berke Bates. That was horrible.

TWEET FROM EMILY GORCENSKI, LOCAL ACTIVIST: These were senseless deaths for a rally that should have never happened.[4]

TERRY MCAULIFFE: After Jay and Berke went down, it was just tremendous anger and tremendous sadness.

DON GATHERS, COFOUNDER, CHARLOTTESVILLE BLACK LIVES MATTER: At that point, I think that the day in and of itself was winding down or had already wound down. And folks began to disperse and head home as quickly and as safely as they could.

CHRIS SUAREZ, REPORTER, CHARLOTTESVILLE *DAILY PROGRESS*: It started to rain.

EMILY BLOUT, UVA PROFESSOR AND MAYOR MIKE SIGNER'S WIFE: I remember the pouring rain after the stifling oppressive day, just a deluge.

ELIZABETH SHILLUE, QUAKER ACTIVIST: I remember thinking, *Thank God for the rain*. And hopefully that was going to end everything. Anything else that might happen was going to be over.

MIKE SIGNER, CHARLOTTESVILLE MAYOR: There was a lot of nervousness about what was going to happen at night. Had they left? Had they really disbanded? And so there was this real nervy, eerie, horror movie feeling as the dark started to settle.

REV. SETH WISPELWEY, PASTOR AND COFOUNDER, CONGREGATE C'VILLE: It's getting later, the shadows longer. At some point, we ate a little bit, we regroup, things are getting quieter. We are going to kind of do our own sweep. There's reports of white supremacists on motorcycles. I remember still sweeping around downtown.

DON GATHERS, AT HOME: My phone did not leave my hand that entire day because I knew at any moment we may have to get out and assemble again, not knowing where they were or what they may be doing at that point. But that we might have to rally en masse and get the troops up and ready to go again.

I'm not certain that I slept that night. Because at this point, I'm looking and listening for any bump in the night outside the house. And just prepared to take whatever action is necessary.

WALT HEINECKE, UVA PROFESSOR AND ACTIVIST: As it became evening time, I was left with just a couple of volunteers. And I figured the parks were kind of trashed, so I cleaned up the parks. I went to each park with trash bags and cleaned them up, and turned off the water that we were using, and just kind of got the parks back in shape.

ANDREW BAXTER, CHARLOTTESVILLE FIRE CHIEF: I slept at the firehouse that night. We were unsure of the degree to which we need to, or should, demobilize.

TWEET FROM EMILY GORCENSKI, LOCAL ACTIVIST, 7:52 P.M.: I don't look forward to my nightmares for the next few weeks.[5]

SUSAN BRO, HEATHER HEYER'S MOTHER, BACK AT HOME: It was a long and hellish evening. I couldn't sleep. Every time I closed my eyes, I was back in the ER with them telling me. And then my brain kind of clicks into practical mode. So I did laundry all night.

L.Q., COUNTERPROTESTER: The first night in the hospital I woke up with my heart racing, terrified that the white supremacists would come to kill me. They are terrorists. I was terrified. After some discussion of what to do, the hospital ended up hiring a security guard for me. I am not sure how protected I was, but I felt better.[6]

KENDALL KING, THIRD-YEAR UVA STUDENT: I remember I was like, *I just wanna go see Nat, I just wanna go see Nat, I just wanna go see Nat.* And a lot of our comrades were like, *Hey, just so you know, there's likely also these people [white nationalists] in the hospital. Decide how you're gonna act, if you see them.*

Marcus Martin refused to even stay the night in the hospital.

MARCUS MARTIN, COUNTERPROTESTER: Didn't trust anybody. Just wanted to be in the comfort of my home.[7] They took me out the back.

STAR PETERSON, LOCAL ACTIVIST AND STREET MEDIC: I remember being super afraid, and asking them not to put my name on the outside, in the hallway on the outside of my room, just because I was so afraid of Nazis. I remember a friend coming to visit me in the hospital and being like, *Oh yeah, just standing next to somebody with Nazi tattoos in the elevator*, because they weren't just treating us.

SUSAN BRO, HEATHER HEYER'S MOTHER: Those of us who miss her, miss her forever.

Her best friend said, *You know, it's kinda weird. I'll get to be an old man and she'll always have been 32.*[8]

LISA DRAINE, LOCAL ACTIVIST: The next week we were able to get in to see an orthopedist at UVa. They still weren't sure how bad was the break? So they then x-rayed Sophie and said, *There's no question. She's gonna need major reconstructive surgery.* Her tibial plateau was broken—the bone around your knee—all of the ligaments around the knee were torn or ruptured. So the next week, she was in the hospital having surgery on the day that she was supposed to start classes for her fourth year. Instead of being in class, she was in the hospital.

Sophie and Rebecca said then, and they'll say now, *We don't regret it*, and I don't regret it. You would think that we would, you know, and then I know there are people that are like, *Why did you let your daughters...?* And of course, it's not like I could really stop them. They were 21 and 23, but I was very convinced that this is something I needed to do, and I would've been fine if they had opted out, but they really wanted to be there and we don't regret it.

I came to find out that Sophie was right next to Heather and Marcus. And so it's very unsettling. I now know Susan Bro, and she is an incredible woman, but it's very hard for me to be around her because I know that I came like this close to *being* her: losing my daughter. And she could not be more gracious—she always asks how Sophie's doing.

For a long time, I beat myself up about going home and not being there. Like, if I had been there, maybe I would've seen the car, maybe I would've been able to push her out of the way, you never know these things. Yeah. But you know, in the end, my daughter's alive and hers isn't and for no reason, but maybe a few inches.

KRISTIN SZAKOS, CHARLOTTESVILLE CITY COUNCILOR: For the next week, you'd see some kind of paunchy, white guy in a baseball cap. And I love some paunchy, white guys in baseball caps, but you see people who look like they might have been at the rally and you think, *Are they planning something else? Are they going to do something? Are they armed?* I found myself really jumpy for a long time after, wondering if they were going to come back.

SABR LYON, COUNTERPROTESTER: For the next couple weeks anytime I left the house, I would drive the neighborhoods, because around where we lived at the time were a lot of predominantly Black neighborhoods. So there was absolutely more than once that there was just a truck full of white dudes driving around trying to harass people.

So yeah, the vibes in the town afterwards, it's high alert. You're on high alert for forever.

HEAPHY REPORT: The City of Charlottesville protected neither free expression nor public safety on August 12.

BRIAN MORAN, SECRETARY, VIRGINIA PUBLIC SAFETY AND HOMELAND SECURITY: I don't think we should blame the law enfor—you know, there was a breakdown in some communications. There was a breakdown in communication. I think our law enforcement is oftentimes held to a standard that we don't hold our leadership to.

Charlottesville did not prepare adequately.

EMILY BLOUT, UVA PROFESSOR AND MAYOR MIKE SIGNER'S WIFE: There was just like one week of unity where people joined together and helped each other and solidarity. After that, it all fell apart. It was like the whole city just fell into itself and it started eating itself alive. It was just so dramatic and so painful because everyone wanted answers. How could such a horrible thing happen? How could the police not intervene and watch people be beat up?

CONSTANCE PAIGE YOUNG, COUNTERPROTESTER: Why didn't y'all stop it? Why didn't you stop it? I mean, because honestly you can't tell me that had there been hundreds of Black people with long guns walking down the street that they would've been able to come back multiple times and rendezvous, terrorize people, fight, scream racial slurs. So I don't want to hear this free speech argument. No, I'm not trying to hear that.

EMILY BLOUT: [Mike] did everything humanly possible and more to try to stop this. Every single step of the way, every single resource he had, every single pathway he could find, or hope to find to stop this or to contain it, was thwarted and undermined by the city government itself. And specifically, the city's lawyers but also Maurice Jones, again, who was *way* over his head and was undermining any attempt that Mike was making to stop this thing.

MIKE SIGNER: In my last [city council] meeting I said...you know, *I want to apologize to Emily Gorcenski, because you did bring that [dossier] to us. And we...* It was like we couldn't legally have stopped the rally. But if there was...I forget exactly what the apology was, but I wanted her to hear that we could have amplified it more.

It was so hard because it didn't meet the legal standard for a credible threat. It didn't. Nothing that was in the dossier met what the FBI standard is, or the Court's.

KRISTIN SZAKOS: After the event, people from Charlottesville got very angry at the city for not protecting them, and I shared that. I was angry too. So, I just took it. Even as they were yelling at us, I couldn't help but love them and feel like we'd let them down. But we also had shared their experience. We felt the same way. At least I did.

DON GATHERS, COFOUNDER, CHARLOTTESVILLE BLACK LIVES MATTER: Where we go from here, I don't know.

It's still laughable when people say, *Well, that's not...that wasn't Charlottesville.* Yeah, it was and yeah it is! This was a community that is very visibly divided. And I just don't see anything on the horizon, bridging those chasms that exist.

REV. BRENDA BROWN-GROOMS, PASTOR, NEW BEGINNINGS CHRISTIAN COMMUNITY: If I heard it once I heard it a million times: Everybody kept saying, *But this is not who we are. This is not who we are.* Yeah. It's exactly who we are. We don't want to admit it, but it's exactly who we are.

Can we be someone else? Of course, we *can* be, but it takes work. It takes commitment. It takes being willing to be uncomfortable.

CONSTANCE PAIGE YOUNG, COUNTER-PROTESTER: There's life before the car attack and there's life after the car attack.

Some of the people who I've met who were also injured in this car attack, I will love for the rest of my life. And I think I am more brave because they are brave. And I can continue to exist here and do good work because they are able to do it too. I found a community of people who keep trying and of people who have lost so much. I mean, we have lost so much and we keep going.

I want people to know that a whole bunch of brave people showed up, regular people. A lot of regular brave folks showed up to do an extraordinary thing that day, and I think we did make a difference and we paid a big price for it. And that's all.

ROSIA PARKER, LOCAL ACTIVIST: We are still fighting.

As elders of the community, it took us a long time to get respect, because they didn't understand why we were going off in the way we were going. We became the angry Black women. Well, why are we angry Black women? Because this has been going on for generations and generations.

We grandmamas out here in the streets, you know, because we was planning for such a time as this. But our babies don't have an understanding. Our babies are constantly coming from trauma. And until you treat that trauma, it is going to get worse.

ALEXIS GRAVELY, SENIOR ASSOCIATE NEWS EDITOR, *CAVALIER DAILY*: We can't just be complacent. If all these people and all these systems just sort of provide the breeding ground for these ideas and these people and these views, then yeah, it's going to happen. And if we don't change anything, then it's going to happen again. It's not just something that you ignore and it goes away.

ROSIA PARKER: It's a continuous fight. All we see is a constant fight, until— Trina, what's your favorite song? We have one particular song, a slave song, that Katrina holds in her heart. And before we leave out the house, she sings it.

KATRINA TURNER, SINGING:

> Oh, freedom, Oh, freedom, Oh freedom over me
> And before I'd be a slave
> I'd be buried in my grave
> And go home to my Lord and be free!

ACKNOWLEDGMENTS

First and foremost, thank you to those whose voices make up these pages. Thank you for trusting me to tell your stories. Thank you for reliving your trauma in order to share the truth. Thank you for the work you have done, and continue to do, to fight fascism. This book is for you and by you.

Thank you to my own Charlottesville community, those who made the city feel like home, and especially my NBC29 family who gave me my first real journalism job and stuck with me as I learned the ropes—and learned how to turn on a broadcast camera.

This book would never have progressed past the idea phase without my inimitable agent, Wendi Gu. Thank you for believing in this book from its inception and continuing to stand by me through the whole process. And to my editor, Catherine Tung, and the whole team at Beacon Press, who saw the importance of this story and helped bring it to life. I'm also so grateful to Noor Alzamami, Arya Royal, and Amalia Schwarzschild for assisting on the oral history and research that forms the backbone of this book.

Thank you also to my colleagues during my time at CNN, who supported this book project from the beginning, especially John Berman, who reviewed an early draft and provided detailed feedback. And special thanks to CNN's Anderson Cooper and Charlie Moore, who trusted me to field-produce their Charlottesville coverage after I had only officially worked for them for a few weeks. And even before that, thank you both for giving me my first journalism internship, my foot in the door at CNN, and the best training as a journalist I could have asked for.

Thank you to my parents, Mike and Karen, and siblings, Jack and Julia, for encouraging me to embark on a book project of this magnitude. Mom and Dad, thank you for editing the very first drafts of this book's proposal, and even more so, for encouraging my journalism and writing careers from as early as I can remember. And thank you to my in-laws, Kendal and Andy, and brother-in-law Gerrit, for being such cheerleaders of my writing career.

Finally, to my spouse, the love of my life, Lex. This book would not exist without you. Thank you for walking alongside me throughout this writing process, cooking me dinner after tough hours-long interviews, and serving as my ultimate sounding board, consultant, editor, and supporter. I love you forever.

NOTES

Chapter 1

1. Mark Kavit, email message to Charlottesville city officials, August 10, 2017, University of Virginia Library of Special Collections, MSS 16386, Unite the Right Rally and Community Response Collection, series 1, subseries 1, Correspondence, etc., box 1, folder 1.
2. Thomas Jefferson, *Notes on the State of Virginia* (Philadelphia, 1785), https://docsouth.unc.edu/southlit/jefferson/jefferson.html.
3. "The Illusion of Progress: Charlottesville's Roots in White Supremacy," Carter G. Woodson Center at the University of Virginia, Citizen Justice Initiative, 2017, https://UValibrary.maps.arcgis.com/apps/Cascade/index.html?appid=3e111d6024 53478cad8452ba551138b6.
4. Wes Bellamy, *Monumental* (Newport News, VA: BlackGold Publishing, 2019), 47.
5. Bellamy, *Monumental*, 102.
6. Screen capture included in email message from local lawyer to friends, May 4, 2017.
7. Screen capture included in email message from local lawyer to friends, May 4, 2017.
8. Email message from local lawyer to friends, May 4, 2017.

Chapter 2

1. Bryan McKenzie, "Police Prep of 2 Fronts," *Daily Progress* (Charlottesville, VA), August 11, 2017.
2. Bellamy, *Monumental*, 102.
3. Emily Gorcenski, "Terry McAuliffe Still Doesn't Understand What Happened in Charlottesville," *Slate,* August 8, 2019.
4. "Solidarity C'ville Documents Threats of Violence Planned for August 12," *Solidarity C'ville,* July 17, 2017, https://solidaritycville.wordpress.com/2017/07/17 /solidarity-cville-documents-threats-of-violence-planned-for-august-12/.
5. Bellamy, *Monumental*, 143.
6. Bellamy, *Monumental*, 150.

Chapter 3

1. Chris Suarez, "Faith Leaders Gather on the Eve of 'Hate-Driven' Unite the Right Rally," *Daily Progress,* August 11, 2017.
2. Joe Heim, "A Stark Contrast Inside and Outside a Charlottesville Church During the Torch March," *Washington Post,* August 19, 2017.
3. Heim, "A Stark Contrast."
4. Nicole Hemmer, host, "The Summer of Hate," *A12: The Story of Charlottesville* (podcast), Miller Center, University of Virginia, https://millercenter.org/A12.
5. Willis Jenkins, "Ethics under Pressure: An Autoethnography of Moral Trauma," in *Charlottesville 2017,* ed. Louis P. Nelson and Claudrena N. Harold (Charlottesville: University of Virginia Press, 2018), 165–66.
6. Heim, "A Stark Contrast."
7. Heim, "A Stark Contrast."
8. "Charlottesville Mass Prayer Service: Dr. Cornel West and Rev. Traci Blackmon Speaking to #CvilleClergyCall," Facebook livestream, August 11, 2017, https://www.facebook.com/SojournersMagazine/videos/10154913829892794.
9. #CvilleClergyCall Mass Prayer Service program, August 11, 2017, University of Virginia Library of Special Collections, MSS 16386, Unite the Right Rally and Community Response Collection, series 1, subseries 1, Correspondence, etc., box 1, folder 4.

Chapter 4

1. Tweet from It's Going Down (@IGD_News), August 11, 2017, https://twitter.com/IGD_News/status/896155204617248768.
2. Tweet from It's Going Down (@IGD_News), August 11, 2017, https://twitter.com/IGD_News/status/896139934116962304.
3. Day 13 official court transcript, *Elizabeth Sines et al., Plaintiffs, v. Jason Kessler et al., Defendants. Sines v. Kessler,* Civil Action No. 3:17-cv-00072, (W.D. Va.), 44.
4. Day 5, *Sines v. Kessler* (hereafter *SvK*), 167.
5. Day 5, *SvK,*167.
6. Day 5, *SvK,* 21.
7. Day 5, *SvK,* 90.

Chapter 5

1. Day 13, *SvK,* 45.
2. Heim, "A Stark Contrast."
3. Hemmer, "The Summer of Hate."
4. Day 8, *SvK,* 118.
5. Day 8, *SvK,* 117–24, 131.
6. Day 5, *SvK,* 22–23.
7. Day 6, *SvK,* 69–70.
8. Day 5, *SvK,* 171.
9. Day 5, *SvK,* 22–23.
10. Day 5, *SvK,* 23.
11. Day 5, *SvK,* 21, 24.
12. Day 5, *SvK,* 172.

13. Day 5, *SvK*, 176.
14. Day 5, *SvK*, 24.

Chapter 6

1. Day 5, *SvK*, 176.
2. Day 5, *SvK*, 172.
3. Day 5, *SvK*, 172.
4. Maggie Mallon, "Elizabeth Sines and Leanne Chia Were in Charlottesville When White Supremacists Descended—This Is What They Saw," *Glamour*, August 18, 2017.
5. Day 5, *SvK*, 25.
6. Day 5, *SvK*, 176.
7. Day 5, *SvK*, 177.
8. Day 5, *SvK*, 28.
9. Day 5, *SvK*, 28–29.
10. Tweet from Chris Suarez (@Suarez_CM), August 11, 2017, https://twitter.com/Suarez_CM/status/896193287257821184?s=20.
11. Day 5, *SvK*, 180.
12. "Documenting Hate," *PBS Frontline*, 2017, https://www.pbs.org/wgbh/frontline/film/documenting-hate-charlottesville/transcript/.
13. Day 5, *SvK*, 181.
14. Day 5, *SvK*, 28.
15. Day 5, *SvK*, 29.
16. "Documenting Hate," *PBS Frontline*.
17. Hemmer, "The Summer of Hate."
18. Michael Signer, *Cry Havoc* (New York: *Hachette,* 2020), 205.
19. Signer, *Cry Havoc*, 205
20. Jenkins, "Ethics under Pressure," 165–66.
21. Jenkins, "Ethics under Pressure," 165–66.
22. Jenkins, "Ethics under Pressure," 165–66.
23. Day 13, *SvK*, 47.
24. Tweet from Jalane Schmidt (@Jalane_Schmidt), August 11, 2017, https://twitter.com/jalane_schmidt/status/896191494020792320.
25. "UVa Prof on UVa's Historical Ties to KKK & White Nationalist Alums Richard Spencer & Jason Kessler," *Democracy Now,* August 14, 2017, https://www.democracynow.org/2017/8/14/UVa_professor_on_schools_historical_ties (these two sentences only).

Chapter 7

1. Day 5, *SvK*, 183–84.
2. Day 5, *SvK*, 30.
3. Day 5, *SvK*, 185.
4. Day 5, *SvK*, 30.
5. Day 5, *SvK*, 186.
6. Day 6, *SvK*, 79.
7. Day 5, *SvK*, 30.

8. Day 5, *SvK*, 30–31.
9. Heim, "A Stark Contrast."
10. Day 13, *SvK*, 46–47
11. Day 13, *SvK*, 49.
12. Day 13, *SvK*, 49.
13. Day 8, *SvK*, 125.
14. Day 5, *SvK*, 31.
15. "Documenting Hate," *PBS Frontline*.
16. Humanity Over Hate Forum, The Leadership Conference on Civil and Human Rights, May 19, 2022, https://m.facebook.com/events/982057595675771/.
17. "My Daughter Was Killed at Charlottesville—Susan Bro—What I've Learnt," *Channel 4 News* (UK), August 12, 2018, https://www.youtube.com/watch?v=YI8vBx967GI.
18. Humanity Over Hate Forum.
19. Humanity Over Hate Forum.

Chapter 8

1. Bellamy, *Monumental*, 156.
2. Day 13, *SvK*, 51; personal interview.
3. Congregate C'ville Facebook livestream, August 12, 2017, https://www.facebook.com/congregatecville/videos/461977134182807.
4. Congregate C'ville Facebook livestream, August 12, 2017, https://www.facebook.com/congregatecville/videos/461977134182807.
5. Congregate C'ville Facebook livestream, August 12, 2017, https://www.facebook.com/congregatecville/videos/461983787515475.
6. Congregate C'ville Facebook livestream, August 12, 2017, https://www.facebook.com/congregatecville/videos/461977134182807.
7. David Straughn, "I Witnessed Terrorism in Charlottesville from a Foot Away," *Scalawag*, August 16, 2017.
8. Bellamy, *Monumental*, 162.
9. Bellamy, *Monumental*, 161.
10. Bellamy, *Monumental*, 162.

Chapter 9

1. Day 5, *SvK*, 191–92.
2. Day 5, *SvK*, 191–92.
3. Day 5, *SvK*, 195.
4. Tweet from Allison Wrabel (@craftypanda), August 12, 2017, https://twitter.com/craftypanda/status/896355589772763136.
5. International Association of Chiefs of Police, "Virginia's Response to the Unite the Right Rally: After-Action Review," 15, https://www.pshs.virginia.gov/media/governorvirginiagov/secretary-of-public-safety-and-homeland-security/pdf/iacp-after-action-review.pdf.

Chapter 10

1. CNN, *Anderson Cooper 360*, August 17, 2017, 8 p.m.
2. Tweet from Allison Wrabel (@craftypanda), August 12, 2017, https://twitter.com/craftypanda/status/896369731506188289.
3. Recorded on personal videos.
4. Recorded on personal videos.

Chapter 11

1. International Association of Chiefs of Police, "Virginia's Response to the Unite the Right Rally," 11.
2. Hemmer, "The Summer of Hate," 25:48.
3. Day 13, *SvK*, 58.
4. Day 13, *SvK*, 60–61.
5. Day 13, *SvK*, 60–61.
6. Day 5, *SvK*, 199.
7. Day 5, *SvK*, 40.
8. Day 5, *SvK*, 40.
9. Day 5, *SvK*, 40–43.
10. Day 5, *SvK*, 208.
11. "Documenting Hate," *PBS Frontline*.
12. "Documenting Hate," *PBS Frontline*.
13. Day 5, *SvK*, 204.
14. Heaphy report, 144.

Chapter 12

1. Alan Zimmerman, "In Charlottesville, the Local Jewish Community Presses On," ReformJudaism.org, https://reformjudaism.org/blog/charlottesville-local-jewish-community-presses.
2. Zimmerman, "In Charlottesville, the Local Jewish Community Presses On."
3. Anti-Defamation League, "Have Hate, Will Travel: The Demographics of Unite the Right," October 8, 2017, https://www.adl.org/resources/blog/have-hate-will-travel-demographics-unite-right.
4. Heaphy report, 144.

Chapter 13

1. Day 5, *SvK*, 211–12.
2. Day 5, *SvK*, 211–12.
3. Hemmer, "The Summer of Hate," 27:55.
4. Tweet from Chris Suarez (@Suarez_CM), August 12, 2017, https://twitter.com/Suarez_CM/status/896402363568795648?s=20.
5. Tweet from Allison Wrabel (@craftypanda), August 12, 2017, https://twitter.com/craftypanda/status/896397870320021507.
6. Official court transcript, *United States of America v. James Alex Fields*, 3:18-cr-00011-MFU, (W.D. Va.), sentencing hearing, 22.

7. Straughn, "I Witnessed Terrorism."

8. Straughn, "I Witnessed Terrorism."

9. Yesha Callahan, "Interview: How Corey Long Fought White Supremacy with Fire," *The Root,* August 14, 2017, https://www.theroot.com/interview-how-corey -long-fought-white-supremacy-with-f-1797831277?rev=1502737785317.

10. Callahan, "Interview."

11. Callahan, "Interview."

12. ACLU of Virginia, "Video Shows Man Firing into Crowd in Charlottesville," as posted by *IBTimes UK,* August 27, 2017, https://www.youtube.com/watch?v= C2ro7U_Yoc4, 0:31.

13. "'I was losing so much blood': Counterprotester Beaten with Poles, Signs in Char-lottesville," WRAL, August 13, 2017, https://www.wral.com/charlottesville-rally -organizer-condemns-violence-gov-says-incident-made-us-stronger-/16877938/.

14. Complaint, "*DeAndre Harris, Plaintiff, v. Jason Kessler et al., Defendants." Harris v. Kessler*, Case No. 3:19-cv-00046, (W.D. Va), 15.

15. Tweet from Chuck Modiano (@ChuckModi1), August 12, 2017, https://twitter .com/ChuckModi1/status/896409728959606789.

16. *Harris v. Kessler*, 2–3.

17. Ian Shapira, "The Parking Garage Beating Lasted 10 Seconds. DeAndre Harris Still Lives with the Damage," *Washington Post,* September 16, 2019.

18. Callahan, "Interview."

19. Callahan, "Interview."

20. Callahan, "Interview."

21. WRAL, "'I was losing so much blood.'"

22. *Harris v. Kessler*, 17.

23. WRAL, "'I was losing so much blood.'"

24. WRAL, "'I was losing so much blood.'"

Chapter 14

1. Mallon, "Elizabeth Sines and Leanne Chia Were in Charlottesville When White Supremacists Descended," *Glamour.*

2. Mallon, "Elizabeth Sines and Leanne Chia."

3. Day 5, *SvK*, 48.

4. Straughn, "I Witnessed Terrorism."

5. Straughn, "I Witnessed Terrorism."

6. Day 12, *SvK*, 17.

7. Mallon, "Elizabeth Sines and Leanne Chia."

8. Day 5, *SvK*, 48.

9. Day 5, *SvK*, 48.

10. Mallon, "Elizabeth Sines and Leanne Chia."

11. Day 15, *SvK*, 64.

12. Day 15, *SvK*, 66.

13. Humanity Over Hate Forum.

14. Mallon, "Elizabeth Sines and Leanne Chia."

Chapter 15

1. CNN, *Anderson Cooper 360*, August 17, 2017, 8 p.m.
2. Day 15, *SvK*, 66.
3. Official court transcript, *United States of America v. James Alex Fields*, 3:18-cr-00011-MFU, (W. D. Va.), sentencing hearing, 90–91.
4. Hemmer, "The Summer of Hate," 30:33.
5. Day 15, *SvK*, 66.
6. Day 15, *SvK*, 66.
7. Day 13, *Svk*, 12.
8. Debbie Elliot, "As Trial Begins in Charlottesville Protest Death, Community Reflects," NPR, November 26, 2018, https://www.npr.org/2018/11/26/669377175/as-trial-begins-in-charlottesville-protest-death-community-reflects.
9. Straughn, "I Witnessed Terrorism in Charlottesville from a Foot Away."
10. Day 15, *SvK*, 67.
11. Official court transcript, *United States of America v. James Alex Fields*, 111–12.
12. *Sines v. Kessler.*
13. Official court transcript, *United States of America v. James Alex Fields*, 90–91.
14. CNN, *Anderson Cooper 360*, August 17, 2017, 8 p.m.
15. Mary Wood, "Standing Up for Charlottesville," University of Virginia School of Law, August 16, 2017, https://www.law.virginia.edu/news/201708/standing-charlottesville.
16. Official court transcript, *United States of America v. James Alex Fields*, 90–91.
17. Official court transcript, *United States of America v. James Alex Fields*, 90–91.
18. Mallon, "Elizabeth Sines and Leanne Chia."
19. Wood, "Standing Up for Charlottesville."
20. Mallon, "Elizabeth Sines and Leanne Chia."
21. Straughn, "I Witnessed Terrorism."
22. Official court transcript, *United States of America v. James Alex Fields*, 90–91.
23. Tweet from Emily Gorcenski (@EmilyGorcenski), August 12, 2017, https://twitter.com/EmilyGorcenski/status/896476017753300992?s=20.
24. Hemmer, "The Summer of Hate," 31:37.
25. Wood, "Standing Up for Charlottesville."
26. Day 5, *SvK*, 51.
27. Hemmer, "The Summer of Hate," 31:37.
28. Mallon, "Elizabeth Sines and Leanne Chia."
29. Day 5, *SvK*, 51.
30. Katti Gray, "Ryan Kelly: 'The Day of the March Was Probably the Most Fear I'd Ever Had,'" The Pulitzer Prizes, https://www.pulitzer.org/article/ryan-kelly-day-march-was-probably-most-fear-id-ever-had.
31. Straughn, "I Witnessed Terrorism."
32. CNN, *Anderson Cooper 360*, August 14, 2017, 8 p.m.
33. Day 5, *SvK*, 52.
34. *Sines v. Kessler.*

Chapter 16

1. Hemmer, "The Summer of Hate," 32:32; Day 13, *SvK*, 62.
2. Day 5, *SvK*, 52–55.
3. Mallon, "Elizabeth Sines and Leanne Chia."
4. Day 15, *SvK*, 68.
5. Tweet from Allison Wrabel (@craftpanda), August 12, 2017, https://twitter.com /craftypanda/status/896427648552927234.

Chapter 17

1. Day 5, *SvK*, 56–57.
2. Day 5, *SvK*, 56–57.
3. Ellie Silverman, "From Wary Observer to Justice Warrior: How Heather Heyer's Death Gave Her Mom a Voice," *Washington Post*, February 1, 2018.
4. CNN, *Anderson Cooper 360,* August 14, 2017, 8 p.m.
5. Humanity Over Hate Forum.
6. Humanity Over Hate Forum.
7. CNN, *Anderson Cooper 360,* August 14, 2017, 8 p.m.
8. Humanity Over Hate Forum.
9. Humanity Over Hate Forum.
10. "My Daughter Was Killed at Charlottesville," *Channel 4 News* (UK).

Chapter 18

1. Terry McAuliffe, *Beyond Charlottesville: Taking a Stand Against White Nationalism* (New York: St. Martin's Publishing Group, 2019), 5, 20, 103.
2. Dean Seal, "2 State Troopers Die in Helicopter Wreck," *Daily Progress,* August 12, 2017.
3. McAuliffe, *Beyond Charlottesville,* 5, 20, 103.
4. Tweet from Emily Gorcenski (@EmilyGorcenski), August 12, 2017, https://twitter .com/EmilyGorcenski/status/896495361166123008?s=20.
5. Tweet from Emily Gorcenski (@EmilyGorcenski), August 12, 2017, https://twitter .com/EmilyGorcenski/status/896519668919291904?s=20.
6. Official court transcript, *United States of America v. James Alex Fields*, 112–13.
7. Day 13, *SvK*, 20.
8. "Documenting Hate," *PBS Frontline.*

INDEX

ABOUT THE AUTHOR

NORA NEUS is an Emmy-nominated journalist whose reporting has appeared in CNN, VICE News, the *Washington Post*, and more. Neus field-produced Anderson Cooper's coverage of the 2017 white nationalist riot in Charlottesville, Virginia for CNN. Before joining CNN, she worked as a local news reporter and fill-in anchor for the CNN affiliate in Charlottesville, WVIR NBC29. She is the coauthor of the young-adult graphic memoir *Muhammad Najem, War Reporter: How One Boy Put the Spotlight on Syria*.

KNEADED TO DEATH

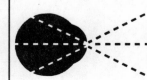

This Large Print Book carries the
Seal of Approval of N.A.V.H.

A BREAD SHOP MYSTERY

Kneaded to Death

Winnie Archer

THORNDIKE PRESS
A part of Gale, Cengage Learning

GALE
CENGAGE Learning

Farmington Hills, Mich • San Francisco • New York • Waterville, Maine
Meriden, Conn • Mason, Ohio • Chicago

LIBRARY OF CONGRESS CATALOGING-IN-PUBLICATION DATA

Names: Archer, Winnie, author.
Title: Kneaded to death / by Winnie Archer.
Description: Large print edition. | Waterville, Maine : Thorndike Press, a part of
    Gale, Cengage Learning, 2017. | Series: A bread shop mystery ; 1 | Series:
    Thorndike Press large print peer picks
Identifiers: LCCN 2017012342| ISBN 9781432840945 (large print : hardcover) | ISBN
    1432840940 (large print : hardcover)
Subjects: LCSH: Murder—Investigation—Fiction. | GSAFD: Mystery fiction.
Classification: LCC PS3601.R3878 K58 2017 | DDC 813/.6—dc23
LC record available at https://lccn.loc.gov/2017012342

Published in 2017 by arrangement with Kensington Books, an imprint
of Kensington Publishing Corp.

Printed in the United States of America
1 2 3 4 5 6 7 21 20 19 18 17

KNEADED TO DEATH

CHAPTER ONE

Santa Sofia is a magical town, nestled between the Santa Lucia Mountain Range and the Pacific Ocean on California's Central Coast. I've always seen it as the perfect place. Not too big, not too small. Historic and true to its commitment to remain a family-oriented place to live. The town accomplished this goal by having more bikes than people, concerts in the park, and a near perfect seventy degrees almost year-round.

I had been gone from my hometown since college but had come back when a horrible accident destroyed our lives as we knew them, taking my mother far too young and leaving my father, my brother, and me bereft and empty. We were still struggling to make sense of what had happened and how a nondescript sedan had backed right into her as she walked behind it in the parking lot at the high school where she'd taught.

"No one saw anything. It was a hit-and-run," my best friend, Emmaline, had told me sadly. "She never saw it coming, and the doctors say she didn't suffer."

That made no sense to me. She was run over by a car. There had to have been pain and suffering, even if it was brief. I relived what I imagined were my mother's last moments. The split second when she saw the truck backing up, realizing that it was coming too fast and that she couldn't get out of the way in time; the impact when it first made contact, hurling her back against the asphalt; the force of the vehicle as it rolled over her. I caught my breath, swallowing the agony I knew she'd felt.

The final result of the tragedy was the emptiness of being back in Santa Sofia without her. The place where I was born and raised no longer filled me with the comfort it used to. Things were different now; six months later, I was still trying to pick up the pieces.

Since I was a little girl, taking photographs had always been my saving grace. Capturing the beauty or heartbreak or pure, unbridled emotions in the world around me showed me how small I was in the scheme of things. At the same time, it allowed me to revel in the moments I captured, treasuring each one as a work of art in and of itself.

My mother had given me a camera when I was nine years old and constantly in her hair. "It'll keep you busy," she'd told me, and it had. I had picked up that camera and had never put it down again. Now I had a degree in design and photography. I'd started a photography blog to keep my creative juices flowing, posting a picture a day. I'd had a vibrant business in Austin. But I was floundering. Since I lost my mother, finding inspiration had become a challenge. My voice had been silenced, it seemed, and I had nothing more to say with the images through the lens.

This lack of direction and the loss of my creative vision are what led me to Yeast of Eden, the bread shop in Santa Sofia. I might be able to end my dry spell if I could find inspiration somewhere. Somehow. But now, as I stood at the doorway, one hand on the handle, I wondered what in the hell I'd been thinking. Baking? A pan of brownies from a boxed mix? Sure. A batch of chocolate chip cookies, courtesy of the recipe on the back of the Nestlé package? Definitely. But from-scratch bread? Not in my wheelhouse. Baking was a far cry from finding beauty through the lens of a camera. The mere thought that I was even contemplating this bit of craziness clearly meant that I was under duress.

True, I'd been to the local bread shop every day since I'd moved back to Santa Sofia. Truth be told, the place was becoming my home away from home, but that did not give me the right to think I could actually make the stuff. And it certainly didn't mean baking would solve my problems. Grief had to run its course. I knew this, but the reality was that I'd never *not* feel the emptiness inside.

An image of my dad popped into my head. "What did you bring today?" he regularly asked me. It was becoming almost a joke, because I'd already cycled through nearly everything Yeast of Eden had to offer . . . twice. Baguettes. Sourdough. Croissants. Rye. Wheat pumpernickel. Focaccia.

Check.

Check.

Check.

Check.

Check.

And check.

There were so many choices, and I loved them all. But I did have my favorites. The flaky, buttery croissant in the morning or a crusty sourdough roll at lunch — these were the staples. On a sunny day, the pumpernickel with sliced turkey and cheese hit the

10

spot. When it was rainy, I bought a round loaf of French bread, turned it into a bread bowl, and filled it with homemade chowder.

But this time I wasn't here to buy bread; I was here to get my hands dirty, so to speak. To plunge them into a bowl of dough and knead, knead, knead. And somehow, despite logic and despite reason, I knew that it was going to be life changing. I had no idea how . . . or why, but as sure as I was standing on the cobbled sidewalk in Santa Sofia, and as sure as the breeze off the Pacific Ocean blew through me, I was 100 percent certain that the bread-baking class at Yeast of Eden was going to send me on a new trajectory.

But was I ready?

Before I had the chance to answer that question in my head, the door opened, and a woman in a colorful caftan and red clogs, hands firmly on her hips, emerged. Her iron-gray hair was cropped short and loose, playful curls danced over her head. Her green eyes, heavily flecked with gold, stared me down. *"Ven aqui, m'ija,"* she said to me in Spanish, as if I could understand her. Which I could not. "You have to come inside to change your life."

I jumped, startled. "To change my . . . what? I'm sorry. What?"

11

"You don't think I recognize you? You, *mi amor,* are here every day. You have discovered the magic of this place, and now you want more." She smiled, her eyebrows lifting in a quick movement that seemed to say "I see this every day." "Come in. We're all waiting."

"You're all . . . ?" I stared. "Who's waiting?"

This time the woman laughed. She threw her head back and gave a hearty guffaw that made me take a step back. Of course, I recognized her, too. Her daily authoritative presence had made it easy to deduce that the woman owned Yeast of Eden. "The rest of the bakers, *por supuesto.*"

Her laughter seeped into me, and despite myself, I felt a smile tilt my lips upward, but I bit down to stop it from being fully realized. Being happy was simply not okay. How could it be when I'd lost my mother just a few short months ago, and when my dad, my brother, and I were hanging on to each other just to get by? My grief had become part of me. It was embedded in my soul. Trapped in my pores. Smiling felt like a betrayal of my sorrow. A betrayal of my mother.

The woman watched me with a gaze that seemed to burrow through every bit of me.

Her voice softened. "It will be all right, you know."

A flurry of goose bumps danced over my skin. I'd spoken to this woman no more than a handful of times, and the interactions were always superficial and cursory, and yet somehow she seemed to know exactly what I was feeling. I tried to school my expression. I tended to show every one of my emotions on my face the very second I felt them; I was working on that particular problem.

"I don't know what you mean," I said, my voice a little more indignant than I'd intended it to be.

She considered me again and then gave a succinct nod. "*Está bien, m'ija.* Come in then." She held the door open, letting me pass. "It is time to bake some bread."

"I'm not . . . I've never . . . I don't cook, you know," I said, already apologizing for the future failure I was afraid might happen once I got into the kitchen.

"Perhaps not yet, but you will . . . ," she said, letting the words trail away, and just like that, I felt as if I really might be able to do the impossible and learn this new, tantalizing skill.

She flipped the sign hanging in the window to show CLOSED and locked the door.

I followed her deeper into the bread shop, the scent of fresh-baked bread swirling around me and enveloping me like a cocoon. As I breathed in, letting it soak into me for just a moment, I felt the grief that was always with me soften around the edges. For the first time since I could remember, it ebbed and I felt my lungs open up.

I followed her flowing caftan–clad body through the swinging doors, which led to the back room. *"La cocina,"* she said, gesturing wide with her arms. "This is my favorite place in the world. Settle in, *m'ija. This* is where you belong."

I didn't know if she was right about that, but I let the comment go, instead looking at the other women gathered around the room. They had been chattering excitedly, but their voices had tapered off as we walked in.

"It's about time," one of the women said, her gaze trained on the bread shop owner. "At long last. *Lista?* Are you finally ready?"

"Keep your *pantalones* on, Consuelo." The iron-haired woman wagged a finger at the one called Consuelo, and I noticed how alike they looked. Sisters. They had to be. Consuelo was a few inches taller and her hair was dyed a deep brown, but they had

14

the same eyes, the same nose, slightly curved down at the end, and the same hollowed cheekbones.

The other women in the kitchen were of varying ages. I placed the owner — I still didn't know her name — in her early sixties; Consuelo, a few years younger; and another woman, who was wearing wide-legged black pants, a T-shirt with a cardigan over it, and slip-on sandals, somewhere in her late fifties. Three others were closer to my age.

I stepped forward and gave a little wave. "I'm Ivy Culpepper."

The owner's eyebrows flicked up again, as if something she'd thought had just been validated. "And I'm Olaya," she said. "Olaya Solis. This is my shop. Bread baked the way it used to be made back in Mexico."

The comfort I'd felt when I'd walked into the shop and breathed in the scent of bread deepened. It almost seemed as if we were connected somehow, this woman and me. But the moment I thought it, I shook the thought away. It was ridiculous. I'd been away from Santa Sofia for nearly a decade, and before I started coming to Yeast of Eden, I'd never laid eyes on Olaya Solis.

But still . . .

Olaya stepped up so that she was even

15

with me, and started pointing. "Consuelo is my sister. *Y tambien . . .* so is Martina."

The woman in the cardigan, Martina, lifted her chin and gave a slight smile and a shy wave.

"Martina is the quiet one in the family," Consuelo said, her own voice booming.

Consuelo definitely was *not* the quiet one. They were three sisters who might be different from one another, but they *had* each other. I had a brother, and while we were close, it wasn't the same as what I imagined having a sister would be like.

"I'm Jolie," one of the younger women said. She looked to be in her mid- to late twenties, maybe not around the corner from my own thirty-six years, but relatively close. She had long, straight black hair, which she'd pulled back into a careless ponytail. I inadvertently touched my own mop of curly ginger locks. I looked just like my mom, which I was grateful for, but as a result, I generally appear just a touch disheveled and not nearly as effortlessly put together as Jolie appeared. My hair looked like it had been shampooed with liquid paprika and made my green eyes sparkle like shiny emeralds. I'd pulled it up, wrapped it around and around, and tied it with a hair band.

My whole childhood, I'd longed for the sleek look that Jolie had, instead of the free spirit presence that I'd inherited from my mother. I waited for that old, familiar feeling of envy to seep in . . . but it didn't. Jolie was a beauty, but for the first time, I consciously realized that while I wasn't gorgeous like she was, I was okay with who I was. More than okay. I loved looking in the mirror and catching a glimpse of where I came from. Of *who* I came from.

"Nice to meet you," I said.

"There was a teacher — Mrs. Culpepper — at the high school. English, I think. Are you . . . ?"

"She was my mother," I said, glancing away.

"Wasn't she . . . was she . . . ," Jolie began, but she trailed off.

One of the other young women finished for her. "There was a hit-and-run at the school a few months ago."

"It was a horrible accident." I managed to keep my voice from quavering.

"Oh!" Jolie's jaw dropped. "I'm sorry."

Olaya placed her hand on my back, a comforting gesture. "Let's get to our baking," she said, sensing that I didn't want to talk about my mother's death. She introduced the other two young women as Sally and Becky. They each lifted their hands in a quick wave, and we all found our spaces at the counter. Each station had a name tag with a name neatly printed on it. Next to the name was a drawing of an apron. From what I could see, each apron was unique. As Olaya directed me to my station, I saw that even I had a name tag.

I spun around to look at her, raising my eyebrows in puzzlement. "How . . . ?"

"I knew you'd be coming," she answered.

I couldn't fathom how she'd known with such certainty that I'd come to this baking class when I hadn't even known for sure. But there was my name, my station, a lovely petit four, and an apron, all waiting for me. Each baking station had been equipped with a large mixing bowl, a container of flour, a jar of yeast, and the other essential ingredients for bread making, as well as a glass of ice water for our own hydration. I immediately took a deep sip, steadying my nerves. Only one empty station — water and petit four untouched — remained. Everyone else seemed to have eaten their sweet treat. I followed suit and nibbled mine.

Olaya took her place behind the stainless-steel center island and began talking. I'd detected a slight accent when she first met me at the door to Yeast of Eden, but now, as she spoke about the history of bread making in Mexico, it became more pronounced. "I know what you are thinking," she said. "Tortillas, yes? The bread of Mexico has always been tortillas. And yes, I make and sell Mexico's traditional fare once in a while. But bread . . ." She gestured toward the swinging doors, which led back to the front of the now closed shop and the display cases that were littered with what was left of the day's baked goods. "I have been baking bread since I was a little girl. Once I started, I never stopped."

I listened, enthralled. Her words seeped into me, and I understood completely. It was all about passion. Mine was photography. I had left California to go to college in Texas and had stayed there for many years, building my business. Circumstances had brought me back, I was starting over, and turning to the lens was the only thing I knew how to do. I imagined the display cases in Yeast of Eden overflowing with the day's offerings every morning, and I had a sudden hankering to photograph them. I made a mental note to myself to bring my camera in the morning and take a few shots, excited to see how the light would be and thinking about how best to capture the delicacy of the bread.

As Olaya continued filling us in on her history as a bread maker, the back door opened and a woman in a knee-length jean skirt and a floral blouse breezed in. "Sorry I'm late!"

"Late?" Olaya said, not missing a beat. "Jackie, five more minutes and I would have locked the door. You would have been stuck outside, with not an ounce of bread. You would have been . . . How do you say it?" She drew a finger across her neck. "Out of luck."

Clearly, Olaya didn't like tardiness with her classes. Duly noted. But I'd detected a light touch in her voice, and there was the faintest hint of a smile on her lips. I suspected that Jackie wasn't often on time and that Olaya had learned to accept this about her.

Jackie looked around and frowned, but Olaya ushered her to her workstation. She grabbed an apron off a hook and handed it to her. "But you are here now. You might as well stay."

"I had my own class to wrap up. Not as meaningful as baking bread, of course, but my livelihood." Her eyes glinted mischievously as she pushed her name tag aside, tied on her apron, took a drink from her ice water, and bit into her petit four. "Did I miss the talk about you baking bread as a child in Mexico?"

"She was just finishing," Consuelo said, and the two women's gazes met.

Jackie mouthed, "Phew!" and a knowing grin crossed each of their faces. Evidently, they had both taken the bread-making classes before and had heard Olaya's stories.

Olaya ignored her sister and her friend. She scanned Jackie up and down, and her gaze settled on the wedge heels. "Very nice shoes you are wearing," she said. "Perfect for baking."

Jackie burst out laughing and boisterously kicked up one leg behind her in an old Hollywood starlet manner. "That's exactly what I thought. You know my philosophy. One should always look her best, and shoes are the instant wardrobe definer." She fluttered her hand. "Carry on, Olaya."

I stood back as the women chattered, taking it all in, absorbing the energy in the kitchen. Memories of being in my childhood kitchen with my mom settled over me like a layer of gauze cloaking me. We'd cooked. We'd baked. She'd taught me everything I knew about being independent, about being strong, about being a woman. The memory slipped and cracked, and once again sorrow leached through me.

21

I drew in a deep breath, stilling my racing heartbeat, tucking the memory of my mom and me in her kitchen into a back corner of my mind. I wouldn't think about it right now.

Olaya reached her hand into a large plastic bin and let a handful of flour cascade through her fingers. "Baking bread is an art," she was saying. "I come in at four thirty every morning, and I produce top-quality breads on a daily basis. Consistency is key. When you bake, you get one shot. You don't know for certain if the bread is going to turn out the way it should until it comes out of the oven. It must look right. It must taste right. There are no additives. There are no shortcuts. My goal is for it always to be perfect, and that takes time. That is the payoff."

My heart beat a little faster, a niggling worry about producing a flawless loaf of bread working its way through me. This was supposed to be fun, not stressful.

Olaya must have sensed the pressure building in the room, because she smiled and patted the air with her hands, as if to calm us down. "You will learn to let your experience guide you. You will learn what to look for, what to feel for, and how to work the dough until you produce bread to be proud of."

I closed my eyes and let Olaya's words and voice float around me. Let my anxiety fade away. If my bread didn't turn out quite right, well, I'd be okay with that. I was doing something new. Doing something I wanted to do. Doing something challenging. And I was excited about the prospect.

Olaya continued. "Do you know my sisters and I come from a long line of *brujas*? Witches," she explained when Jolie asked what that meant. "Family legend has it that a *bruja,* many generations past, had been wronged by a man —"

"What else is new?" Jackie snarked.

"Is there any other way?" Consuelo added. She winked at Jackie.

Martina, the quiet one, piped up. "*Cállate,* both of you. You choose badly, so what do you expect?"

Consuelo and Jackie sniggered to each other, and Olaya continued as if there hadn't been an interruption at all. "To protect the future women in her line, the *bruja* in our *familia* made it so that mothers and daughters, *abuelitas* and *nietas,* aunts and nieces, *madrinas* and *comadres* — these relationships would last and sustain themselves better than any other. She blessed the women in my line with the ability to cook.

To bake. And that is how this tradition started in my family."

She continued, "Me? I have no choice. I must bake bread. You?" She pointed at each of us. "You are each here for your own reasons. I will be your guide. I will show you how to create your own bread, and you will form your own traditions. You will come to understand the power of bread. No. The power of *baking.* Of creating with your hands. Your mind. Your *soul.* We women are strong, and bread is healing. It can give you strength you did not know you had."

I didn't know what to make of the Solis women, the magic they put into bread making, and the fact that they thought they came from an ancient line of witches. But I went with it. There was something about them. I liked them all, especially Olaya, and being in her kitchen . . . in her *cocina* . . . gave me a sense of peace I hadn't felt since my mother died.

We spent the next hour measuring and mixing the ingredients for *conchas.*

"Mexican sweet bread is an easy way to start the bread-making process," Olaya said.

We went through the lesson by mixing the yeast and warm water, adding the milk, sugar, butter, eggs, and flour, and finally kneading the mixture until a soft, pliable dough formed.

"Much of the bread I make here is to be long cultured," she continued. "Forty-eight hours or more, to get the best rise and flavor possible. But the sweet bread, the *conchas,* can rise much more quickly."

We left the dough in our greased bowls covered with a thin dishcloth and went to the front of the shop, where Olaya walked us through the different breads still remaining in the display cases, telling us the history of her experiences making sourdough loaves, French baguettes, boules, brioche, *tartine* country bread, challah, festive breads, and so much more. Part way through the bread tour, Jackie's cell phone rang, sounding like the harsh ring of an old-fashioned phone from twenty years ago. Jackie answered, avoiding Olaya's disapproving glare.

"I can't," she whispered into the smart-phone. "I'm in the middle of a class."

Whoever was on the other end of the line said something that caused the color to drain from Jackie's face. She turned a ghostly white and glanced around, her spooked gaze skittering over each of us. Turning her back to us again, she cupped her hand over the phone and lowered her voice even more. "No. She's not. It was my decision. My life, not yours."

She talked for another minute, but her words were muted. Unintelligible.

Finally, she pressed the OFF button and shoved her phone into her pocket. The next instant, her phone rang again. "Kids," she said when she'd looked at the caller ID. "I told you, I'm busy, Jasmine," she said, but she looked at Olaya, rolled her eyes, and pushed through the swinging doors, disappearing back into the kitchen.

The three sisters gave each other some sort of knowing look, as if they knew something about Jackie's phone calls from Jasmine that gave them all pause, but Olaya picked up right where she'd left off in her talk.

"Artisan bread is handcrafted. They are hearth-baked loaves, and now I am going to tell you the secret. Are you ready?" she asked, a twinkle in her eyes.

We all nodded. I'd heard the stories about Yeast of Eden and the magic in the bread here. If you had a cold, people around Santa Sofia said that a loaf of traditional French bread from Yeast of Eden could cure it. If you'd had too little sleep, the five-grain bread was sure to wake you up. Heartbroken? Choose the sundried tomato and black olive or the fig and almond loaf. Either would mend the sadness. I wanted to know the secret to Olaya's magic as much as everyone else did, but part of me wondered if knowing would lessen the impact the bread could have or, worse, somehow take away altogether the magic it held. My daily visits had helped me cope with losing my mother; I didn't want that to stop.

Olaya forged on. "The secret," she said, her voice low and conspiratorial, "is wet dough."

I laughed spontaneously. I'd been expecting some mystical truth, but Olaya, although she might well be a *bruja,* was a realist. Wet dough. Okay, then.

"But the *conchas* dough wasn't wet," Becky, one of the younger class members, said.

Olaya nodded. "True. *Bueno.* That is a good observation. *Conchas* are lovely sweet breads, but they are not artisan breads. I do not want to scare you away too fast. You must learn the basics first, and then slowly you can increase your repertoire."

After another few minutes, we took a ten-minute bathroom break and then followed Olaya back into the kitchen and resumed our places at our stations with our bowls of sweet bread dough. Mine was a creamy white and had doubled, the previously dense dough now light and airy.

Olaya stood at the island, and we all looked at the mirror that was positioned above it, angled so that we could see exactly what she was doing. She'd told us how she'd had the mirror installed the previous year so she could teach others the art of bread making. As I watched her reflection mix the topping ingredients for the *conchas,* I could honestly say that the mirror was a great tool. We could all see everything she was doing so clearly, and we effortlessly followed her every move.

I followed her directions, step by step, beating the sugar and butter, stirring in flour until the mixture was the consistency of a thick paste, and then mixing in cinnamon.

Next, she turned her *conchas* dough out onto her stainless-steel counter. I followed suit, then rolled the dough into a log and cut it into twelve even pieces. After rolling the pieces into balls, I placed them onto the greased cookie sheet I'd already prepared. Olaya led us as we divided the topping paste into balls, then flattened each one, placed one on top of each of the *conchas* balls, and patted each one down lightly with our open palms.

"The last step," she said, "is to take your knife and cut grooves into the topping. Like a clamshell," she added. "*Y lista.* It is ready. Now it must rise again for about forty-five minutes, and we will bake."

It was at that moment that Consuelo looked around and asked, "Where's Jackie?"

I turned to Jackie's baking station. She wasn't there. I'd been so wrapped up in the baking process that I hadn't noticed. Neither, apparently, had anyone else.

"*Hijo de la chingada.* Of course it is Jasmine," Olaya said. "Now she wants to talk, and Jackie jumps. The girl cannot have it both ways."

"She is her daughter," Martina said softly. She definitely was the quiet sister, as Consuelo had said, but if she had an opinion, she seemed more than willing to share it.

A bowl crashed to the floor, breaking the tension.

"Sorry," Becky said.

Jolie dropped to her knees to pick up the ceramic fragments. "No, no. It was my fault."

But no one paid either of them any mind. Olaya and Consuelo headed out the back door of the kitchen. It had grown dark while we'd been baking, but the typically peaceful beach sounds of Santa Sofia weren't what we heard. Instead, the sound of male voices floated in the air. And then, like rolling thunder in the sky, at first distant, but growing louder, familiar yet at the same time ominous, an old, familiar voice crept into my consciousness. Memories from high school. Memories of my broken heart being torn apart and stomped on. Memories of the face behind all that old pain.

My heart seized. It was Miguel Baptista . . . and he was still right here in Santa Sofia.

CHAPTER TWO

After stepping outside with the other women in the bread-making class, I saw trouble with a capital *T.* Miguel Baptista and I had dated during my junior year (his senior year). I'd fallen head over heels, and I'd thought Miguel had, too, but his desire to get out of Santa Sofia had been greater than whatever he'd felt for me. He had graduated from high school and had taken the next bus out of town. I didn't think he'd ever looked back. I'd been nothing but a blip in his love life, but I'd always wondered if he was the one that got away.

Except here he was, arguing with a man I didn't know in the parking lot behind Yeast of Eden, their figures illuminated by the old-fashioned streetlights around the perimeter of the lot.

Seeing him reaffirmed something for me. He was the one I'd never fully gotten out of my system.

31

"Is that Randy Russell?" Sally asked, peering at the man Miguel was arguing with.

"What's he got in his hand?" Becky drew in a sharp breath and took a step backward. "Oh my God. It's a gun!"

A shot of panic surged through my veins. A gun?

There was a burst of lavender and hydrangeas in the planter beds on either side of the door, and we all instantly dodged behind them, trampling the columbine, bellflower, coralbells, and daisies that were also planted there. Of course, I realized too late that the fronds and flowers of these pretty planter beds wouldn't actually do anything to stop a stray bullet that might happen to come our way.

I peered through the lacy flowers and saw a man waving what looked like an old pistol. The light was dim, but the streetlights illuminated the scene well enough. I could see that his cheeks were ruddy, the color creeping up from his neck. "Who is he?" I said under my breath to the other women hiding beside me in the flower bushes.

"Randy co-owns the antique store across the street with Gus Makers," Jolie whispered.

Sally pulled apart two enormous hydrangea blooms to peer more closely. "What is wrong with him?"

I couldn't hear what Miguel and Randy were saying to each other, but Randy's voice was raised. He was definitely upset about something. Miguel patted the air with his open palms, working to calm him down. We all recoiled as Randy waved his arms around. Something seemed off. I peered into the waning light, trying to get a better look at the weapon in his hand. Realization struck me.

"It's not a gun." I heaved a relieved sigh and repeated, "It's not a gun."

In fact, it looked more like an antique billy club. How any of us could have mistaken the short brown club for a gun, I was not sure. All I knew was that I heaved an enormous sigh of relief.

Olaya seemed to realize the same thing. She muttered something in Spanish, blew out a loud breath, and suddenly charged forward. "Enough. Randy Russell. *Qué paso?* What are you doing?"

Randy stopped and slowly turned around. "Back off, Olaya," he said with a hiss.

"I will not, Randy. You interrupt my class, and you act like a crazy person."

He flung his head this way and that, as if he were looking for someone. Then he raised his hand, the billy club clenched tight.

I and the women flanking me in the flower beds gasped in unison.

"Oh my God," Jolie said.

"What's he going to do?" Becky muttered.

Sally suddenly clasped her hand on my shoulder.

I willed them all to relax, and at the same time, I willed Olaya to back away and not bait him anymore. Even though it wasn't a gun, a lot of damage could be done with a club. Unfortunately, I didn't have the magical ability to communicate telepathically with her. Instead of retreating, as I'd hoped, she advanced on him.

"Randy Russell, you hothead, you need to put that stick away, go home, and sober up. Gus and Jackie are not your business. They are old news," she told him.

Behind him, Miguel seemed to make eye contact with Olaya. She continued to distract Randy Russell, and as I watched, Miguel crept for ward like a panther. In one lightning quick move, he threw one arm around him and grabbed his wrist with his other hand. "You don't want to do this, pal," he said, and the next thing I knew, Miguel had yanked the man's hand down until it was behind his back and the club was no longer in his grip. In ten seconds flat, Miguel had disarmed the lunatic, a siren blared and grew deafening as a police cruiser skidded into the parking lot, and Randy Russell broke free and took off running. Stumbling. Running.

A female officer jettisoned out of the police car before it even stopped, and took up chase. Moments later, she tackled Randy Russell and it was over.

Just as we had made a collective gasp a minute before, the four of us in the bushes let out the breaths we'd been holding, releasing sighs of relief.

"Did you think the lavender would protect you if he'd actually had a gun?" a voice said.

I looked up to see Olaya staring down at me and the other wannabe bakers still crouched behind the flowers. The white apron she'd had on all evening still covered her clothing.

"I already realized the folly," I said, "but hiding was instinct. This was the best we could do."

"Let us hope your baking talent is better than your self-preservation skills," she said. We unfurled ourselves from our crouched positions, and she ushered us out from behind the hydrangeas and lavender.

"Miguel Baptista," I muttered, sneaking another look at the boy — now the man — who'd broken my heart once upon a time.

He looked the same, yet somehow completely different. A little bit weathered. Experienced. Intense. Six feet, dark hair, swarthy skin, end-of-the-day stubble, and elongated creases that ran from the side of his mouth to his chin, like exaggerated dimples. Miguel Baptista made my heart contract in my chest.

Olaya paused, considering me once again. "You know him?"

"We went to school together," I said, leaving it at that. I already felt as if Olaya could see right through me; she didn't need to know the heartbreak of my youth.

"He knows how to handle himself, doesn't he?" Jolie said, a smitten expression on her face, and I felt an unreasonable and wholly unwarranted stab of jealousy. Where had *that* come from? I had no claim on Miguel Baptista. Less than none.

"Ten years in the military will do that for a man," Olaya said. "So yes, he can handle himself quite well." She patted her iron-gray hair and looked around, frowning, and I remembered that we'd come outside in the first place to look for Jackie.

Olaya's voice, this time full of concern, made me turn around. "That's Jackie's car," she said to Consuelo and Martina. She took a step toward it. "Is she . . . ?"

"Sitting in it?" Consuelo said, finishing the question. Instantly, the three sisters started across the parking lot, headed for the silver sedan parked smack in the middle. It was in one of the darker areas, away from the light of the street lamps.

The police officers had Randy Russell handcuffed and in the back of their cruiser and were now talking to Miguel Baptista. He stood firmly rooted to the ground, his arms folded over his chest, hands pressed flat beneath his armpits. All that had changed about him was the fact that he'd grown from the attractive young man he'd been in high school into the ruggedly good-looking man who'd just single-handedly saved the day.

My heart went from clenching to fluttering, and I kicked myself. Getting involved with Miguel Baptista again was *not* going to happen. And yet —

A bloodcurdling scream broke through my thoughts.

"Jackie!" Consuelo's voice was raw and fragile.

Even in the dark, I could see Olaya make the sign of the cross, touching her fingers to her forehead, the center of her chest, her left shoulder, and then her right. *"Dios mio!"*

At the first scream, Miguel was running

37

toward the women and Jackie's car, the two police officers right behind him.

Martina had backed away from the sedan. Consuelo had buckled over, looking like she was hyperventilating. Only Olaya seemed to have kept herself under control.

"She's dead," I heard her say. "It's Jackie. I think she's . . . Yes . . . she's dead."

CHAPTER THREE

The town of Santa Sofia would always be part of me, the memory of my mom firmly rooted in every part of the town, every corner I turned, every street I walked down. It was a curse and a blessing. Eventually, I hoped I'd be able to let go of the sadness and revel only in the memories.

My dad and my brother, Billy, would do anything for me, and I felt the same about them. Family was everything, and they were mine. Then there was Agatha. About eighteen pounds and cute as a button, she was my little pug. I'd rescued her back in Texas just after my divorce, and she was my little shadow. We'd helped each other in our times of need, and now she was my greatest comfort.

But in the years I'd been away from Santa Sofia, Emmaline Davis had been my other constant. Emmaline had graduated college with a degree in criminal justice and had become a deputy sheriff in Santa Sofia. When I'd first heard about her position, I'd wondered if Santa Sofia even needed a deputy sheriff. Did anything criminal ever happen here?

I hadn't thought so, but the night before I'd been proven dead wrong. Jackie Makers, the woman in the jean skirt and wedge heels, was dead. And according to the officers at the site, not only was she dead, but she also quite possibly had been killed.

As in murdered.

I'd met a woman, albeit briefly, whose life had been suddenly, and purposefully, ripped from her.

And Emmaline Davis was going to be central to bringing the woman's murderer to justice.

My thoughts went back to Miguel and the scene I'd witnessed the night before. Even if he held a long petrified place in my heart, I didn't pine for him. If I'd never seen him again, I'd have been fine with that. I'd moved on. So seeing him right here in the back parking lot of Yeast of Eden, facing down a man on the proverbial ledge, had sent my blood pressure skyrocketing and now sent me straight to the phone to call Emmaline.

"Miguel Baptista lives in Santa Sofia," I

said, clutching the phone between my ear and shoulder as I whipped off my ball cap, tucked my hair back behind my ears, and jammed the cap back on my head.

I heard the *tap-tap-tap* of Emmaline's fingers on her computer keyboard. She was a pro at multitasking. I imagined her digging into the murder of Jackie Makers. Maybe they'd already charged Randy Russell. He'd been in the right place at the right time, after all, and he might not have had a gun, but he'd had a few screws loose in his head. He seemed to be the perfect suspect.

"Why is he back here?" I asked, back to Miguel.

"His dad passed away about a year ago. He came back to take over the restaurant. His mom was in no shape," Emmaline said, distracted.

"I can't believe you never told me he was back," I said, feeling irrationally hurt.

"You and Miguel are such old news. I didn't think you'd care."

"We are," I said. "And you're right, I don't." Did I?

The death of Mr. Baptista explained it all. Miguel might have had some wild oats to sow way back when, but he came from good stock, and he knew that family was at the heart of everything good and dear. His mama had needed him, and it didn't take much to deduce that he'd done the right thing by her, coming home to save the restaurant named after the family. And none of it had even the remotest thing to do with me.

I told myself that, but Emmaline read between the lines. "Ivy Culpepper, you should just march on over there to Baptista's and say your hellos. You know you want to."

I mustered up a good dose of indignant dismay. "I most certainly do not. . . ."

The typing stopped abruptly. "You most certainly do, and don't you deny it. That man has been a thorn in your side ever since he left you, hasn't he? He probably ruined your marriage to what's-his-name —"

"My marriage was ruined by what's-his-name's lack of backbone and immature infidelity," I interrupted.

She didn't miss a beat. "And it's been forever. Get him out of your system once and for all so some other worthy man can steal your heart."

"Been there, done that. I'm destined to be single. Which I'm fine with."

"You're still pining for Miguel," she said.

"Ha! No. I'm not. And don't even talk to me about pining for someone, Em. Talk about the pot calling the kettle black. You don't have a leg to stand on." She and my brother, Billy, had been on and off again for years, had been flirting for even more years, and had each been in long-term relationships with other people but had never gotten to the commitment stage of their own affair.

"I'm black, he's white, and —" she began, as if the simple statement was meant to explain why she would have an unrequited love for the rest of her life.

"And this is California, and it's the twenty-first century, not nineteen fifty Mississippi. If you and Billy love each other, you should be together. Period."

"I know," she said from her end of the phone line, but she sounded dejected. "But you know how hard it is to cross a huge ravine without a bridge."

"You're making a ravine where there is none, Em," I said, "and even if there was some uncrossable canyon between you two, Billy would *be* the bridge. He loves you. He always has."

My brother hadn't ever confided in me about how he felt about Emmaline, but I'd seen the way he looked at her, the lovesick expression in his eyes whenever she entered the room, and their star-crossed lover thing had been going on for years. I was 100 percent sure that he'd lay down his life for her, so why they both felt circumstances had conspired against them and their love was baffling.

"So, about Miguel," Emmaline said in a not so subtle change of subject. Maybe this was why she and Billy had never really got together and stayed together. Neither one of them could stand to get serious and have the hard conversation.

"There's nothing to say. I'm back. He's here. That's all I wanted to tell you. You could have mentioned it, is all."

"You just stay away from him, then," she said, playing devil's advocate. If only her staying away from Billy, or Billy from her, made a bit of difference in how they actually felt, I might have taken her seriously. As it was, I let the pink elephant in the room quietly slip out.

"So what's the story with Jackie Makers?" I asked. This time I was the one who was not so subtly changing the subject. After discovering the body, Olaya had abruptly canceled the baking class. The police had come in, and the bread shop's kitchen had become a crime scene. They'd taken pictures and, I presumed, collected evidence. After they'd gone, I'd stayed behind and helped Martina and Consuelo dump the *conchas* dough in the garbage. But since then I'd been on edge, wondering what had happened to Jackie. Who in the world could have killed her?

The tap-tap-tapping on the other end of the line stopped, and suddenly I had Emmaline's full attention. "You tell me. You saw her before she died, right?"

"Yes," I answered, wishing anything I could tell her would actually make a difference in her investigation. "But she got to Yeast of Eden late, and then we started baking right away."

"Since when do you bake bread?" she asked.

"Since this big hole in my heart appeared."

Silence. I hadn't meant to snap at her, but the death of my mother brought a constant array of different emotions out in me, and sometimes I couldn't control them. "Yeah. Makes sense," she said.

"So, Jackie Makers?" I nudged her back to a subject I was more comfortable with. Anything not to think about how much I missed my mom.

"Randy Russell is no longer a suspect," she said. "We released him this morning."

I drew in a startled breath. "But the club

45

in his hand, and his ranting —"

"He knew the victim, but we have no evidence pointing to a motive. He was on a bender, and it's common knowledge that he has a lot of pent-up resentment toward Jackie. She was the woman who hurt his best friend so badly," she explained. "But she was definitely *not* beaten to death, and he didn't seem to know she was there."

"Okay," I conceded. "So do you have a different suspect? Surely not Miguel . . . ?"

"No. Relax. As far as I can tell, Miguel didn't even know the woman. Right now we're sort of nowhere. We have a few people of possible interest. The bread shop owner. Her sisters. All the women in the class, in fact. Except you, of course."

My heart felt like it stopped cold in my chest. "You think one of the Solis sisters might have killed their friend? No way," I said. "Impossible."

"How are you so sure?" she asked, and I imagined her eyebrows pulling together as she waited for my response.

"I was with them all evening. We were baking bread. We listened to a talk about the history of bread in Mexico —" I broke off, drawing in another breath, but this time it was sharp and sudden.

"What?" Emmaline prompted.

"No, nothing," I answered. "How did she die?" It certainly hadn't been obvious to me as a bystander.

"There'll be an autopsy. There was no visible wound, so the logical assumption is poison of some sort. It'll be a month, maybe more, before we know for sure."

A month or more? That seemed like forever. Real life certainly didn't work like "life" did on TV. I went with Emmaline's logic and thought about Jackie being poisoned. Could it have happened while she was at Yeast of Eden? Did poison act that quickly?

I thought about the possibilities. Jackie hadn't been at the bread shop for very long, but I had one distinct recollection. We'd each had a glass of water at our stations. Olaya had directed Jackie to her baking station, and Jackie had taken a good long drink. But I didn't tell Emmaline this. I couldn't. It might have been misguided, but I couldn't stand the thought that I could have so drastically misjudged a person. Olaya Solis couldn't have killed her friend Jackie.

Could she?

CHAPTER FOUR

The Historic Society of Santa Sofia was a political hotbed on par with . . . with . . . with the worst of the presidential elections in the United States. Or at least that was how I saw things now that I was back in my hometown. My dad was the city manager and oversaw the historic society. It mostly seemed like this particular department was full of infighting and petty battles, but he loved it, and now I was walking alongside him as he took stock of a renovation project on Maple Street, in the historic district.

My dad and I walked down the sidewalk, my fawn pug, Agatha, trotting beside me in her tiny harness. Her ears were back, and her tail was curled happily. She'd been the last dog surrendered by a backyard breeder. From sitting on the couch, trembling, to scampering about in joy, she'd come a long way.

We stopped in front of a sunny yellow

clapboard house. Agatha instantly sat beside me, waiting as I took in the details of the house. The front porch was adorned with a hanging bench on one side, a ceramic planter draped with green ivy, and two red Adirondack chairs. "It's so cute," I said. "What's the problem?"

My dad pinched his thumb and index finger together, pressed them against the space above his upper lip, and stroked his mustache. "Stupidity. The problem, Ivy, is pure stupidity."

Every house on the street was at least fifty years old, and some, like the one under renovation, was closer to a hundred, at least.

"How so?"

"The Mastersons, over there," he said, pointing to the pale and worn pink house next to the one being renovated, "pretty much want to destroy the Rabels."

"The Rabels own the yellow house?"

My dad stroked his mustache again and nodded. "The house was falling apart when they bought it. Was literally falling apart right in front of our eyes. It was actually sinking. Only the fireplace in the center was holding it in place. They bought it and had to rebuild the foundation and lift everything up. It's been years, and they're still working on it. From what I can see and know of them, it's been a labor of love for them."

I looked at the house while he continued, admiring the unassuming design. It was a simple square. The front door had a glass center, allowing for a clear view through to the back. A staircase on the left led upstairs, a hallway led straight back, and the main living space appeared to be on the right. "It's beautiful." I crouched down and scratched my dog's head. "We could live in a place like this, couldn't we, Agatha?"

Agatha glanced up at me with her giant, bulbous eyes. Her upper lip was caught on her top teeth. It looked like a grimace, but I called it a smile. An old home full of history and charm was exactly the type of place I envisioned myself in. Someday. My years in Austin, Texas, and the derailment of my marriage had taken a mental and financial toll. I'd been saving, but I wasn't quite there. Yet.

For now I'd just have to dream.

"So the Rabels fixed a house that was falling apart. I don't get what the problem is."

"Meet the Mastersons," he said, and he looked pointedly at the house next door to the Rabels'.

"But why? The renovations have only made the Rabels' house better, right? They'd rather have an eyesore?"

My dad cupped one hand over his eyes to block the sun. "That's logical, Ivy. Too bad the Mastersons aren't subject to using logic. They're . . . How should I put this? They have a few screws loose. They cause a lot of trouble for the city, always complaining and issuing ultimatums."

We stood side by side for another minute, and then turned to head back to my Dad's Silverado just as the door to the house behind us opened and an elderly woman stepped onto the porch. "Hallo!" she called. Her voice was surprisingly robust. Or maybe I was just expecting a halting, wavering sound, given the snow white of her hair and the map of wrinkles on her face.

My dad lifted his hand in greeting. "Afternoon, Mrs. Branford. You're looking lovely today."

She dismissed his comment with a wave of her hand, but she gave an embarrassed smile, and the thin skin of her cheeks tinged pink. "Oh, pshaw. Mr. Culpepper, how you do go on."

I had to agree with my dad. Mrs. Branford, in her lavender velour sweat suit, looked spritely and hip. She had to be eighty-five if she was a day, and although she held the handle of a cane in one hand, she wasn't leaning on it, which made me

51

wonder how much she really needed it.

"Mrs. Branford, do you remember my daughter, Ivy?" He put his hand on my back and ushered Agatha and me forward.

An equally good question was whether I remembered Mrs. Branford. Truthfully, I had a vague recollection of having met her once or twice, but my memories didn't go any deeper than that.

"Oh yes, of course, but you were a little girl. Or maybe a teenager last time I saw you."

I smiled, my mind pretty much blank. Santa Sofia was home to almost sixty-three thousand people, plus the barrage of tourists who descended throughout the year. The fact that Mrs. Branford and I had not crossed paths in the last twenty years or so wasn't terribly surprising.

Together my dad and I walked up the uneven brick pathway toward the elderly woman. Agatha brought up the rear. As we approached, I noticed the tilt of the porch. The slope was so pronounced that if I dropped a ball on one end, it would roll right to the other end, gathering speed as it went.

"Nice to meet you . . . or see you again, I guess, ma'am," I said.

She looked at me with a twinkle in her

eye and said, "Enough of the ma'am stuff. You just call me Penny. I taught school for a million years, but not anymore. My days of ma'am are long gone." She paused, taking in my hair, my eyes, my face. "You are the spitting image of your mother," she said.

Speechlessness was not usually one of my traits, but at this moment I could, quite literally, not think of anything to say. My mind felt slack. It was not that I hadn't heard the sentiment before. I knew I looked like my mom, and I treasured that. But somehow Penny Branford expressing it cut something loose inside me.

My dad came to the rescue. He cleared his throat and ran his fingers over his mustache. "She got all of Anna's best qualities," he said. I didn't think most people would be able to detect it, but I heard the faint quiver in his voice. It had been nearly six months since my mom had died, and my dad was stoic, but the veneer cracked every now and then. This was one of those moments.

I was stoic, too. Most of the time, anyway. I got that from my dad. He didn't cry, and neither did I. Losing Mom had left a hole in both of our hearts, but we stuffed the empty space with bread and music and walks in the historic district, but deep down nothing could really shore up the hollow-ness we both felt. So, like I said, I was a tough cookie, managing my emotions on an expert level so that nobody would even know I'd lost my mom, who'd also been my best friend. But this elderly woman . . . this Mrs. Penny Branford . . . Her eight simple words had sliced into me like a blade, opening my grief like an old wound until the ache and sorrow spilled out like sand from an overturned bucket.

"How did you know my mother?" I asked, my voice far more shaky than my dad's had been.

Mrs. Branford lifted her cane and pointed it at me. "How did I know her? Owen, does she know nothing?" My dad just shrugged, and she continued. "I taught your mother when she was knee high to a grasshopper, and when she went on to become a teacher herself? Why, I took that as a personal compliment." She pressed one gnarled hand against her chest. "I am entirely sure that I am the reason she went into education, you see."

"What grade did you teach?" I asked, the hole inside me growing wider, a craving for information taking over. If I were pregnant, surely I'd be wanting pickles and ice cream, the feeling was that strong.

"Ha. What grade *didn't* I teach? That would be a better question, I reckon. But what you're really asking is what grade did I teach when your mother was a girl. Am I right about that?"

I gave a little laugh. "Yes, ma'am, er, Mrs. Branford, you are."

"Polite young woman," she said, nodding with approval. She turned to my dad. "You and Anna did good with this one. Oh, don't get me wrong. Billy's a fine young man, too, but a sweet and polite young woman is a treasure. Anna's smiling down this very minute. Of that I'm sure."

My smile faltered as each of her words fell over me like a blanket. I wasn't sure if I felt stifled or comforted that this old woman, this Mrs. Branford, praised my parents' raising of me and felt my mother was watching down on me. I crossed my arms, letting my right hand spread on my chest, as if it were pressing my beating heart back into submission. Mrs. Branford had stirred up emotions I'd successfully kept at bay, and I wasn't sure I was ready to face them yet. The six months my mom had been gone felt like an eternity in some ways, but in others it felt as if it had been mere seconds, and I still couldn't make sense of a world without her in it.

"Your mother was beautiful. You look just like her. More importantly, she was the top student in my tenth grade honors English class," Mrs. Branford said. "I convinced her to join the newspaper staff, which, of course, she did, and she went on to be the best staff photographer we had, and during her senior year, she was editor in chief. She could have been an investigative reporter, you know, as she was that good. A nose like a blood-hound's, I'd venture to say."

"I can't picture her as a sixteen-year-old." My voice got a little dreamy, as I was trying to imagine her running around the high school, taking pictures, her ginger hair pulled up into a ponytail, her green eyes clear and excited, her skin freckled and fair. Sensing the emotion coursing through me, Agatha rubbed against my leg. "She was beautiful," people said every time they told me I looked just like her. I had never internalized that sentence quite the way I had when Penny Branford said it.

"She was smart as a whip and as strong willed a young woman as you'd ever meet. Girls from her generation, why, they had the good fortune of growing up after the sexual revolution, you know. Women's equality had a good foothold, and she took advantage of it. Went to college. First in her family, if I remember correctly."

"That's right," my dad said. I could tell he was choked up. His eyes glistened, and his chin quivered slightly. This was a conversation I knew he wanted to have. If he didn't, he'd have already made up some excuse and we'd have been out of here. But wanting to hear what Mrs. Branford had to say didn't mean it was easy. I knew he felt the loss just as keenly as I did. More so. They'd shared a life for almost forty years. "She wasn't supposed to go first," my dad had told me through his tears after she died. "She wasn't supposed to go first."

"Now you," Mrs. Branford said, pointing her cane directly at me. "You went to college, right? Your mother told me as much, but with this old mind, I'm not sure if I'm remembering that right."

"Yes, ma'am, that's right. University of Texas in Austin, but I'm back home now."

"Penny," she scolded, and I felt myself blush.

"Penny." I said the name, but it felt wrong. Presumptuous. Intimate. This woman had life experience. Wisdom. I needed the formality of her surname. She was Mrs. Branford, plain and simple.

"And what are you doing now that you're back in Santa Sofia? Because let me tell you something. It doesn't do you a whip of good to come back here and wallow in your sorrow. Your mother would not have wanted that. Would she have, Owen?" She dropped the end of her cane back to the ground, the rubber-cupped base making a loud thump on the porch, and looked at my dad.

"No. Mrs. Branford, you have that exactly right. She wouldn't want any of us to wallow." He wrapped his arm around me and pulled me next to him. "But I'm awful glad to have Ivy home, even if it is because Anna's gone from us now."

His voice quavered, sinking into the deepest part of me, and just like that, a tear dislodged from where it had been tucked away for half a year. It fell down my cheek, a lone symbol of the love I would always have for my mom and of the sadness that seeped through me.

"What's going on with the Rabels' house, Mrs. Branford?" My dad's change of subject was the opposite of subtle, but it worked, and I squeezed his hand. Our emotions were raw and on the surface, and we'd both had enough for today.

Mrs. Branford turned her body slowly, like a music box dancer whose tune was coming to a halt, until she faced the yellow house under construction across the street. "Nothing's changed, Owen. As long as that Buck Masterson is next door, the Rabels are going to suffer. He's done it to everyone on the street, one by one by one."

"Done what?" I asked, curious about the historic district gossip and politics.

"Buck Masterson is a piece of work," Mrs. Branford said. "Think of him like a virus, slowly infiltrating until he takes hold and knocks you flat on your back. He's alienated most of the people of the neighborhood with his reports to the city. His own house is a mess, but he holds everyone else to some impossible standard, proclaiming himself to be the king of the street. The ones he hasn't alienated are just like him. Oh, he starts out as Mr. Jovial, all peaches and cream. But underneath that smile — and it's a smarmy smile, if you ask me — there's arsenic. Goes with all that old lace in that eyesore of a house of his. Ha! Arsenic and old lace. That about sums it up."

My dad and I turned to look at the Mastersons' house, and I found myself agreeing with Mrs. Branford's assessment. It *was* a bit of an eyesore. Old, yes. But well kept and appealing? Not so much. The faded pink color looked like watered-down Pepto-Bismol. The paint was peeling along the windowsills, and scaffolding balanced precariously on the upper-story roofline. From the looks of it, the Mastersons complaining about the Rabels' renovation was definitely irony at its finest.

I looked up and down the street. The sunlight beamed down on the old historic houses. No cars passed by, and the green canopies of trees rustled in the light breeze. I was struck by what it must have been like to live here when the street was young and new. This was the type of street I wanted to live on. Maybe even *this* street specifically. It was the place I belonged.

"I hear you were at the bread shop when Jackie Makers died," Mrs. Branford said. She clearly wasn't one to beat around the bush. I liked that about her and immediately thought that Olaya Solis and Penny Branford needed to meet. They were two peas in a pod.

"I was," I said, nodding my confirmation.

"I heard it was" — she lowered her voice to an ominous whisper — "murder."

"That's what I heard, too." I looked over my shoulder, as if someone might be there listening. Someone like the murderer.

Next to me, Agatha pulled on her leash. She growled, recoiled, and then let out a high-pitched bark. She scooted back slightly, drew in a hoarse breath, then let loose a barrage of barks aimed at the street.

"Speak of the devil," Mrs. Branford said, notching her chin in the direction of Agatha's attention. I turned all the way around and saw a square-faced, stocky man standing in the middle of his yard, blatantly staring at us.

Penny Branford raised her lavender velour arm and waved. "Afternoon, Buck," she said over Agatha's yowling.

His upper lip flared in what I imagined he thought was a smile. He flipped a hand up in the barest semblance of a wave before turning and disappearing around the side of his pale pink house.

Mrs. Branford grimaced as she looked back at me and lowered her voice. "I don't know how," she said, "but *he* probably did it. *He* probably killed that poor woman."

My dad and I both stared at her. "Do you really think so?" I asked her.

Mrs. Branford tapped her cane on her slanted porch. "Most definitely," she said. "I think it is quite possible. Probable even. Quite probable."

CHAPTER FIVE

Jackie Makers's funeral took place a few days later at Liberty Methodist Church, which was down the street from the bakery and catty-corner to the old antique mini-mall. The pews were filled. Tears streamed down faces. Tissues dabbed eyes. Low sobs filled the sanctuary. It was an all too familiar scene, and one that I didn't relish reliving. But I'd felt obligated to come given that I was one of the last few people to see her alive.

"She was born and bred here," Olaya said through her own swallowed sorrow. She looked at the townspeople all around us and pointed out folks, as if she were introducing me to the who's who of Santa Sofia. My dad sat in one of the back pews. In the very front and on the opposite side of the church were Consuelo and Martina. "That's Jasmine next to Martina," Olaya said. All I could see was a close crop of black hair and a long, elegant neck with skin the color of a latte, warm and rich. "She is — was — Jackie's daughter."

Jasmine was clearly a mix of her mother's fair white skin and her father's presumably black skin. When she turned, I caught a glimpse of her profile. She was beautiful, with a refined nose and high and defined cheekbones. From the way Olaya and her sisters had reacted to the phone call Jackie had taken from her, I'd thought she was a teenager, but now, looking at her, I placed her in her early to mid-twenties. She was one of those lucky women who would age well, with beautiful, clear skin that would keep her looking young.

"They were talking on the phone during the class," I recalled, not mentioning that the conversation had seemed less than amiable.

Olaya pursed her lips. Her eyes were red rimmed, and the tip of her nose was chapped. She had cried herself out and now seemed determined to focus on anything but her grief. "They've had a strained relationship for a while now. More than a year. Jackie and I were good friends. Best friends, even. But she had not been telling me everything lately. She would never say anything against Jasmine, just that things were not good."

A stab of sorrow for Jasmine sliced my chest. No matter what their issues were about, I knew from experience that she'd never forget her last conversation with her mother. If she was anything like me, it would haunt her for the rest of her life. The last conversation I'd had with my mom wasn't bad or drama filled. On the contrary, it was banal. Ordinary. Boring, even. It had been a normal conversation, just like the one we'd had every week since I'd moved away from Santa Sofia. I'd played the last conversation over and over and over, wishing I'd been sweeter, or that I'd apologized for the teenage years. Or that I'd told her I loved her and that she was my best friend.

But I'd said none of those things, and it was a huge regret.

"Have you talked to her?" I asked Olaya.

"To Jasmine?" She shook her head. "She won't take my calls."

Before I could ask her why she thought Jackie's daughter wasn't responding, Olaya pointed to a man I recognized. "That's Randy Russell."

I'd never be able to erase Randy Russell's face from my memory. It was seared there, right alongside Miguel Baptista's, although for different reasons. "He's the one Miguel was trying to talk down the day Jackie . . . died."

She acknowledged the connection with the faintest nod and then moved on to the man next to the ruddy-cheeked Randy. He was black, his head was bald, and his build lean and muscular. "That's his business partner, Augustus Makers. They own the antique mini-mall across from the bread shop. Jackie and Gus were married for twenty-five years or so. They divorced about a year ago now. In case you haven't noticed," she added wryly, "Santa Sofia is like a soap opera. Everybody is connected to everybody."

I remembered that about the town where I'd grown up. The idea that it takes a village had taken root here long before Hillary Clinton wrote a book about it. Everyone was in everyone else's business. That was just the way it was. My mom had taken the idea to heart. As a teacher, she'd been involved in all her students' lives. As a kid, I'd been oblivious, but now I saw the benefit — and the detriment — of being too connected with your neighbors and townsfolk.

"What were Randy and Miguel fighting about the other night? Why was he even there?" I followed the first two questions with another. "I think he should be in jail, don't you?"

"Randy is just a hothead," she said, as if that explained and excused everything.

"But what was the whole thing about?" I pressed.

So far, Olaya had been pretty forthcoming, but this time she lifted her shoulders dismissively and her voice lowered. "I do not pretend to know what goes on in Randy's head. We are not exactly on good terms."

I let my voice match hers. "Why not? What happened between you?"

She looked over her shoulder, the silver spikes in her hair catching the light in the church. She dropped her voice a smidge more. "Randy is a . . . What is the word? A bodybusy?"

I grinned. "A busybody."

"Right. Yes. A busybody. He is in everybody's business, when none of it concerns him. Yeast of Eden is a strong business. Many tourists. Many local customers. A good reputation. The antique mini-mall, on the other hand, is hit and miss. People, especially the tourists, ask me about it when they are in the bread shop. 'Should I stop by? Do they have authentic antiques? Is it good quality?' I am always honest. I tell them that if they have time to poke around and search through the rubbish, then it is certainly worth a visit. It is consignment, so I cannot speak to the authenticity or quality of anything there. That is the truth, and that is what I say."

"And Randy got wind of that?"

"He's convinced it is a personal vendetta I have against him, which could not be further from the truth."

A thought struck me suddenly, and I drew in a sharp breath. "That night, when he was in the back parking lot, was he there to see you? Is he . . . Oh my God, Olaya. Is he off the rails? Had he come to threaten you with that billy club?"

A look of utter disbelief crossed her face. "No. No," she repeated firmly. She sounded convinced, but she trained her eyes on Randy Russell, sitting in the pews, and nodded once. "And yet . . ."

He must have felt the intensity of her stare, because he turned around in his seat, his gaze met hers, and an electric charge seemed to spark between them. And not a smoldering, romantic one. No, this was more like a battle of wills, with one powerful superhero vying for power over another.

She didn't break her gaze with him as she spoke to me. "What had he been planning?" she mused.

My question exactly. That antique club

he'd been wielding came to mind again, and my first thought was, Thank God he hadn't seen Olaya. But it was my second thought that made me pause. Thank God Miguel Baptista had been passing by to stop Randy Russell from inflicting harm on anyone.

With my peripheral vision, I saw a hand come down on Olaya's shoulder. At the same time a man said, "Ms. Solis?"

The current connecting Olaya and Randy Russell was severed as Olaya jumped and turned around. I turned, too, and, speak of the devil, there stood Miguel Baptista.

"Miguel," she said. *"Cómo estás?"*

"Bien, señora. Y tu?"

"Así así," she said, waggling one hand to show how she was feeling.

He hadn't looked at me yet, and I took a step backward to avoid an awkward encounter and let him say whatever it was he needed to tell Olaya, but, damn him, he was a gentleman. Slowly, a polite and slightly crooked smile graced his face. He always had been chivalrous, even back in high school. He moved to the side as he looked at me; he hesitated, as if working to place my familiar face. Something in his expression changed, his smile dropped, and his face seemed to tighten.

"Ivy?"

My dad always said I showed every single emotion I was having on my face the moment I was feeling it. I tried hard to control it, but I was 100 percent sure that I was not successful at masking anything at that moment. "In the flesh." The response sounded far coyer than I'd wanted to, which I'd actually not wanted to sound at all. I uttered a curse under my breath before saying, "Miguel Baptista. It's been a long time."

Olaya cleared her throat, which broke Miguel's concentration. "You know each other?" She shot me a pointed look since she already knew that we did.

The left corner of Miguel's mouth quirked up into grin. "Oh, we know each other, Ms. Solis. Very well, in fact."

The way he said them made the words sound almost ominous. It wasn't as if we shared some dark, secret past, but we did *have* a past. I couldn't get a read on what he meant by his tone or what he thought. His expression was almost amused, although his leaving me the split second he'd graduated from high school, and his subsequent years in the military, were anything but amusing to me. He'd been my first real love . . . and my first utter heartbreak. And here he was, grinning at me as if it had all been one big joke to him.

"Oh yes, we know each other," I agreed. "Miguel walked out of Santa Sofia without a backward glance, if I remember correctly. And look, here you are, back again. Guess escaping wasn't all it was cracked up to be." I regretted the contemptuous tone of the comment the moment it left my lips, given what Emmaline had told me about his father passing and Miguel returning to help his mother with their restaurant. Still, he deserved my anger. He had left me high and dry, after all.

"Guess I realized what a great town Santa Sofia is. Something I couldn't appreciate when I was eighteen years old."

"Humph," I uttered under my breath, but it came out louder than I'd intended.

"Santa Sofia isn't the only thing I didn't appreciate," he said, but before I could even process what he'd said and fully wonder if he was referring to me . . . or us . . . he turned back to Olaya. "Ma'am, I haven't had a chance to talk to you about the other night. The sheriff isn't pressing charges against Randy. That being said, I think you need to steer clear of him."

"I always do," she said.

"What does he have against Olaya?" I asked, wanting to dig a little deeper. Mrs. Branford's claim about my mother being a

70

bloodhound crossed my mind. Like her, I always wanted to ferret out the truth. After the hit-and-run that had caused my mom's death, I had gone back to the scene, had looked for skid marks, thinking I could somehow match them to the culprit's tires. I'd been determined to bring her cowardly killer to justice. When there hadn't been any marks on the pavement, I was flummoxed. Had the driver not even bothered to slow down? Had he not seen her, or had he thought he could miss her by speeding up instead of stopping? As much as I'd searched for the truth, I couldn't get any closer to it. There were no leads, and so I'd pushed my questions about how the accident had happened aside and focused on helping my dad get through his grief.

I might never understand the details of my mother's death, but I could dig a little and figure out why Randy Russell had been in the back parking lot of Yeast of Eden.

Miguel had turned to me as I spoke, but now he looked back at Olaya. "No idea."

"He is a business rival, nothing more," Olaya said.

"He looked suspicious to me," Miguel said. "I saw him in the parking lot. Saw the club in his hand. And when I asked him what he was doing, he got pretty belligerent, said it was none of my business —"

"I know very well how he can be," Olaya said.

"I talked him down, and then you all found Ms. Makers in her car." He gave a weighty pause and then said, "Just be careful."

Olaya nodded solemnly. We stood there in an awkward silence for a few seconds. I didn't know what I might have said to Miguel if I'd had the chance, but the pastor stepped to the altar and the service began. Coming face-to-face with my past would have to wait. A look passed between us before Miguel walked away and took a seat on the left side of the church. Olaya took my hand and pulled me to the opposite side of the church.

"What is your story with him?" she whispered as soon as we were seated.

I kept my eyes on the pastor but shrugged. "No story."

She looked at me skeptically, her eyes bright with tears again. "That I do not believe. I loved a man once." Her voice became melancholy. "I thought James was the love of my life, but there were too many years between us."

I tried to mask the surprise on my face. I didn't know why Olaya was opening up to me, but it proved that she felt the same connection to me that I felt to her. My heart swelled just a little bit. "What do you mean? He was older than you?"

"Yes. By fifteen years. I didn't care, but he was married, and, well, he loved his wife. He was a rule follower. I could never fault him for that, although I wish things had turned out differently."

"I'm sorry," I said as I tried to wrap my head around the fact that Olaya had loved a married man. I tried to lighten the situation. "Love. Who needs it?"

She grimaced and said, "You do. There's nothing more important. You feel it. You need it. You just don't want to admit it to yourself."

This gave me pause. Just like my mom, Olaya seemed to have a sixth sense about me. Given that I hardly knew her, I couldn't imagine how she had her pulse on my history and my emotions. But I realized in that moment that it wasn't worth trying to hide anything from her. I knew she'd already figured me out . . . and I hadn't even figured me out. "Miguel and I were high school sweethearts," I said, "but, you know, he left. That about sums it up."

"That I also do not believe. There has to be more to the story. You thought he was the one —"

I nodded, just once. "But he didn't," I said, finishing her sentence.

She glanced at Miguel, then at me. "I'm not so sure about that, *m'ija,*" she said, squeezing my hand. "Sometimes the one comes around again, and you have a second chance together."

My view of Miguel was of the back of his head. He looked straight ahead, listening to the pastor delivering the sermon for Jackie's funeral. Whatever Olaya had seen between us in the brief few minutes we'd spoken, I couldn't say, but all I saw was our past, and it felt just like the bridge Emmaline had said was uncrossable between her and Billy. Any connection Miguel and I had had was long gone.

I felt the unmistakable sensation of someone's eyes on me. My attention shifted and was drawn to the man next to Miguel. A chill ran down my spine. Randy Russell was looking over his shoulder, but not at me. He was staring menacingly at Olaya.

CHAPTER SIX

I stood in the *cocina* at Yeast of Eden, ready for my second baking lesson. Olaya had postponed for a week after Jackie Makers's death, and she still didn't look ready to launch into class again. She'd wanted to cancel altogether, but I'd talked her out of it. "You're always going to miss Jackie," I'd told her, "but doing normal activities is the best thing you can do. Plus, remember you told me I belonged here. That you'd teach me the art of baking bread."

"Keep busy," she'd said in response, but her voice had been flat.

"Yes, keep busy." It was another thing I knew from experience. Going about everyday activities was the only thing that had kept me sane after my mom died. Being idle meant only that I had too much time to think, and thinking was the one thing I'd wanted not to do at the time.

Olaya had agreed, but her heart wasn't in

it. If only she could eat a slice of some magical bread to mend her broken heart. But with the depth of her grief, I suspected it didn't work that way. In fact, I hoped that her sadness wasn't instead seeping into the bread she made daily, only to be passed along to her patrons.

"Do not worry," she said, as if she'd just read my mind. "Our bread is as pure as it ever was."

"What are we baking?" Sally asked.

Last time there had been a chalkboard with the word *Conchas* written in beautiful cursive, colorful drawings of the sweet breads alongside. Today the chalkboard was blank. Olaya walked into the bakery's kitchen. She stopped at the chalkboard, her back to us, and wrote on the black surface with a practiced hand. A minute later she turned around and revealed the day's task: fig and almond loaf. She'd also sketched a picture of a bâtard-shaped loaf of bread, its markings crisscrossed on the top.

"Bread is healing," she said, and a sliver of relief wove through me. She was turning to what she knew, to the comfort of her baking. Yes, she was grieving, as I was, but we'd both get through it.

"I can attest to that," a voice said.

We all turned to see who had spoken. My

jaw dropped. Penny Branford, dressed in a coral velour sweat suit just like the lavender one she'd been wearing the first time I met her sashayed right into the kitchen, cane swinging, a lightness in her step. On her feet were snazzy white leather sneakers, and her snowy hair was wound into tight curls on her head. I couldn't help but smile. She was a sight to see, and I knew she was a force to be reckoned with.

As my smile lit up, Olaya's dulled. "Can I help you?" Her voice was almost accusatory.

If Mrs. Branford noticed the lack of warmth in Olaya's welcome, she didn't let on. "I'm here to bake bread. Like you said, it's healing. It's one of the things that keeps me so young and spritely." The twinkle in her eyes seemed to have extra glow going on, and I wondered if she had a personal testimonial about the healing powers Olaya had mentioned.

Despite Mrs. Branford's enthusiasm, something about Olaya's expression made me think she might turn the spritely woman away. I surged forward and took Mrs. Branford's free hand in mine. "You can be at the station next to me," I said, thankful that it wasn't the area Jackie Makers had used during the first class. I felt, as I think Olaya did, that that space needed to remain a tribute to Jackie, which meant no other baker should use it. At least for the time being.

Olaya frowned, but a moment later the grimace vanished as she got the materials ready for Mrs. Branford to join the class. "Here you go," she said, holding out a floral apron with layers of ruffles, a little smirk on her face. "You definitely want to protect that lovely sweat suit."

I flinched at the sarcasm coming from Olaya. I'd never heard that from her. Her reaction to Penny Branford's entrance had raised a red flag, but now I knew. There was some bad blood between these two. I'd bet my life on it.

Mrs. Branford's expression tightened as she started to reach for the apron, but then she dropped her hand, gave a weighty pause, then up and marched right past Olaya. She bent to look in the drawer the apron had come from. Ten seconds later she straightened up, a triumphant smile on her face and a bright blue half apron in her hand. No frills. No ruffles. But stylishly cut and sewn, and definitely more her style than the one Olaya had initially proffered.

As Penny Branford's smile grew, Olaya's faded. This, I thought, was going to be interesting.

Olaya flung her shoulders back, stood up straighter, and headed to her workstation. I could tell that she was ready to move on and stop letting whatever existed between her and Mrs. Branford interrupt her class. "As I was saying," she said, her voice crisp, "bread is healing. Anyone who doubts it has not experienced authentic bread made by hands with the power to heal."

As if we'd been prompted by her words, all of us class members, including Penny Branford in her newly donned apron, studied our own hands, flipping them over to look at the palms, then back to contemplate the backs. My hands looked ordinary, and I doubted that I'd ever get to the point where they had the power to heal. I did, however, notice a few more wrinkles than I'd had the last time I'd taken a close look.

While I was pretty sure I'd never be a bread-making healer right out of the gate, an hour later I was also positive I'd never be a professional bread maker. We'd dusted a jelly-roll pan with cornmeal, had snipped the stems from a cup of Calimyrna figs and let them steep in boiling water, had let the yeast froth in warm water, had mixed the dough and let it rest, and had added un-blanched almonds and chopped figs to the mixture. Now we were letting the dough rise in a covered bowl. None of it was particularly difficult, but the stress of exact measurements and hoping the mixture would turn into a delectable bread had worn me out. The process of baking didn't seem to come naturally to me.

Despite the conflict between my perfectionist nature and my baking struggles, I was, I admit, excited for the outcome. We went through the steps to turn the dough, a bowl of water nearby to keep the sticky mess off our hands.

"Why can't we just knead it?" Sally asked. Working side by side for two sessions now had allowed me to discover something about each of the women in the class. Sally was on the whiny side. I imagined her with her siblings, one of them catching her with an arm over her shoulders, giving her a noogie, and her struggling and saying in her best ten-year-old whine, "Stooop. Dooon't."

"We allow the dough to develop as it ferments," Olaya said. She demonstrated the process of grabbing the underside of the dough, stretching it up, and folding it back over the rest of the dough. We dipped our hands in the water after each turn. Thirty minutes later, the dough had started to puff.

"Fermentation!" Olaya's giddy expression

was contagious as each of us noticed our own bowl of dough rising with air. We all looked around at each other. Martina and Consuelo nodded at each other, holding out their bowls to show the other. They each shot a glance at Jackie's empty workstation, a wash of sadness skimming both of their faces. The vacant spot in the kitchen left a heavy feeling of darkness hanging over the space.

Jolie, with her perfectly straight black hair, which was once again pulled back into a carelessly perfect ponytail, stared at her bowl, her mouth downturned. "Mine isn't doing that puffy thing. It looks flat."

Olaya strode over and stood by Jolie's side, and the two of them studied the failed almond and fig dough. After a moment, she raised her gaze to Jolie's and asked, "Did you add the yeast?"

Jolie rolled her eyes. "Of course I did," she said, her tone calling Olaya out for asking such a ridiculous question.

Olaya ignored the attitude and focused only on the bread. "No, I am quite certain you did not, actually."

"But I did." She held up the squat brown jar of yeast. "It's right he —" she started to say, but she stopped when Olaya took the jar right from her hands.

81

"See this depression in the lid?" Olaya ran her finger over the top. I looked at my jar of yeast, and from the corners of my eyes, I saw the other women in the kitchen do the same, each of them feeling the top of the lid.

"This is still sealed," Olaya said. "Once it's opened, this little button area is raised."

"Is your dough rising, Ivy?" Olaya asked me.

The depression in the yeast jar was not there, and my dough was fluffy. It was coated with a fine layer of tiny air bubbles. Yeast successfully added. "Rising," I confirmed.

One by one, Olaya checked each of the bakers' doughs, nodding as she looked and poked and sniffed at each station. As she approached Mrs. Branford, her expression once again tightened. "I didn't know you still baked, Penelope."

"Once you learn, you never forget. I'm eighty-six years old, but I'm not senile. Or incompetent."

"If you say so," Olaya said with a smirk. "Did your dough rise?"

"Like the sun every morning," Mrs. Branford said. She pulled her bowl forward so Olaya could see.

Olaya frowned "So it did." I got the feeling Olaya would have grinned happily if Mrs. Branford's dough had been a fail. As it was, she said, "Ladies, entertain yourselves for a moment. We have a bread emergency." She glanced at what had been Jackie Makers's workstation, a veil of sadness clouding her face. I saw her steel herself against her emotions, pushing away her grief, as she turned back to Jolie and they began the recipe from the beginning.

"Well," Mrs. Branford huffed, "this is going to take longer than a moment."

I'd thought that Olaya Solis and Penny Branford would get along, that they were two peas in a pod — both strong, smart, assertive, and accomplished. But maybe they were too much alike, because a friendship between them clearly wasn't going to happen. They had some history, these two. The bad blood I'd sensed was simmering just below the surface, and I wanted to know more.

"How do you know Olaya?" I asked.

Mrs. Branford wasn't biting. At least not at this moment. "That, my dear, is a story for another time."

"I'm holding you to that," I said, pressing. "When?"

Mrs. Branford laughed, her already wrinkled face compressing into a crisscrossed map of lines. She considered me for a moment, her hand over her chin, her fingers on one side of her mouth, tapping. "Hmmm. I do believe I could use a bit of help around the house."

I cracked a smile. "Do you, now?"

"Those cupboards in my kitchen are abnormally tall." She looked me up and down. "And you're, well, perhaps not abnormally so, but you are also tall."

I was a mere five feet eight, but that was definitely taller than her five feet five inches or so. I went with it. "I guess I am."

"Tomorrow morning, then. Eight o'clock. Don't be late, my dear."

"I wouldn't dream of it," I said, liking Mrs. Branford more and more with each passing second.

Sally strode toward us, drying her hands on a kelly-green dish towel. "Don't be late for what?"

Mrs. Branford grinned. "This lovely girl is going to help organize my kitchen tomorrow."

Judging by the frown on her face, Sally didn't seem to think that sorting through Mrs. Branford's dishes and pans sounded all that appealing.

"I take it you don't want to come along and help?" I said with a laugh, already knowing she'd decline.

"Come along where?" This time it was Becky who'd come over.

"Cleaning house," Sally said. "Not something I like to do in my own place, let alone in someone else's."

"You leave your kitchen how you like it, but you have to clean up *here,*" Olaya announced, a glint in her eyes. She'd been busy with Jolie, but she was aware of absolutely everything in her kitchen. Eyes in the back of her head and all that.

A blush of pink spread from Sally's neck to her cheeks. "Oh, of course!"

Olaya winked at her, and then she turned her attention to Mrs. Branford and her expression hardened. "Penelope, it's just like you to put this poor girl to work."

"Nonsense," Mrs. Branford said. "Ivy is not a *poor* girl. She's tough, just like her mother was."

"I can hear you, you know," I said, "and I wouldn't say I'm a 'girl.' "

"I'm knocking on eighty-seven's door, my dear. You can't be more than what? Thirty-five —"

"Thirty-six," I said, correcting her. Exactly fifty years her junior, which was crazy to think about. She had instantly become my role model. I wanted to *be* her in fifty years.

85

"A spring chicken," Penny Branford said, a twinkle in her eye that made her seem more like the spritely young thing she was describing me as.

"I'm happy to help sort the kitchen. I'll bring my camera, too," I said. The words came unexpectedly, but the second I spoke them, I knew I wanted nothing more than to photograph the street I'd instantly fallen in love with the moment I walked the sidewalks there. Maybe my creative voice wasn't entirely gone. "I want to take some pictures of the houses on Maple."

Mrs. Branford nodded sagely. "There is never a dull moment on Maple Street."

I suspected there was never a dull moment with Penelope Branford. "Tell me more."

This time, instead of twinkling, Mrs. Branford's eyes became hooded. "That Buck Masterson, you know, the one who lives across the street from me? He thinks he's a one-man neighborhood watch."

Ah, the intrusive Buck Masterson. I wondered if he was the only thing "going on" on Maple Street. He rubbed Mrs. Branford the wrong way — there was no doubt about that — but was her perspective entirely reliable? "Right. You said he keeps an eye on the whole street."

"A self-appointed eye, and that does not

give him a green light to go into people's houses. He calls it entitlement. I call it breaking and entering."

I stared. "Wait. He went into someone's house?"

"Oh yes," Mrs. Branford said. Her voice dropped to a whisper. "He's a sneaky one. Or at least he *thinks* he is. I'm sure he thought no one was watching. But me? I. Am. *Always.* Watching. What else do I have to do, after all?"

Before I could ask whose house Mr. Masterson had snuck into, Olaya clapped her hands and brought us all back to attention. "We are nearly ready to bake bread," she announced.

We spent the next few minutes dividing our dough into two equal pieces; rounding each piece by pushing against the bottom with the sides of our hands, our palms facing up; working and shaping our fermented dough into spheres; covering the spheres and allowing them to rest, rise, and proof until they were 50 percent larger than when we'd started.

"The last step," Olaya said, "is to take your serrated knife and draw it across the center. Then make a second perpendicular slice. Not too deep, mind you. Just enough to mark it as the bread bakes."

We all followed her directions, brushed our loaves with water, and baked them for thirty minutes. By the time the loaves were lightly browned and cooked through, the kitchen and all our workstations, except for that of Jolie, who was behind in her process, were spotless and the kitchen smelled of freshly baked bread.

While Olaya and Jolie waited for her loaf to finish up, the rest of us brushed our baked loaves with melted butter and took our masterpieces home. I felt a throb of sorrow in the pit of my stomach. Though she was trying to hide it, I could feel Olaya's sadness, and Jackie Makers's absence in the baking class was palpable, her empty station like a beacon re-announcing her death.

CHAPTER SEVEN

Bright and early the next morning, Agatha and I drove from my parents' house to Maple Street, purposely parking at the east end of the block so I could walk down the sidewalk and take pictures. I stopped at each house, Agatha on her harness and leash beside me, getting the full effect and studying the rooflines, the dormers, the porches, and the other details that made each one unique. The houses were each beautiful in their own way and gave the street its historic and distinct personality. Once again the longing to live on Maple Street hit me square between the eyes. I saw myself here, felt the pull of the history, wanting so much to be part of it.

I found myself following the light, the shadows, and focusing on pieces of each house: a window here, a cornice there. When I got back to my computer, I'd upload my shots and try to see them from an objective perspective. I was hoping I'd be able to recapture some of my creative voice right here in the historic district of Santa Sofia.

One house in particular struck me. It was a red Tudor-style home that drew me closer. It was crafted of old brick, had the traditional half-timber exterior, a steep gable, and a high-pitched roofline. The wavy-edge siding at the gable peaks was a deep red, a warm and welcoming color in my world. Pulling Agatha along beside me, I crossed the street to get a closer look, loving how the tall trees softened the fairy-tale gingerbread look of the house, noting the cobbled walkway up to the arched front door, and admiring the blush of color the flower beds brought to the home.

I sighed, and after another minute I made my way up the street toward Penelope Branford's Victorian. But as I walked, I kept looking over my shoulder at the Tudor. I tossed up a wish that one day I'd live in a place just as beautiful and filled with as much character as that house.

Fifteen minutes later I was ensconced in Mrs. Branford's kitchen, a cup of tea on the table in front of me. Agatha was lying by the side of my chair, a rawhide bone I'd brought along stabilized under her front paws. She licked and chewed loudly, but happily. Mrs. Branford's house looked like it had gone through a few careful renovations over the years; the interior was compartmentalized, with a wide center hallway in the entry, which had doors leading to a library, a den, the parlor, and the dining room. French doors separated the dining room and parlor, and another pass-through was situated between the dining room and the kitchen.

"This is a beautiful house," I commented, absorbing every detail of the kitchen. Parts of the room seemed to be original, while some, like the floors and countertops, had been remodeled. On the floor were black-and-white checkerboard tiles. Instead of a traditional tile backsplash, worn, nicked beadboard lined the walls, accenting the off-white, green-specked granite countertops. Rustic green ceramic tiles added a splash of vintage color behind the old off-white ceramic stove. The avocado-green refrigerator looked like it was from another era, but it was comforting, and when taken together, the entire room was as welcoming as pot roast on a cold, blustery day. "How long have you lived here?"

Mrs. Branford glanced up to the ceiling, her lips moving as she counted. "Let's see.

My grandparents built this house back in eighteen ninety-nine. My mother grew up here. My parents left it to me. Jimmy — that's my husband — we moved in here forty-two years ago."

"And Jimmy . . ." I felt a memory or a thought tug at the back of my mind, but I couldn't pull it out. I let the sentence hanging there.

Her voice became tinged with sadness. "I lost my Jimmy."

"I'm sorry."

She pressed her lips together and nodded. "It's been, oh, ten years now. It's true what they say. I miss him every day, but time heals. You'll heal, too, Ivy."

I knew she was right. My sorrow would lessen, and I'd be left with memories that would fill me with a melancholy joy. "I think you brought me here under false pretenses," I said. Not a dish seemed out of place, not a speck of food littered the counter, and Mrs. Branford didn't appear to need a bit of help with anything. I'd bet my life that she was the most self-sufficient, organized, and capable eighty-six-year-old woman on the planet. In fact, if she were pitted against any woman of any age, I'd lay odds on Penelope Branford.

She grinned sheepishly. "I wanted the

chance to talk to you. This seemed as good a ruse as any."

Other than meeting Mrs. Branford with my dad, I didn't remember ever laying eyes on her. I couldn't imagine what she'd want to talk with me about. Still, I felt nervous for some reason. "Oh?"

She patted the air. "Now, now. Don't panic."

"Is it about my mother?" That was the only thing we had in common . . . that I knew of, anyway. Any progress I'd made — or thought I'd made — in dealing with my grief was fleeting. Talking about my mom might be therapeutic at times, but it was also torture. At this moment, I was pretty sure the agony would outweigh any healing that might happen.

"No, dear. Your mother was a beautiful soul, but you knew her far better than I did. No, I have a . . . proposition for you."

The nerves gave way to relief. "What kind of proposition?"

"Pictures."

"Pictures," I repeated, not following.

"Photographs," she said, clarifying the matter.

She leaned forward, rested her elbows on the table. I tried not to focus on the tight curls of her snowy hair, but they were so

93

perfect that they drew my eye. Not only was she spry, but she was stylish, too. Just looking at her made me smile.

"I'm not as young as I used to be," she began, as if I wouldn't have discerned that tidbit on my own. I covered my smile as she continued. "I can see you agree. It's well established, in fact. An eighty-six-year-old woman is no longer in her salad days, even if she still feels like she's forty inside. You know, I used to say that I felt as if I were still twenty years old. Now I see what shenanigans so many twenty-year-olds are up to that I'm grateful I'm well beyond that. My forties, yes. Now, those were good years."

I couldn't help but take her perspective to heart. I was fast approaching my forties, so to hear that I was heading toward a great decade made me feel rather happy.

She continued. "Because I'm not in my forties anymore, however, I can't always do the things I'd like to do. Like take pictures. My hands aren't as steady as they used to be. Arthritis, you know. They ache and don't bend like they should." She held her hands out for me to see the trembling.

"That would make it hard to hold a camera," I agreed, "but what do you want to take pictures of?"

She lowered her voice to a whisper, as if someone might hear us. "The neighborhood," she said.

"I'm already doing that. Such beautiful houses here," I said.

"No! That's not what I mean." She practically jumped up from her chair, went to a drawer next to the refrigerator, and returned, holding a spiral-bound journal. The cover was pale green and adorned with butterflies. As she flipped through the book, I caught a glimpse of page after page after page of lists. Finally, she found the one she was looking for and turned the notebook for me to see.

"What's this?" I asked.

"Buck Masterson's comings and goings."

She stopped talking, letting the statement hang there between us.

I tamped down my surprise — and concern — that Mrs. Branford clearly spent too much time documenting her neighbor. Was she just a busybody with excess time on her hands, or had she observed something about Buck Masterson that had given rise to a legitimate concern? As I contemplated these possibilities, I skimmed the list, noting random events dating back six months.

12:03 p.m. Left house. Returned at 2:30

p.m. Historic district committee meeting. Buck led the attack against the Rabels' construction. Inciting.

8:21 a.m. Snuck into Jackie's backyard. Exited five minutes later.

3:55 p.m. Buck and Nanette sat on porch and stared at my house until 5:03 p.m. Stared. And never looked away.

The list went on and on. "You could be a private investigator," I said.

She patted the curls of her hair. "I have often thought the same thing, my dear. I might say that I missed my calling, but I loved teaching."

I looked back at the list. "They just sat and stared at your house?"

"For more than an hour. I don't think they even blinked."

"But why would they do that?"

She slapped the table with an open hand. "Exactly my question. I want you to help me figure it out. That man has no right snooping around other people's homes, causing trouble with the historic district, and trying to intimidate people. Luckily, I'm not so easily bullied."

"No, you're not, are you?"

"He's trouble, that Buck Masterson. I just need to prove it. And I need your help."

I sighed. "I'm not a private investigator, Mrs. Branford."

Her spine straightened. "If you're anything like your mother, you have a nose for it. Why, I remember when she was back in high school, she single-handedly uncovered a cheating ring among the students. This was before computers, mind you. Some of the students would write their notes and adhere them to a water bottle. The water acted like a magnifying glass, and no one was the wiser. It was quite a scandal when your mother broke the story."

I stared. I knew she had often nosed around to ferret out the truth of something, but my mom had never told me that story. I felt a mixture of gratefulness at learning something new about her and an odd emptiness that there were missing pieces to my mother's history, pieces that I didn't know about. Pieces I'd never know about. Knowing this about her sent my curiosity into overdrive, and a rogue thought entered my consciousness. My mother had died so suddenly, and the hit-and-run had some oddities about it. No skid marks, for example. And no witnesses. Maybe it wasn't an accident like we all thought. Was that possible?

I shook my head, dislodging the idea. Of course it wasn't possible. No one would want my mother dead.

"I can see it in your eyes. You're just like her," Mrs. Branford said. "You always get to the bottom of things, don't you?"

Her comment brought me back to Mrs. Branford's kitchen. I directed my gaze to the ceiling as I considered that question. Did I? "I guess so." I had, after all, deduced the affair my former husband had been having. He'd done a good job of hiding the evidence and operating on the down low. But secrets, I found, were meant to be discovered. An unfamiliar number on the cell phone bill, a lip gloss container on the floor of his car, late nights at work but no answer at the office when I'd called. Bit by bit, I'd pieced together the clues. And then I'd divorced his cheating ass.

"Buck Masterson is up to no good, Ivy, and I want to catch him in the act. I *will* catch him in the act."

"In the act of doing whatever it is he does —"

"Exactly."

"Like sitting on the porch and staring at your house?"

"Well, no. That wouldn't be very exciting, now, would it?" She leaned forward. "We need to do a stakeout and catch him breaking and entering."

98

"Breaking and entering?" This was sounding way out of my league. "Maybe we should call the police and let *them* know what he's doing. If he's breaking and entering, that *is* illegal. They'd be able to stop him. Arrest him. Something."

"He's come uninvited into my house, you know. Opened the door and waltzed right in, acting like we're old friends. He's intrusive, and it has to stop. He's got some nerve, don't you think? And, no, I don't want to go to the police. I'm perfectly capable of handling issues in my neighborhood."

Except she wasn't. She needed me to help her handle the issues in her neighborhood. And if I was being honest with myself, I was happy Penny Branford had come to me for assistance if it meant I could form a tenuous connection between myself and who my mother had been when she was a girl. Add to that that my mind was going to be more occupied than it had been in months, and I was sold, any danger in staking out Buck Masterson notwithstanding. Distraction was something I desperately needed.

"Now if Jimmy were alive, he'd have skinned Buck's hide."

The scraping of Agatha's teeth against her bone stopped, and she peered up, almost as if she'd understood and didn't like the idea of any hide being skinned.

Mrs. Branford continued. "He was a rule follower, my Jimmy. He might have teetered on the line once in a while, but he never crossed it. Buck Masterson would be thinking twice if Jimmy were still around."

At the mention of Jimmy's name, that inkling of a feeling came back. There was something . . . It hit me like a fifty-pound sack of flour. The bad blood between Penny Branford and Olaya Solis. The love of Olaya's life. Olaya had said he'd been a rule follower, just like Penny Branford's Jimmy. Jimmy and James. Could they be the same person?

The more I thought about, the more sense it made. Which led me to my next thought. Perhaps it wasn't so crazy to think I'd be able to catch Buck Masterson up to no good. Who knew? Maybe I'd even be able to figure out what had happened to Jackie Makers. After all, if I was right, I'd just identified the source of the feud between two women who otherwise would be great friends. I knew that in my heart. They were more alike than they probably realized.

I sat back, sipped my tea, and concocted a plan with Mrs. Branford to stake out Maple

Street to spy on Buck Masterson. It was turning into an interesting day.

CHAPTER EIGHT

Mrs. Branford waved to me from her front door. "Can't wait for tonight," she said, beaming.

"Six thirty. See you then."

I walked down the street, stopping to let Agatha take care of business and cleaning it up with a plastic doggy bag. I took a few pictures along the way. An old freestanding red gas pump caught my eye. It stood to the side of a detached garage. I walked as close as I dared. With the camera in my hand, I doubted I'd be accused of trespassing, but walking on someone else's property felt wrong. Even though I stayed as far back as I could, I was still halfway up the driveway. I hadn't brought my best telephoto lens, but I was able to zoom in enough to capture detail without compromising stability.

My cell phone ringing made me jump. Agatha yelped, and together we hightailed it to the sidewalk.

Olaya Solis's voice filled my ear. *"Dónde estás, m'ija?"*

I had a basic knowledge of Spanish, thanks to high school, college, and a childhood spent in California. "On Maple Street," I answered, smiling inside that Olaya didn't feel the need to make small talk or offer pleasantries. It was like we were family . . . or old friends. We were neither, but I had the feeling we'd get there sooner rather than later.

"Qué bueno! Great minds," she said.

"Oh?"

"I am also on Maple Street. Come join me."

I spun around, looking up and down the street, thinking she might materialize right in front of me. "You're here? Where? Why?" I asked.

"Aquí, Ivy, *aquí!"*

I heard her voice calling me and turned to follow the sound. Finally, I spotted her. She waved her hands over her head. "I am here!"

My jaw dropped. She stood on the front porch of the Tudor house I'd instantly fallen in love with just hours before. I checked the street for cars. The coast was clear, so I jogged across the street, Agatha keeping pace with me. "Is this your house?" I asked as I slowed to a walk on the cobbled path and joined her on the stone porch.

"No, no," she said. Her smile didn't reach her glassy eyes. "This is . . . was . . . Jackie's house."

I hadn't been expecting that, and a new wave of sadness washed over me. It was easy to see a person who'd died as simply gone. I hadn't even known Jackie Makers, and her horrible demise had shaken me. But at this moment, she became more to me than just a woman I'd briefly met who died. Looking around and into the house, I began crafting together the life she had lived. She'd picked out the furniture. She'd created this space. She'd had a daughter and friends and a job and enemies and people who felt hollow inside with the loss of her.

Jackie Makers suddenly became 1000 percent real to me, and I ached inside for Olaya. I knew what she was going through. I knew firsthand the emptiness she felt. I knew, and it made my own ache grow even stronger.

Olaya opened the door for me to follow her in, but I stopped, pointing to Agatha.

"What a sweet baby!" She crouched down and used the pads of her fingers to scratch Agatha's compact little head. Looking up at me, she asked, "Is she housebroken?"

"Completely." It had taken a good year or more for Agatha to realize that I wasn't going to abuse her. When she crossed that hurdle, she also figured out that outside was the place for pottying. It had been a tough year for both of us, but now I couldn't imagine my world without her.

"Come on, then," Olaya said, stepping aside for us to enter.

Olaya followed me and Agatha in. I gazed at the arched doorway as I passed through. I hadn't even seen the inside yet, but something about the house filled me with warmth and comfort.

"The police have finished their search," she said, answering the unspoken question in my mind as to why she was here. "Jasmine finally called. Said she wanted to start sorting through her mother's stuff and asked if I'd help."

"So here you are."

"Here I am." Her voice cracked with emotion, and her chin quivered. She swallowed hard. "It feels too soon. I cannot understand. She is gone, and Jasmine wants to forget."

"People grieve differently," I said, laying my hand on her arm in comfort. "Can I help?"

She let herself smile slightly. "Just what I

was hoping you would say."

"You're boxing things?"

"Jasmine wants to sell the house." She gave me a quick tour. The master bedroom had French doors leading to the immaculate backyard. Jackie had had a knack for gardening. Flowers bloomed in abundance, and it was more of an oasis than any backyard I'd ever seen. The room itself was a pale, warm yellow and had the same arches and architectural details as the front entry.

There were two other bedrooms, a living room, and a small informal family room off the kitchen. The garage, also off the kitchen, housed two cars.

"The police towed Jackie's car back here," Olaya said. "The other one is Jasmine's old one. There are a few dents. Some chipped paint. I guess we will get them fixed and sell them, also."

"What room are you starting with?" I asked as we came back in from the garage.

"The kitchen. Jackie loved to cook. I'm the baker, but if I brought her a chicken and some vegetables, she could whip up a gourmet meal." She ran her fingers under her damp eyes. "Chicken and dumplings. That was her specialty."

The kitchen had a brick arch over the stove, with a window behind it overlooking

106

the front yard. An island in the middle with bar stools gave it a homey look, and the pale yellow cupboards were the perfect complement to the honey-colored wood floors. An empty pink bakery box with cupcake remnants was open on the counter. Fruit flies buzzed around the rotting bananas and apples in a three-tiered rack. It was a beautiful kitchen.

"My mom loved to cook, but she always said we could and should hone our skills. 'There's nothing worse than growing old and growing lazy,' " I said, quoting her when a memory spirited into my consciousness. "She and my dad were taking lessons together. She had decided that he should finally learn to cook like a Food Network chef."

It was as if my mom had had a premonition, I realized. Maybe not that she was going to die, but that for whatever reason, my dad should learn to cook for himself.

Olaya's brows tugged together. "Did she? I wonder . . ."

I pushed the emotions of my mother's sixth sense away. "Wonder what?"

"Jackie ran a cooking school. Well Done. It's a little kitchen over on Bissonet Street. Is that where your mom and dad took their classes?"

Well Done. I repeated the name of the cooking school in my head. It didn't ring a bell, but then again my mother might never have mentioned the name of the actual business. "That would be a small world, wouldn't it?" Another way Olaya and I were connected, even if that particular thread was tenuous.

"I wouldn't be surprised. Jackie's was the best cooking school in Santa Sofia. There was competition for a while. What was that place called?" She tapped her chin with one finger, thinking. "Divine Cuisine, I think. Anyway, it went out of business, and Well Done had a corner on the market. Now I guess I'm it for cooking classes in town."

"Why did she take baking classes from you if she ran a school of her own?"

Olaya took a cookbook from one of the two black baker's rack shelves and flipped through it. It was based on the blog *Smitten Kitchen.* I'd read posts by Deb Perelman and drooled over the photos of her recipes. If Jackie had used all these cookbooks in her cooking school, no wonder it had been so successful.

Except, of course, that she'd been killed. Viciously murdered. Could her death have had anything to do with her school? I guessed there was no way to know the

108

answer to that.

It was so tragic that Santa Sofia had lost two successful, smart, and accomplished women in Jackie Makers and my mother, Anna Culpepper, in just six short months.

"When you think of chefs," Olaya said, "they tend to specialize in something. Perhaps one is a saucier or a pantry chef or, like me, a pastry chef. Even I specialize within the realm of baking. Bread is my passion, although I am perfectly skilled at producing sublime cookies and cakes and pies and anything else dessert related. Jackie was trained at the Culinary Institute in the Napa Valley. She was a personal chef for many years. She took the required pastry classes, of course, but that was never her specialty. But when she opened up her business, she wanted to incorporate pastry and bread components into her sessions."

"But didn't that conflict with your classes?"

Olaya waved away the question. "Not one bit. What I do is magical. People like Becky and Sally may learn the fundamentals of baking, but they will never come away with the deeper understanding of how bread can change lives. You, on the other hand . . . There is something about you that makes me think you have something different inside you. Maybe because your mother taught you to cook. Or maybe because you see things through the lens of a camera. You see the details. The creativity that exists in baking. The cracks in the crust. The texture of the dough. The final crumb.

"These are things that can be taught, but you, I think, already possess them. Jolie shows promise. So does Jasmine, but then her mother was gifted, so that makes good sense. My sisters, of course, have it, although not to the degree that I do. Penelope Branford." Olaya drew in a deep breath and held it for a moment, as if she was deciding how kind to be about Mrs. Branford. "She has it."

She paused for a second, letting her angst about Mrs. Branford slip back into a corner of her mind before she continued. "Jackie didn't want to delve into baking bread like I do. She wanted to master her own skills so she could incorporate a bit of baking into her school and her catering business."

From the way Olaya spoke, I could tell there had been no competition between the two friends. People killed for all sorts of irrational reasons. A business rivalry wasn't too far-fetched as a motive. Emmaline telling me that the Solis sisters were suspects had never left my mind, so to hear Olaya dismiss any conflict was a relief for a worry I hadn't known I'd been feeling.

Once Olaya found a soft blanket for Agatha, my little pug promptly went to sleep. She and I then worked in companionable silence, starting with Jackie's cookbooks. I handed them to Olaya, and she perused them and then placed them into one of two piles: books to keep and books to donate.

"Jasmine doesn't want to go through them?" I asked after a few minutes. My brother, Billy, my dad, and I still hadn't gone through my mom's things. It was too emotional of a job, and we'd been putting it off. It was a step we needed to take, a step Jasmine Makers was taking already. If we followed suit, then maybe we could start to heal and accept my mother's death.

But it wasn't healing that Jasmine was doing, apparently.

Olaya said, "She's eighteen. She's holding on to her grudge. She won't have anything to do with any of this. She just wants it done."

How could she hang on to her anger? I wondered. What was her anger even about? Her mother was gone. For good. The complicated relationship my mother and I had had — that any mother and daughter had — had evaporated into simple grief when she died. It was a loss I could never fully accept. It had happened too quickly. Too unexpectedly. In the end, none of the rest of our ups and downs or disagreements mattered. I couldn't understand Jasmine's distance.

"So she's leaving it for you to do?"

Olaya nodded as she picked up a copy of *Joy of Cooking.* "I don't mind," she said. "We were friends for thirty years. She was with me through so much."

"Through losing James?" I asked, testing the waters.

Olaya's head snapped up. "That and more."

She handed me *Joy of Cooking.* "This is a keeper," she said.

"For Jasmine?"

"For me. Jasmine doesn't want to keep anything. Nada."

One by one, we went through the shelves of cookbooks. Olaya had commentary on about half of them, and she kept that many in her keeper pile.

"Tell me about James," I said to her after another stretch of silence.

She raised an eyebrow and shot me a suspicious glance. "Why?"

I shrugged. "Just curious. Was there never anyone else . . . after?"

112

Olaya picked up the next cookbook, this one a tome on vegetarian cooking. "Love is love. Sometimes things are not meant to be, that is all. I never wanted anyone else."

"But don't you think there's more than one person we can fall in love with?" I asked. An image of Miguel Baptista came to me. He was my first love, but I'd been in relationships since. I'd been married and divorced, but I didn't want to believe that my relationship failures were because Miguel was my one and only.

"For most people, yes," she said, sensing my disappointment. "It was simply not in the cards for me."

"He was older than you?"

She straightened up. "You remember everything, yes?"

I nodded, smiling. I was blessed with a good memory.

"The years, I am afraid, were significant."

They were, I agreed, but if I was right, it was more significant that he was married. "Is that why it didn't work out?" I was fishing, searching for confirmation that the love of Olaya Solis's life was also Penelope Branford's deceased husband, but Olaya waved her hand in the air, and it was clear she'd decided she was done talking about her past relationships.

"Would you go through the papers in this? Make sure there is nothing important stuck in there?" she asked me, handing me a file folder filled with recipes that looked as if they'd been printed from the Internet.

I sat on a backless wooden stool at the kitchen's center island. The island itself was painted a warm olive gray-green and had open shelving on either end. Coffee cups and a few decorative cookbooks adorned the shelves. The dark wood of the island countertop was pristine. The buttery white of the cabinets, complemented by wrought-iron hardware, and the dark wood frames of the leaded windows gave the kitchen an old-world feel reminiscent of the 1920s or 1930s. I glanced at the wrought-iron light fixture above the island. It was a horizontal circle with six yellow glass tubes affixed to it. They mimicked the look of candlelight. The light fixture illuminated the exposed dark beams on the peaked ceiling above. The kitchen was a place I never wanted to leave. Cooking here would be a dream.

I opened the file folder and flipped through the pages one by one. I read recipe after recipe, observing the notes written in neat script in the margins. Measurements had been crossed out and adjusted. Cooking times had been changed. Wine pairings had been added. Jackie Makers was thorough and looked at every aspect of her cooking, I thought.

The last few pages in the folder were not recipes. I started skimming the first page, then paused and started again, this time reading more slowly. It was a photocopy of an essay, typed and double-spaced, but there was no name on it, and no title, date, or other identifying information. Those had all been removed before the copy made. Still, I felt sure it was a high school paper. The prompt was written on a sticky note, which was paper clipped to the top of the page.

Write a story about a time when you taught something to someone. What you taught could be a song, an activity, a game, a way of figuring out a homework problem, or something else. Be sure to narrate an event or a series of events and to include specific details so that the reader can follow your story.

I read the prompt, then went back to the essay, all the while wondering why it was here in Jackie's recipe folder. The essay itself was decent, well written, even if it didn't quite address the prompt. The author had written about teaching a lesson rather than a skill, song, or activity. It felt cryptic somehow, although I couldn't quite put my finger on why or how. The whole thing was about choices and how one decision could impact that person's life, as well as the lives of others. There were a few comments written in the margins. Things like *More detail needed. What is the lesson, specifically? This touches the surface; go deeper.* And *How do you factor into this lesson?*

I left the folder on the counter and went back to the cookbook shelf Olaya was still going through. "I don't think anything much in the folder is worth saving. They're all recipes and nothing original of Jackie's," I said. "But," I added, "I did find this." I handed her the essay.

She put down the book she'd been perusing and scanned the page. She frowned and uttered a puzzled "Huh."

"There's no name on it."

She tucked it into the oversize brown leather bag that was on the floor next to her. "I'll ask Jasmine about it. Must be hers."

I nodded. Of course. That made perfect sense. Jackie would keep her daughter's essay. Odd that it was randomly tucked into the file folder of recipes, but I often stuck things somewhere convenient rather than taking the time to put them away where they belonged. It was a bad habit and one my mother had tried to break me of. To no avail. Her propensity for organization hadn't been passed on to me. She'd organized every bit of her classroom and every corner of the house she shared with my dad. She knew where everything was, and she had a firm philosophy about loose papers and random stuff. File it, deal with it, or toss it. If you couldn't do one of those three things, your life would end up in disarray. It was true; I was living proof. I had stacks of bills and papers that stymied me. I didn't know where to begin, and so I did nothing, and the stacks grew until I was forced to tackle them in their entirety. My mother had tried to teach me, but my brain didn't work that way.

Maybe Jackie's hadn't, either.

Olaya and I spent another twenty minutes finishing the cookbooks and were just ready to move on to the first cupboard when a knock came at the front door. Olaya peered through the kitchen window, then quickly withdrew so she wouldn't be seen. I leaned over her and saw Penny Branford.

"What does she want?" Olaya demanded, as if I had invited Mrs. Branford and was personally responsible for the fact that she was now standing, stoop shouldered, on the old brick porch.

I shrugged helplessly. I liked both of these women, but it seemed evident that they were never going to like each other. I couldn't choose between them, but somehow I got the impression that this was what Olaya wanted. "I'll go see."

A minute later, I walked back into the kitchen. Mrs. Branford sauntered in behind me, the hook of her cane looped over her wrist.

"I'm sure I'm the last person you want to see, Olaya. Believe me, I feel the same. However, this is important." Olaya scoffed, but Mrs. Branford ignored her and continued. "About a week ago, Jackie stopped by —"

Olaya's head snapped up. "She stopped by to see you?"

"We were neighbors, Olaya. The fact that we were on friendly terms wasn't a betrayal of you."

Olaya's nostrils flared slightly as she drew in a deep breath. *"Por supuesto,"* she said. "I know that."

"Anyway," Mrs. Branford continued, "I just remembered this morning — after you left, Ivy — that she'd been in a state."

"What does that mean, in a state?" Olaya asked.

"She was worried. She asked me if I could keep a secret, which of course I can —"

"Yes, I'm sure you can."

Mrs. Branford drew herself up, throwing her hunched shoulders back as much as she could and lifting her chin indignantly. "Look here, Olaya Solis. You . . . *you* fell in love with my husband, not the other way around." She pointed a gnarled finger at Olaya. "*I* should be angry with *you*. For many years I *have* been angry with you. But life is too short. Jimmy's gone. Jackie's gone. Everything can change in a single moment, and we need to be grateful for the things we have. The friends. The family. The love. This" — she waved her finger back and forth between the two of them — "this animosity doesn't do either of us any good."

"James stayed with you," Olaya said, her voice quiet and laced with hurt and regret. "He stayed with you."

"He was my husband. Should he have left me for you?"

"I loved him."

Mrs. Branford's expression softened. "I've no doubt you did. And I believe he probably loved you, too."

"But you were his wife," Olaya said with

resignation.

"I was his wife."

A heavy moment of silence passed between them, and then Olaya said, "I never meant for it to happen, you understand." Her gaze finally met Mrs. Branford's, and a thread of understanding seemed to pass between them.

Mrs. Branford nodded solemnly. "I know, my dear. I've always known *that.* Jimmy didn't, either."

Olaya shook off the emotion flooding her, swallowing and blinking away the tears that had been pooling in her eyes. They'd had a breakthrough. I didn't know if it would last, but I was happy, for the moment, to have them in the same room without the heat of anger heavy between them.

"Have a seat," Olaya said, gesturing to the kitchen table.

Mrs. Branford plopped herself onto a cushioned chair, then leaned her cane against the distressed wood table.

"Now," Olaya continued, "what were you saying about Jackie?"

"She was upset about something that day," Mrs. Branford said. "I'd completely forgotten. My old, addled brain, you know."

"You remembered," I said, encouraging her to go on. "That's what matters."

"I haven't remembered much," she said, clarifying. "She looked over her shoulder a few times, as if someone might be following her. She was afraid. I'm sure of it now that I'm looking back on that day. She was definitely afraid."

Olaya's cheeks had tinged pink, and her hands had balled into fists. "I knew it."

"Knew what?" I asked.

"Something was going on with her. Something she would not share with me."

I sucked in a sharp breath. When I'd first met Mrs. Branford, we'd seen Buck Masterson, and she'd made an offhand remark that he probably killed Jackie Makers. Could there be truth behind that? Was Jackie afraid of her own neighbor?

"But who would she have feared?" Olaya asked, pondering aloud.

"Buck Masterson?" I offered. I looked at Mrs. Branford. "You said he'd gone into your house uninvited." The invasion of privacy would certainly have me on edge if it had happened to me.

"He did?" Olaya asked.

Mrs. Branford nodded. "He's a menace to the neighborhood," she declared. "But," she added, "I'm not sure if that's who Jackie was afraid of. Quite possibly. She mentioned Jasmine that day."

"She and Jasmine were not getting along, but she wasn't afraid of her own daughter," Olaya said.

"No, no, that's not what I mean. I don't believe so, either," Mrs. Branford said. "But there was something going on there. Something that had her on edge."

"We could ask Jasmine," I suggested. Seemed to me that if you had a question or concern, you simply needed to go to the source.

Olaya shook her head. "I told you. She will not return my phone calls."

"I don't know her," Mrs. Branford said. "Never had her in my class, and while I've seen her around over the years, it's been a long time."

They both looked at me expectantly. "You could reach out to her," Olaya suggested.

I spit out a laugh, chagrined. Were they serious? "Are you serious?"

They both nodded.

"I've never even seen her," I said, then proceeded to rattle off other reasons why I should not be the one to contact Jasmine about her mother's murder. "She'll think I'm a freak if I just randomly show up and start asking her questions about her relationship with her mother," I paused. "I have no idea how to even find her. I'm really pretty shy," I lied. "There's no way!"

"You are the farthest thing from shy," Mrs. Branford said.

"The farthest," Olaya agreed. "And I have her home and work address."

"Of course you can't just show up and start quizzing her about her mother. But, Ivy," Mrs. Branford said, "you're your mother's daughter. You're curious. You're smart. Think about the stories your mother broke when she was in high school and on the newspaper. You just have to be creative and dig a little."

"You mean lie." I'd have to visit Jasmine Makers on some false pretense. I couldn't even imagine what that might be.

Mrs. Branford shook her head. "Not a lie, Ivy. A manipulation of the truth. You can do this."

"For Jackie." Olaya said.

I held back a scoff. Telling a lie and manipulating the truth were one and the same, but I kept my thoughts on that to myself. My shoulders sagged. Despite my misgivings, I knew I'd give in.

As I accepted what I knew would happen, it occurred to me that we still didn't know why Jackie Makers had shown up at Penny Branford's house. "What did she want that day?" I asked.

"Oh!" Mrs. Branford exclaimed. She slid a gray canvas daypack off her back. "I don't care for purses," she said when she noticed me looking at it.

"That is quite practical," Olaya said with approval.

"It is," she agreed. She reached into her daypack and pulled out an eight-by-ten goldenrod envelope on the table between us. "She'd been having trouble with Buck Masterson." She grimaced. "Of course."

"She talked about him, this Buck Masterson," Olaya said, looking from me to Mrs. Branford and back.

"Only because he's the biggest menace to Santa Sofia and the historic district since Richard Nixon," Mrs. Branford said.

I stared. "Um, Richard Nixon?"

"Okay, forget Nixon. Buck Masterson is the biggest menace to Santa Sofia. Period."

Olaya shook her head, puzzled. "How have I never met this menace?"

Mrs. Branford patted Olaya's hand. "You're better off, my dear."

I covered my mouth with my hand, hiding my grin. I knew they were meant to be friends, and now, despite the Jimmy/James situation, their friendship destiny might be secure.

"Buck wanted Jackie to tear out the patio

124

cover she added in her backyard. Tear it right out." Mrs. Branford slapped her hand on the table. "It probably cost Jackie ten thousand dollars. Tear it out, indeed. That man is horrible!"

"She told me about that. She said a neighborhood committee was giving her a difficult time about the work she'd done. That she did not have it approved by the historic district before she did the work."

Mrs. Branford folded her left hand on top of her right, nodding. "But her backyard work was actually done in . . . the . . . backyard. Not visible from the street. Not attached to the house. Not required to get approval by the historic district."

"What is this guy's problem? How did he even know about the work she did?" I asked.

Mrs. Branford tilted her head as she responded. "Remember I told you he'd been sneaking into houses on the street?"

I gasped. "Jackie's house? *This* house?"

She nodded solemnly. "*This* house. I saw him with my own two eyes, and let me tell you, I called Jackie right away. Of course she was in her kitchen. Buck had carte blanche to break and enter without Jackie's knowledge," she said. "But he didn't count on me," she added, shaking her head. "He could have known about the work she did only by being in the house or in the back-yard. And Jackie did not give him permission."

"Let me understand this," Olaya said. "You saw him enter Jackie's house. You called Jackie to tell her. And then she came over to your house and brought this envelope?"

"Yes. Oh! Yes." Mrs. Branford flipped the golden-rod envelope over and unclasped it. "She came to find out what I'd seen. We got to talking, you know. I do miss her."

"I miss her, too," Olaya said quietly.

Mrs. Branford continued. "As I said, we got to talking. I told her that I'd seen Buck walk down the sidewalk, all nonchalant-like. He looked over his shoulder, then up and down the street. Quite suspicious, if you ask me."

Olaya and I both nodded. "Very," I said.

"We talked for a while. Just chitchat about her work, her daughter, life's mysteries." Mrs. Branford chuckled. "I have sons, so I couldn't really help her much with the issues she was having with her daughter. She said that no matter what she said, her daughter didn't understand. Couldn't understand."

Olaya frowned. "This is why I never had children."

126

"Hey now," I said. "Jasmine may not be daughter of the year, but some of us are pretty good kids. *I'm* a pretty good kid." I'd probably driven my parents crazy as a teenager, and moving to Texas had been hard on both of them. My divorce had taken its toll on them. But in my heart I knew that most parents thought their children were worth all the grief and frustration.

She patted my hand. "I know you are. Your parents, they are good ones."

"Yes, they were. Are." I swallowed the lump in my throat and let my fingertips touch the edge of the envelope. "Back to the mysterious envelope. She gave it to you?"

"No, no," Mrs. Branford said. "She left it behind. I confess that I looked in it." Mrs. Branford's eyes glazed, and she seemed distressed. "I snuck a peek, and then I tucked it away until I could give it back to Jackie. And then . . ." She paused, twisting her fingers around each other. "And then I forgot all about it."

Suddenly her face looked more worn than it had just a few minutes ago, her wrinkles etched deeper into her skin. She was an old woman, and it seemed she was going through the experiencing some forgetfulness, as so many elderly people did.

"It happens," Olaya said, giving Mrs. Branford a sympathetic glance. "It is nothing to be concerned about."

Mrs. Branford held up her hand, silencing any more discussion about any gaps in her memory. "I happened upon the envelope again this morning, after you left, Ivy. In the freezer, behind the gallon of ice cream, if you can believe that."

That was an unusual place for it, which was an understatement, and it raised a bit of concern. I set that worry away for another time and unclasped the envelope, slid out the papers from inside it, and took a quick glance. "They're letters to the historic district." There were six, and each one was dated within the last month and signed by someone with a Maple Street address.

"Yes! From the looks of it, Jackie was gathering ammunition to oust Buck Masterson from his seat on the council. She must have come by that day to ask me to write a letter. I'm sure that was her intent."

Olaya asked the obvious question. "But?"

"But she got a phone call. Her daughter, she said. And then she dashed off —"

"To save Jasmine from herself," Olaya said, finishing the sentence, her sarcasm heavy.

I hadn't met Jasmine yet, but if I were to

describe her, *selfish* was the word that came to mind. She didn't strike me as someone I'd be inclined to hang out with.

We spread the letters across the table. One by one, Olaya and I read them, sliding them back and forth as we finished one and reached for the next.

"This one's pretty direct," I said, considering a handwritten missive from Mr. Harold Reiny. The writing was neat and precise, slanting slightly to the left. I was no handwriting analyst, but if I had to guess, I'd say Mr. Reiny was a tough old guy who didn't take any crap from anyone, least of all a devious man like Buck Masterson.

Granted, I hadn't actually met Buck Masterson, either, although I'd seen him from across the street while I'd been at Mrs. Branford's. I hadn't met a lot of the players in this crime drama in which I was living, but I was getting a good handle on many of them despite my lack of personal knowledge.

I read aloud a snippet from Mr. Reiny's letter: "Buck Masterson is single-handedly destroying Maple Street. He manages to make people think he has good intentions and only wants the old houses here cared for, but in reality, the man is power hungry and is a menace to his neighbors. He does not represent me, my house, my family, or my interests."

Each of the letters had a similar message. The good people on Maple Street did not want Buck Masterson involved in their lives and the decisions made regarding their homes and properties.

Half an idea started to form in my mind. "Do you think Jackie initiated this letter campaign?"

Olaya considered the question. "If she did, she never told me about it, but it sounds like something she would do. She did not like that man."

"None of us do," Mrs. Branford muttered.

"But do you think . . ." I trailed off, not sure how I felt about what I was thinking.

Both the older women who were suddenly part of my life prompted me to continue. Olaya rolled her hand in the air, and Mrs. Branford patted my arm and asked, "Do we think what, dear?"

I formed the thought into words. "Do you think it's possible that Buck Masterson got wind of the letters and Jackie's campaign against him? Do you think he really could be behind her death?"

Olaya and Mrs. Branford looked at each other, looked at me, and then looked back at each other. Olaya clasped her hand over her open mouth. Mrs. Branford gasped.

"Buck Masterson, a murderer. A murderer?" Mrs. Branford said it as if she were testing the idea out to see how it sounded, then repeated it again. "Buck Masterson. A murderer."

"I do not know the man, but a killer? Jackie's killer?" Olaya leaned back, pondering.

"Someone in this town killed her," I said. "Someone who had some strong feelings against her. Why not Buck Masterson? If she was behind trying to stop his antics here on Maple Street and with the historic district, he might have seen that as a vendetta against him. Maybe he's unhinged —"

"Unhinged." Mrs. Branford tried that word on for size. "Buck Masterson, unhinged. Breaking and entering. Sneaking around. Inserting himself into other people's business. His smarmy smile." She nodded. "I'd say that he most definitely could be a trifle unhinged."

Olaya spoke up, the voice of reason. "None of those things make him a murderer."

Mrs. Branford agreed. "No, but as Ivy said, someone killed Jackie. Now we know that Buck actually has . . . had . . . a motive."

"Okay, look," I said. "We're being arm-chair detectives, and the truth is we aren't the ones to solve this. Why don't I take the letters to the deputy sheriff? Let her investigate Buck Masterson if she feels like it's warranted?"

After another few minutes of debate, they both agreed. Emmaline Davis would be able to determine if Buck Masterson was a killer or just a know-it-all busybody.

CHAPTER NINE

Easier said than done. My phone calls to Emmaline went unanswered. I had a few hours before I was to meet back up with Mrs. Branford for our stakeout, so I tucked the envelope of letters into my camera bag and headed back to my dad's house. I'd try Emmaline again before I headed back to Maple Street at dusk. Or, I thought deviously, I could give the envelope to Billy and ask him to deliver it. A little matchmaking never hurt anyone.

The house was empty when I got home. As the city manager, my dad was always busy with a million tasks. He probably wouldn't be home until after nine. Since my mom died, his hours had gotten later and later. "Nothing to come home to," he'd told Billy and me.

Agatha jumped from my car and zoomed to the gate leading to the backyard. I let her off her harness and leash, and she instantly took off at a high-speed run. She slowed, spun in happy circles, leapt straight up into the air, and then took off again like the Tasmanian Devil, cutting hard to make a tight turn, her normally curled tail elongated with the force of her run.

I let her run, tossing a tennis ball for her to chase, until she slowed down, panting, and was finally worn out. Once inside, she settled down in her bed, happily chewing on a knotted length of braid, and although the house was deathly quiet, I was glad for the solitude. I wanted to look through some of my mom's things, which I hadn't been able to bring myself to do yet. After spending the morning with Mrs. Branford and then with Olaya at Jackie's house, I felt ready. Ready to think about my mom and the life she'd led. Ready to face the raw emotions that hovered on the surface of my mind. Ready. Just ready.

I dropped my purse and camera bag on the white slipcovered couch and headed straight for the garage. My dad had carefully placed all my mom's school and classroom supplies along the left side of the garage, but no one had been able to muster up the courage to look at them since. They were obstructed by my mom's car, which also hadn't moved in the past six months.

"Should we sell it?" Billy had asked me when I first returned to Santa Sofia.

"I think it would break his heart. He needs to hold on to her."

I wasn't sure Billy understood what my dad was going through or why his emotions were tied to every little thing that my mother had touched, but I got it. If he started to get rid of things, he'd be shedding his memories of her bit by bit. I think he saw that as a betrayal of her. That somehow, from wherever she was, she'd look down and see that he'd moved on and that she wasn't mourned anymore. It was not true, of course, but he had to grieve in his own way and at his own pace.

We all did.

I needed to start today.

I walked into the kitchen, took the only set of car keys hanging from the mounted hook there, went back to the garage, and rounded the back end of the pearl-white Fiat crossover my mom had loved. Once inside it, I started the engine. It roared to life, and seconds later I backed the car out and parked it on the driveway. I had considered a short jaunt around the block but had decided against it. Baby steps. Even sitting in the car, surrounded by the still new-smelling black interior, made me choke up.

"Big enough for grandkids," Mom had told me with a smile and a wink when she'd picked it out.

Grandkids she'd never get to meet. Babies who'd never know their grandmother. I choked back the lump that had risen in my throat. It was just a car, but remembering how carefully my mom had picked it out, how she'd envisioned driving around her grandbabies in it, and how she'd loved it made my dad's decision to keep it all the more reasonable. I didn't want him to sell it, either.

I drew in a bolstering breath as I got out of the car and went back into the garage. "Stay focused," I told myself. "Just one box."

I set up one of my dad's collapsible lawn chairs, grabbed the first box, hauled it from the stack along the wall, and sat down with it. The box was labeled CLASSROOM BOOKS, and sure enough, it was full of teaching manuals, books on instructional strategies, and games for the high school English classroom. I searched through the box, flipping through a few books in case there was anything personal tucked away, but there was nothing. This was truly just a box of books my mom had felt were important enough to own print copies of.

I overlapped the cardboard flaps, closing the box again, and retrieved the next box from the stack. This one, labeled DESK, held all the miscellaneous stuff my mom had kept in her desk drawers. Clear acrylic containers of paper clips, staples, Post-it notes, a vast collection of pens and pencils, with a heavy emphasis on colorful Paper Mate Flair pens. "They're perfect for grading papers," she'd told me once when she'd bought a jumbo pack of them. "I try to stay away from the dreaded red. Grading in purple makes me happy."

I closed up the box, set it aside, and took another one down. STUDENT WORK. Inside was a series of file folders holding students' essays. The folders were dated and organized by year and went back a decade. Each folder held anywhere from one to five essays.

I took a closer look at a few of the writing pieces. They weren't originals but had been photocopied. Just like the one I'd found in Jackie's kitchen. I got to thinking. Had my mom been Jasmine's teacher? I ran through some possibilities in my mind and finally settled on the idea that if Jasmine *had* been in my mom's class, my mother might have created a copy of the essay because of the cryptic nature of it and given it to Jasmine's mother. What really struck me, however, was that it was quite possible that my mother had actually known Jackie Makers, that they'd been connected, even if it was only slightly. The realization gave me a chill.

I refocused on the essays. Did teachers regularly keep copies of their students' writing? Pastel-colored sticky notes adhered to many of the samples. Notes my mother had made. One said: *College admittance UCLA.* On another she'd written: *3/15 Contacted counselor and mother Re: cutting.* A third noted: *Use as exemplary next year.*

My mom had copied and kept select student writings for a variety of reasons, ranging from concern to pride. I had a faint recollection of overhearing my mom telling my dad, "Somebody was Barack Obama's teacher. Someone taught Ronald Reagan and Angelina Jolie and Johnny Depp. One of my students may go on to do great things. If they do, maybe I'll be able to say, 'Look! Here's an essay Frances wrote on Julius Caesar back in her sophomore year of high school!' "

I laughed at the memory. My mom, the dreamer. She knew she was making a difference in the lives of her students. They came to her with their problems, their failures, and their triumphs. They trusted her, and she loved them. She respected them. And right here in front of me was the proof.

I pulled out a random file from the box. It was filled with copies of several essays from the previous year. They were all literary responses to *Bless Me, Ultima; Death of a Salesman; The Grapes of Wrath;* and *The Great Gatsby,* among others. I smiled, proud. My mom knew how to challenge her students.

I spent another hour looking through her boxes, memories flooding me. How many hours had I spent helping her set up her classroom every August, and then helping pack it all up again at the end of each school year so the room could be cleaned or so she could move to a new room? Countless. As a teenager, I'd hated being asked to spend days of my summer vacation helping, but looking back now just made me smile. Those were good memories. Time with my mom that I now treasured and wouldn't trade for anything.

My cell phone beeped, bringing me back to the present. It was a text from Emmaline.

Back in the office. Call whenever.

A moment later a car door slammed, and my younger brother, Billy, strode into the garage, set down a bag he was carrying, then stooped to give me a peck on the cheek. "What's going on here?"

"Looking at some of mom's school stuff."

Billy had gotten my dad's dark brown hair and hazel eyes, as well as his tall, lean build. At thirty-three, he was an eligible bachelor in Santa Sofia. But his heart, if only he'd admit it, belonged to Emmaline Davis.

He sank to his haunches and pulled a random file from the box I still had open. "Anything interesting?"

"These are old student essays Mom kept copies of. This box goes back ten years."

He glanced at the stack of twenty-plus boxes still lining the garage wall. "She taught for what? Twenty-eight years?"

She'd gotten her teaching credentials when Billy and I were little. I couldn't remember exactly when, though. "Something like that."

He flipped through the file folder, nodding. "Wish I could have had her as my teacher. My friends always loved her. Said she really 'got' them."

"My friends said the same thing." School policy had been that, because she was our mom, we couldn't be in her class, so we'd both had Mrs. Jameson for sophomore English, then Mr. Lemon as seniors, when my mom had changed to twelfth grade English.

"She was a good teacher," Billy said.

"And an even better mom," I said.

"Are you looking for something in particular?"

I wondered if there was something that I was subconsciously hunting for, something I knew my mom had had in her classroom that I was hoping to find. I'd racked my brain, but if there was, it wasn't rising to the surface. "No, nothing. I just wanted to be close to her. I miss her," I said softly.

He moved closer and rested his hand on my back. "I do, too."

We restacked the boxes, and I pulled the car back into the garage. Billy retrieved the bag he'd brought, and handed it to me.

"That's a lot of kiwis," I said.

He winked. "You know how Dad loves 'em."

That he did. Kiwis. Berries. Mangos. Pretty much any fruit made our dad happy.

"Could you do a favor for me?" I asked, taking a kiwi from the bag and turning the fuzzy brown sphere around in my hand.

"Sure." He didn't even ask what it was. That was my brother. He was an inherently good guy. He followed me into the house. I set the kiwis down, went to the couch, and returned to the kitchen holding out the envelope from Mrs. Branford. "Can you drop this at the sheriff's office for me?"

His hand stopped in midair. "Uh, why? What is it?"

I gave him an abbreviated version of the Maple Street saga, ending with the letter campaign initiated by Jackie Makers against Buck Masterson. I concluded by saying, "Emmaline needs to see them."

"You think this Masterson character might have had something to do with that woman's murder?"

Leave it to Billy to sum it up in one succinct sentence. I answered with Mrs. Branford's words. "Someone killed Jackie. And this guy, this Buck Masterson, he had a pretty good motive."

"And you want Emmaline to take a look at the letters."

Again, he cut to the chase.

"She's in charge of the investigation," I said by way of an answer.

Billy was nobody's fool, least of all mine. He'd seen through me the second I mentioned Emmaline's name. "Your matchmaking isn't going to work, Ivy."

"Relax, Billy. It's not a date. You're just dropping off an envelope."

"And why, exactly, can't you do it, when

you need to explain the situation to her, anyway?"

It took it as a rhetorical question, so I didn't bother to answer. Instead, I went with, "You know you and Emmaline are meant to be together."

Billy closed his eyes, his eyelids fluttering with frustration. "We had our chance, Ivy. It didn't work out."

"You wouldn't let it work out. There's a difference. She cares about you. You care about her. So why can't you just do something about it? You're being stupid. Didn't losing Mom teach you anything? Life is too short. You're letting your chance at love slip right through your fingers."

My brother was a handsome man. Five feet eleven inches, a gentle wave to his dark brown hair, broad shouldered, and fit. But when he scowled, like he was doing now, he looked a little menacing. I knew when to leave well enough alone.

But he surprised me by taking the envelope. "I'll leave it with the receptionist," he growled.

"That's fine. Thanks. I'll call Em later to fill her in."

He snatched an apple from the fruit bowl and headed back out through the garage, leaving me to get ready for my stakeout with Penelope Branford.

CHAPTER TEN

This was my first stakeout, and I had the feeling it might be my last. Mrs. Branford was antsy in the passenger seat of my tiny car, and the potential hours we could sit here together stretched before me.

"What kind of car do you have? Maybe we should use it instead," I suggested.

"Oh no, dear. I long since stopped driving," she answered. "It's been sitting in my garage for years. Who even knows if it would start at this point?"

I sighed, wishing I had a bigger car with more legroom and interior space. As it was, my little economy car barely let me turn my body and prop my camera in the open driver's side window. If I ever did another stakeout, I'd find a different solution. Of course, I'd never have a reason to do another stakeout, so really it was a moot issue.

I considered our current situation and why we were here. Buck Masterson had a motive to want Jackie Makers out of his way. If he had anything to do with her murder, that gave me double the reason to want to catch him doing something incriminating.

I had my camera out, as well as a U-shaped beanbag support, which I'd propped over the window frame. Thankfully, it was a temperate seventy degrees this evening. I imagined those funny graphic T-shirts geared toward people who loved to sew and their resulting self-descriptions as fabricaholics. My passion for photography meant I had more camera equipment than any reasonable person might collect. Every spare dime I saved went to Nikon gear and paraphernalia. And every dime was well spent. Fabric was to a seamstress what camera lenses were to me. My own graphic T-shirt might say IF I CAN'T BRING MY CAMERA, I'M NOT GOING OR I FLASH PEOPLE.

For the stakeout tonight, I'd chosen an 85mm lens with an f-stop of f/1.4. It was the fastest lens I owned. To the layman, this meant absolutely nothing and probably filled him or her with anxiety. Given the minimal ambient light on the street, to me the specs on this lens meant the difference between a black screen with no image, a mess of movement as the camera tried to capture light in the dark, and a halfway decent shot. Getting a shot of Buck Masterson and his wrongdoings was, in theory, possible. Now we just had to wait for the subject in question.

"That's quite a setup you have," Mrs. Branford commented once I had the four-inch camera lens propped on the beanbag.

I focused and took a practice shot, examining the digital screen to gauge the lighting and the adjustments I needed to make. "Let's hope it pays off," I said, but truth be told, I was a little doubtful. Buck Masterson would have to be a Class A idiot to do something blatantly illegal in full view of the neighborhood, and in my wildest dreams, I couldn't actually fathom what we could catch him in the act of doing, anyway. But I wanted to make Mrs. Branford happy, and who knew? Maybe we'd get lucky and bust him doing something diabolical and nefarious. Stranger things had happened.

Ninety minutes later, we'd fallen silent. My rear end was numb, my neck ached from continually looking up and down the street for evidence of Buck Masterson, I was sleepy, and my back was stiff from the way I was angled in the seat of the car.

"I say we give it another thirty minutes, then call it a night," I said grudgingly. I wanted to see what my lens could capture in the dark, but without a subject and short of sending Mrs. Branford out into the street to be a test subject for me, it seemed unlikely that I was going to get the opportunity.

Mrs. Branford's response was a snort through her nose and a burst of air blowing between her lips. I snuck a look at her — sound asleep — and stifled a grin. I didn't blame her. My eyelids were heavy with the weight of boredom. I'd fought the urge to give in to letting them close; Mrs. Branford had lost that fight.

A movement from across the street caught my attention. We were far enough away that only someone with bionic vision would be able to detect us sitting there. Still, I shrank back in my seat. We weren't doing anything wrong, but I'd rather not explain to anyone about our stakeout. I peered through the eyehole in my camera, letting my super-powerful lens do the work for me. I drew in a sharp breath as recognition hit me. Buck Masterson was actually striding down Maple Street, but he wasn't alone. Next to him was a woman with what looked to be red hair. She had a round middle and skinny legs, and her arms swung purposefully as she walked alongside Buck. Surely, *this* was

Nanette, the wife and the person who'd stared intimidatingly at Mrs. Branford from the front porch.

I didn't know her, but I already didn't like her.

As they walked down the street, I depressed the shutter button on my camera, checked to make sure I was getting decent images, and waited. I continued to watch through my lens. The zoom allowed me to see their faces, gestures, and actions. Nanette Masterson turned her head and said something to her husband. He nodded and ushered her forward with a wave of his arm. She glanced over her shoulder once, then continued on at a brisker pace.

Suspicious. "Where is she going?" I muttered.

Next to me, Mrs. Branford stirred. "Where is who going?" Her words were slurred, but I caught the gist.

Buck and Nanette were on the opposite side of the street and far enough away that there was no way they could hear me, but still, I kept my voice at a stage whisper. "The Mastersons."

Mrs. Branford sat bolt upright. Or at least as upright as her hunched shoulders and back would allow her to. "They're out there?" She leaned forward to peer out the front windshield. "Where? Where are they?"

Instinctively, I shushed her, extending my arm and pointing south. "Right there. They were walking together, but Nanette said something to Buck, and then she started walking faster. They look like they're up to something, but —" I didn't have the chance to finish my thought before I knew exactly where Nanette was headed. "Jackie's house."

Mrs. Branford clapped her hands triumphantly. "I knew it! Did you get a picture?"

Oh! In my excitement to see where Nanette Masterson was heading, I'd almost forgotten. Nanette was darting across the grass, bypassing the front walkway and door in favor of the side gate leading to the backyard. The area was tangentially lit from the street lamps. I hoped it was enough light to allow for some clear images. *Click. Click. Click.* I snapped picture after picture as she snuck onto Jackie Makers's property, her husband following. But Buck didn't go all the way through the gate to the backyard. Instead, he stood sentry at the fence, what looked like a cell phone in his hand. A security light shone down from the corner of the house, illuminating the area enough for me to get some halfway decent shots.

"Got 'em," I said, taking a few more as

Buck put his phone to his ear and spoke to someone.

I glanced at the front of the Tudor house as the blinds in the front living room parted and someone stared out. Buck had probably been talking to Nanette. Testing their covert operation and alert process, I presumed. Buck was the lookout, and Nanette had done the breaking and entering.

"They could be looking for the letters," I said.

"But how would they even know about them?" Mrs. Branford mused.

"Remember that one man, Harold Reiny? He was pretty straightforward in his letter. Maybe he told Buck that his days on the historic district's council were numbered."

Mrs. Branford sat back, considering. Finally she nodded. "Yes, I think that's possible. Harold is a pistol. He doesn't mince words, and it's gotten him in trouble on more than one occasion. Buck has no boundaries, and Harold has no filter. They're like oil and water, you know. They have never gotten on."

I debated our play. We hadn't really thought about what our play would be if we actually saw the Mastersons doing something nefarious. We could continue to watch, document with pictures, and keep the incident to ourselves. After all, I hadn't seen Nanette break into Jackie's house, and although I took a picture of the cracked blinds, I knew there was no way I actually got a shot that captured her face.

For the time being, more photos of Buck Masterson were out of the question. He'd shrunk into the shadows and all but disappeared.

After a moment, I made a decision. If they had anything to do with Jackie Makers's death, then keeping their illicit actions quiet was a mistake. I would alert someone who'd actually know what to do. With one eye still on the house, I picked up my cell phone, went to favorites, and dialed Emmaline.

"About time," she said by way of answer.

"Hello to you, too."

She ignored my sarcasm. "Thanks for the heads-up," she said. "I was *not* prepared for that."

In the distance, Buck Masterson appeared under the security light beside the fence, cell phone at his ear. I snapped another picture. It wouldn't give me any additional information, but I took it, anyway. "Prepared for what?"

"Playing dumb does not become you, Ivy Culpepper. Next time you send Billy on an errand for you, give me fair warning."

"Oh, shoot. Sorry, Em." I played contrite, but inside I was smiling. So Billy hadn't dropped the envelope of letters off with the receptionist at the sheriff's office. He'd opted to pay a personal visit to his soul mate. Explaining to Emmaline that he hadn't wanted or planned to see her, but that he'd apparently changed his mind didn't seem like the right response. Instead I repeated, "Sorry."

Mrs. Branford waved her craggy hand in front of my face. "To whom are you speaking?" she said dramatically.

Emmaline, ever the detective, promptly asked, "To whom are you speaking, indeed? Please tell me, pray tell, with whom are you spending your time, Ivy?"

I answered Mrs. Branford first. "To the deputy sheriff. Her name's Emmaline Davis."

"My question next," Emmaline said into my ear.

"I'm sitting with Mrs. Penelope Branford on Maple Street. We just observed Nanette Masterson entering Jackie Makers's house. Her husband, Buck, is standing guard at the side gate leading to the backyard."

Emmaline didn't miss a beat. "Number one, how is it that you and Mrs. Branford were able to observe this alleged breaking and entering at this time of night and in the dark? Number two, why are you so interested in Jackie Makers's death? And number three, how did you come by these letters Billy delivered for you today?"

I answered in reverse order. "Olaya Solis and I were cleaning out some of Ms. Makers's things, and Mrs. Branford stopped by. Jackie had left the envelope with the letters at Mrs. Branford's house a few weeks ago."

"Don't you dare tell her I found them in my freezer," Mrs. Branford said, still leaning forward and peering through the windshield at the Tudor house.

Emmaline cleared her throat. "You might tell her that I can actually *hear* her."

I ignored them both, moving on to Em's second question. "I'm interested in Jackie Makers's death because she was good friends with Olaya Solis and Mrs. Branford. That makes me a friend —"

"Or acquaintance —"

"By association. Plus, I guess I have a curious side."

Mrs. Branford leaned back and gave me a pointed look. "And you've got that investigative gene your mother had."

I answered Emmaline's final question. "And lastly, we are on a stakeout on Maple Street."

Emmaline interrupted me with an indignant "What? You're on a *what*?"

"A stakeout. Buck Masterson, as those letters Billy brought you explain, is in everybody's business on this street. Mrs. Branford has seen him sneaking into houses. He's threatened her and others on the street. So we've been sitting here, seeing if we could catch him in the act. Which, I might add, we did."

She covered the receiver of her phone, and I heard her say something to someone. When she came back, she let out a heavy sigh. "I have some problems with this whole thing, Ivy. I can look into the letters, of course. I'll need to talk to Mrs. Branford and Ms. Solis. So that's all fine. But you should know that curiosity killed the cat. You're staking out someone who, by all intents and purposes, appears to have had a motive to kill Jackie Makers. I'm not saying this Buck Masterson or his wife is guilty of murder, but if, by chance, they are, you're getting in their way. Whoever killed Jackie did it for a reason. He, she, they won't hesitate to do it again. And finally . . . and most importantly . . ."

Sirens blared in the distance. She'd reported the breaking and entering, I realized. The sirens, though, had also reached Buck

Masterson's ears. The cell phone was glued to his face again, and a moment later Nanette joined him at the gate. Together they raced down the street, back the way they'd come. Just as a police cruiser appeared on Maple Street, Buck and Nanette Masterson disappeared into the darkness in the distance, and presumably into their own house.

"All you've done by staking out Maple Street is alert the Mastersons that we're on to them. Which makes my job that much harder."

I let out my own exasperated sigh. "But you wouldn't be on to them if we *hadn't* staked out Maple Street," I said. "And actually," I added, bringing her down off her sheriff's high horse, "I think *you* alerted them with the sirens. A little stealth can go a long way."

Another heavy exhale. She couldn't argue with me. We'd had this conversation so many times. I had never understood why the police always announced themselves with their lights and sirens when it seemed to me that they could catch bad guys in the act if they were more subtle about their approach.

"The house is secure," Emmaline said. "You should leave the stakeouts to the

156

professionals, Ivy."

"Tell that to Mrs. Branford."

Mrs. Branford stirred beside me when she heard her name mentioned. "Tell me what?"

"Deputy Sheriff Davis says we should hang up our private-eye hats."

Mrs. Branford, bless her, blew a raspberry through her pursed lips. "Why would we go and do a thing like that when we clearly excel at it?"

I grinned, silently agreeing with her. We'd caught the Mastersons in the act of breaking and entering, we'd gotten photographs, although I didn't really know what good they'd do anyone, and we'd put the fear of God in them. If they had killed Jackie Makers, hopefully they wouldn't target anyone else, and if they hadn't killed her, at the very least, maybe they'd think twice before continuing their Maple Street shenanigans.

CHAPTER ELEVEN

Before dawn the next morning, I took Agatha for a long walk at Wayside Beach, my favorite stretch of sand in Santa Sofia. I yawned, struggling to get energized at that early hour. I must have been crazy to agree to meet Olaya at such an ungodly time. "What was I thinking?" I asked Agatha.

Agatha looked up at me from her lazy stride beside me. I could tell she agreed that it was far too early, even if we were walking on the beach, something that had become her very favorite thing to do since we'd moved back home. She'd been born and bred in Texas's Hill Country, so sand and ocean had been foreign concepts to her. She'd adjusted like a champ.

After our walk, I left her crated at my dad's house, then met Olaya at Yeast of Eden. The sun was barely peeking over the horizon.

"How do you do this every day?" I asked

her, stifling my tenth yawn of the morning.

"Early to bed, early to rise . . . Is that not how the saying goes?"

"It *is* how the saying goes. But still . . ."

"I run a bakery. It is how the business works."

Photography wasn't much different. The best photographs happened in the wee hours of the morning, usually just after sunrise, when the light was soft, warm, and dimensional. It was, in short, magical. Shadows were long and fluid, and everything seemed more dynamic.

Which was why I was at Yeast of Eden so early. I was shooting the pictures for a new brochure for the bakery, and I wanted the best shot possible of the front facade. The striped awning, the colorful Mexican garlands strung in the windows, the old-fashioned tables and chairs, the potted plants with geraniums and pansies all added to the quaint ambiance of the bakery. Waiting until midday would have made the whole shot harsh and bright, but the magical hour after sunrise meant the colors would be warm and welcoming: exactly what we wanted to make the place look its most inviting.

Olaya and her staff had filled the window racks with the day's offerings of fresh bread, the aroma drifting out to the sidewalk and even across the street, where I stood. I'd switched out the lens from the night before, going with a 24–70mm zoom lens, all that was necessary given the short distance from across the street to the bakery. Since the sun was up, I set the ISO to 100 and the f-stop to f/5 so I had enough depth of field to keep everything in focus. I didn't want my camera to home in on any one element of the storefront; instead, I wanted to capture the whole thing in its entirety.

I walked up and down, shooting from different angles to see what would work best. I'd brought my laptop with me to upload the shots so Olaya could look at them when I was finished and I joined her inside Yeast of Eden. At that point we could decide in which direction to go and if more shots were needed.

"Wanna take some of my place?"

I jumped, spooked by the voice behind me, and then remembered Olaya's comment about my startle factor. I hadn't heard anyone approach, which meant my situational awareness was not very good at the moment. I turned to see a bald man with skin the color of dark-roast coffee. He had a fair share of wrinkles lining his face, but they didn't age him. Instead, he was rugged and good-looking. I pegged him to be somewhere in his fifties.

"Oh!" I stumbled back, widening the area between us.

He guffawed, his infectious smile reaching to his penetrating brown eyes. "Didn't mean to startle you, young lady."

I resisted correcting him on that point. Thirty-six meant I wasn't quite a young lady anymore. "It's okay."

He offered his knobby hand. "Gus Makers."

Gus Makers. As in Augustus. As in Jackie Makers's ex-husband.

"I own the antique mini-mall down the street."

Right. And he was partners with the crazy man, Randy Russell.

"Ivy Culpepper," I said. "Nice to meet you, Mr. Makers."

"Mr. Makers was my pop," he said, "and he's long gone. Call me Gus."

I smiled at how normal and pleasant he seemed. Much different from the sketchy business partner he had. "Well, nice to meet you, Gus."

"Tell me what you're up to over here. Does Olaya know you're snapping pictures of her place?"

"She does," I answered, thinking how nice

161

it was, despite the divorce he'd been through with her best friend, that Gus was watching out for Olaya. It was the neighborly thing to do, but people didn't always act in a neighborly fashion, as Buck Masterson had so aptly proved to the people of Maple Street. "She asked me to, in fact."

"Why's that?" he asked.

He was also blatantly nosy, but I didn't mind. Turn around was fair play, after all. "She's creating a new brochure for Yeast of Eden. I'm shooting photos for the front of it."

Traffic had started to pick up on the Pacific coastal road, and the parking spaces in front of Yeast of Eden were now filled. The bread shop sold only bread, but that didn't stop people from indulging or making two stops if they also wanted doughnuts or cookies or some other bakery delicacy. "Unadulterated bread is what I offer," Olaya had told me that first day. "And it's what people want. If they wanted the tasteless stuff, they could simply get it at the supermarket. Yeast of Eden is for the connoisseurs. It's for the people who really care about their bread and what they put in their mouths."

Personally, I was a convert.

"Good for her," Gus said, nodding his approval. "We compete with the beach, and with Broadway, where all the historic downtown shops are. Olaya's reputation brings a lot of folks to our neck of the woods, though."

So, Gus liked and respected Olaya, while his partner, Randy Russell, had waved a billy club around, threatening to shoot her because she no longer referred people to the mini-mall. Randy might be a hothead, but at least he was honest about it. A little part of me wondered if Gus Makers had the same anger toward Olaya and just hid it, or if he really was as pleasant and innocuous as he seemed. Had his divorce from Jackie Makers been amicable, or did he have animosity that had spilled over onto Olaya because of her friendship with Jackie?

I figured there was no harm in digging a little to find out. After all, I didn't relish Randy Russell appearing again, and if Gus here was anything like Randy, I wanted to know.

"Doesn't Randy Russell own the mini-mall, too?" I asked innocently.

Gus's smile never dropped, but I sensed a change in him nonetheless. A slight tightening of the jaw? Or maybe it was a dulling in the eyes. "Do you know Randy?"

I shrugged and did my best to look sheepish. "I was taking a bread-making class at Yeast of Eden when the, uh, incident happened."

"Aha."

He didn't offer any more than that quick utterance, but I pressed. After all, if Randy Russell had spotted Olaya and attacked, things could have gotten really bad really fast. Or worse, if he'd had a gun instead of a club, I could well have been caught in the cross fire. "We were all pretty unsettled."

Finally, his smile faded into a grimace. "I bet you were."

"What was that about, anyway, with the stick?"

Gus Makers shrugged. "He was having a bad day."

I tried to stop my jaw from dropping, but I didn't succeed. Having a bad day, for me, meant I was grumbly, snappy, and didn't much want to be around people. It didn't mean I went around waving a weapon and threatening people. With all the shootings in the country, the idea that this unhinged anger was okay as a response to having a bad day left me with a sour taste in my mouth. "Really? And so he came to threaten Olaya?"

Gus's whole demeanor had changed. He was deadly serious, and his anger seemed almost to ooze from his pores. "Randy's not the nicest man anymore. I admit it. That's why I try to look out for the people around here. He's basically harmless."

"Basically harmless" was not a soaring recommendation, but I let it go. The sun had risen over the buildings now, that soft morning light giving way to the more severe light of the day. I shaded my eyes. "Do you think he'll try it again?"

It took him a few moments, but he finally answered, "I can't say. I hope not."

That was not a ringing endorsement of our safety. "You think he should have been arrested?"

Gus contemplated this question. "I don't know how to answer that. We've been business partners for a long time, and friends for even longer."

"Sounds like he has some secrets, though." Randy's anger that night in the back parking lot of Yeast of Eden, and again at Jackie's funeral, was almost palpable. He had been out for blood, but who knew why? And what if he still was?

Gus grimaced, his lips twisting into an angry frown. "Doesn't everyone, Ms. Culpepper? Doesn't everyone?"

CHAPTER TWELVE

Everywhere I went, it seemed that Miguel Baptista lurked nearby. Okay, maybe *lurked* wasn't the best word to describe his presence. Santa Sofia was a smallish town, after all. It wasn't surprising that I'd see him around. But I felt as if I were newly pregnant, and suddenly, around every corner was a woman with a baby in utero.

Of course, I saw pregnant women everywhere, too, and I was not even close to having a baby. Divorced. No boyfriend. No prospects. That meant motherhood was not in my near future, yet my biological clock was ticking. It was Murphy's Law . . . or something.

This time, it wasn't a baby bump that struck me. It was Miguel. Gus Makers had gone back toward the antiques mini-mall, and I had packed up my camera bag, my back to the street and to Yeast of Eden. I jumped at the sound of three short horn blasts, then whipped around instinctively and just barely in time to see Miguel, his hand raised in a stationary greeting, driving past.

"As if a honk and a wave wipe away you being . . . you," I muttered. I couldn't quite call him a name. It didn't fit. He'd graduated high school and left to pursue his own dreams. I couldn't really fault him for that. We had been teenagers, after all, and that had been nearly twenty years ago.

But despite the logic of my argument not to hold him leaving me against him, I held fast to my anger. And I didn't plan on letting go of it anytime soon. Miguel Baptista maintained a special place in my heart, right smack in the middle of the fissure he'd created when he broke it for the very first time.

Olaya walked up to me at that moment. "Let it go, *m'ija.*"

"I'm trying to, believe me," I said. I gathered my things and followed her across the street and into Yeast of Eden. She had a little office just off the kitchen. Off-white faux blinds covered the two large windows, which were currently pulled up. The activity in the kitchen was hectic, yet organized. The staff worked quickly, jogging from one station to another, but together they operated like a well-oiled machine.

We spent the better part of ninety minutes arranging and shooting all the different bread choices Yeast of Eden had. "What did Gus want?" Olaya asked as we set up the last shot. At my direction, she placed a single rustic sourdough round on a worn teak cutting board lightly dusted with flour.

I adjusted the aperture and shot, moving around to get some different angles. "He was looking out for you, actually. Wondering why I was taking pictures of the bread shop."

"Hmm," she said, and it sounded like a mixture of surprise and approval.

"He was telling me a little about Randy Russell. I'm still worried about him. That he might come back."

She dismissed my concern with the wave of a hand. "He is harmless."

"That's what everyone says . . . until someone comes unhinged and shoots up a senior center . . . or a school. Then they're not so harmless anymore. What if *he* killed Jackie? What if he comes back and tries to kill *you*?"

She put the bread back on the professional-grade metal bread rack, then wiped the cutting board clean with a damp cloth. "He had no reason to kill Jackie, and he certainly has no reason to want to kill me. We don't get along. I'll give you that. But he is not a killer, Ivy."

I'd dropped the subject as we set up my laptop in her office and I uploaded the pictures. She sat in her plush black office chair, and I pulled up a smaller, less comfortable chair, then pulled up the photos.

"Gorgeous," she said as I scrolled through the shots.

"The lighting was perfect."

She went back and forth between several but finally zeroed in on one particular shot. I'd stood directly across the street and centered the storefront in my lens. With the pink awning and shutters, the quaint green table and chairs, the pots overflowing with flowers, and the bread artfully and delectably arranged in the windows, it was the perfect choice. "This is it," she said.

"It's a good one," I agreed.

We spent another hour selecting the interior brochure shots, flipping through the different bread types, evaluating the shape, size, and the overall appeal of each one. Finally, we had a solid selection, one she felt represented the vast yet traditional offerings of Yeast of Eden.

Just as I was closing the folder on my laptop screen, she put her hand on mine, stopping me. With her other hand, she pointed to a folder labeled "MapleStreet _May10." "Are those the pictures from last night?"

"Yes." I double clicked on the folder, opening it up. "I had my best lens, but it was dark. They turned out pretty grainy."

The first series was of Buck and Nanette Masterson walking down the sidewalk, then stopping to confer before they closed the distance to Jackie Makers's house.

"Nothing notable there, is there?" Olaya said.

"Not at that moment, no."

I moved on to the next series, which showed Buck standing sentry at the gate to the right of Jackie's house. I scrolled through the photos one by one, allowing enough time for Olaya to take a good look before moving on to the next shot.

"Look at the window of the house," I said, pointing to the shadowy face behind the blinds on the right side of the house.

"They actually broke into Jackie's house." Olaya's voice was incredulous. She muttered under her breath, ending with, "*Hijo de su madre.* I cannot believe they would do such a thing."

I still couldn't believe it, either. I hadn't gone by to show the pictures to Emmaline yet. I hadn't even had a chance to look at all of them myself. After the police had left the scene, I'd driven the short distance to Mrs. Branford's house, parked in the driveway, and walked her inside. I had no reason to suspect that she was in any type of danger, but I'd still wanted to be sure her house was buttoned up tightly. Back at my dad's place, I'd uploaded the pictures, then glanced at a few to confirm what I already knew. The quality was as good as I could have hoped for given the light conditions and my powerful camera lens, but they still weren't, by any definition, acceptable.

Now, with Olaya next to me, I moved through the next few frames. I'd taken multiples of each shot, so I flipped through them quickly, but once again, Olaya stopped me.

"What was that?" she asked.

I pressed the BACK button and returned to the previous frame. "What?" It was the same shot: Nanette in silhouette as she peaked through the blinds.

"No, not that one. Go forward."

A moment later, we both stared at the picture, stunned.

"Is that . . . ?"

She nodded, and a chill swept over me as she whispered, "Someone else was in the house."

Chapter Thirteen

I pointed to the upstairs window, showing Emmaline the figure Olaya had spotted in the picture.

"Wait," she said. "Go back a few frames."

I knew what she was doing. Looking at a series of pictures in a row, all of which looked basically the same, was like looking at one of those old cartoon flip books that showed a hand-drawn cartoon character going through some simple motion. Mickey Mouse spinning Minnie in a sweet dance move. Popeye downing a can of spinach and flexing his bicep. Curious George doing somersaults.

I went back to the first shot, which showed the shadowy image of Nanette Masterson peering through the downstairs window of Jackie Makers's house. Clicking the right arrow, I advanced through the next few photos one by one until we saw the change.

She stared at the screen. "Unbelievable."

In the previous frame, the upstairs window had been dark, but this frame held the clear image of a figure, backlit by ambient light from somewhere in the house. It was eerie and ghostlike, the way the upstairs window had been dark and now it was filled with a human shape.

"Male or female?" Emmaline posed the question aloud, but I knew she didn't expect me to answer. There was no way to know. Even with super crime center–enhanced imaging equipment, which I was pretty certain Santa Sofia didn't have, I didn't think there was any way to get more details from the photograph.

I scrolled through the next few pictures, stopping when the window upstairs went dark again.

"Nanette Masterson's gone, too," Emmaline commented.

Sure enough, the downstairs window was dark again, the blinds closed tight, not a speck of light coming from inside.

"I think that's when we first heard the sirens," I said, lowering my chin slightly as I looked at her to drive home my stance that in a situation like this, sirens did more harm than good.

She ignored me, instead scooting the laptop closer to her and taking over the touch pad. She went back to the beginning and scrolled through the entire collection slowly and methodically, taking notes on a pad of paper she'd pulled from her desk drawer. "So you started your stakeout around eight thirty?"

"Right. We wanted to wait until the sun went down. Mrs. Branford seemed to think the Mastersons wouldn't venture out and do anything nefarious until it was dark. We settled in a little before the sun went down."

"I guess she was right about the cover of darkness," Emmaline commented. "And you first saw them at —"

"About ten o'clock. Can I just say, as an aside, that stakeouts are not fun?"

She arched her perfectly coiffed eyebrows, tucking her thick black hair behind her ears. "You don't say."

"Watching grass grow, and all that." *Or maybe watching bread dough rise,* I thought. That was about as exciting as the stakeout had been before we hit pay dirt with the Mastersons' appearance. "I do say. I was ready to call it a night. I'd just told Mrs. Branford that we should give it thirty more minutes, then *bam*! There they were."

"And then what happened?"

I took her through the events, aligning them with the captured moments from my camera, ending with seeing Nanette and Buck Masterson make a hasty retreat from Jackie Makers's house back down the street to their own just as the police car pulled up.

"You stayed until the police left?"

"We stayed in the car, which was parked down the street. We waited a while longer after the police cruiser left, just in case the Mastersons came back."

"But they didn't," she said, still taking her notes.

"Not that I saw."

She stopped again at the photos showing the dark shadowed figure in the upstairs window. "And you never saw anyone else enter or leave the house?"

I shook my head. "No. Either they snuck out through the back somehow or they were still inside when Mrs. Branford and I left."

"Male or female?" she asked herself again.

"It could have been her daughter," I said, realizing that Jasmine very well might have decided to end her ban on all things having to do with her mother. I filled Emmaline in on what little I knew about Jasmine and the feud she'd been in with Jackie. "She came to the funeral," I said, "but she refused to help Olaya —"

"Solis? The bread shop woman?" Emmaline asked

"Right. She refused to help her clean out Jackie's house. Maybe she had a change of heart. She'd have every right to be in the house. Except . . ."

"Except that the lights weren't on. Which means it probably wasn't Jasmine." Still, Emmaline turned the page of her notepad and wrote down Jasmine's name. "So she and her mother didn't get along. She refused to help clean up the house and pack up Ms. Makers's effects. If she changed her mind and *was* there last night — although, again, why would she remain in the dark? — she would have been surprised by someone else sneaking into the house."

"Right!" I slammed my open palm against the desk. "Which is why she would have looked out the window, so she could see if she could spot anyone. A car, another person, anything to tell her who might be in the house."

"Any other ideas, Ivy?"

Buck Masterson was the only other person I could think of who'd had it in for Jackie Makers. He was already in the mix, so beyond that, I was drawing a blank. "No. Nothing," I said.

We rehashed the events of the stakeout one more time before calling it a night. "Dinner?" she said as she shut down her computer.

"Yes." As if on cue, my stomach growled. I'd had a chocolate croissant at Yeast of Eden earlier in the day, but nothing since. And I was starving. "Where should we go? Chinese? Thai? That new sandwich shop on Acorn?"

"We can talk about it in the car," she said, already halfway out the door. "I'm driving."

I figured we'd take her civilian car, but instead she got in the driver's side of a police-issued SUV.

"What happened to your Jeep?"

"It's at home. I just drive this most weekdays and save the Jeep for the weekends."

"I didn't think you took weekends off."

"This is Santa Sofia, Ivy. Pretty much nothing all that exciting or extreme happens here that warrants weekend work. Until now, of course. I won't sleep until we find Jackie Makers's murderer."

I hadn't paid any attention to where she was driving until we pulled into the parking lot of Baptista's Cantina and Grill. I bolted upright in the passenger seat. "Oh no," I said. "We aren't having dinner here."

"It's by far the best Mexican food in town, Ivy, and I need some chips and salsa. And *queso.*"

My left eye narrowed suspiciously, and I

tilted my head to the side. She'd zeroed in on my weakness. The gooey, melted deliciousness that was *chili con queso* had me salivating. It was everywhere in Texas, but not so prevalent in California. "They have *queso*?"

"They do, indeed. The best."

I harrumphed fairly indignantly. "I doubt that. I lived in Austin, remember? I don't know if anyone in California can make it as good as they do back there."

There was a glint in her eyes. "Wanna bet?"

I weighed my options. Miguel might be in there. It was his restaurant, after all. So I could refuse to go in, acting like an immature twentysomething, or I could deal with my past heartbreak and have cheese dip.

I was no fool. I held out my hand. "Winner treats."

She shook my hand rather vigorously and grinned, her teeth bright and white against the milky chocolate color of her skin. "Deal. Better bring your wallet."

Twenty minutes later, I took my wallet out of my purse and laid it on the table. Our main course hadn't arrived yet, but our large order of *queso* and the basket of tortilla chips were both gone. "You win. My treat."

She laughed. "Told you. Wait till you taste the Tacos Diablos."

We'd ordered one dinner plate to share. I was already stuffed, but when it arrived, it looked too good to pass up. Three home-made corn tortillas were cradled in a metal contraption made just to house tacos. Bacon and jalapeño-wrapped shrimp filled the bottom of each tortilla and were topped with shredded cabbage slaw and creamy lime-chipotle mayo.

I took a bite, and a bit of the sauce dribbled down my chin. My cheeks were bulging when someone approached our table, a shadow looming over us. "Welcome to Baptista's," a familiar baritone voice said.

Miguel.

My mouth was on fire from the jalapeño. I peered up at him through my watering eyes. I quickly chewed, then swallowed in one dangerously large gulp. Before I was forced to answer his greeting, with cabbage probably still in my teeth, Emmaline spoke up.

"Delicious as always, Miguel."

He rocked back on his heels, hands in his slacks pockets, a satisfied grin on his sun-kissed face. "Glad you think so." He swiveled his gaze to me, his grin lifting on one side. "And do you agree, Ivy?"

I swallowed the last of the food in my mouth, swiped a napkin across my chin, took a sip of water, and finally attempted a smile. "Definitely. Very good stuff."

Good stuff? I cringed at the lame comment on his restaurant's food.

His gaze found the empty bowl on our table. "Liked the *queso,* too, I see."

"Apparently, *queso* is Ivy's favorite," Emmaline said. "A result of living in Texas. She was skeptical, but yours passed muster."

I remembered Miguel as having one of those faces that was hard to read. He had never put his feelings out there on his sleeve for everyone to see. He masked his expressions, making it impossible to know what he was really thinking behind a smirk. Looking at him now, I could see he hadn't changed in that respect. The mildly cocky grin was still there, but what was churning in his mind behind it was anybody's guess.

"Glad to hear it," he said. "I wouldn't want you to be disappointed in the *queso,* Ivy."

My eyes narrowed involuntarily. I couldn't tell if he was being facetious or sincere. "Mmm-hmm," I said noncommittally.

"Take a load off, Señor Baptista." Emmaline scooted over, making room for Miguel on her side of the booth.

I tilted my head. "*Señor* Baptista?" I mouthed, eyebrows raised.

"Ah, he knows I'm just messing with him, don't you, Miguel?"

"I'd expect nothing less, Em."

Em? How well did these two know each other? The world had turned topsy-turvy.

They continued chatting, and it was clear that they were comfortable with each other. No, more than comfortable, they were downright friendly. I didn't know if I should feel betrayed by Emmaline for her friendliness with Miguel or if I was being hypersensitive about a man I had no business being sensitive about. Still, for a brief second I wondered if the reason Emmaline was still resisting Billy might be Miguel. But after a few minutes Miguel rested his forearms on the table, his attention fully focused on me.

"How long are you in Santa Sofia for, Ivy?"

Inside my stomach was in knots. I couldn't deny it; Miguel Baptista still had a hold on me. But outside I played it cool. Or at least I tried. "Cut right to the chase, why don't you, *Señor Baptista.*"

"It's all the military training, I bet," Emmaline interjected. "No time for small talk when you're in a ditch, fighting for freedom."

"Guess not," he said with a chuckle, but his eyes never left me. "So?"

"I'm here to stay."

Emmaline dropped her fork with a clang. "You are?" she said at the same time Miguel said, "Hmm."

I could have sworn I'd told Emmaline about my plans to stay in town, but now that I thought about it more carefully, I realized I'd only intended to tell her. I hadn't ever actually gotten around to it.

"I want to be here for my dad," I said.

Miguel dipped his chin in a single nod, and I knew we had some common ground. He understood.

From across the table, Emmaline grabbed my hand. "Texas's loss, but our gain."

"I mean, don't get me wrong. I'll miss Austin. It's a great city. But —"

"But since you found *queso* here," Miguel said, "you'll be fine in Santa Sofia."

"That's right," I said with a coy smile. "*Queso* and the bread shop."

Emmaline and Miguel both nodded in agreement.

"Olaya Solis is a master," Miguel said reverently.

"For a little while, Em thought she might

be capable of murder."

"What?" Miguel's spine went stiff as he sat bolt upright. "No way. That woman helps people. She doesn't kill them."

"I have to agree," Emmaline said. "I've been digging all day, and I have zilch for a motive. I'm still looking at the other Solis sisters, but I haven't been able to find anything on them, either."

Miguel whistled softly and shook his head. "Hard to believe there's a murderer walking around Santa Sofia."

Just as I was wondering how good a friendship Emmaline and Miguel had, and if Em would reveal the theory we'd tossed around about Jackie Makers's daughter, Jasmine, having a motive, her cell phone rang. She glanced at the screen, instantly muttering something unintelligible under her breath and holding up one finger. "I have to take this."

She answered with a curt "Davis," then listened. A moment later she had hung up and was gathering her bag, shoving her phone inside it, and sliding toward the booth's exit. "I gotta go, guys."

Miguel stood to let her slip out. I slung my purse strap over my shoulder, ready to join her, but Emmaline held out her hand, palm facing out, stopping me. But instead of talking to me, she turned to Miguel.

"Hate to ask, but would you take Ivy back to her car? It's at the station."

"Uh, no. Don't worry about it, Miguel," I said. "I'll just go with Em."

But Emmaline was already heading to the door. "Can't. There's a . . . a situation. I'm heading in the opposite direction. No time, really. Sorry. Talk tomorrow, Ivy."

"Sure," I muttered, but she was already gone.

"I won't bite," Miguel said, sliding back into the booth. He pushed the plate of Tacos Diablos toward my side of the table. "Enjoy. They're on me."

What the hell. Em had abandoned me, so it wasn't as if I had much choice. I didn't have to sacrifice my dinner just to hurry up and be free of Miguel's company.

"The *queso,* too?" I asked.

He laughed. "The *queso,* too."

A silence descended for an awkward minute before he spoke again. "I was really sorry about what happened to your mom."

The bite of shrimp in my mouth turned into a tasteless lump. "Thanks. I heard about your dad, too."

"Yeah. It was pretty sudden. My mom's still having a rough time of it."

"My dad, too. He tries to be stoic and

184

strong, but it's hard."

Another awkward silence filled the space between us. I took the time to look more closely at the man Miguel Baptista had become. With his six feet, broad shoulders, and lean physique, courtesy of years of military training, no doubt, he was definitely someone you'd want on your side in a dark alley. His already normal olive skin was tanned from hours in the sun, his hair was shorn close to the scalp, and faint smile lines on either side of his mouth softened his hard jawline. But it was those massive dimples that weren't exactly dimples curving around his mouth that clinched the deal. He was still the most attractive man this side of, well, anywhere. He was a cross between Mark Harmon and Enrique Iglesias. An odd combination, I knew, but there it was.

And, damn it, I still found him sexy and appealing.

As if he'd read my mind, he said, "You look good, Ivy."

I gave a self-deprecating laugh. "Divorce and death will do that."

"Yeah, I heard about the divorce, too."

"Good news travels fast in Santa Sofia, eh?"

He shrugged. "I run into Billy every now

and then."

I silently cursed my brother for sharing my business with the man who was supposed to have been my soul mate. But I had to check myself. After all, I shared his business with his soul mate.

"You never settled down?" I cringed at how the question sounded as it left my lips. It might as well have been Mrs. Branford asking, it had sounded so dull and middle-aged.

The corner of his mouth rose in a half grin. "No, I never settled down. I still have a few good years in me."

I tried to play off my ineptitude at small talk. "Of course you do. Lots of time."

"You, however, had better hurry." He tapped the face of his watch with his finger. "Tick tock."

I felt my eyes narrow, my glare piercing. "Tick tock? Seriously?"

He chuckled. "Yes, Ivy. Seriously. You're thirty-six," he said, his voice laced with sarcasm. "Practically over the hill."

I breathed in, holding in the rash response hovering on my tongue. Clearly, I still harbored a good amount of anger at Miguel. I was ready to pounce and take him down, but the glint in his eyes and the tone of his voice helped me check myself. He was pushing my buttons, something he had always been good at and had done in flirtatious fun. It looked like he was channeling the old days. Once again, I spoke without thinking. "Since we're both past our salad days, we might as well commit to each other right here, right now."

His grin morphed into something smoldering. "Done. We can meet at the top of the Transamerica Pyramid in the city on New Year's Eve five years from now."

My jaw dropped, and words failed me. He knew about Cary Grant and Deborah Kerr in *An Affair to Remember*? Or maybe he knew about Tom Hanks and Meg Ryan in *Sleepless in Seattle*. Whichever movie he'd connected with, the romantic gesture was unmistakable, and I didn't know what had just happened. But before I could even begin to formulate a response, three women bounded up to the table. Jolie, Becky, and Sally from Yeast of Eden's bread-making class stood there, all teeth and smiles.

"Ivy!" Jolie clutched her cross-body purse, barely containing her excitement. "I thought that was you. I told the girls here that it was, and Sally was like, 'No, that's not her,' but I swore it was, and, look, it is!"

I blinked, switching gears from the cryptic conversation I'd been having with Miguel to Jolie's "train of thought" speech. "Different setting, right? We're not covered in flour —"

"And Olaya isn't on your back." Sally's grimace seemed to be in commiseration with Jolie, although I didn't get the sense that Jolie herself was displeased with Olaya.

"Sal, she wasn't on my back," Jolie said. "I forgot the yeast. She was helping me fix the *conchas.*"

I'd already pegged Sally as whiny, but now I amended my earlier assessment. She was whiny by proxy. It didn't have to be her own issue she complained about, and it also didn't seem to matter whether the so-called wronged person was actually upset. Interesting. I filed the information away, thinking it might help me understand her even better at some point.

Becky, the quiet one of the group, cleared her throat.

Jolie instantly picked up on the cue, shot a glance at Miguel, and raised her eyebrows suggestively. "Who's this?"

Inside I cringed. My mother's death had sealed my heart. Introducing Miguel to the Yeast of Eden baking group felt too intimate somehow, as if I was opening up some part of my past to this bevy of strangers.

Miguel saved the day. "Miguel Baptista,"

he said, nodding at them collectively.

Jolie tucked a loose strand of her jet-black hair behind her ear and tilted her head coyly. "Hold the phone. Baptista? As in this restaurant, Baptista's?"

He smiled, and if I'd had to qualify it, I'd have said his smile was almost modest. "Family owned," he confirmed. Modesty. It was a side of Miguel that I hadn't seen, one he had developed in his adult years.

Jolie had a slew of questions, some about the restaurant and others that skirted around flirtation. She didn't come right out and ask about it, but she was fishing for information about Miguel's availability. "And Mrs. Baptista," she finally said when Miguel didn't take the bait. "Does she work here, too?"

This time Miguel's smile lifted on one side. It was a flirtatious look I knew too well, and the fact that it was directed toward Jolie sent a tiny sliver of jealousy through me. Irrational, I knew, but there it was.

"She does, as a matter of fact," he said. "Occasionally."

I did a double take. "She does?" Inside I formulated a different question. There was a Mrs. Baptista?

His brow furrowed, his head tilted to one side, and I got the sense he was trying to communicate something to me.

"Ah, oh, yes, she does. Of course she does!" I said, the truth of his statement hitting me like a ton of bricks. The only Mrs. Baptista in Miguel's life was his mother.

Before Jolie could inquire more about Señora Baptista, Sally swatted Jolie with the back of her hand, and this was followed quickly by the same knock against Becky's arm. "Isn't that the crazy guy from the antique store? The guy with the stick from that night that lady Jackie died?"

We all turned to follow her gaze. Sure enough, Randy Russell had sauntered into Baptista's. At that moment he looked around and spotted Miguel.

The three women seemed to stiffen in unison, their spines practically crackling with instant nerves.

"What's he doing here?" Sally asked under her breath, her voice thready with anxiety. She drew in a sharp breath. "Oh my God, he's coming over here. Why is he coming over here?"

It was true. Randy Russell was heading right toward us.

"Be cool, girls." Jolie seemed to have taken on the role of queen bee in this little group, and like any leader, she knew what to say to calm her followers. "He's not here to see us."

They stepped aside, making space for Randy Russell as he sauntered right up to the table. He glanced at the three of them, one at a time, glared at Jolie for an extra beat, gave me a cursory look, and then directed his attention to Miguel. "We need to talk."

The softness that had been in Miguel's expression a minute ago had been replaced with hard edges and lines, but he nodded. "What's up, Randy?"

Randy looked at us again, his eyes clouded with doubt. "Privately."

Jolie read between the lines and cleared her throat. "We'll just go now. Good to see you, Ivy. Nice to meet you, Miguel." She turned to her friends, gestured with a quick nod of her head, and off they went. Randy watched them go, waiting. Sally sent a nervous backward glance over her shoulder, but as the young women left the restaurant, Randy turned back to Miguel.

Miguel folded his hands on the table. "Anything you want to say to me, you can say in front of Ivy. She's one of my oldest friends."

Randy hesitated, seemed to consider this, then finally drew in a deep breath through his flared nostrils. Up close he was more weathered than I'd realized.

"That night . . . in the parking lot?" Randy began. "At Yeast of Eden?"

"What about it?" Miguel asked.

"I'd gone to the Broken Horse before I headed to the bread shop."

Miguel grimaced. "Yeah, I smelled the booze on you."

"Nothing wrong with a drink," Randy said, a defensive tone seeping in. I wasn't sure if he actually believed what he was saying, or if it was just what he told himself to get by.

"Nothing wrong with it," Miguel agreed.

I melted into the shadow of the booth, wishing I could be invisible so maybe Randy would get to his point a little sooner.

He must have read my mind, because the next second, he blurted out, "Someone else was there."

Instead of hiding under the invisibility cloak I'd wished for a split second before, I sat bolt upright, leaning eagerly over the table. Maybe he was talking about Jackie's murderer. "When? You saw someone in the parking lot?"

I really think Randy had forgotten that I was there. He took a wobbly step backward, and I wondered if he'd stopped by the

Broken Horse for a shot of courage before coming to Baptista's tonight. But he gave a deep nod and said, "Yes. With Jackie."

I waved my hands, trying to process what he was saying. "Back up a second," I said. "You got to the parking lot of Yeast of Eden. Kind of belligerent, I might add. You were heading to what? Have it out with Olaya Solis for some reason?"

Randy dipped his head in a solitary nod. "She's screwing with my livelihood."

I didn't want to touch that can of worms. Whatever issues he had with Olaya had to be dealt with by her. As long as she wasn't in imminent danger from Randy Russell, I was more than happy to let her handle him herself. I redirected the conversation. "So you got there and what happened? What did you see?"

"I didn't know what I saw," he said. "Not then, anyway."

Talking to Randy felt like pulling teeth. "But now you do?" I asked.

He hesitated again, as if he were weighing his options. Should he tell us, or should he not? Finally, he made up his mind. "Jackie was in her car . . . with a man."

I stared. "Wait. What?"

"You're saying someone was in the car with her?" Miguel asked.

193

"I saw him, sure as you two are sitting here. He was right beside her. I musta blinked or turned around, 'cause when I looked back, he was gone."

"When did you get there? To the parking lot?" Miguel demanded.

Randy drew back, thinking. "I didn't check the time, dude. I'm just telling you, she was with someone."

That niggle of doubt about Miguel being involved in Jackie's murder taunted me again. Surely he'd had nothing to do with it. I couldn't imagine him involved in anything criminal. But he was a man, and suddenly he'd been there to fend off Randy and his billy club.

I turned to Miguel, and for my own peace of mind, I asked the question that had been in the back of my mind since I saw him in that parking lot. "Why were you there?"

His eyebrows angled together, and I got the distinct impression that he knew why I was asking. He answered, anyway. "I was dropping off my weekend order. Nobody makes *pan dulce* and *tres leches* cake like Olaya."

"*Tres leches* cake? But she bakes bread."

"She makes it special just for Baptista's," he said patiently, as if explaining himself to an old girlfriend and giving his alibi for the time of a murder were second nature. "I was hoping she had a leftover sourdough from the day," he added, "but I never did get the chance to ask."

Randy slapped his hand against the table-top, bringing our attention back to him. "As I was saying. Someone was in her car. I couldn't see clearly, but someone was there."

"You didn't tell the police?" I asked. Telling Emmaline what Randy saw was the first thing I was going to do. She needed to know there was a suspect who had been right there and had slipped away. My mind went straight to Buck Masterson.

"With the chaos and the fight, and then hearing that Jackie was dead . . . I just . . . I don't know. Forgot? That doesn't sound right. Doesn't sound possible." He sucked in a bolstering breath. "But it's the truth, man. Someone was there with her."

He got the implausible part right. How could you forget you'd seen a man in the car in which your best friend's ex-wife was just found dead?

"Maybe I had more than one drink at the Broken Horse," he said reluctantly.

Miguel and I shared a knowing look. Like three or four or five drinks, maybe. That many might blur the senses enough.

"And you just remembered?" I prompted. I didn't want to alienate him, but I also wanted to get as much information as he was able to give.

"He was on the tall side," Randy said by way of answering. "Brown hair. A jacket. Maybe blue. Or black. Hard to say." His voice cracked, the first sign of emotion I'd seen from him, his anger notwithstanding. Truthfully, I was glad for it. He had to have known Jackie for years and years. A little sorrow at her death seemed in order.

From what I'd gathered, Randy had lived in Santa Sofia for a long time. So had Buck Masterson. Surely they'd crossed paths at one point or another. The description was a little vague and generic, but it *could* fit the man from Maple Street. I'd seen him only from a distance, and he didn't seem inordinately tall to me, but then again, Randy looked to be about my height. So to a man who stood five feet eight inches, someone five-eleven might seem tall.

"Have you ever seen this man around town?" I asked.

Randy shrugged heavily. "Nah. Maybe. I don't know."

"You need to tell the police," Miguel said.

Randy lifted his upper lip revealing an expanse of pink gums. "I reckoned if you

196

saw the guy, too, then it wouldn't look so bad that I didn't say nothin'," he said.

Miguel shook his head. "Sorry, man. I saw you talking to yourself, walking in circles, and then heading toward the back door of Yeast of Eden. If there was someone else in the parking lot, he was gone before I got there."

Randy nodded, looking resigned. "I'll call the deputy in the morning. That man — maybe he killed Jackie."

Maybe. Except that from what Emmaline had said, the theory was that Jackie had been poisoned. It seemed improbable to me that she could have met up with someone in her car and been poisoned with something that killed almost instantaneously. But what did I know? Anything was possible.

A little while later, I sat in Miguel's truck in the parking lot of the police station, where I'd left my car. I was still processing what Randy Russell had said, wondering if he really would call Emmaline Davis in the morning. There was no sign of her cruiser, and the light in her office was off. Either she was still at the crime scene that had pulled her away from our dinner or she had wrapped it all up and had gone home for the night.

"It was good to see you tonight, Ivy." Miguel's voice was low and sincere, and it hung there between us like a warm blanket.

I had my hand on the door handle. Being here with him felt like old times, and I had a fleeting thought that he might lean over and kiss me.

He didn't.

I waited, maybe a second too long, and an awkward silence replaced the warmth I'd thought I felt. Finally, I opened the door. "Yeah," I said, going for nonchalant but sounding impetuous. "You too, Miguel."

CHAPTER FOURTEEN

Randy Russell's confession the night before at Baptista's had stuck with me. Who had the mysterious person in Jackie Makers's car been, and did he have anything to do with her murder? I couldn't shake the feeling that he did.

But more than that, I had a niggling thought about something else. When I'd gone through my mother's boxes in the garage, she'd had photocopied essays — just like the one I'd found in Jackie's kitchen. Clearly, they'd known each other, at least on a cursory level. I also thought about my conversation with Olaya about Jackie's cooking school and the classes my mother and father had taken. I finally put into words the thought that had been circling my mind. Could my mother's death be connected to Jackie's? It didn't make a single bit of sense to me, but then again, nothing seemed to these days.

After walking Agatha along the beach-front, I headed straight to Yeast of Eden. I'd asked Penny Branford to meet me there, and I summoned Olaya outside. The three of us sat at one of the bistro tables under the awning. The morning sun was just beginning to peak over the mountains to the east, the dappled light softening the morning. It was too early for the street to be busy with tourists, but a few locals strolled along the sidewalk. Agatha was not a barker. She stared at passersby but stuck close to me. Her tail curled when she was happy, but she was a skittish thing, and the activity on the street had her on edge. Her tail was currently hanging down stick straight. Something was making her nervous.

"Shhh, shhh, shhh, *perrita.*" Olaya ran her hand over Agatha's shiny hair, calming her. To me, she said, "She is a wary one."

"Being wary can get a person far in this world," Mrs. Branford said. "Leaping in headfirst and without a plan can mean disaster."

I definitely agreed with that. Agatha would never run away from me or go willingly with a stranger. She stuck to me like glue, and I was absolutely fine with that. "I rescued her. She was the last dog surrendered from a backyard breeder in Texas. I never could find out the full story, but I was pretty sure she was abused."

We all looked lovingly at sweet Agatha. Her tail curved a little, and I sat back. I wanted to talk about my mother and Jackie, but I couldn't quite do it. Instead, I went with the other thing on my mind. "I saw Randy Russell last night," I said, and I spilled the whole story.

Olaya stared at me, then beyond the businesses across the street to the blue of the ocean. After a few minutes, she looked back at me. "He is sure someone else was with Jackie in her car?"

So she couldn't corroborate Randy's story. "You didn't see anyone?" I asked her. It hadn't occurred to me the night before, but on top of nobody seeing anyone in the car with Jackie, and no one seeing a person leaving the parking lot, no one had heard a car door slam. Maybe Randy Russell had had more at the Broken Horse than he'd conveyed and those drinks had had him seeing things.

She shook her head. "No one. I was thinking only of Randy and Miguel. That fight. It was not until later that we saw Jackie in her car. And she was alone."

Mrs. Branford grimaced. "And she was dead."

At first, the comment struck me as a bit heartless, but Mrs. Branford's expression was anything but. She was simply stating the sad fact that had led us to this conversation.

Olaya's eyes glassed over. Her tough facade had cracked for a moment, the idea of the killer made more real by Randy's assertion.

"It could have been Buck Masterson," Mrs. Branford said.

"My thought exactly, but how do we find out?" I mused. We'd already done a stakeout, and all it had shown us was that Masterson and his wife had broken into Jackie Makers's house. The why was still an unknown, but aside from following the man, I couldn't think of a way to figure out what he was up to.

Olaya's face lit up. "What if Mrs. Masterson wins a free baking class? We'd have her in the kitchen with us for a few hours and maybe —"

"She'd spill all her husband's secrets without even knowing what she was doing." Mrs. Branford clapped her hands with glee. "Brilliant!"

"Assuming she takes the bait and shows

up," I said, the voice of reason. It was a good idea, but Nanette Masterson was an unknown, in my opinion.

"Then we need to make it irresistible," Olaya said. "We will create a certificate —"

"I can do that," I said, getting on board with the idea.

We brainstormed ideas and finally settled on the concept of Yeast of Eden reaching out to members of the Santa Sofia community and offering free bread-making classes as a way to attract new customers and thank existing ones.

We moved from the bistro table in front of the bakery to Olaya's office. We gathered around the desk, me at the keyboard, and set to work on a Yeast of Eden "free baking class" certificate. An hour later the three of us sat back to admire our handiwork.

"I might incorporate this idea into the business," Olaya said, holding the printed document.

"It does look good," I said. We'd used the Yeast of Eden logo, which was a simple oval with "Yeast of Eden" prominently written in a typed font, and "Artisan Bread Shop" beneath it in a readable cursive. It was classic and accessible, like Olaya herself.

"How are we going to explain how she won it?" Mrs. Branford had asked midway through the production.

"The accompanying letter," I'd said.

Now Olaya directed me on opening up the letterhead for the bread shop, and I started typing. A short while later, I printed the letter and read it aloud to them.

Dear Friend,

Yeast of Eden has been part of the Santa Sofia community for more than fifteen years. Our bread is a testament to the artisan practice of bread making the old-fashioned way, and we've been fortunate enough to do what we love for many years. Our continued success is due, in great part, to people like you. If you're an existing customer, we'd like to say thank you. If we're unfamiliar to you, we'd like to introduce ourselves. We're offering you free registration in our exclusive bread-making classes. Learn how to make some of your favorites in la cocina, the bread shop's kitchen. Please call to register. Hurry! Spaces are filling up fast.

With appreciation,
Olaya Solis

Mrs. Branford clapped her hands. "Perfect! You have a way with words, Ivy, just like your mother did."

I waited for the tug of sorrow I'd grown accustomed to feeling whenever my mom was mentioned, but for the first time it didn't come. Instead, I felt pride. It started as a sliver of a feeling in my heart and spread outward, giving each of my limbs a pleasant sensation of warmth.

"Thank you," I said, smiling, savoring the connection Mrs. Branford had shared.

Olaya put her hand on my shoulder, and I recognized the gesture as a sign of her gratitude. She wasn't effusive; I'd already learned that about her. But she managed to show her appreciation with a single touch. I laid my hand on top of hers, and in that instant the connection between us grew. I understood suddenly what the Grinch must have felt as his heart grew three sizes. I was filled with what I could describe only as love, both from and for these two women. It wouldn't ever replace the relationship and connection I'd had with my mother, but it was the next best thing. There was something about a bond between women that fed the soul. I'd been missing that since I'd been back in Santa Sofia, and since my mother's death. But now it was rekindled, both with Emmaline Davis, my oldest friend, and now with Penny Branford and

Olaya Solis.

The moment faded, but the feeling of contentment remained. Olaya handed me an envelope, Mrs. Branford rattled off the Mastersons' address, and I folded the letter and the certificate, then slipped them inside the envelope. We stamped it, and minutes later, Agatha and I were walking down the street toward the post office to mail the summons to Nanette Masterson.

CHAPTER FIFTEEN

"She never called to register," Olaya said a few days later. I'd picked up Mrs. Branford on my way to class, and we'd arrived at Yeast of Eden, ready to bake.

"I tried to run into her in the neighborhood," Mrs. Branford said, "but she's been in hiding or something. Nary a sight or sound from that house all week." She shrugged. "Truly, I thought about calling someone to check on them. But I didn't. I'm nosy, but I'm not *that* nosy."

"I guess we'll see," I said.

I tied my floral apron on and then tied the back of Mrs. Branford's utilitarian number for her, and we set to inspecting the ingredients at our stations. I photographed the canisters of flour and sugar that sat on the counter, grouping and arranging them artistically, framing them in the lens to capture interesting angles and portions of the bags and clear plastic containers, spoons, and measuring cups.

I had reactivated my blog and had been posting more regularly. Most of my photographs lately had been of food, and more specifically bread. I had a good sprinkling of coastal images I'd taken on my morning walks with Agatha, and I'd started capturing the birds I saw around town, too. But the *cocina* at Yeast of Eden was chock-full of interesting things that I was loving photographing. Bit by bit, I was recapturing my creativity and was feeling more like myself.

The other class participants began trickling in. Sally, Consuelo, and Becky came in first, and then a few minutes later Martina showed up. Jolie trailed in last, just as Olaya was getting under way with the class.

No Nanette Masterson.

"Bienvenidos a todos," she said, a chipper quality to her voice, which I was pretty sure was manufactured. She was just as anxious about Nanette coming as Mrs. Branford and I were. We all hoped she'd hold some vital key to figuring out what had happened to Jackie Makers, most importantly if her husband had been with Jackie in her car just before she died.

I listened as Olaya talked about the baguettes we'd be making. "Baguettes are a

French staple. The flour is the absolute key ingredient. Sixty percent of the bread by weight is flour. We use only the best quality," she said, pointing to the canister at her station. "It is ambitious to be making baguettes at this point in our adventure together, but why not, as they say, go for the gold? Baguettes are just flour, yeast, water, and salt. And time. Always time."

"Why is it so complicated when it seems so easy?" Jolie asked.

Olaya smiled. "As I said, it comes down to time. All of us, we are too impatient. Cell phones. Social media. Work. We want to rush, rush, rush, but with the baguette, we cannot rush. We will wait while the flour and water and salt do their work in the bowl. It is magical. We will knead, we will let the dough rest, and we will let it rise. We will wait and let time work its magic with the dough."

Sally piped up. "But we're not here all night to do that. I have to help my mom later. I have other things to do."

Once again Olaya smiled. "*No problema, señorita.* I have the different steps of the process completed for you. We will work in stages."

We started by mixing together the flour, water, and a pinch of yeast. We each mixed our concoction and set it aside.

"Ivy," Olaya said. *Ven aqui. Ayúdame.*"

I stared at her, trying to piece together the three words she'd spoken to figure out what she wanted me to do.

"She wants you to help her," someone said from the doorway.

I turned, as we all did, to see Nanette Masterson walking in.

"Nanette!" Penny Branford lunged forward, an enormous smile on her face. She clasped her neighbor's hand ardently. I didn't know how well Nanette Masterson knew Mrs. Branford, but it seemed obvious to me that her enthusiasm was overexaggerated.

"Oh, uh, hi. Hi there, Mrs. Branford," she said, taking a step back.

Mrs. Branford didn't let up. "How wonderful to see you here! I didn't know you were a baker."

I stifled a laugh. Those were pretty much the same words Olaya had said to Mrs. Branford when she'd shown up at Yeast of Eden.

Nanette Masterson held out the certificate we'd so carefully created. "I don't bake. Much. I got this in the mail, so I thought I'd . . . check it out." Her gaze found Olaya's. "I meant to call ahead, but —"

Olaya waved her hand, dismissing Nanette's excuse before she had time to utter it. "We happen to have room in this particular class."

I met Olaya's eyes and grinned. Inside I did a silent cheer. Our ruse had worked! Olaya sent me a look that said to take it slow and not spook Nanette. I nodded, completely agreeing. If Nanette knew anything that could be helpful about Jackie Makers's murder, she wasn't going to just blurt it out. And if she or her husband *was* involved, then she'd work triple hard to keep her mouth shut. Which meant Olaya, Mrs. Branford, and I had to play this carefully.

"What did you need help with?" I asked Olaya.

She beckoned me to the back counter near the large walk-in refrigerator. We were too visible for us to have any sort of private conversation, but we shared another satisfied glance. Bowl after bowl was laid out across the stainless steel, each one filled with an odd bubbly white goop.

"Take one of these to each baker," Olaya instructed.

"Ew. What is it?" Sally asked, wrinkling her nose and taking a tentative sniff after I handed a bowl to her.

"That," Olaya said, "is the starter. What

you just created with the flour, yeast, and water will turn to this after many hours. We are speeding things up. I made these early this morning. This, *mis estudiantes,* is what yeast looks like when it starts growing. It is exactly what we want. *Exactamente.*"

I passed out the rest of the bowls before going back to my own station, giving Mrs. Branford a wink as I went by.

She waggled her eyebrows in response, and I stifled a laugh. She was not the subtlest person, but I doubted Nanette Masterson would equate Mrs. Branford and her wiggly salt-and-pepper brows with the subterfuge we were in the middle of.

Olaya showed Nanette to the station next to mine, then handed her an apron and a bowl of starter. "It is Mrs. Masterson. Is that correct?" she asked, feigning ignorance. She did it quite well, I had to admit.

"Nanette's fine."

Olaya clasped her hands together. "*Qué bueno.* And this is Ivy Culpepper. Ivy, *mi amor,* will you help Nanette if she needs it?"

"Oh, sure," I said, hoping my innocent act was as convincing as Olaya's. Of course we'd planned the whole thing in advance. Olaya had reconfigured the stations, moving Jolie to Jackie Makers's spot and sliding

Mrs. Branford over one. This had left the space next to me open and ready for Nanette . . . if she showed up.

Which she had.

I felt slightly diabolical and thought about rubbing my hands together, throwing my head back like Maleficent, and letting out a twisted "mwahahaha."

Instead, I smiled at Nanette.

Working with the starter as our base, we added flour and salt to our mixers, then put warm water into the starter bowl to loosen up all the little tidbits of goop stuck to the sides of the bowl. "You want every last bit," Olaya said, demonstrating how to scrape the bowl with a spatula. The water turned slightly opaque, the starter bits floating around in it. Next, we added another dose of yeast to the milky water and stirred to mix it in.

"Like this?" Nanette asked me.

I glanced over at her handiwork. "Looks right to me." I held up my camera. "Do you mind?"

Her mouth pulled down on both sides in a heavy frown. "Uh, no, thank you. I don't want a photo taken of me."

"Oh, no. I was talking about the yeast concoction."

"Why not take it of your own?" she asked,

glancing at the mixer on my counter.

"You can take a picture of mine," Jolie said. She took the stainless-steel bowl from her mixer and held it in front of her. I had to admit, I thought it would make an excellent picture. She had on a white and red apron with a red- and white-checked gingham ruffle and succulent-looking cherries as the fabric's main pattern. She clasped the bowl on either side with her hands, her fingernails painted red, grinning at her handiwork.

I aimed, focused my lens, and shot, focusing on the contents in the bowl only and blurring the rest. "That's actually perfect, Jolie. Thanks."

Olaya directed us to add water and the starter mixture to the ingredients already in our mixers and let the beaters do their magic, churning just until the dough formed a cohesive ball. "Now, at this point," she said, "we could switch to a dough hook and let the mixer do the work, but we are not going to do that."

Sally grimaced at the sticky mess in her stainless bowl. "We're not?"

"We are most certainly not," Olaya confirmed.

Consuelo piped up from her corner station. "My sister likes to make us work harder than we actually need to. We're going to knead this dough by hand."

Martina smiled, nodding. "Always. When we were little girls back in Mexico, she would make us sit under the single tree in ouryard, mix water with dirt, and make mud pies. If we did not do it right, we had to start again."

"*Otra vez,*" Consuelo said with a laugh. "*Otra vez!* Those were her favorite two words. *Otra vez!*"

"*Es verdad,*" Olaya said, completely serious, but I could see a glint of amusement in her gold-flecked eyes. "*Y hoy también.* Do not do this bread correctly and you begin again. *Otra vez.*"

Martina and Consuelo burst into laughter, then chanted, "*Otra vez! Otra vez!*"

Olaya dismissed them with the practiced look of an older sister at her younger, irritating siblings. "*Entonces . . .* my sisters can have their big laugh. We will continue. Knead until the dough is soft and elastic."

Nanette was the first to dig her hands into her bowl of prepared dough.

Olaya rushed over to her. "Turn it onto your floured surface first. We knead here, not in the bowl."

A pink tinge colored Nanette's cheeks. "Oh. Right." She grabbed hold of the soft

215

dough and plopped it on the floured counter. Everyone else followed suit, and a moment later we were each wrist deep in our dough, attacking it, kneading it, and turning it.

"Not too much," Olaya warned. "It should still be a bit rough. The yeast will keep working, allowing the gluten in the bread to develop. If you knead too much, the dough will overdevelop and be difficult to shape in the end. Not too smooth, *pero* not too rough."

I felt my dough, trying to gauge what would be just rough enough but not too smooth. Olaya came up beside me, touched the mound on the counter, and proclaimed it perfect.

One by one she moved to each station, making a determination if more kneading was necessary or if, as was the case with Sally, the person had over-kneaded.

Sally bit her lower lip and stepped back. "Will it be okay?"

"It is not too far gone," Olaya said.

"Oh, *Dios mio!* It will be just fine," Consuelo said. "Olaya, stop tormenting the poor girl. It is just bread."

Olaya turned on her sister, fire in her eyes. "There is no such thing as *just* bread." The blaze in her subsided, and she patted Sally on the shoulder. "I am instructing, not tormenting."

Sally nodded, but the expression on her face was sheepish and hesitant. She eyed her dough, clearly not sure if she could successfully turn it into the baguettes it was meant to become.

Olaya directed us to grease the clear glass bowls she'd placed at each station. "Put the dough in the greased bowl. It will rise for one hour."

Jolie worked two stations down from me. "She wasn't kidding when she said this would be an extended class," she said to Becky.

Becky brushed her hair away from her face with the back of her hand, leaving a trail of flour behind. "Good thing I canceled my dinner plans."

"Oh, give us the details," Mrs. Branford said.

Becky blushed. "It's not that big of a deal."

Mrs. Branford pshawed. "You know, dear, I'm far too old to go out on dates of my own. I must live vicariously through others."

"That's putting it mildly," Nanette said under her breath beside me.

"What?" I had heard her perfectly well but wanted to see if I could get her talking.

She kept her voice low so only I could hear. "That woman is a busybody. Always in other people's business. She's too old to get a life, but she needs one."

"She seems nice to me." It was an understatement, but I was playing a role. My hackles were up, and I wanted to defend Mrs. Branford. From what I'd already seen, Nanette Masterson was the one in everybody's business. In Jackie Makers's, anyway.

"Don't let the sweet old lady performance fool you. It's just that, a performance. She's . . ." She looked around to make sure no one was listening and then dropped her voice a bit more. "She's diabolical. She's turned the Historic Landmark Commission against my husband and me. We are looking out for our entire district. For all the home owners. For everyone! But that's not good enough. No, the HLC has called us out. Like we're the bad guys. She's almost as bad as Jackie was. The two of them have been thorns in our sides for as long as I can remember."

I couldn't believe she'd opened the door for me by bringing up Jackie Makers. I feigned disbelief. "Really? That's awful."

"This one?" She held her thumb up like she was hitchhiking and directed it at Mrs. Branford. "She's underhanded."

218

I had kept tabs on the other women in the class, noting that they had all left their bread to rise and had gone to wash their hands at the sink in the back corner of the kitchen. Nanette Masterson and I were alone.

"But why would she want to get you in trouble with the HLC?"

Nanette threw her flour- and dough-covered hands up. "Good question."

"How do you know it was Mrs. Branford? Maybe it was Ms. Makers?"

She hesitated. "I think it was both of them. My husband? He confronted Jackie the day she died. Told her to back the hell off and leave us alone. Do you know what she said?"

I shook my head, holding my breath, afraid that the slightest move or sound would wake her up and make her realize the extent to which she was spilling the beans.

"That we deserved her wrath. She actually used that word. *Wrath.* Well, someone got wise to her and gave her a dose of their wrath." She blinked, and her eyes suddenly grew wide. Realization had hit, and suddenly she was backtracking. "Not that I'm glad she was murdered," she quickly said. "Oh my, no. And not that we had anything to do with it. Buck — that's my husband —

he told me Jackie wasn't feeling too well, so he just up and left. Told her he'd talk to her about their issues some other day."

"So he left her in the car?"

"She was alive when he left —" She stopped, eyeing me sharply. "I didn't say they met in a car."

Shoot. I kicked myself for revealing that tidbit. "Oh, it was just a guess. Jackie said she had been at her own class, then had rushed over here. When you said they talked before she died, I assumed you meant *right* before she died."

She still looked suspicious, but she relaxed slightly. "She was alive when he left her," she repeated, as if saying it enough times would make people believe it was true.

"Did you tell the police? It could help them with the investigation."

She grimaced. "Yeah, by giving them a suspect with motive and opportunity. We're not fools, Ms. Culpepper."

"Don't you think they'll find out?"

"Why? Are you going to tell them? What's any of it to you?" She sounded harsh, but it was an act. I could see the fear in her eyes. She didn't know me from Adam, and yet she'd just handed me a suspect and motive for the murder of Jackie Makers. I couldn't help but rationalize that if Buck Masterson was involved, then my earlier thought that my mother's and Jackie's death were somehow related had simply been a case of my imagination getting the better of me.

"I was just making conversation, Mrs. Masterson. Don't worry about me." It was an outright lie, but what could I say? Emmaline's warning that Buck and Nanette might be the killers, and that if they were, they'd be willing to kill again to stop the truth from coming to light, surfaced front and center in my mind. Diffusing the situation was the only sane thing to do.

"People like her and that Jackie Makers," she said, glancing once again at Mrs. Branford, "they're the menace."

I bit my tongue, stopping myself from accusing her and her husband of exactly the same type of behavior. "Hmmm," I said, as noncommittal a response as I could muster.

I studied Nanette Masterson. Her dyed red hair was short and in need of a wash. She couldn't be older than fifty — at least that was my guess — but her frumpy clothes gave her an extra ten years. She had thin lips, which she was pursing. Her anger was palpable . . . and from where I sat, it seemed wholly unwarranted.

"They shouldn't get involved in things that don't concern them," she said.

I wanted to set her straight, tell her what Mrs. Branford had said, warn her to mind her own business, but instead I said, "Huh." I waited a moment, watching Olaya lead the other class members to the front lobby of the bakery, and then said, "So you and Jackie weren't friends, I take it."

"Not even close. I didn't wish her dead. Let me be clear about that. But now that she is, let's just say we sleep easier at night knowing we aren't going to wake up to some new terror she decided to inflict on us."

All I could think to say was, "Wow," but I kept that to myself. Nanette Masterson was a piece of work. "I helped Olaya clean out some things in Jackie's kitchen," I said, wanting Nanette to know I'd been on Maple Street.

She pursed her lips tighter. "Is that right?"

"Beautiful kitchen. Beautiful house, actually."

She grimaced. "She ruined it. Painted authentic wood trim inside. White. Why would she destroy something that had been so carefully crafted? That's the problem with the people in the historic district. My husband and I work to preserve our town's history, but people like Jackie Makers, they just destroy it on a whim."

"You mean the moldings? What's wrong

with white?"

"Not. Authentic."

"But it's pretty. It makes the house feel so clean and open. And it was her house, right?"

She gave me a withering look that I could translate only as "You're an idiot." "You don't move to the historic district and ruin a landmark house. The people who live there want to preserve history, just like me and Buck. That house . . ." She shook her head, as if she still couldn't believe what Jackie had done to it. "It should not have a green roof. And new windows? What was she thinking? You never replace windows in a historic house. The windows are its soul. That house has lost its soul."

"Because of new windows?" I happened to think the white grids and frames of the windows, edged by brick-red trim, were lovely. And new windows were probably far more energy efficient. If that house were mine, I wouldn't change a thing. In my opinion, it had plenty of soul.

"Clearly, you are *not* a historic home owner."

"No, not yet. Hopefully someday," I said, once again feeling that my future did include living in a house like Jackie Makers's or Mrs. Branford's.

She eyed me, seeming to take a closer look. "Have we met?"

Not in so many words, I thought, remembering seeing her and her husband the first day I'd met Mrs. Branford, not to mention the stakeout, during which I'd seen Nanette Masterson break into a dead woman's house. "I don't think so," I said.

She wasn't going to let it go. "You look familiar."

I shrugged it off. "I must have one of those faces."

"Red hair, freckles, those green eyes. You definitely do not have one of those faces." She stopped suddenly, and I could see her mind working. "Wait a minute. Six months ago. Maybe longer. I saw you at Jackie Makers's house."

I shook my head. "Um, no."

"Oh yes. I'm sure it was."

"It couldn't have been. Six months ago I lived in Austin. I came back here when my mother died —"

She inhaled sharply. "The woman who died in that hit-and-run?"

I breathed in, bracing myself for the wave of emotion that always came when talking about the tragedy. "Anna Culpepper."

"You look like her, don't you?"

"Most people think so."

"Then it must have been her I saw."

"I think she took cooking classes from Jackie, but I don't think they were friends."

As I said the words, I wondered if they were true. I hadn't lived in Santa Sofia for years; there was no way to know if my mom had become friends with her cooking teacher — and maybe the parent of a former student.

Nanette shrugged, her mouth pulled down in an exaggerated frown. "Perhaps not, but I'm sure I saw her —" She broke off, and a lightbulb seemed to go off in her brain. She pointed at me. "Wait. I know where I saw you. You were on Maple Street."

My nerves stabbed in my gut. Had she seen me in the stakeout car, spying on her? "Um —"

"I saw you on Penny Branford's porch. It must have been a few weeks ago. You *do* know her." She leaned against her workstation, accusation in her voice.

I feigned innocence. "I remember! I was looking at the houses on your street with my father. He's the city manager."

"And Penny —"

This line of questioning felt like the Inquisition. At least she hadn't noticed the stakeout. I resisted filling the empty space with further explanation and just said, "She was outside."

"What? Are you watching the dough rise?" Nanette and I both turned as Sally sashayed into the kitchen. "Come on. Olaya sliced a lavender loaf."

We joined the group and savored a slice of heaven.

Mrs. Branford caught me by the arm as we retreated to the kitchen afterward. "Got anything good? Did she confess, for example?"

"Ha! Not even close." I recounted the conversation as quickly as I could. "She doesn't like you."

She swung her cane and tapped the floor with the rubber-tipped base. She definitely didn't need it. "The feeling's mutual."

I separated from her before Nanette saw us talking, and then I returned to my station. As if by magic, my baguette dough had risen and was full of bubbles.

Olaya came around and punched each of our bubbly loaves, deflating them by releasing the air. "Now, we let them rise again for three hours."

A series of gasps and disbelief circulated in the room.

"Three hours!"

"That's crazy!"

"I have things to do tonight!"

"*Cálmense.* Relax." Olaya smiled, and I knew we wouldn't be here all night long. She disappeared back into her secret corner of the kitchen and returned a minute later with a shiny silver baking tray dotted with perfectly smooth and rounded dough mounds. "I have prepared the dough to this stage for you all."

She made the rounds, stopping once again at all our stations. We each took one of the soft, elastic mounds Following her directions, I divided my dough into three equal pieces. After flattening them into ovals, we let them rest for a few minutes. "So the gluten can relax like you just did," Olaya said.

She modeled the next step at her teacher's station, and we observed by watching her in the angled mirror above her area and followed her lead. First, we shaped one of the ovals into a rectangle. Next, we folded the rectangle in half and sealed the edges with our fingers. We flattened, folded, and sealed it again.

"Now look!" Olaya held her hands together in a prayer-like position. "See how it has stretched from about eight inches to ten? It is magical. It is bread."

It *was* pretty amazing. We laid the seam side down and gently rolled our rectangles

227

with our hands, working from the center to the outer edges.

"Not too hard," Olaya warned. "We don't want to make the dough tough."

After going through the same process with the other two pieces of dough, we placed the three fifteen-inch loaves on the three-welled baguette baking trays Olaya had given us.

"Your loaves will bake on your baguette pans, but I will have to move mine. I use a couche to let the dough rise rather than the baguette pan. It is the French method," Olaya said. She demonstrated with the loaves at her station, first sprinkling flour on a linen towel and then rubbing it in. She laid her three loaves on the towel, cradling them between the folds she created.

We cleaned our stations while the loaves rose for the final time.

"The final step," Olaya said when we were finished and after she'd moved her loaves to a baking sheet, "is to spritz them with water. This will give them their crunchy outside." She then scored each loaf three times at a forty-five-degree angle. "This gives the baguette its signature look."

"I don't care about their signature look anymore," Sally whined. "I'm tired."

"You will care when they come out of the oven."

The loaves were placed in the kitchen's professional-grade ovens.

"Four hundred fifty degrees until they are a golden brown," Olaya told the women.

Before long, the aroma of baking bread filled the space.

"Okay, maybe I do care. When will they be done?" Sally asked, and everyone laughed.

Olaya grinned. "Soon."

"Time to set the table," Consuelo announced. She'd stepped into a closet. When she came back out, her arms were laden with brightly colored place mats, spoons, bowls, and small plates.

We all followed her to a back area of the kitchen. Cream window panels hung on either side of an archway. Martina pushed them aside, letting Consuelo and the other women pass through. I hadn't known this cute room existed. A rectangular walnut table sat in the middle of the space. Twelve chairs were positioned around the table. They were red, turquoise, yellow, and green and were arranged around the table in a pattern.

"It's beautiful!" Jolie walked the perimeter of the room, taking in the delicate lamp in the corner, the story quilt hanging on the wall, the metal sheet with the words *Buen Provecho* cut out in an angled cursive font. A primary-colored Mexican flag banner was strung across the top edge of one wall.

Consuelo and Martina quickly set the table. They did it with an expertise that told me this wasn't their first time doing this particular job. When they were finished, candles flickered across a lace table runner, and each place setting had a sprig of lavender tied to the napkin. I completely agreed with Jolie. It was warm and inviting.

"Did someone order soup?"

I immediately recognized that male voice. Miguel stood in the archway. His mahogany hair was windswept, and his smile was enticing. He met my gaze, and I got the feeling the smile was just for me.

Olaya surged toward him. "Just in time." She took one of the bags he held, set it on the sideboard, and removed two tall containers. "Poblano corn chowder. *Perfecto,* Miguel. *Muchas gracias.*"

"De nada," he said, unloading the second bag.

Martina set two soup tureens on the sideboard, and Olaya carefully poured the soup, one container at a time, into them. Miguel carried them to the table and placed one on either end, between the candles.

Consuelo had disappeared back into the kitchen and soon returned with a wooden tray and three of the freshly baked baguettes.

We sat at the table and broke bread as Miguel ladled soup into our bowls.

Mrs. Branford sat next to me. She took a bite of the bread and breathed in the scent of the chowder. A slow smile spread across her face. "Olaya Solis, it pains me to admit it, but this is quite spectacular."

Olaya bowed her head once in acknowledgment. I could see the pride on her face. Coming from the woman who had been her archenemy just days before, this was a big deal. "I also hate to admit it, but, Penelope, your approval, it makes me quite happy."

CHAPTER SIXTEEN

I brought leftover poblano corn chowder and baguettes home. The hours my dad was working were getting longer and longer — a way to escape his pain — which I understood, but I missed him. And I worried about him. I'd texted him that I was bringing dinner, but he wasn't home when I got there. I set the table and readied the soup and bread so that I could reheat them.

And then I leashed Agatha and headed out for a walk. Instead of taking our normal path to the beach, I stayed on the sidewalk and in the neighborhood. Agatha trotted along, her bug eyes facing forward, her ears flattened back as she walked, her tail curled up tightly in a little loop. She didn't have a care in the world. I was envious.

As I was heading back, I saw my dad's car parked in the driveway. I pushed my worry aside for the time being, and my pace quickened. Agatha's little legs worked double time. A short while later, we were sitting at the kitchen table.

"Good day?" I asked. The small talk seemed so banal and pointless, yet I knew we had to keep moving forward in hopes that one day the unimportant stuff in our day-to-day lives would be worth thinking and talking about again.

"Normal day, I guess," he said. "Soup's good."

Billy, Dad, and I had all had to redefine what ordinary was. Billy was a lone wolf, so I didn't actually know how he was coping. He internalized everything and didn't share what he was feeling. My dad was the same way. He had nothing new to take his mind off things. Work, work, and more work was his only outlet. I, on the other hand, had Olaya Solis and Penelope Branford and my newfound baking classes, not to mention the amateur sleuthing I was becoming slightly obsessed with. It didn't make coping easier, but it did give me something else to think about.

"You'll never guess who made it."

He looked at me, the interest on his face genuine, if clouded by his numbed emotions. "Who?"

"Miguel Baptista. You remember him, right?"

Dad half scoffed, half chuckled. "How could I not? I think you cried for six months after he left Santa Sofia."

I slapped his hand playfully. "No, no. Maybe six weeks. He did break my heart, after all."

We sat in silence for a while. My stomach was in knots, in part because of the emptiness inside me, but the truth was that I couldn't push my thoughts to some remote corner of my mind. They escaped and returned front and center. Nanette Masterson had said that she'd seen my mother talking to Jackie Makers at Jackie's house, but as far as I knew, they hadn't been friends. No matter how I looked at the situation, it didn't feel right. I wanted my dad to tell me that Nanette Masterson had been mistaken. That Mom knew Jackie Makers only from the cooking classes they'd taken. That my mom's death had been an accident.

But deep down I suddenly wasn't sure. My mind whirled around the idea that my mom and Jackie were connected in some way, and that what we thought we knew about my mother's death might not actually be the truth.

I drew in a deep breath and launched into the conversation I'd had with Nanette.

"Were they friends?" I asked when I was done.

With his elbows on the table, he folded his hands and propped his chin on them. I took the moment to study him. His hair had always been a sleek dark brown, and while his mustache had been salt and pepper for the past seven or so years, the pepper had all but vanished. New gray hair had sprouted at his sideburns and temples. I hadn't realized it until this moment, but he'd aged ten years in the past six months. My heart broke for him all over again.

"Not that I'm aware. We took the cooking classes, like I told you."

"That's what I thought, but Nanette was sure she saw Mom and Jackie Makers on Maple Street."

His brow furrowed, and I could tell he'd thought of something.

"What is it, Dad?"

Instead of answering, he pushed back from the table and disappeared down the hall. A moment later he came back, sat down again, and slid a cloth-covered journal across the table to me.

I stared, afraid to touch it. "Mom's?"

"It's not a diary. Not exactly, anyway. Your mom jotted down notes and . . . just . . . stuff." He pushed it toward me. "I haven't looked at it. Haven't wanted to. It's too tough for me, Ivy. I hope you understand that. But if you want to know more about your mom, look in there."

I stayed up into the wee hours of the morning reading my mom's journals. Turned out the one my dad gave me at dinner wasn't the only one my mom had. There were eight altogether. I had figured out the order and had lined them up on my bed from the earliest to the most recent. I'd been afraid that starting at the beginning would take me on an emotional journey I wasn't ready to take. Starting with the most recent would be difficult enough, but that was the journal that could potentially tell me about her connection to Jackie Makers. And that was the thing I wanted to know about more than anything.

But once I'd got started, I couldn't stop. Page after page, I read about her students, her passion for everything French, sketches of the Eiffel Tower, and random pictures of birds, which had been her favorite thing to photograph. As I read her poems and snippets of ideas for stories and articles, my mom seemed to unfold before me. I saw her thoughts, her desires, her soul . . . all in new ways. I began to see her not as my mother, but as a woman.

I'd thought that not reading the early journals would make it easier somehow, but it hadn't. What I realized was that while I knew my mother, I knew only the part of her that she had shared with me. And she was so much more than that. She'd been a woman, a mother, a wife, a friend, a teacher, a writer. . . . She'd been so much more than I'd ever recognized. I could see why my dad didn't want to read her journals yet. It was too soon, and seeing on the page all that we were missing with her not here was salt in the wound.

I had made it to the last pages of the most recent journal and had all but given up on finding anything in it about Jackie Makers. Then I turned the page.

Jesus. I *knew* I was right. *Knew. It.* I won't tell Owen yet, not until I talk to Jackie. He wouldn't want me getting involved. The problem is that she doesn't really know me. Will she trust that I want to help?

How to approach her? Not at cooking class. Maybe I'll stop by her house. Yes. That's what I'll do. But what about Gus? That's what I still don't know.

I reread the entry, trying to read between

the lines. What was she right about? If she'd ended up telling my dad whatever had been on her mind, he would have mentioned it, so maybe whatever she'd thought hadn't panned out. I read the entry again, zeroing in on Gus's name. What about him? Could my mother have discovered an affair? It was possible, but my mom was not a gossip. She'd always made a point to steer clear of the riffraff in her school, staying above the fray. I didn't think she'd get involved in an affair that Jackie or Gus had been having. She didn't *know* them, so why get tangled in anything they were doing? Plus, they were divorced, and this journal entry of hers had been written long after Jackie and Gus had called it quits.

I turned to the next page, but it was blank. So this was the last entry. Flipping back, I checked the date of the last thing she'd written, but she hadn't noted it. I turned to the previous page. I read the date. Blinked. Reread it. It couldn't be.

But it was.

My heart caught in my throat.

The last dated entry had been written two days before my mother died.

I tossed and turned the rest of the night, mulling things over, trying to talk myself out of what I now suspected. But I woke up the next morning more sure than I'd been a few hours ago, and I made the call I'd wanted to make at two in the morning. I worried that 6:00 a.m. was still too early, but the bright, clear tone of Emmaline Davis's voice erased that concern. Ever since college, she'd been an early bird. Earlier than me, and that was saying something, since my favorite thing to do, even back then, was to photograph the sunrise. That meant I was often up before the sun. Even so, Emmaline usually beat me.

I launched in the second she answered the phone, and told her about my mother's journals and the entry about Jackie Makers. "Em, she knew something, and that's why she died. I'm sure of it."

"I don't know, Ivy —"

"I know I'm right. I feel it in my gut. I didn't think my mom knew Jackie Makers outside the cooking classes she and my dad were taking —"

"Which is so cute, by the way. I love that they did that."

I had, too. After thirty-seven years of marriage, they'd still loved each other and been sweet with each other. Another nail in the coffin of my dad's misery.

"But maybe she did *know* her," I said. "She learned about something. And she was . . . was . . . killed for it."

I stumbled getting the sentence out. I didn't know why, but I knew in my heart that her death hadn't been accidental. My mother . . . my mom . . . had been murdered.

CHAPTER SEVENTEEN

I looked for Gus Makers at the antiques mini-mall. I hadn't been in the building in years and years. Under different circumstances, I would be drawn to the vintage treasures. I would be educating my taste, which was all I could do given that I didn't have a house in which to put anything.

For now I walked straight to the front counter, bypassing the nooks and crannies of the shop, each filled with old china, crystal, record albums, bags and purses, vintage clothing, ceramics, reclaimed wood, shutters, old doors, and more. It wasn't Gus I found, however. It was Randy Russell.

My heart seized a tiny bit, his volatile encounter with Miguel that night in the parking lot of Yeast of Eden resurfacing front and center in my mind, quickly followed by his assertion to Miguel and me that someone had been in the car with Jackie Makers the night she died.

Which had proved to be true, according to Nanette Masterson.

He eyed me suspiciously as I approached the U-shaped counter. "You're that girl who was with Baptista the other night, aren't you?"

"Yes, sir. Ivy Culpepper. Good to see you again."

A blondish ring of hair ran like a horseshoe around his head, the top portion completely bald. He ran his hand over it. "Didn't I see you at Jackie's funeral, too? You knew her?"

"No, not really. I'd met her only once," I said, glad for the opening. At least I didn't have to try to come up with some vague story line so I could try to get information. "My mom knew her, though."

He looked skeptical, and his voice was rough, like he'd smoked a pack a day for the past thirty years and it had destroyed his vocal chords. His was a hard life lived, from what I could tell. "Did she, now? And who is your mom?"

"Anna Culpepper. She was a teacher at the high school in town. She, um, she died about six months ago."

His narrowed eyes opened wide as recognition took hold. "I remember that. She was hit by a car in the parking lot." The gravel in his voice loosened. "Darlin', I'm sorry for your loss."

I hadn't expected any compassion from him, and it softened his rough edges in my mind, despite the belligerence I'd witnessed and Gus Makers telling me that his business partner and friend was a bit of a loose cannon. "Thank you."

"What can I do you for? In the market for some antiques?"

"No house to put anything like that in right now. I'm staying with my dad."

"Okay, so what do you need, Ms. Culpepper?"

"I was actually looking for Gus. Is he around?"

Randy's eyes rolled up for a split second, and something in his expression made me think there was a lot of baggage in their friendship that neither one hid very well. "He'll be in later."

I tried to hide my disappointment. "Okay. Thanks. I'll come back."

He hesitated for a second and then seemed to make up his mind about what he was going to say next. "Gus hasn't mentioned you. You're friends?"

"No, no. I've met him only once or twice. It's just, my mom . . . her death. I'm trying to piece together some things that happened before she died, and I thought Gus could help me."

The creases of his weathered face deepened as he frowned. "I've known Gus since we were kids. He didn't know your mother. That I can guarantee."

"Oh." I felt my face fall. "How can you be so sure?"

"We've worked together nearly every day of our adult lives, darlin'. Pretty hard to keep secrets. I've managed to have a few, but Gus? He wears his damn heart on his sleeve. He don't know the meaning of the word *vault*."

I'd intended to try to get information from Gus about his ex-wife and whatever connection she might have had to my mother, but if what Randy said was true, then he might very well have his own information. "My mom talked to Jackie Makers right before she was ki—" I swallowed the emotion clogging my throat. "Right before she died," I amended. "I can't ask Jackie about it, obviously —"

"Obviously," he parroted.

"So I thought I'd ask Gus about it. Since he'd been married to Jackie and all."

"They were divorced."

"I heard they were still friendly, though."

He shrugged. "For Jasmine's sake."

I rested my elbows on the glass counter

and leaned in, lowering my voice to a level that suggested conspiracy. "I'm always curious about people. Why'd they get divorced?"

But if I'd thought Randy Russell would just spill the beans and tell me his best friend's dirty secrets, I'd been wrong. "Not my story to tell," he said. "I do know the meaning of the word *vault,* and this, Ms. Culpepper, is locked up tight."

"It's my story, so I guess I can tell it."

I jumped at the voice behind me and turned to see Gus Makers and his affable smile entering the store, the door silently swinging shut behind him. They really needed a bell on that door to announce customers. And owners.

I swallowed my guilt, hoping he hadn't heard our entire conversation. "Hi, Mr. Makers."

"Just Gus, remember?"

I smiled, tamping down the nerves in my gut. For all I knew, Gus Makers could have had something to do with my mother's death. She'd specifically mentioned him in her journal. Maybe she hadn't spoken only with Jackie. Maybe she'd sought out Gus, too. Did he have a secret worth killing for? "Gus. I was just . . . I stopped by to . . ."

"She wants to know if her mother and Jackie were friends," Randy said, jumping in as I stumbled over my words.

Whereas Randy had a ring of blondish hair that still crowned his head, Gus was completely bald. If he'd had a dark covering of hair, he would have been the spitting image of Denzel Washington, complete with the wide smile and the intelligence emanating from his eyes. He wasn't going to let his lack of hair define him; instead he had taken charge, had shaved it all, and had remained in control. The difference between him and Randy was night and day. Gus was Mr. Cool compared to Randy's curmudgeonly persona. They were both good-looking men, but completely different from one another.

"Your mother?" Gus asked.

This time I was determined to get through my own story without my voice cracking or the words catching in my throat. "My mom died about six months ago. I ran into someone who said she saw her talking to your ex-wife a few days before." I drew in a quick breath to steady my emotions. "I didn't know they knew each other, and I'm just trying to piece together the time before my mom died."

Gus folded his arms over his chest. "And your mother is . . . was who?"

"Anna Culpepper. She was a teacher at the high school. She and my dad were taking cooking classes from Jackie at Well Done." I studied him, looking for a reaction or a sign of recognition.

He gave me neither.

"So there you go," he said. "They knew each other from the class she was taking, right? Seems logical to me."

I tapped my fingers on the glass. "That's what I thought at first, but they were outside of Jackie's house." I didn't mention that his daughter might have been in my mom's English class. That was something to dig into separately.

Gus and Randy looked at each other. Gus raised his eyebrows, as if he were silently communicating that maybe I was a bit off my rocker. "Ms. Culpepper, maybe they *became* friends. It happens, you know."

That was, of course, a logical conclusion for someone who was not privy to the entry my mom had written in her journal. "Maybe . . ."

"Not maybe. Probably. You seem to be looking for some cryptic explanation. Let me tell you something I've learned over the years. The most obvious reason is usually the correct reason."

I sighed and spoke honestly. "I guess. I just . . . It's been hard, you know, losing my mom. I'm sure you understand. I miss her.

I'm just trying to get closer to her —"

"I do understand. I ask myself all the time why my wife — ex-wife — did the things she did, what she thought and felt, her choices and decisions. I can never know these things, and the last year isn't how I want to remember her. I choose to remember her the way she was when we were together. When we were raising our daughter. Before things fell apart for us."

He'd given me an opening, and I jumped. "What happened, if you don't mind me asking?" It was a bold question, but I needed to know if I was right and if my mother was actually murdered, and the only way I knew how to do that was to be bold.

Another look passed between Gus and Randy. Randy made a face, his brow crinkling, as he shrugged at his friend. The message seemed to be that it was Gus's life, so it was up to him if he wanted to share his dirty laundry.

"Let's just say that relationships are complicated. Secrets and lies. Secrets and lies are nothing but destructive," Gus said.

I hadn't expected that level of honesty from him, even though it was cryptic. From that response, I had no idea which one of them, Jackie or Gus, had kept secrets and told lies. Maybe both. I didn't come away with anything that would help me understand what my mom had discovered about Jackie and if that had had anything to do with her death, but I couldn't, in good conscience, pry any more than I already had. I said good-bye and headed across the street to Yeast of Eden to regroup and figure out what to do next.

CHAPTER EIGHTEEN

Olaya Solis had a style all her own. Loose-fitting dresses and caftans were her go-to apparel. I'd always classified such clothing in the housedress category, but on Olaya, they looked stylish and hip. Today she wore a flowing dress with a colorful symmetrical tribal pattern. The vibrant black, blue, and coral colors made her skin glow. She had bangles on her left wrist and gladiator sandals on her feet. She was a modern-day Aztec goddess — in her early sixties.

We sat down at a little bistro table in front of Yeast of Eden, and I told her about my mom's journal, the last entry, my conversation with Randy Russell and Gus Makers, and the niggling fear I had that my mother's death hadn't been accidental.

Once I'd finished, we sat in silence for a minute.

Only the sudden pallor of Olaya's skin showed she was shaken. "Murder?" She looked stricken, her green eyes wide and clouded. "Do you really think so, Ivy?"

"It makes sense. My mother *knew* something." I recited the words I'd memorized from my mom's journal. "Jesus. I *knew* I was right. *Knew. It.* I won't tell Owen yet, not until I talk to Jackie. He wouldn't want me getting involved. The problem is that she doesn't really know me. How to approach her? Not at cooking class. Maybe I'll stop by her house. Yes. That's what I'll do. But what about Gus? That's what I still don't know."

I went on. "Nanette Masterson said she saw my mom talking to Jackie on Maple Street. It had to be around the same time as the journal entry my mom had written. She knew something . . . *something* . . . and she went to talk to Jackie about it."

"But no, that does not make sense. If someone saw them talking and was worried about some secret coming out into the open, Jackie would have been killed then, too, yes?"

"But she was."

That simple statement hung between us for a minute.

"Maybe my mom told someone else what she knew. Or somehow someone, meaning the killer, found out. He or she killed my

251

mother to keep her quiet."

"And six months later Jackie was killed," Olaya said.

"They *have* to be related."

She took a bite of the chocolate croissant she'd brought out with her, and continued a moment later. "*Entonces,* Jackie died because she knew the same thing your mother did?"

I shrugged helplessly. Truly, I had no idea. I could speculate all I wanted, but as of now, all I had was a feeling. Intuition. A suspicion. And Emmaline was forever telling me that only hard and fast proof was worth anything in the eyes of the law.

"Hola!" Consuelo strode down the sidewalk toward us, waving her hand. Her style was so completely opposite of Olaya's. She wore jeans and a T-shirt that hung loosely on her rounded midsection. She was casual, whereas Olaya had style. Still, it was obvious they were sisters. Same nose. Same lips. Same almond-shaped eyes.

Martina trailed behind Consuelo, her cell phone pressed to her ear. I looked at the three sisters, noticing how different Martina looked. I already knew she was the quiet one, but she also had a much darker complexion, dark eyes instead of the green of her sisters, and almost black hair. Her features were more refined than those of her sisters. An aquiline nose, big round eyes, and defined lips. She was trim and was dressed in white fitted capris and a blue and white tunic. Her style was younger and hipper than her sisters', and she was definitely the one who stood out and didn't look like the others. Still, it was clear that their connection ran deep.

"Buenos días, mis amores," Consuelo bellowed as she reached us. She breathed in. "Ah, *qué rico.* I love the smell of the bread shop, even from outside. Eh, Martina?"

Martina had put her phone away, and now her eyes were closed and a soft smile graced her lips. "Oh yes. *Delicioso.*"

Consuelo looked from Olaya to me and back. *"Qué pasa?* What is going on with you two this morning?"

With a nod, I gave Olaya my okay to share what we'd been talking about. After Olaya brought her sisters up to speed, Consuelo tapped her finger against her upper lip.

"Many rumors went around about Jackie and Gus's divorce. Jackie never talked about it to us. Not even to Olaya, and they were closer than any of us," she said.

"What kind of rumors?" I asked.

"Some people said Gus had an affair, but I don't believe that," Olaya said. "He loved

Jackie. But he never would say what happened. He said it was his business and no one else's. I have to respect the man for that."

"I can't figure out what my mom meant when she said, 'But what about Gus?' To me that means that whatever my mom knew and wanted to talk to Jackie about affected Gus somehow." I'd been thinking about it. Could it have had to do with their house? "Was Gus okay with moving out?"

Olaya answered. "Yes, yes. Jackie bought him out when the divorce was final. He didn't care about that house —"

"It wasn't the house," Martina said. "He hated the politics of that street."

Olaya nodded to me. "Ask Penny Branford about that. Jackie said Gus got into it a few times with someone on the street."

I'd lay odds that that someone had been Buck Masterson.

Olaya went on. "After the divorce, Gus moved out. After twenty-five years, it was over. It all happened so fast, but now that I look back on it, I think it was actually a long time in the making. She always did her best to be happy, *pero* I know she was not."

Martina swallowed the bite of her sister's croissant she'd taken. "I remember there was a time when I stopped by her kitchen

254

to drop off bread for you, Olaya. When I went to the back office, I found Jackie crying."

"*Yo recuerdo,*" Olaya said. "You called me, and I came over right away. Hugged her and hugged her, but she would not say what had her so upset."

I remembered what Gus had said to me earlier. *Relationships are complicated. Secrets and lies.* "Was she always secretive?"

"No, not at all. That is the strange thing, you know. Jackie and me, we have been friends for many, many years. We told each other everything. But then divorce . . . and even before that . . . something changed."

I remembered what Olaya had said about the falling-out between Jackie and her daughter. "With Jasmine, too, you said?"

"Jasmine was so angry, but I do not know why. Jackie kept it — how do you say? — close to the chest."

I tried to put myself in Emmaline's police shoes. What would she do next? "Maybe we should talk with Jasmine," I suggested. Even if they'd been at odds, she was still Jackie's daughter. Without police resources, it seemed like the logical next step to me.

Without missing a beat, Olaya sauntered inside. We followed and gathered around as she picked up the phone and dialed. A moment later she was talking to Jasmine.

"*Cómo estás, m'ija?*" she said. They talked for a minute, and then Olaya cut to the chase. "*Bueno.* See you then."

I hadn't realized I'd been holding my breath until Olaya hung up the phone. What if the secret my mother had uncovered had to do with Jasmine? What if Jasmine Makers, daughter of Jackie and Gus, had killed my mother, then killed her own mom? It seemed unfathomable, and yet I knew stranger things had happened. Emmaline had told me on more than one occasion that people killed for the most trivial reasons. And as Gus had said, the most obvious reason was usually the right reason. I doubted my mom had somehow become privy to an elaborate corporate embezzling scheme or some political corruption in Santa Sofia. Her discovery had probably been about something so banal that she never could have imagined someone would kill over it.

I released the air trapped in my lungs. But someone *had* killed over it.

"You will come with me," Olaya said to me. "If Jasmine knows anything, we may be able to get it out of her."

"Look at you two," Consuelo said. "You are like two real-life detectives. *Como* Jennifer Lopez in that police show."

Whereas Consuelo looked amused, Martina seemed far more serious. "*Con cuidado.* You must be careful. Remember, someone killed Jackie. And if you are right, Ivy, someone killed your mother, too."

It was sobering, but accurate — and exactly what Emmaline had said to me. Olaya and I had to be very careful. This was no game. This was murder.

CHAPTER NINETEEN

I'd seen Jasmine Makers from the back as she sat in a front pew at Jackie's funeral, but now, at Jackie's house, I had the opportunity to get a closer look and really develop a first impression. I'd seen her father up close more than I'd seen her mother, but there was no doubt that she was a combination of the two. With a white mother and a black father, she'd ended up with blue eyes and skin the color of milky hot chocolate. With her cropped hair, she was refined and stunning from head to toe.

Olaya greeted her at the front door. Jasmine gave her mother's oldest friend a hug, and from where I stood, it seemed genuine.

"M'ija," Olaya said. "You look good."

Jasmine smiled wanly. "I guess."

As I watched them, I felt for Jasmine. Beautiful as she was, she looked worn out, with dark circles under her eyes. I wondered if she'd slept a full night since her mother's death.

"I brought you something," Olaya said, leading her into the kitchen.

"Olive loaf?" Jasmine asked. Her eyes remained flat, though, a sign that she was trying, but that her emotions had a strong hold on her.

"Your favorite. You have not been in to the bread shop in a long while."

"I know. I'm sorry. Just busy, I guess."

Olaya gestured at me. "Have you met Ivy Culpepper? She is a wonderful photographer, *pero* now she is my apprentice at the shop."

I was? Her apprentice? That was news to me. I was loving baking bread, but I didn't think I had the inherent talent to be Olaya's apprentice. Nevertheless, I smiled softly and greeted Jasmine. "Nice to meet you. I'm very sorry about your mother."

She gave me the same detached smile, and I suddenly understood the depth of the rift between her and Jackie. It was a deep chasm that, at least for Jasmine, seemed unbridgeable even in death.

"Ivy lost her mother about six months ago," Olaya said, pulling out a chair at the kitchen table. She sat, and then Jasmine and I followed suit. "She was a teacher at Santa

259

Sofia High School."

Understanding crossed Jasmine's face. "That was your mom? The one hit by a car?"

I blinked away the emotion. "Mmm-hmm. It's been difficult. I know just what you're going through."

A hardness settled onto her expression. "No offence, Ivy, but I don't think you do. Your mom . . . the accident. That was tragic, but my mom was killed. Murdered."

"Jasmine!" Olaya pronounced the name as any Spanish speaker would, saying the J like a Y. "They are both tragedies."

I brushed aside Olaya's indignation. "It's okay, really. But, Jasmine, I want to tell you this. The reason I'm here."

She looked at me, a wall still up between us. "Okay . . . ?"

I'd contemplated how to approach the subject. Should I be cagey and subtle and try to pull information from an unwitting suspect, or should I be direct? In the end, I opted for direct. I wasn't trained to investigate anything except a sunrise with my camera and the best light in which to photograph someone. Trying to act like Miss Marple or Jessica Fletcher seemed like a very bad idea. "I've come to believe that my mom was also . . . ." I swallowed hard to get the final word out. "Murdered."

Whatever reaction I'd been expecting from Jasmine, it wasn't what she gave me. She scoffed. "So, what? You want to form a murdered daughters' club? Bond over our dead mothers and sing 'Kumbaya'?"

I felt like I'd been slapped, but Olaya reacted for me. "*M'ija,* what is wrong with you?"

Jasmine shoved back from the table, nearly knocking the chair over behind her. "What's wrong with me is that people need to stop thinking they know what I'm feeling. Olaya, I love you. But you don't know what my mom did. She betrayed me. She betrayed my dad. She . . . she . . ."

Olaya reached for her hand, pulled her close until she could wrap her up in a mama bear hug. "It is okay, *m'ija.* People make mistakes. Holding on to your anger, it is hurting you. Only you."

Jasmine's hard exterior cracked under Olaya's motherly embrace. Her shoulders heaved, and a sob escaped, muffled against Olaya's shoulder. "She lied. All these years, she'd been lying to us."

I held my breath, hardly daring to exhale for fear any sound would snap Jasmine out of her safe zone and back to her protected reality.

Olaya patted her back, comforting her.

Encouraging her. She wanted the truth as much as I did. More maybe, since Jackie had been her closest friend. "Lying about what, *m'ija*?"

Jasmine pulled away, wiping away a tear with the back of her hand. So she wasn't the coldhearted young woman she presented herself as. She was hurt. Betrayed. And I felt for her. "She had a baby, Olaya." She sucked in a shaky breath. "A daughter." She shook her head, as if she were clearing cobwebs away, and her voice dropped to a whisper. "I have an older sister somewhere."

Olaya looked taken aback. It was clear she'd never suspected that *this* was the source of discontent between Jackie and Jasmine. "A daughter," she said quietly, as if she were trying to make sense of that bit of information and the fact that she hadn't known about it. How was that even possible? She snapped her head up. "Are you sure?"

"I'm positive. I got a letter in the mail. At first I thought it was a joke, right? I didn't believe it. But I asked her." Her voice escalated. "I asked her straight out, and she couldn't deny it."

I rewound. "You said you got a letter in the mail?"

She nodded.

"When was that?" I asked.

"I don't know. A year and a half ago?"

So that explained the big falling-out Jackie and Jasmine had had, then.

"Where is she? Your si . . . , Jackie's other dau . . . child?" I said.

Jasmine shrugged and looked at Olaya. "She cheated on my dad, you know. He was in the marines way back before I was born. They hadn't been married that long, but she got pregnant by someone else. She kept it a secret for a few months, and then he was deployed. She had the baby while he was gone, and gave it up for adoption."

"And years and years later your father found out," Olaya said, nodding to herself, as if it all suddenly made sense. "The reason for the divorce."

When I'd first heard of the rift between Jackie and her daughter, I'd thought that Jasmine was selfish and not a very likable person. That was before I'd heard her story and learned about the bombshell dropped on her life. My perception of her had been instantly reshaped, and I felt for her. I still wished, for her sake, that she'd been able to be in a better place with her mom before her death, but I understood now why they'd fallen away.

Gus's words came back to me. *Secrets and*

lies. They were hard to overcome. "Your dad must have been devastated."

"That's one way to put it. He always said she was the love of his life, but when he found out, he just couldn't forgive her. It wasn't even that she'd cheated on him and had another baby — okay, well, it was — but it was more that she'd lied about it for so long. He said their entire marriage had been built on this faulty foundation, you know? Everything was a lie."

Olaya looked shell-shocked. "How could I not have known?"

"You were friends back then?" I asked.

Olaya nodded. "Oh yes. She was the first person I met when I moved to Santa Sofia. It has been, oh, thirty years now. *Pero* she was not pregnant —" She broke off, her eyebrows lifting as she realized something. "After Gus, your dad, was deployed, she went away for a few months. I'm trying to remember. . . ." She thought for a minute, then snapped her fingers. "I think it was for a cooking program, but I wonder . . ."

"Maybe it was so she could go off and have the baby?" I asked.

"It is the only thing that makes sense. If she was here, she could not have hidden it."

For more than twenty-five years, Jackie had kept her secret well hidden. She must have felt unhinged when Jasmine confronted her about the child she'd long since forgotten.

The child who had found her birth mother and her sister.

I slipped my cell phone from my back pocket, stepped away from the table, and leaned against the slick cement countertop in Jackie's kitchen. Jasmine's story had created an entirely new possibility for Jackie's murder, and I had to tell Emmaline. I quickly texted her the abridged version of Jasmine's story, ending with:

Maybe Jackie's daughter was mad enough to kill her mother over being abandoned by her. It's possible. And if my mom figured it out somehow . . . it could all be connected.

I tapped the pads of my fingers on the counter while I awaited her reply. "Come on, Em," I said under my breath. She was taking too long.

Finally, her response came.

Wow. What a soap opera. Good work, Detective Culpepper. I'll see what I can find out.

Another text came immediately after.

265

Could you be careful, though? Statistically, if a person has killed once, it's easier for them to kill again. I prefer you alive.

I told her I'd be on high alert at all times, then smiled to myself. I was proud. I wasn't a detective, but I'd succeeded in finding a new possible motive for Jackie Makers's murder.

What I hadn't done, however, was find a link between that and my own mother's death. But a possibility came to me the next second. "That essay," I said.

Olaya and Jasmine both looked at me.

"What essay?" Jasmine asked.

"Olaya, that day we went through the cookbooks. We found a school essay with Jackie's things. We thought it might have been yours, Jasmine, but what if it wasn't?" My heart was in my throat. Had I just figured out how my mom was involved and why she was killed? I leaned forward. "Olaya, do you still have it?"

Her face clouded for a moment and then cleared as she realized why I was asking. She went to the cookbook shelves we'd sorted through and searched through a stack of papers and books she'd set aside. "Right here," she said, holding out the sheet of paper.

The typed and double-spaced piece of writing felt powerful in my hands. I knew that it held a clue to my mother's death. I reread the prompt, silently at first, then aloud to Jasmine and Olaya. "Write a story about a time when you taught something to someone. What you taught could be a song, an activity, a game, a way of figuring out a homework problem, or something else. Be sure to narrate an event or a series of events and to include specific details so that the reader can follow your story."

Jasmine looked from Olaya to me. "I don't understand. What is that?"

I tried to tamp down my beating heart and the wave of heat that was pooling in my head. "I think this is the reason my mom was killed."

CHAPTER TWENTY

First, I studied the notes in the margin. They were faded and scribbled, but the more I looked at them, the more confident I was that they'd been written by my mother. This prompt had been given to her students. Which, if I was right, meant that Jackie Makers's other daughter had been the one in my mom's class.

What it didn't necessarily mean was that the girl was a killer. It was one thing to write an anonymous letter to your sister saying that you existed, but it was quite another to kill your birth mother over giving you up for adoption. It was a stretch that even I couldn't quite believe.

And it didn't explain a motive for killing my mother, either.

When I'd first read the essay, I'd thought, as my mother had commented on in her margin notes, that it was cryptic and incomplete. Some lesson was alluded to but never stated directly. But now, as I reread it from the lens of it being Jackie's unwanted daughter, I filled in the blanks. It felt more like a threat than anything else. The lesson was that people made their choices and had to live with the consequences. If I read between the lines, the message was that Jackie had chosen to give her child up, and now, years later, she had to face the truth about that decision with her other child and her husband. The secondary message was that the decision to give up her child hadn't affected only her. Decisions, by their very nature, had a long reach, often far beyond what we thought they did. In Jackie's case, the choice to give up her daughter had affected the child's life, of course, but much later it had also had a major impact on Jasmine's and Gus's lives.

The last line of the essay echoed in my mind. "Was it worth it?"

I could answer that quickly and honestly, because another piece of collateral damage to Jackie's choice so long ago was that my mother had died. No, it was not worth it. And it was not fair.

I gasped, rolling over in my bed, my eyes flying open. My sleep had been fitful, one face flashing in my mind over and over.

"There was a teacher — Mrs. Culpepper," she'd said when I first met her. She was the right age, in her mid- to late twenties. A few years older than Jasmine Makers.

Could she be the one?

Could Jolie, from the Yeast of Eden baking classes, be Jackie's other daughter?

CHAPTER TWENTY-ONE

I sat in the restaurant lobby of Baptista's, waiting for Miguel. I didn't know what to do with my dream and what I thought might be the truth about Jolie. I'd scoured my mother's teaching boxes again, looking for some shred of proof that Jolie had been one of her students. I'd found a stack of photocopied essays with the same writing prompt as the one we'd found among Jackie's cookbooks, but I'd seen nothing with Jolie's name. Which indicated that the one in Jackie's possession could well belong to her.

My cell phone rang.

"You got my message?" I said by way of answering. I had called Olaya to find out Jolie's last name from her Yeast of Eden class registration — Jolie Flemming — then had passed it on to Emmaline.

"Yep," Em replied.

"Are you going to question her?"

"I don't know, Ivy. It's not much to go

on. Let me dig around a little more."

"We have class at Yeast of Eden tomorrow," I offered. "Four o'clock."

"I need more, Ivy. I need proof."

"I'll get it for you," I said, more determined than I'd been about anything in my life.

Miguel walked through the dining room of the restaurant just as I hung up with Emmaline. "This is a surprise," he said.

"Sorry for just dropping by, but I had a question, and it couldn't wait." I had to speak over the din of the lunch crowd.

"I'm not sorry," he said, his strong jawline and grin revealing those two deep dimple-like crevices on either side of his mouth. "Want to walk?"

We left Baptista's and headed toward the pier. The restaurant's location had to be the best in town. It was on the right side of the pier, with an expanse of windows facing the ocean. They boasted the freshest seafood dishes in town, all with a Latin American flare. I had had a few minutes to look at the menu while I waited and had noted the house specialties. The bacon and jalapeño-wrapped shrimp tacos, which I'd had and loved, had looked to be a crowd favorite. The crab- and shrimp-stuffed avocados had caught my eye. I'd have to bring Olaya and

Mrs. Branford here for dinner one night. Girls' night out, multigenerational-style.

Miguel and I walked in companionable silence for a few minutes.

"See the seals?" he said, breaking into my thoughts. "They sun themselves on those rocks every single day. Watching them is one of my favorite things to do."

I could see why. The salt air, the soft breeze, and the slick black water mammals would make a perfect afternoon for me, too.

I wasn't sure how much to tell him about what I'd learned. We weren't exactly friends anymore, yet I still felt linked to him. Maybe more than I did with any of my other old connections in Santa Sofia, with the exception of Emmaline. I guessed history had a way of erasing the years we'd spent apart.

We leaned against the railing of the pier, the breeze blowing gently, the bright blue sky dotted with puffs of white clouds. I could see why he loved being out here. It was the same reason I loved to walk with Agatha along the beachfront. Being so close to the surf brought me a sense of calm that I couldn't find anywhere else. I'd missed it the years I'd been in Texas, but now that I was back, I didn't think I could ever leave. I breathed in the fresh, damp salt air, and as I exhaled, the tension I'd been holding was released.

Miguel turned to face me, one elbow propped on the railing. "What did you want to ask me?"

I debated simply asking the question, but instead I opted for the full account of what I'd learned, beginning with Jackie Makers's attempt to oust Buck Masterson from the historic district's council, Nanette Masterson breaking into Jackie's house, Gus Makers's comment about secrets and lies, and Jasmine's confession that Jackie had had another daughter. I ended with my belief that my mom had not died accidentally but had been murdered. "I'm sure they're connected," I said, gauging his reaction. So far, he'd schooled his face, keeping it noncommittal.

"So tell me what you think."

I looked back at the seals, wishing for a moment that life could be as simple as lying on a rock and soaking in the sun. Then I remembered that there were sharks out there just waiting for their next meal, and usually that meant a poor unsuspecting seal. No creature was safe.

"What I think is that my mom realized one of her students was Jackie's daughter. I'm not sure how, but it has something to do with the essay that we found at Jackie's house. I think she met with Jackie and gave her the essay. But somehow, someone found out and wanted to keep my mom quiet. That's why she was killed."

"By someone, you mean the other daughter?"

Did I? I wasn't sure, because I didn't understand that as a motive for murder. "Maybe?"

Miguel's brows pinched together slightly, creases appearing on his forehead. "Let me play devil's advocate."

"Okay." I braced myself for him to discount my theories completely and tell me to leave well enough alone. Why dredge up my mother's death? She was gone, and I should hang on to the best memories I had of her.

"If you're right and this woman, Jolie, is Jackie's daughter, and that's a big if since it's just a guess on your part, right?" I nodded, and he continued. "She wouldn't have had a reason to kill your mom. That is, assuming she's the one who sent the letter to Jasmine telling her about her existence. By the time your mom figured it out, Jasmine knew, Jackie knew Jolie was back, Gus and Jackie had got divorced. Jackie's world had already fallen apart, right?"

I breathed a sigh of relief. On the one

hand, Miguel hadn't dismissed my effort to ferret out the truth, like I'd feared he might. But, on the other hand, he had put into words what I'd just thought, and I was back to square one. He was right; the time frame didn't work. I went through what I knew in my head, making a mental list in the order that things had happened:

- Jasmine gets an anonymous letter about the sister she didn't know about.
- Jasmine confronts her mom and presumably tells her dad.
- Jasmine and Jackie have a huge falling-out that lasts until Jackie's death.
- Gus and Jackie get divorced.
- My mom puts two and two together and realizes that Jolie is Jackie's daughter.
- Mom meets with Jackie, possibly gives her the essay Jolie wrote, and what? Warns her? But Jolie's already made herself known, so she has nothing to hold over Jackie.
- My mom dies.
- Six months later, Jackie dies.

"You're right," I said. "It doesn't make any sense."

Miguel started walking again, heading

toward the end of the pier. I fell into step beside him. We passed a bait-and-tackle shop; a surf-wear shop that sold swimsuits, touristy T-shirts, boogie boards, and miscellaneous knickknacks; and a glassblowing shop run by a local family of glass artists. The Glassblowing Shop, as it was so creatively named, had been on the pier for as long as I could remember and sold hand-blown glassware, as well as novelty items and unique gifts. I stopped to gaze in the window. Galileo thermometers were artfully arranged on a table, each cylindrical container filled with liquid and then smaller floating glass vessels, which rose or fell depending on the temperature. I'd always loved the colorful fluid in the small upside-down teardrops inside the thermometers.

My gaze settled on the largest cylinder, and I watched as a blue glass teardrop inside rose to the top, displacing a yellow-filled one. This was how I needed to look at the situation, I realized. I might be wrong about what my mom had discovered and talked with Jackie about, but the fact was, she'd discovered something, and she'd met with Jackie. Nanette had seen her, and my mom had written about it in her journal. Those were the facts.

Like the thermometer, I needed to displace the old theory, push it down, so I could allow a new idea to rise to the surface.

Miguel seemed to read my mind. "You've been focusing on the theory that the big secret Jackie had was about the child she gave up for adoption, making your theory fit the facts rather than letting the facts guide the theory. It wasn't widely known, but Jasmine and Gus knew about it. I don't think anyone would have killed your mom over that in order to keep her quiet."

He was completely right. I picked up the thread, thinking aloud. "So my mom must have discovered some other secret about someone, and she was killed to keep her quiet. Secrets and lies." I remembered a line in her journal. *But what about Gus?* Did she find out something inflammatory about him? Could *he* have killed her?

Deep down I hoped not. Jasmine had already lost her mom. I couldn't imagine the pain she'd experience if her dad turned out to be a murderer.

A horrible thought crossed my mind. "What if . . ."

I trailed off, not wanting to say it aloud, but Miguel pressed. "What if . . . ?"

I walked to the edge of the pier, stared out at a barge anchored offshore. The new idea that had surfaced in my mind was not one I wanted to put into words. It was not one I wanted even to think about. But I had no choice. I turned to face Miguel, drew in a breath, and shared the theory.

"What if my mom discovered something about Jackie that Jackie wanted to keep quiet? I've been thinking all along that she discovered this long-lost daughter and that maybe the daughter was up to no good, blackmailing Jackie or something."

Miguel was six feet tall and stood four inches over me. I looked up at him, meeting his gaze, wishing I were wrong. But deep down I knew I wasn't. I'd been swayed by Olaya's friendship with Jackie, and by the fact that she was a victim, too. But before Jackie was killed, what if she'd *done* the killing?

"I guess I didn't want to think that Jackie could be the bad guy here." I blinked away the moisture gathering in my eyes. "But what if she was?"

CHAPTER TWENTY-TWO

After Miguel and I walked back to Baptista's, I did the logical thing. I sat in a corner booth, ate chips and *queso,* ordered the crab- and shrimp-stuffed avocado, and called Emmaline again.

"It's a good theory, Ivy," she said when I was done filling her in on my thought process, "but I think you should talk to your dad. He may know something and not even realize it."

"Billy too," I said, thinking aloud. "My mom might have mentioned something to him. Who knows?"

"Um, yeah. Good idea." Emmaline's voice sounded strange. Even the mere mention of Billy sent her reeling. God, love was just ridiculous sometimes. It was unspoken, but I was relieved that Miguel and I had somehow come to the point where we could be friends.

I paused long enough to take a few bites

of the avocado, my eyes rolling back in my head at the sublime combination of tastes. Once I'd recovered, I called my dad, told him that I wanted a family meeting.

"What's going on, Ivy?" He sounded tired.

"It's important, Dad. Please?"

He agreed, and we arranged to meet at the house at seven that night. I called Billy next.

"You have something you want to talk about?" he asked me before I could pose the question.

My intuition flared. His response was almost too quick. Red flag. I'd told Emmaline I wanted to talk to Billy, as well as to my dad. Maybe her strained voice wasn't so much about her angst over not having Billy. Maybe it was because she was keeping her own secret from me, namely, that she and Billy had something going on. "How'd you know?"

"Brotherly intuition."

"Uh-huh." I remembered the other night, when she'd hightailed it out of Baptista's, leaving me to catch a ride back to my car with Miguel. What if it hadn't been a case she'd had to rush off to? What if it had been Billy? It would certainly explain her caginess and the fact that she never called me back that night.

I filed my theory away to a back corner of my mind. I had more pressing matters to think about. Billy and Emmaline could wait.

"Hey, I'm perceptive," he said, his tone playful, but I wasn't buying it.

"If you say so," I said, letting it go. I had bigger fish to fry. Emmaline and Billy were adults. If they chose to pussyfoot around a relationship — or whatever they called it — that was their business, not mine. "Family meeting, Billy. Tonight, okay?"

He nodded and we went our separate ways.

I'd found that baking was becoming a way to clear my mind, so I spent the rest of the afternoon baking bread. I didn't try anything as ambitious as baguettes, not on my own. Instead, I tried dinner rolls to go with the chicken salad and French onion soup I'd decided to make for my dad and Billy. We hadn't had a family meal since my mom died. If I was going to broach a difficult subject tonight, I wanted to offer them a good meal, complete with home-baked bread. It was the least I could do as I tore their worlds apart for the second time in a year.

They arrived at the house at the same time, Billy coming through the front door and

Dad coming in through the garage. Billy came straight to the kitchen and leaned down to kiss my cheek.

"Turning into Betty Crocker, huh?"

I swatted him away.

"She's brought some pretty good stuff home to her old man," my dad said. Once again, he was trying to engage, but it was only on the surface.

While our dad went into the backyard to water his garden, Billy stayed with me, stirring the pot of soup I had simmering on the stove. "He's not any better," he commented, stooping to slurp a spoonful of the oniony beef broth. "Mmm, good."

"Wait till I top it with the day-old baguette and broil it to melt the Gruyère."

He reached for a ladle and started to spoon the broth into a bowl. "You could have made boxed mac and cheese and I'd have been happy. I haven't had a home-cooked meal in forever."

I took the ladle and bowl from him and poured the soup back into the pot. "You really should learn your way around a kitchen, you know. Women like a man who can cook. Bobby Flay. Michael Simon. Emeril Lagasse. Ever heard of them?"

He arched an eyebrow. "Miguel Baptista."

"It *is* romantic when a man cooks for a

woman —"

"Even if it's his job?"

"Miguel doesn't cook for me."

"But if he did —"

"If he did, I'd enjoy every bite, I'm sure. But that is not the point. You're thirty-three, Billy. You should learn to make something besides scrambled eggs."

"I can. I do. Ask E—"

He stopped, but I filled in the blank. *Ask Emmaline.* So my intuition was right on the money. He and my best friend had finally gotten over whatever hang-ups they had and were seeing each other.

"Aha! I knew it!" I said with a grin. "I'll get the scoop from Em, you know."

"Not *all* of it," he said with a wink.

I resisted throwing a precious dinner roll at him and instead grinned stupidly. "It's about time. That's all I have to say."

Billy just shrugged. I'd already set the table. He tossed the freshly baked dinner rolls into a basket, and I ladled the soup, finishing just as Dad came back in. I placed the chicken salad in the center of the table, and without any fanfare, we began our first meal together since my mom's funeral.

"So what's the occasion, Ivy?" Billy finally asked after we'd exhausted all our small talk.

The thrumming of my heart in my chest

echoed in my ears. This was not a conversation I wanted to have, yet I had no choice. I released a shaky breath and plunged right into it. "I think Mom was killed."

They stared at me like I'd lost my mind. "Uh, yeah, Ivy. We know that."

"That's not what I meant." I closed my eyes and regrouped. "I mean, I think someone killed her on purpose. She was a target. What I mean is, Mom was murdered."

It took an hour to explain my thought process, field questions, and offer explanations. Finally, disbelief gave way to acceptance.

"Knowing mom, she was probably trying to help someone," Billy said with a frustrated shake of his head.

Dad pushed his dinner dishes away and placed his palms flat on the table, but he kept silent.

Billy cupped his hand over his forehead. "You think she discovered something about the woman who was just killed? What was her name?"

"Jackie Makers," I said, tucking my hair behind my ears. "And yeah, I think it's possible."

My dad leaned back in his chair and folded his arms over his chest. It was his typical stance. He was closed off, protecting himself. After a minute, he finally spoke. "It doesn't matter, Ivy. She's gone."

I stared at him. "It does matter, Dad. Someone murdered her."

"And you think Jackie may have done it? Mom discovered something, and she was killed over it, and now that same woman, Jackie, is dead, too. Where will it stop, Ivy? You're going to dig around and try to vindicate your mom, try to make sense of what happened, but why? You'll end up dead, too, if you're not careful. And no matter what you find, it's not going to bring her back."

Billy clasped my hand, then squeezed. "I get what you want to do, Ivy, but Dad's right. It's not going to bring her back. And if you're right and she was killed by Jackie Makers, then it doesn't matter, anyway, because Jackie's already dead. There's no justice to be had here."

Heat crawled up my chest, then spread like tendrils through my body. I wrenched my hand free. "How can you say that? Don't you want to know what happened to her?"

My dad stood and calmly gathered his soup bowl and plate. "Good dinner, Ivy." He rinsed the dishes, stuck them in the dishwasher, and with a quiet good night, he disappeared into the bedroom he'd shared with my mom for nearly forty years.

CHAPTER TWENTY-THREE

I left Billy to clean up the kitchen. I didn't agree with the two men in my family. I wanted to know what my mom had discovered. I wanted to understand why she had died. I wanted to let go of the unknown and come to peace with it, and the only way I knew how to do that was to find out the truth.

The only thing I could think to do was to start with the most tangible theory I had — that Jolie was Jackie's oldest daughter. I texted Olaya to get Jolie's address. When she didn't reply, I unlocked my phone and dialed her directly.

"Why do you want it?" she asked.

I didn't want to tell Olaya my suspicions about Jackie being behind my mother's death, so I kept my answer vague. "I don't think she had anything to do with her mother's murder, but I want to ask her a question. Please, Olaya."

She hesitated but gave me the address. Ten minutes later I pulled into a guest parking spot at Beachfront Apartments, a mid-range complex on State Street. It wasn't actually beachfront, but it sounded good. According to her registration form at Yeast of Eden, Jolie lived in apartment 232. I tried to open the front door, but without a key fob, there was no entrance. I found her name on the directory and pushed the intercom buzzer.

It took about thirty seconds before she answered with a short "Yes?"

"Jolie? It's Ivy. Culpepper. From baking class?"

"Ivy!"

There was a buzzing sound, followed by a click as the door to the building unlocked. I grabbed the handle and let myself in, then headed up the stairs and down the hall until I reached her apartment.

She was waiting at the door, a huge smile on her face. Her black hair was piled up in a loose topknot. She had on jogging shorts and a tank top, was barefoot, and had not a stitch of makeup on her beautiful face. She hadn't been expecting company, but if she had, I didn't think she would have changed a thing. She was one of those perfect specimens that made other women crazy with jealousy and men fall at her feet.

"What a surprise!" She grabbed my hand and pulled me into her apartment. I quickly took in the interior. It was sparse, but tasteful. Neat and tidy. A book was open and facedown on the sofa.

"Sorry to barge in on you."

She waved away my apology. "Something to drink? I tried to bake some bread earlier today, but it was a complete bust. I should probably get my money back and give up on the baking classes."

"I tried dinner rolls today. They weren't bad. I'm not sure Olaya would agree, but we ate them."

"It's a lot harder than I thought it would be. Baking, I mean. I figured it would be easy and I'd be able to bake and bake and bake."

I'd thought the very same thing. So far it seemed my success inside and outside class was better than Jolie's.

She poured two glasses of cabernet, and we sat on her white sofa, chatting about baking and Yeast of Eden. After a while I broached the subject I'd been waiting to bring up.

"You went to Santa Sofia High School?"

"Yes! Good school. Good teachers," she said, sympathy in her eyes.

"Did you grow up here?" I'd wondered whom Jackie had given her baby to. Someone in town, if Jolie went to the local high school.

"Born in San Francisco but raised here. I don't know if I could ever leave, actually. I love it here. You must, too, since you came back. You were in Texas, right?"

"Yep. Austin. Now that I'm back, I realize how much I missed it. There's something about the ocean air. It's clean. Fresh."

"I know what you mean!" She said everything with such enthusiasm; it was hard not to smile. "I keep the windows open as much as I can, which is pretty much whenever I'm home."

I leaned forward, elbows on my knees, cupping my wineglass in my hand. "Can I ask you something?"

She drew her lips into a straight line, which I took to be her serious look. "Is something wrong?"

"No. Well, yes. Kind of."

"Ask me anything."

I was fishing and felt completely incompetent as a sleuth, but I kept my focus. If I asked enough questions, and somehow one or two of them were the right ones, I might discover something that would help me get to the truth. I decided not to mince words.

"Do you know Jasmine Makers?"

Whatever she thought I'd ask, it wasn't that. Her persona completely changed, the happy-go-lucky Jolie replaced by a reticent, nervous young woman. "Wh-what?"

"Jasmine Makers. She told me about . . . her mom and . . ." I just went for it and dropped the bomb. "You."

Her jaw dropped, and she looked away. Her voice dipped low. "Did she say she wanted to see me?"

That was all the confirmation I needed. I'd been right. Jolie was Jackie's other daughter. But from the raw emotion emanating from Jolie, I didn't feel like it was a victory. The crack in Jolie's optimistic veneer was painful. She was an upbeat person, but the estrangement from her biological family had broken her on some level. She wanted to connect with her sister. The fact that Jackie had gotten pregnant and had given Jolie up wasn't her fault. Jasmine needed to recognize that. I hoped that she would someday and that the two could become real sisters.

"We, uh, didn't talk about that. She told me about you — about her mom's other child. About her mom giving you up for adoption."

"I get it, you know. She was married, and

Gus is black." She gave a wry laugh. "Look at me. Not much chance of her trying to hide the truth from him."

"Do you know who your father is?" It was a blunt question, but I didn't know how to ask it subtly. In that instant, a new theory surfaced. It was possible that Jolie's biological father could have been so angry at losing all those years as a parent that he killed Jackie out of anger. It was also possible that my mom had somehow learned who he was, confronted her about it, and was killed by Jackie to protect *that* secret.

But she shook her head. "I wanted to talk to her about it that night at the bread shop. I had it all planned out. I was going to pull her aside during one of our breaks and come right out and ask her."

"But she died before you had the chance."

"Don't get me wrong," she said suddenly. "My parents were great. I don't know how Jackie found them, but they were good to me. They died when I was seventeen, just before I graduated. It was a horrible car accident down in Santa Barbara. I loved them, but eventually, with them gone, I just really wanted to find out where I came from. Who my biological mother was."

"Is Flemming the name you used in school?"

"No. I got married right out of high school. Big mistake. It lasted only six months, but I kept the name."

I sipped my wine as I thought about what to ask next. "Did Jackie know you were her daughter? You'd met?"

"She knew. I mailed her a letter. God, must have been more than a year ago now. I sent one to Jasmine, too. It took three more letters and four months before Jackie finally replied and agreed to meet me."

"How was that?"

She set her wineglass on the glass coffee table and stood, then folded her arms over her chest and walked to the sliding glass door. "Not what I expected," she said after a moment. "She was distracted. Looking over her shoulder. She kept saying that she had to get back to the kitchen. She definitely didn't want to be meeting me."

"That was it?" I could see why Jolie's naturally exuberant personality was tamed when talking about Jackie. It certainly hadn't been a fairy-tale reunion between a mother and her long-lost daughter.

"Pretty much. She said it was a mistake. That she didn't mean to. Get pregnant, I mean." Jolie's eyes pinched as she remembered. "But you know, even though she said it, I didn't ever feel like she was talking to me. Like she really meant it. But then she never called me. Never tried to meet me again. I tried a few more times, but it was pretty clear she wasn't interested, so finally I gave up. She was really focused on her business, so maybe she just didn't have time for me. The other cooking school in town had just closed. She said something about her being the better chef and now she'd have the chance to prove it.

"She kept looking at her watch and checking the door, like she was expecting someone else. Finally, she just got up. She told me that she couldn't 'do this' right now. *Do what?* I thought. She couldn't make time to meet her daughter? The one she'd given up without a second thought? Before she left, she told me that she'd done things she wasn't proud of, and that other people had paid the price. She said she was sorry and that she'd make things right." Jolie wiped away a tear. "And then she left."

"And did she? Make things right?"

Jolie shook her head sadly. "I waited for her to call. To reach out to me. But she never did."

I didn't want to beat a dead horse, so I redirected the subject. "Did you know she'd be at the baking class? Because you said you were going to ask about your biological father."

"I knew. I love the bread shop, although, as you know, I'm not a natural. Olaya mentioned the classes to me one day when I was in there getting my daily fix. She pulled out the sign-up sheet, in case I was interested, and Jackie's name was right there. I thought, *Maybe it's fate. Maybe this will give us the opportunity to get to know each other.* No pressure, right?" She sighed. "But it didn't quite work out that way. She never even looked at me that night."

We finished our wine, and I got up to leave. "Will you be there tomorrow?" I asked.

"With bells on. I am determined to learn how to bake halfway decent. It's in my genes, after all."

Before I left, I gave her a hug. I didn't know if I was a good judge of character, but I liked her. She'd been dealt a bum hand, what with Jackie giving her up, a sister who wanted nothing to do with her, and her adoptive parents being dead. "See you tomorrow," I said, adding to myself that maybe I'd have some answers by then.

Chapter Twenty-Four

My dad was waiting up for me when I got home, Agatha curled up at his side. My pug lifted her head as I walked in, her ears twitching back when she heard my voice.

My dad sounded tired. "Sit down, Ivy."

I perched on the edge of the coffee table opposite him. I knew my dad, and I knew that he had something he wanted to say to me. I couldn't rush it, so I waited.

Finally, he spoke. "You're right. I know it, but that doesn't make it easy."

I leaned forward, reaching for his hand. "I know, Dad. I just want the truth. It may not help at all, but then again, it might."

He didn't look like he thought the truth would bring any peace, but I appreciated the effort he was giving. What he needed and what I needed were two different things. He might not agree with me, but he could respect me. "You're looking for a reason, Ivy. You'll never find one that's good enough. Mom died, and she shouldn't have. But if you're determined to look for answers, then I'll help you."

Heat pricked the skin on my face, and my nostrils flared with emotion. I fought the tears that burned in my eyes. "Thank you, Dad."

"You said you thought Jackie Makers had some sort of secret."

"More than one, I think. She gave up a daughter for adoption before she and Gus had Jasmine, but I think Mom figured out something else."

"You can retrace Mom's steps. Maybe that'll help you."

"What do you mean, retrace her steps?"

"You know your mom. She never went anywhere without her planner."

I felt as if a lightbulb had suddenly gone off in my head. My mom had written down everything, in a million different places. She'd had her lesson plan book. Even though the school district had gone to an online method of tracking and submitting lesson plans, my mom had kept her old-school spiral book. She'd had her journals for her writing and inspirations. And she'd always kept a day planner. The one my dad handed me now was called a Spark Notebook The hard black cover gave it a utilitarian look, but inside it was filled with graphic elements, quotes, spaces to write and doodle, and prompts to make you think about your desires, accomplishments, and goals.

I flipped through it and immediately saw what my dad had seen. My mom's appointments were noted on the calendar pages, along with a few anecdotal notes here and there. I started at the end — her last entries.

The last few pages were mostly school related. Department meeting, parent-teacher conference, staff meeting. She'd made an appointment to take her car in for service the week before she died. There'd been a community cleanup day she'd noted. But the thing I zeroed in on was a ten o'clock Saturday meeting with someone named Renee at Divine Cuisine. The business's name rang a bell, but I couldn't put my finger on why.

"What's Divine Cuisine?" I asked my dad.

He had been scratching Agatha's head. Now he stopped and let his hand run from her head to her curled-up tail. "One of the cooking schools your mom was looking at for our classes."

"But didn't you start the sessions with Well Done and Jackie Makers?"

"We went to three or four be-before the accident."

That was what I'd thought, which was why it seemed odd that my mom had made an appointment with someone from Divine Cuisine.

"Did Mom like the classes?"

"At Well Done?"

I nodded.

"I think so," he said. "She never said she didn't. She came home pretty inspired. Mostly, though, I think she just liked that I did it with her. Being an empty nester was hard for her. Harder on women than on men. She was always looking for something we could do together. She suggested salsa dancing. Do you believe that? I said no way in hell was she getting me on a dance floor, but now I wish . . ."

He left the sentence unfinished. I imagined that the what-ifs and the wishes could eat him up alive if he let them.

"Dad . . ."

He swallowed down the emotions bubbling up in him and tensed his jaw. "Why? What do you see in there?"

I pointed to the Divine Cuisine appointment.

He frowned, peering to get a closer look. "You know your mother."

I did. She was a thinker and a doer. "Why would she meet with another cooking school if she was happy with Well Done?" I mused aloud.

"That is definitely a puzzler."

"Right? If she was happy with Well Done, would she want to switch to another school?"

"Maybe she thought the other place had an interesting concept or something. Who knows? Your mom was always looking for new things. But no, that's not what doesn't make sense."

"What is it, then?"

"Divine Cuisine," he said, and at that moment, it came back to me. Olaya had told me about it. It had been the other cooking school in Santa Sofia, but it had closed down. "They shut down. A year ago or so. Maybe a little more."

"Why?"

He looked to the ceiling, thinking. "Something with the owner. An accident, I think."

"Was it bad?"

"I don't remember the details," he said, "but yes. Bad enough that they had to close their doors."

"And they didn't reopen?"

"Ivy, you're asking the wrong person. I've been a little distracted. Haven't kept up with the local cooking schools." He almost said it as a joke, but as always, the undercurrent of pain was evident.

"I know, Dad."

He thought for a second and then shook his head. "Now that I think of it, though, I don't think it reopened."

"So . . ." I trailed off, processing my thoughts before speaking up again. "If Divine Cuisine shut down more than a year ago, then Mom couldn't have scheduled a meeting with this Renee woman to talk about classes."

"No, I don't suppose that's what it was about," he said.

We fell silent because neither of us had any inkling what might have been behind the meeting my mom had scheduled with Renee at Divine Cuisine.

Finally, my dad squeezed my hand, his eyes glassy and his skin cold to the touch. "Be careful, Ivy. I can't stand the thought of losing you, too."

"I will, Dad. I will."

As I climbed into bed a little while later, my cell phone beeped. A text from Mrs. Branford came through.

Community meeting at Mastersons' tomorrow morning. Come with me!

I turned my smartphone sideways and

quickly tapped in my response.

What time?
Ten o'clock.

I told her I'd see her there, and then I turned off the light. My head sank into my pillow, as if it were cradling the myriad thoughts ricocheting in my brain. As I drifted off to sleep, I wondered what tomorrow would bring.

CHAPTER TWENTY-FIVE

I parked at Mrs. Branford's, arriving thirty minutes early.

"Step right in," she said, ushering me through the living room and into the kitchen. This room, I'd come to realize, was where Mrs. Branford lived her life.

"What's this meeting about?" I asked. I did not have a stake in the neighborhood, although I wished I did. Regardless, I was happy to tag along — if only to see inside Nanette and Buck's historic house.

She offered me a cup of tea in a dainty floral cup. Mrs. Branford was a tough bird, but she had a soft side underneath it all. She sat down at the kitchen table, and her usually bright smile tempered. "Ivy, I want to talk about something with you."

Worry instantly coursed through me. I took a close look at her. She didn't appear sick. Her cheeks were rosy, and the jovial twinkle was still in her eyes, despite her serious expression.

I sat down across from her. "What is it? Are you okay?"

"I don't think so." She looked around, as if someone might be listening. "Remember the envelope in the freezer?"

"I remember." It had been only a week ago that she'd brought it across the street to Olaya and me.

"I found another one."

"Another envelope in the freezer?"

"An envelope, yes, but not in the freezer. This one was under the cushion of the couch."

Curious. "That's, um, an interesting place to keep an envelope. What's in it?"

"Pictures."

"Pictures?" I realized that I was repeating everything she was saying, but I was stymied by her confession. Mrs. Branford had found an envelope filled with pictures under the couch cushion. It felt like a game of *Clue.* Professor Plum in the library with a candlestick.

She stretched her hand behind the fruit bowl and slid out a five-by-seven manila envelope. Just as she'd said, inside was a stack of photographs.

I slipped them out and quickly scanned them, then slowed my pace to take a closer look at each one. The first was a picture of Buck Masterson in his front yard, hose in hand. He stared across the street, his bad comb-over thready on his forehead. It felt like he was looking right at Penny Branford's house.

"Did you take this picture?" I asked.

"You'd think I did, wouldn't you? But no. You've seen my shaky hands. I couldn't take a good picture to save my life."

"Then who?"

She looked pointedly at me. "That's the winning question, dear."

The next photo was of Nanette Masterson, hand on a door handle, her head turned to the side, as if she were looking over her shoulder.

"Whose house is that?"

"Jackie's." With a bony finger, she pointed to the flowerpot on the front porch, to the left of where Nanette stood. "I helped her plant that pot not two months ago. See how the impatiens have grown? They started as single-stalk flowers."

In the photo, the flowers were full and colorful. The picture, then, had to have been taken fairly recently.

"You think Jackie took these?"

Mrs. Branford threw up her hands, clearly exasperated. "I don't know. Why would she hide in my yard and take a picture of Buck? And how would she be outside, across the street and hidden, in order to take that one of Nanette?" She rubbed her temples. "My dear, my head hurts."

I looked at that picture again, noticing the almost menacing look on Buck's face. It was as if he was staring straight at the camera. "What if she — Jackie, I guess — *was* in your yard to take a picture of Buck?"

Mrs. Branford looked at me like I was short a few marbles. "It's puzzling, but at the same time it seems fairly obvious, dear."

"No, no. I mean what if she wasn't hiding? What if she stood there, plain as day, and was snapping pictures?"

"Why would she do that?"

I looked at the next photo in the stack. Buck had dropped the hose and was on the edge of his yard, still looking at the camera. His hand was raised, as if he were scolding an errant child, and his mouth was open. I could almost hear the vitriolic words spewing from him. "Leverage?"

"Explain that to me, Ivy."

"We know Jackie was trying to oust Buck from the historic district's council. She gathered all those letters against him, and the petition to remove him from his position."

She nodded. "Correct."

"What if she was trying to intimidate him? Play at his own game?" I slapped my hand on my thigh. "What if she discovered that Buck and Nanette had broken into her house, looking for something? The letters, probably, which is why she'd hidden them in your freezer."

"But why would she stake out her own house and photograph someone trying to break in? Why not confront Nanette? Jackie was not a shrinking violet."

I smiled to myself. Such an old-fashioned expression. "What if she wanted to catch them in the act of breaking in so she could prove it? Hold it over them or show the council?"

"Okay, but why would she put the pictures under my couch cushion?"

I thought about this. If Jackie knew Nanette and Buck were regularly breaking into her house, she'd want them to be safe. "She didn't give them to you to hold for her? Or to hide?"

"If she did, I have absolutely no recollection of that. Maybe I'm losing my marbles. I'm no spring chicken anymore, so it's possible, you know."

Once again, things didn't quite add up. "Mrs. Branford, I think you'd remember if someone gave you an envelope. Two envelopes," I corrected. The first, with the stack of letters against Buck Masterson, had ended up in her freezer somehow. Now she'd found these pictures. "It had to be Jackie, and she's the one who had to have hidden them."

She seemed to breathe a little easier. Realizing you weren't completely losing your faculties would be a relief, I imagined. "It makes sense for the letters. She was the one going after Buck. But these photos, I don't understand them. There's nothing in here worth hiding."

I had to agree. It didn't make sense.

"Would you keep them, dear?" Mrs. Branford said. "I don't want to misplace them again."

I squeezed her hand. "Mrs. Branford, I don't think you misplaced them in the first place."

Mrs. Branford's hand trembled slightly, the tea in her cup sloshing from the movement. She braced her cup with her left hand, controlling the motion. "Will you keep them, anyway?"

"Of course," I said, and I slid the pictures back into the envelope and tucked the envelope in my purse. "For safekeeping."

I took our teacups, rinsed them, and

placed them in the drying rack to the left of the sink. "Shall we go?"

"No time like the present."

Mrs. Branford stood, took her cane, and together we crossed the street to the Masterson house. She shook her head as we walked up the crumbling brick pathway.

"If I break a hip —"

"You're not going to break a hip," I said, but I took her by the elbow just in case.

As we climbed the porch steps, Mrs. Branford pulled free of my protective guidance and kept walking, bypassing the door. I hurried after her.

"Where are you going?"

"Odd ducks, the Mastersons. You have to enter over here."

I looked back over my shoulder. The walkway led to the porch, which led to the front door. "They don't use the main entrance? Why?"

She stopped walking and leaned against her cane. "There's no accounting for anything they do," she said. "I used to try to make sense of them, but no more."

The side door was open. We stepped in, and I made the mistake of breathing. I nearly choked and covered my nose and mouth. I moved my hand to whisper, "Cats?"

Mrs. Branford pinched her nose with her thumb and forefinger. "About five million of them. And I think they pee wherever they want to."

I grimaced, trying hard not to breathe and hoping I didn't step on one of the five million tabbies that surely must be lurking in the house. I looked around. We stood in the entryway to the side door. An overstuffed period chair sat in the left corner, and a small round table was in the middle of the space. Jars of jelly were lined up around a bowl of plums. A stack of printed notes was next to the bowl. I picked one up and read it.

Our neighborhood is only as strong as the individual people in it. A weak link jeopardizes us all. Take this plum jam, homemade from our trees, as a symbol of how committed we are to the Maple/Elm Historic District in Santa Sofia.

I handed the note to Mrs. Branford. I'd lay money down that in the Mastersons' world, Jackie had been the weak link.

A low chatter came from a back room.

"They're in the kitchen," Mrs. Branford said. She led the way, walking to the dining room. An embossed silver ceiling, heavy wood moldings and trim, and floral wall-paper made the room feel closed in and dark. Oppressive. It was as if they were trying to recapture every bit of life more than a hundred years ago. They seemed to have succeeded in capturing the look, but then they'd kept going, somehow choking the soul from it in the process.

A few people sat at the rectangular dining table. Mrs. Branford stopped to chat and introduced me to a few of them. I smiled and waved.

"Do you live in the neighborhood?" a middle-aged man asked me.

"No, just friends with Mrs. Branford," I said. "Tagging along."

I followed Mrs. Branford into the kitchen and stopped to take it all in. *Cluttered* was an understatement. There were pots and pans hanging from a makeshift pot rack made from an old pulley system. Flower-pots, some with dying plants, lined the back of the counter, intermixed with container after container of cooking utensils. In one corner, a stack of papers, magazines, and books teetered precariously. It was an odd kitchen space, and despite the food offerings on the island and the cooking paraphernalia all around, I wondered if any cooking actually happened here. My gut was telling me that it didn't.

"Penelope. Good of you to come," Buck Masterson said, hand extended. He had what I could describe only as a smarmy smile on his face. There was something untrustworthy about him, and although his words said otherwise, he seemed absolutely less than happy to actually *see* Mrs. Branford.

"Wouldn't have missed this for anything," she replied, a saccharine smile on her lips. "You remember Ivy Culpepper. Owen's daughter."

His nostrils flared, but he kept up his facade. "Of course. Are you here as Penelope's home health nurse? Getting older is a terrible thing, isn't it, Penny?"

I did a double take. Was he intentionally trying to get Mrs. Branford's goat, or was he inordinately socially awkward? Mrs. Branford rallied, bless her heart.

"It is indeed, Buck, as you know firsthand, but Ivy is not here as my nurse. In fact, she knew Jackie and has been helping finish up a few things the poor woman started."

The color drained from Buck's face. He whipped his head around to look at me more closely. "Is that so? What sort of things, exactly?"

"Oh, Mr. Masterson, I don't want to bore

you with city business," I said as coyly as I could.

"Actually, city business fascinates me. I'm the representative of the Maple/Elm Historic District, which I believe you know. Any city business involving our historic designation *must* go through me."

Mrs. Branford cocked her head. She looked like the perfect grandmother, with her fluffy white hair, her velour sweat suit, which was powder blue today, and her sweet face, but underneath, I knew, she was tough as nails and would do whatever it took to bring down Buck Masterson. "Must it? Everything?" she said, quite innocently, but I knew and he knew that she would never answer to Buck.

"You know that, Penny. I'm your representative. I know the ins and outs of the district, the zoning, the city officials and how they are always trying to screw us. No one else is watching out for us. It's me. I take care of everyone in our district."

"Don't forget me," Nanette said, sidling up to her husband. Her dyed red hair hung in two stringy sheets on either side of her head. It was a nice cut, but with her heavy jowls and chin, the straight hair looked plastered to her head in a particularly unflattering way. "There's always a good woman behind a successful man."

I did believe that old expression to be true, but I liked to think more progressively than that. Behind every successful woman was a smart man. That was my belief, and I needed a man who believed it, too. I phrased my response carefully. Specific enough to make them worry, but vague enough not to give anything away. "I'm sure you both do everything you can for your neighbors. I'll let you know if I have any questions as I go through Jackie's papers." I patted my purse for good measure. "Now that I know you're the go-to people."

The skin around Buck's neck reddened and the flush spread upward, coloring his cheeks first and then the entire flat surface of his face. He managed to remain expressionless, despite the fact that he was the color of a tomato. "You have some of her papers?"

I turned to survey the other people in the small kitchen, trying to be nonchalant. Buck's feathers were clearly ruffled. Outside of Mrs. Branford's tales and our surveillance, I didn't know Buck Masterson at all. Despite that, I was pretty sure that playing coy about what I knew or didn't know was going to drive him nuts. "Papers, some notes, and some letters, I think. Is that right,

Mrs. Branford?"

My elderly friend puffed her cheeks and nodded innocently. "And pictures," she said. "Don't forget the pictures."

"Right!" I looked him in the eyes and tilted my head, as if I were puzzled. "I'm surprised you didn't work together on some of your district projects. She was pretty involved in the neighborhood, too, from what I've seen so far."

Nanette choked, then broke into a cough. She patted her chest with her palm. "Sorry. Something caught in my throat." She and Buck shared a look that I couldn't decipher; then she turned to me. "Will you be at the baking class tomorrow? I sure did enjoy my time there the other day." The fake saccharine in her voice revealed the truth behind her innocent words.

I smiled as naturally as I could, although I knew she was fishing. "Oh, I'll be there. Of course! I'm Olaya Solis's apprentice."

"Doesn't your dad work long hours these days, Ivy?" Mrs. Branford was getting in on the game, trying to give the Mastersons an opportunity to do some snooping while I was gone at Yeast of Eden.

"He's hardly ever home. It's easier for him to keep his mind busy at work."

"Poor fellow," Buck said.

I rolled my eyes. As if he actually cared.

Nanette squeezed my arm. "And that's where you're living right now? With your father?"

I had to give her credit. Her attempt at subtly gathering intel about my situation wasn't half bad. If I didn't know that was what she was doing, I might have been snowed.

"Me and Agatha."

She cocked a faded red eyebrow.

"My pug," I explained. "She's my little shadow."

"Ah. We're cat people." Her tone said she thought cat people were far superior to dog people. I'd read the studies. Cat people were smarter, blah, blah, blah. Maybe so, but I'd take Agatha any day of the week. She was loyal, loving, and as warm as a basket full of freshly baked dinner rolls.

"I'm sorry," Mrs. Branford said with an exaggerated sniff.

Nanette's face flamed red, and I stifled a laugh.

Nanette scowled, then turned her body so she had her back partially to Mrs. Branford. "I'm sure it's terribly difficult for your dad to be home alone."

I took the bait. "Oh, it is, Nanette. So tough. I usually call him when I'm on my way home from the bread shop, or wherever I'm at, so we get home about the same time."

She shot her husband a look, and I met Mrs. Branford's eyes. Nanette was like a fly caught in a spider's web, and I was the spider. I knew right then and there that they'd be coming up with some plan to search my dad's house for Jackie's "papers" while I was at Yeast of Eden. All we had to do was set a trap to catch them in the act of breaking and entering. They certainly wanted whatever Jackie had had her hands in. There was no question about that. What I still didn't know, however, was if they'd killed her over it.

CHAPTER TWENTY-SIX

Early the next morning, Olaya phoned and asked me to help her at the front counter at Yeast of Eden. "One of my regular girls called in sick, so we're shorthanded."

I hightailed it over just as soon as I walked Agatha and got her situated with a bowl of food, water, and a chew toy. The weather had taken a turn. The beautiful spring days we were having had become cold and windy. I grabbed a jacket before I left the house, and gave my dad a quick kiss on the cheek.

"I also have baking class," I said, feeling a little like I was back in high school, accounting for my time and outings. "I'll come back to check on Agatha, though."

"You're allowed to have a life, Ivy," he said. "I can take care of myself. I'm going to have to, you know."

I sighed. He was right. We were both going to have to cut the ties and figure out how to move forward, and that meant I'd have to find a place of my own and he'd have to figure out what his life looked like without my mom. "I know, Dad."

"Stay out late. Go on a date. I don't want to be the one holding you back."

"You're not holding me back from anything. I don't want to be doing anything else right now."

"Not while you're playing detective," he said with a frown.

"I'm trying," I said, leaving it at that. I didn't want him to get upset again over the digging I was doing.

The line for bread was ten people deep when I walked in the door of Yeast of Eden.

"Here," Olaya said, calling me over. She handed me a bakery apron and a small order pad. "Write down the orders here, give a receipt if the customer wants one, and put the original here," she said, pointing to a metal base with a long, pointed spike. A stack of order sheets had been speared onto it. "I track everything that we sell at the end of the day. It helps me know how we do with each item and how much I need to bake. I compare the inventory to the receipts. It is how I balance the books, so to speak."

It sounded like a lot of paperwork, but aside from the phenomenal bread, this was definitely why Olaya and her business were so successful. We worked for an hour and a half before the line finally died down and we could breathe again.

"Is it always like this?" I asked. I'd been in at various times of the day, but I'd never seen it so swamped.

"When the temperature drops and the wind picks up, it is always busier."

Outside the wind howled. The heavy breeze from earlier had turned into whistling gusts. I could see why people would want the comfort of freshly baked, warm bread. I went back to check on Agatha. Back at the bread shop, we worked for the rest of the day, closing the door and flipping the OPEN sign over at four o'clock. One of Olaya's afternoon workers came in to help with the day's cleanup, which allowed Olaya and me to set up for the evening's baking class.

One by one, the women in the class trickled in. Becky, Sally, and Jolie came in together, followed by Consuelo and Martina. As usual, Mrs. Branford sauntered in last, swinging her cane, apron on, white hair perfectly coiffed. She looked around.

"No Nanette?" she asked.

I frowned. "Not yet," I said, but at that moment, Nanette Masterson walked into the kitchen. Her thin bright red hair was slicked back, and her heavily drawn eyebrows framed her eyes.

"Bienvenidos, Señora Masterson," Olaya said. "Glad to see you back here."

Nanette checked her watch and nodded. "I wouldn't miss it. What are we making today?"

"Seeded pull-apart rolls," Olaya answered.

Sally placed her hand flat on her stomach. "Sounds so good," she said.

Becky grabbed Sally's arm. "Doesn't it? My stomach's growling!"

We all went to our stations and followed Olaya's directions for making whole-wheat dough. "The pull-apart rolls begin with this," she said. We followed the process of mixing the ingredients and setting our dough aside to rise. Meanwhile, as with the baguettes, Olaya began pulling out dough she had mixed and readied for us the day before. "This is one of those recipes that you can make a day ahead. In the interest of time, I have prepared the dough. Now we will create the seeded rolls."

I glanced at the clock hanging above the door that led to the bread shop lobby. Five on the dot. I peeked at Nanette and caught her looking at her watch. I'd been doubting my intuition, wondering if I was completely off the mark about what I suspected, but seeing her check her watch again two minutes later alleviated my misgivings. Something was definitely up, and if I was right, Buck Masterson was en route to my dad's house at this very minute.

I moved quickly, rolling my dough into a rectangle, then cutting it into twenty-four pieces. The women in the class laughed and chatted, none as focused as I was, because none of them had somewhere to be, like I did. I rolled each piece of dough into a ball, then rolled each of the balls in one of the three bowls of seeds I had set out. Before long, I had twenty-four balls, each coated in either toasted white sesame seeds, untoasted white sesame seeds, or black poppy seeds, laid out on a cookie sheet.

Nanette was at the station next to me, still pressing her ball of dough into a rectangle. "You're fast," she said, eyeing my tray of seeded dough balls.

"Getting better every day. I love it!" I took my camera out and snapped a few pictures, then left the camera on the counter. "I'll be back in a minute," I whispered to Nanette. "Watch my rolls?"

"Where are you going?"

I held up my cell phone. "Checking on my dad. He's working late tonight."

"What a good daughter," she said. Her smile reached to her eyes, but I suspected it was because it meant clear sailing for her husband's breaking-and-entering gig at the Culpepper house, not because I had compassion for my father.

"I try." I nodded toward my phone and walked out of the kitchen.

Once I was out of sight, I grabbed my purse from behind the counter and hightailed it out of Yeast of Eden. If I was right, Nanette was on her own phone, giving her husband the "all clear" signal. I had only a few minutes to get to the house.

I made it in record time. I parked down the street, just in case Buck Masterson was lurking around somewhere already. I'd grown up on this street, and I knew every nook and cranny. Billy and I had spent our childhoods climbing fences, sneaking through backyards, and being as stealthy as we could to stay out as late as we could. Now, nearly twenty years later, I was reliving those moments on Pacific Grove Street. I tucked my purse under the front seat of my old car, pocketed my keys, and cut through Mr. and Mrs. Buffington's side yard. They lived two houses down from our house. They'd been in their sixties when I was a teenager, so by now they were in their

324

eighties. I hoped me sneaking around their property didn't send them into heart failure. I'd have to explain it to them later.

Sneaking through their yard, I felt like Peter Rabbit hopping around Mr. McGregor's garden. I jumped the fence between the Buffingtons' yard and the Martinezes', dodged the Martinezes' German shepherd, and climbed under their fence to sneak into my childhood backyard. I looked high and low. No sign of Buck Masterson. I let myself into the house through the back door, got to work, and a few minutes later I sat down by Agatha to wait.

Twenty minutes passed. My eyes drooped, and I'd begun to wonder if I'd completely missed the mark. Just as I stood to stretch my legs, Agatha's ears perked. She jumped up and faced my dad's bedroom. She was on full alert. Any second, she'd bark and wreck my plan. I snatched her up, shushing her, and cuddled her like an upset child. Agatha held her bark. We sank back into the shadows just as the bedroom door opened.

Agatha started to growl, but I quickly held her flattened pug muzzle and whispered in her ear. She relaxed and seemed to accept that the stranger in the house was, at least in this instant, okay.

I watched as the figure crept forward. With

the fading sun, I couldn't make out any details. The man slunk closer, then quickly closed the blinds in the front windows. My heart beat wildly. My dad's worry and Emmaline's warning that I be careful resurfaced. What was I doing?

But my trepidation couldn't stop me now; I was in it up to my neck, and there was no backing down. I took in his stringy hair, which was slicked back; his narrow eyes; and his thin lips, drawn into a tight line. Buck Masterson stood across the room, just as I'd known he would.

It took him only seconds before he spotted the dining-room table. I held my breath, and he made a beeline for it. He bent over the table and grumbled under his breath. "I knew it."

He acted quickly, gathering up the pictures I'd laid out on the table, the pictures Mrs. Branford had found under her couch cushion. He rifled through them and then tucked them in his jacket pocket. But he didn't turn to leave. Just as I knew he would, he turned to his right. It took a few seconds before he surged forward, staring at the second set of photographs I'd arranged on the kitchen counter.

"Son of a . . . ," he snapped, leaning over to get a closer look. These were the photos

I'd taken on my stakeout with Mrs. Branford. They weren't the highest-quality pictures, but they certainly did their job. Buck Masterson's hands shook as he gathered up the pictures. Several fell to the floor. He crouched and collected them, then stood slowly.

His phone buzzed, and he looked at the incoming text. "What the —"

As he raced to the window, cracked the blinds, and peered outside, I realized what the text must have been: Nanette alerting him that I hadn't come back after the phone call to my dad. He was afraid I was on my way to the house.

Too bad for him, I was already here.

Instead of seeing a car pull into the driveway, though, he heard a siren. I gasped, dropping Agatha. The pug zipped toward Buck Masterson, letting loose the barks she'd been holding back while I'd held her. Agatha was mostly bark and little bite, but she charged him, looking up and down, growling, yapping in her high-pitched way, then backed up, sucking in a raspy breath, and charged forward again.

He whipped around and finally spotted me. "What the —"

I moved into the light but kept my distance. This was the one risk in my plan. I didn't know if Buck Masterson had killed my mom or Jackie Makers, and I had no idea what he'd do if he was backed into a corner. "I see you found the pictures I left for you."

He scowled, waving the prints at me. "You took these?"

"I did. I was pretty surprised to see your wife sneak into Jackie's house. Were you looking for the pictures or for the letters the neighbors wrote against you?"

His face turned beet red. "Wh-what letters?"

Agatha had run back to stand next to me, but her tail was straight and hung down at her back legs, and her tiny teeth were bared.

"Seems to me that the neighborhood is pretty divided. It was Team Buck or Team Jackie."

He scoffed. "She didn't understand that I only want to help the historic district. She was a thorn in my side. She needed to be stopped."

"A thorn in your side," I repeated. They'd been the exact words Nanette had used at Yeast of Eden.

His upper lip curled. "It's like she had a vendetta against me."

The sirens that I'd heard passed, and it was completely quiet outside. Another drawback in my plan was that I hadn't planned for the cavalry to ride in and help wrap things up. No one, aside from Mrs. Branford, actually knew I'd left Yeast of Eden, and no one, except Mrs. Branford, knew I'd planted enough seeds in hopes that Buck Masterson would do just what he did and break into my dad's house. I was on my own, but thankfully, Buck hadn't budged from where he stood near the kitchen counter.

"She must have thought she was doing the right thing," I said.

"The right thing. Pft." The way his upper lip caught on one of his teeth made him look a little like Agatha. "She was messing with my reputation. I asked her to stop. I asked for her *support*," he said, as if asking was all he'd needed to do. "She wouldn't stop."

I'd set this little sting up, thinking he hadn't hurt Jackie, but the way he was talking made me wary. I didn't want to ask, but I had to. "Did you . . . were you the one . . . Did you kill her?"

He recoiled, flinging his hand to his chest. "Me? Are you crazy?"

"No, not crazy," I said. "You just said she needed to be stopped."

"But not by murder!" His voice was shrill.

"And definitely not by me. That was just dumb luck."

He charged toward the door, the pictures still clutched in his shaking hand. Just as he reached for the door handle, someone on the outside turned it. My dad!

Buck jumped back, looking shocked and trapped. I'd moved forward, effectively blocking his path back to my dad's bedroom, where he'd managed to break into the house, and to the kitchen, which was the only other way out. He couldn't go anywhere unless he barreled right past me, knocking me over in the process.

It wasn't my dad's voice I heard, but my brother's. He laughed and talked, and then a woman responded. I could almost see the wheels turning in Buck's head. If he made a run for it, there'd be a chase, and it would be three against one. The odds were not in his favor.

I called out to my brother. "Billy! We have a little situation in here."

He stopped short just as he came into view. "I thought you were at your baking class," he said, but then his attention shifted to Buck Masterson, who was standing in the center of the room, looking like a kid who'd gotten caught with his hand in the cookie jar. "Hello. What's this?" He sounded casual, but his body tensed, and I knew he'd gone on high alert.

"This," I said, "is Buck Masterson."

Billy's smile vanished, and he stood light on his feet, ready to break into a run if Buck took off. "Should I know that name, Ivy?"

"He broke into Dad's house —"

I stopped as I caught a glimpse of the woman Billy was with. Her black hair hung in curls around her face, and her cell phone was pressed to her ear. Deputy Sheriff Emmaline Davis. She wore civilian clothes — a flirty floral dress with coral flats. She looked beautiful, but at the moment, she did not look relaxed. *Of course not,* I thought. I'd interrupted their long overdue date.

She shot me a look that said, "What in the hell are you doing, Ivy?"

"I'm stopping him from stealing something that doesn't belong to him," I said, answering the question she didn't actually ask me.

Buck spun around, looked from Billy to Emmaline to me. The color had drained from his face, taking it from tomato to ghostly white. "It's just a misunderstanding."

"Oh yeah? How'd you get in?" Billy asked, folding his arms over his chest.

Buck glanced toward the bedroom.

"Well now. Let's try this again. If my sister didn't let you in the front door, did you break in?"

"It's a mistake —"

"It's a yes-or-no answer," Billy snapped. "Either you broke in or you didn't. Which is it?"

Buck's eyes bugged. He was busted, and there wasn't any way he could talk his way out of it. "Y-yes, but —" He flung his hand out, pointing at me. "It doesn't belong to her."

Emmaline stepped past Billy, her phone in her hand, her purse slung over her shoulder. She patted the air with her hands to calm him down. "What doesn't belong to Ivy?"

He crumpled the photographs in his hand.

Emmaline's gaze dropped to his fist. "What do you have there, Mr. Masterson?"

He tightened his fist. "Nothing."

Outside the front door, tires squealed and doors slammed. Two uniformed police officers rushed in, then stopped to take in the scene and confer with Emmaline. She directed one of them to the bedroom.

"Check the window," she ordered.

The officer returned a minute later with the report that the window had been jim-

332

mied from the outside.

Emmaline looked at Buck. "Breaking and entering? Mr. Masterson, you have the right to remain silent." She proceeded to read him his rights, and her officers took him into custody. "Bag the photographs," she told them. The officers gathered up all the photos and slipped them into a clear plastic bag. "Did he take anything else, Ivy?" she asked as the officers led Buck to their cruiser.

"That's it. That's what he was after."

"I don't think he's the one who killed your mother, Ivy. There's no motive. No connection."

I hung my head. What had any of this accomplished, other than payback for him making Mrs. Branford's life miserable? "I know, Em. I know."

CHAPTER TWENTY-SEVEN

Emmaline's words invaded my sleep. "I don't think he's the one who killed your mother, Ivy."

I felt as if I were an airplane circling the landing strip, but there was no chance of ever getting clearance to touch down. I might not have had an ounce of proof — yet — but I knew in my gut that my mom had been murdered. I had theories, sure, but in reality, I was no closer to figuring out why and by whom than I'd been a week ago. All I'd succeeded in doing was getting Buck arrested for breaking and entering. It was a minor win for Jackie Makers, but not for my mom. I ran through the possibilities in my head, along with the hows and the whys, jotting down my own notes in the back of my mom's journal.

Buck Masterson. He'd said he'd had nothing to do with any killing, and I believed him. I didn't think he was guilty of killing the two women, but could his wife, Nanette, be? Maybe she'd been so angry with Jackie over her vendetta against Buck that she'd taken matters into her own hands.

Jasmine Makers. She and Jackie had been at odds because of Jolie and the lies. Could she have felt so betrayed by her mother that she'd kill her?

Jolie Flemming. The daughter Jackie gave up could certainly have been hurt and angry enough to have killed her mother for revenge.

Gus Makers. He and Jackie had ended up divorced, according to Jasmine, at least in part because of the affair Jackie had had years and years ago, and the daughter she had had and had given up. Maybe he'd killed his ex-wife over her betrayal of him. In his eyes, their entire marriage might have been nothing but a giant lie.

Jolie's father, whoever that was. He'd been deprived of being a father for twentysomething years. Was that enough for him to kill Jackie over? Of course this theory hinged on some assumptions, namely, that Jolie's father had discovered that Jackie had had a child that she'd given up for adoption, and that he'd actually been upset that he'd not had the opportunity to be a father to her. An added complication was that, with Jackie gone, there was literally no way to know who the father was.

I breathed out a frustrated sigh. Any of these could have been a motive for killing Jackie; I had no way of knowing which was most likely or which was the truth. And none of these scenarios helped me figure out my own mother's connection.

Everything, I realized, came down to what my mom knew . . . and who she told. If I was operating under the notion that my mom's and Jackie's deaths were connected, then my mom was collateral damage. Which of the scenarios was bad enough that my mom was killed to keep her quiet?

I had one last thought. It was more of a Hail Mary than a fleshed-out concept, but I wrote it down, anyway. According to my mom's calendar, she'd been planning to meet with the owner of Divine Cuisine. Renee. Meeting with her was now on my list of things to do.

The more I thought of all of this, the more I knew I needed someone to bounce ideas off of. I considered whom I wanted to call to talk this all through with. Olaya? I was beginning to think of her as an aunt. I worried that I was using her to fill the void in my heart from my mom. I wanted to turn to her, to confide in her, to tell her every-

336

thing, but I also wanted to pull back, not to overstep, to be cautious.

Mrs. Branford? I wanted to *be* Penelope Branford when I was in my eighties. She was spritely, feisty, and still quick-witted. But I didn't want to burden her with all the different scenarios. I'd seen what Buck Masterson had done to her, and I didn't want to add to her load.

I considered waking up my dad or calling Billy. I even considered Miguel, but in the end I went with my oldest friend. We'd always told each other everything. Or at least we had . . . until she'd stopped.

"You and Billy," I blurted when she picked up.

Her voice was groggy. "It's two in the morning, Ivy."

"Sorry," I grumbled. "But Billy?"

"What do you mean, 'but Billy'? You've been wanting me and Billy to get together for years and years. We finally are."

"Together?" I squealed. "You're together?"

"We are." I could hear the smile in her voice.

I grinned. This *was* exactly what I wanted. What needed to happen. And I was so happy about it. "How?"

"It *is* the twenty-first century, as you have reminded me so often. I called him up and asked him out."

"That night at Baptista's when you left me there with Miguel, was it a case like you said or were you going to meet Billy?"

She hesitated for a split second and then admitted it. "Billy."

I slapped the bed. "I knew it!"

We broke into a fit of laughter. In the background, I heard the low rumble of a man's voice. Billy was there. My heart filled with warmth. Emmaline and Billy. Billy and Emmaline.

"Sorry to wake you," I said. "Can I run something by you? Real quick."

She gave me a sleepy okay and then listened while I told her all my theories. "You missed your calling," she said, not for the first time.

"You really think so?"

I could almost see her nodding. "Absolutely."

"If only I could figure out what actually happened."

"You will!" Billy shouted into the phone. And then his voice grew more somber. "You will, Ivy. But tomorrow. Go to bed."

After what felt like a million fitful hours, I finally fell asleep, but I woke up with a start sometime later. *Josephine Jeffries! Of course!*

Josephine was my mom's best friend and

taught social studies at Santa Sofia High School. Just like Emmaline and me, she and my mom had told each other everything. Why hadn't I thought about talking to her before? My mom might have kept her suspicions from my dad, not wanting to upset him, but from Josephine? Not likely.

I drifted back to sleep, relieved to have a plan for the morning.

CHAPTER TWENTY-EIGHT

Like clockwork, I awoke just before sunrise. I threw on a pair of black leggings, a Santa Sofia sweatshirt, brushed my teeth, and harnessed Agatha. Five minutes after I'd climbed out of bed, my sweet pug and I were in the fresh air and heading toward the beachfront. I stopped at the highest point of the small hill my parents' house was on, readied my camera, and captured the layered colors as the sun made its entrance for the day.

We made quick work of our walk; it was a school day, and I needed to get to Santa Sofia High School to meet Josephine before her first class. She'd always been Aunt Josie to me outside of school, and when we were within the walls of Santa Sofia High School, she'd been Mrs. Jeffries, but at some point she'd insisted I transition to her first name. Not an easy thing to do; even being around her made me feel as if I was back in high school and just sixteen years old.

I held my breath as I walked through the hallways of the school, a wave of nausea rolling through me. It was too familiar, but not because of my own years there. My unease was because of the connection to my mother. This had been her home away from home. Everywhere I turned, I remembered something about her. I could picture a bulletin board she'd created for the journalism club. I had a vision of the time we'd gone to the school musical and she'd brought a bouquet of roses for one of her students who'd had a supporting role. The girl had been overwhelmed. Her own family hadn't come to a single performance, but my mom had been there for her. I remembered the academic decathlon teams she'd led to victory.

Maybe it was a mistake to come here. It was too soon. I stopped, ready to turn around and high-tail it out of the there, but Josephine called my name from the doorway of her classroom. "Right here, Ivy."

I felt as if I'd been caught red-handed. Slowly, I turned back around. Josephine looked just like she had the last time I'd seen her. Her short auburn hair was streaked blond in the front, framing her face with soft waves. She had never looked like a stereotypical teacher. No slacks or clogs or vests for Josephine Jeffries. She had on skinny jeans, ankle boots, and a draped top that flattered her soft-around-the-edges body. She was a few years older than my mom had been, but even at sixty, Josephine looked hipper than many of her teenage students.

I met her gaze, and I felt as if an opera singer had just hit the highest soprano note and shattered every bit of glass in sight. I crumpled, my nose pricking with emotion, tears pooling in my eyes. I stumbled forward, and we fell into each other's arms. She wrapped me up, her hand on the back of my head, calming me with her touch.

"It's okay, baby," she said. "I know. It's okay."

I hadn't seen Josephine since my mom's funeral, and now I knew exactly why I'd been avoiding her. Just seeing her brought out every last shred of emotion I had so carefully packed away. I felt myself cracking, my grief just as real in this moment as it had been when I'd gotten the phone call from Billy, when I'd rushed back to Santa Sofia on the first flight out of Texas and seen my dad, when we'd buried my mom, the three of us each tossing white rose petals into her grave, tears streaming down our faces.

I pulled away and ran my fingers under my eyes to clear away my tears. "I'm sorry, Josephine. I'm not normally so . . . so . . ."

She held up a hand to stop me. "There's no normal anymore, sweetheart," she said. "It's fine."

She led me into her classroom. It was like the calm before the storm. Her handwriting scrawled across the whiteboard, posing questions about *The Sun Also Rises*. I realized I didn't know anything about Josephine's life since my mom died. She'd been the conduit to my previous life in Santa Sofia.

"You still teach tenth grade?"

"Still. Always. They'll have to take me out of here kicking and screaming."

"I don't know how you and Mom did it," I said. "Do it," I added, correcting myself.

She laughed. "Some people say it's a calling. Some people say it's craziness."

"And you? What do you say?"

She shrugged. "I guess it's a little of both." She checked her watch — a leather strap that wound around her wrist three times. "Class starts in a few minutes, Ivy. What did you want to talk about?"

I sat down at one of the student desks and

leaned my chin on my fisted hands. I had only a few minutes, so I launched into my tale, trying to keep my emotions at bay. "I think my mom was killed because she knew something," I summed up. The more I said it, the more normal it was sounding.

I couldn't remember ever seeing Josephine at a loss for words, but she certainly was now. She stared at me.

"She was killed, Josephine. *Purposely killed,*" I said, driving my point home.

Finally, she found her voice. "It was an accident, Ivy. She was in the wrong place at the wrong time."

"No. No! Josephine, I'm right about this. She knew something."

"She was a teacher, Ivy. What could she know?"

"That's what I wanted to ask you about. She and my dad were taking cooking classes at Well Done with Jackie Makers, the woman who was just killed. But she had an appointment with someone from Divine Cuisine."

"So?"

"So it doesn't make sense to me. She was happy with the classes at Well Done. You know Mom. Once she finds something she likes, that's it. I don't know if it was a secret, but she didn't tell my dad about it."

Josephine looked at me with her sympathetic brown eyes. "I think you're trying to find an explanation for what happened, Ivy, but there isn't one. It was a horrible accident."

My dad had said basically the same thing. Maybe they were right. Maybe I was reaching, but deep down I didn't think so. Focusing on discovering the truth kept my emotions at bay. I rallied, asking the questions I'd come to ask. "She never seemed strange to you in the days before she died?"

"Strange?"

"You know, distracted or preoccupied?"

Josephine shook her head. "Not really —" She stopped, her eyes clouding. "Well, there was this one thing."

I leaned forward. "What thing?"

"She was concerned about one of her students. She thought the girl was in trouble or something. Of course, that was nothing new. The concern, not the girl in trouble."

"In trouble how?"

Josephine cupped her hand over her forehead, thinking. Finally, she shook her head. "Something about an essay she wrote raised a red flag for your mom. She was afraid the girl might *do* something."

"What does that mean, *do* something?"

Josephine ran her index finger under the band of her watch. "I can't quite remember,

Ivy. It was a while ago."

I put my hand on hers. "Please, Josie."

She pressed her fingertips to her temples, nodding. "I remember when she mentioned it to me the first time. She stopped by my classroom after school one day with this essay in her hand." She closed her eyes, as if she were reliving the memory. "She's going to hurt someone."

"What? Who?"

"That's what she said. 'She's going to hurt someone.' "

I stared. "Like who? Who was she going to hurt? Who was the student?"

"I don't know."

"You didn't ask?"

Josephine shook her head. "I did, but then we started talking about something else, and she never said." She paused, then added, "That had to have been a few months before the accident, though, Ivy. You don't think —"

"I don't know. Maybe." I looked at her, wishing she felt what I did, wishing she was as convinced as I was that something about my mother's death wasn't right. "I think it might be. Related, I mean."

"I don't have the essay."

And just like that, a lightbulb when off above my head. The essay I'd found in

Jackie's kitchen. "Did my mom have a student . . . Jasmine Makers?" I asked.

Josephine nodded. "Yeah, of course. Jasmine graduated in May. Why? You think she might have been the student your mom was worried about?"

"Maybe," I said. But inside I was more convinced than I let on. It made sense. I didn't know how it might factor into my mom's death. Maybe it didn't. But it felt like progress, nonetheless.

I'd read the essay, and I hadn't gotten any red flags about the state of mind of the author, but then again, I wasn't a teacher with years of experience dealing with hormonal and emotional teenagers. I grabbed my cell phone and texted Olaya, asking her to bring the essay we'd found to Yeast of Eden. I wanted to have another look.

The first bell rang. The storm came as a group of students careened into the room.

"Thank you, Aunt Josie." I fell back on the name I'd grown up calling her. She wasn't related by blood, but she was as close to an aunt as I had, and suddenly I wanted to have that connection with her.

"I miss her, too, Ivy." She stood and began greeting her students. "This place isn't the same without her."

CHAPTER TWENTY-NINE

What I lacked in a plan, I oozed in determination. I left Santa Sofia High School and headed east to Divine Cuisine. I'd Googled and read about the car accident that had befallen Renee Ranson, the owner of Divine Cuisine. It had forced her to close shop, but now she was reopening her cooking school/catering business, and I hoped to find her there.

My mind was swirling with a million thoughts. Jackie Makers. The cooking schools. My mom's planner. The student she was worried about. The historic district and Buck Masterson. It felt like all the ingredients to a complex bread dough that I just had to mix together and let rest.

The whole Divine Cuisine lead could be a big, fat dead end, but I felt I needed to talk to Renee. If nothing else, it would help me understand what was going through my mom's mind before she died. I parked on the street in front of the building. It was in a warehouse area, so it didn't have the quaintness of so many businesses in Santa Sofia. Next to it was an embroidery and uniform shop, and on the other side was a cheerleading and tumbling studio.

The front door was unlocked. I let myself in and called out, "Hello? Ms. Ranson?"

I heard a noise to my right and turned as a woman in a wheelchair rolled out. She leaned forward, her hands on the wheels, propelling herself forward. She looked up at me. "We aren't open yet. Can I help you?"

"I hope so. My name is Ivy Culpepper."

She angled her head slightly. "Culpepper?"

"My mother was Anna Culpepper."

Her expression didn't change, but she said, "I remember. A car accident."

"Yes. At the high school."

She gestured to her wheelchair. "I know a little something about hit-and-runs."

"Is that what happened?"

She grimaced. "That's what happened. It was like some bad scene from a movie. One minute I was standing there, and the next I was flattened. I woke up without the use of my legs. This," she said with a sweeping gesture, "is my lovely future."

"I'm so sorry."

"Yeah, me, too." Bitterness spilled from every syllable.

I had the impression that she wanted to talk about it. People who were wronged often did, I'd realized over the years. I waited, giving her the space and permission to speak, and in another few seconds, she continued.

"I was unloading my catering van. Minding my own business. My shop — this shop — was doing great. A full calendar of catering gigs, cooking classes. I worked damn hard for this place, then *bam*!" She slapped her hands together. "Just like that, it was over. A car came out of nowhere. All I saw was a white blur, then nothing. It hit me head-on, and then it backed up and ran right over my legs as it backed away."

I tried to hide the shudder that rolled through my body. In the blink of an eye, her life had completely changed. In a similar flash, my mom's life had ended. It wasn't fair.

"Do you know who did it?" I asked, knowing full well that the driver had never been caught.

"Oh yes. I know exactly who it was."

A flare of excitement shot through me. "Really?"

She lowered her voice, as if she were

imparting some deep, dark secret. "The owner of Well Done. It's a cooking school and catering business in town. Her name is — well, was — Jackie Makers. She's the one who ran me over."

My mouth gaped, and I was speechless for a minute. "Are you sure?" I asked once I found my voice.

She hesitated. "Well, I didn't see her behind the wheel, but it was pretty obvious after a while. She came around to check on me at the hospital, trying to be a" — she made air quotation marks with her fingers — "Good Samaritan. Right. As if I couldn't see right through that. She was my competition, and suddenly I was out of the way. Her cooking school started to take off. Since I was out of commission, the catering jobs that had been on my schedule moved over to her. Guilt must have gotten the better of her. She wouldn't freaking leave me alone. *Always* bothering me, calling to see if I needed anything. Finally, I told her like it was. That if she couldn't rewind time and stop herself from mowing me down in my own parking lot, then leave me the hell alone."

I was flabbergasted, but I managed to ask another question. "And did she?"

"She had the gall to deny it. 'I didn't run

you over, Renee.' Yeah, right. And I have a million-dollar piece of swampland for sale."

"Did you tell the police?"

She pinched her nose and closed her eyes for a beat. "What do you think? Of course I did. But there was" — more air quotes — "no evidence. No witnesses. No reason for them to believe me." She tapped the tires of her wheelchair. "Put me in this thing for life, and she got off scot-free."

"Well, she did meet her own tragic death, so not scot-free." I couldn't believe that Jackie had been behind the hit-and-run. It wasn't at all what I'd expected, and it didn't help me figure out who, then, had killed *her*. Maybe one of Renee Ranson's family? Revenge for the accident that had stolen their wife and mother? And once again, it didn't help figure out what had happened to my mom.

The face Renee made indicated that she didn't seem to think Jackie's murder was enough payback for what had happened to her, but she said, "Whatever. I'm moving on. My business has reopened. My family and I are working round the clock to get back to where we were. My son is the new chef. My daughter is talented in the kitchen, too, but she's a numbers girl. She's doing the books. My husband is the driver and all-around muscle. I'm contracting some things out. Hiring temp workers for ser vice, getting bread from a local bakery, and keeping one full-time employee on staff for everything else. Dishwashing, loading, prep. And me, I'm the delegator. Because — ha! — that's all I can do. Raise my voice and yell at people."

Her bitterness was understandable, but it was wearing. I hoped she could come to terms with what had happened and let her anger go, otherwise it would eat her up, bit by bit by bit.

"They never caught who killed my mom, either," I said, turning the conversation back to the reason for my visit. "That's kind of why I'm here."

"Sit," she said, indicating a low stool at the stainless-steel counter.

The seat of the stool was shaped like a bike seat, only without the cushion. It was oddly comfortable.

"My mother came to see you the week before she died."

She nodded, and from her expression, I knew that she remembered my mom. "That's right. She thought she might know something about my accident, but she wasn't sure. She'd wanted to ask me a few questions."

My heart thrummed. Finally, I might get some answers. "You mean about Jackie?"

Renee tucked a mass of hair behind her ears. Her cheeks were flushed, small red splotches marking the angles of her face. "No. I told her what I thought, but she wouldn't say if that's what she *knew.* Said she couldn't, in good conscience, until she was certain. Those were her words exactly."

That sounded just like my mom. "Err on the side of caution," she'd always said. She would never throw someone under the proverbial bus if she wasn't 100 percent positive about the situation. Still, I was disappointed not to get some nugget that might help.

"When I heard she'd died, I thought, *That's it. There goes my last chance at finding out the truth.*"

"So you thought she really did know something?"

Renee tapped her fingers absently on her wheels. "Hard to know. I thought maybe she'd somehow pony up the evidence against Jackie Makers that I needed."

"What did she ask you?"

"Same as the police. Did I see the driver? Description of the car. License plate. Anything else I remembered. It all happened too fast. I've racked my brain. I've gone to therapy. Hell, I even tried hypnosis. I never saw it coming."

"Can I ask you one more thing?"

"Ask me anything. Like I said, if it might lead to proof, then I'm there. I don't care that the woman already died. I want her crucified for what she did to me."

"Do you think it was intentional?"

"I've asked myself that over and over. I'm basically a good person. I don't have enemies. I haven't done anything to warrant . . . this. But how could it *not* be? Isn't it too much of a coincidence that my one competitor in town is the person who ran me over?"

Allegedly ran you over, I thought. She was ready to convict without a shred of proof, but I wasn't so sure. I couldn't say why, but I felt there was something missing from the story. If Renee Ranson was right and Jackie had run her over, how did my mom know? What did any of it have to do with her? And why would my mom even get involved? Then again, she did go see Jackie, and shortly after that, she was run over. Coincidence?

I couldn't think of anything else to ask, so I stood, ready to leave. Renee stopped me.

"You know . . ."

I sat back down. "Yes?"

"About a month ago I got a strange

e-mail. It had a list of people and e-mail addresses. Some of them were city e-mail addresses, a few were school district, and there were others that were just Gmail or Yahoo or whatnot. Your mom was on there."

I let this information sink in. A list of random e-mails, including my mom's. "You don't know who sent it?"

"No idea. I responded, but it bounced, saying the e-mail was not valid."

"Did you share this with the authorities?"

"Not at all. Until this moment, I didn't think there was a connection to anything, but now I'm wondering."

"There was no message?"

"Nothing. Just the list."

"Could Jackie have sent it? A list of clients for you to — I don't know — add to your mailing list?"

"More retribution." She nodded circumspectly. "Could be."

"Thank you for talking to me," I said.

"Ivy, right?"

I nodded.

"The not knowing is hard. It's always in the back of my mind. Why me? I'm sure you feel the same about your mother. I hope you find what you're looking for."

So did I.

CHAPTER THIRTY

Next stop, Yeast of Eden. I barreled in, anxious to reread the essay Olaya and I had found among Jackie's cookbooks and piles of papers, the one I thought was written by Jasmine Makers.

Olaya greeted me with a smile, her eyes crinkling at the corners. She took one look at my face, reached under the counter for the single paper, and said, "It's right here."

"Thank you!" I took it and sat at a little bistro table, not even taking the time to ask for a luscious popover or croissant. My mother and Jackie were both dead, and nothing I did was going to change that, but discovering the truth felt urgent, nonetheless.

I read the essay through once, then again, more slowly, looking for any clues or evidence that the content might relate to Renee Ranson and what happened to her. If I worked under the assumption that this was, in fact, the essay my mom had taken to share with Josephine Jeffries, and then later with Jackie Makers, then it also made sense that it was also this essay that had led her to Renee Ranson.

But if it was, I couldn't find the obvious clues. There were parts that said things like *I've always been hotheaded. I'm like my dad in that way. I react first, think later. It may be my greatest fault.* And *Sometimes my actions have horrible consequences. It's like that butterfly effect. Something happens here, and then way down the line, somewhere else, something happens that you could never have predicted.*

The prompt had been about a lesson taught. I skipped to the last paragraph of the essay and stopped cold. *I meant to teach a lesson, but really all I did was hurt everyone. Collateral damage. If I could take it back, I would. If only I could.*

This had to have been what alerted my mom. I went back to my assumption that Jasmine Makers had written the essay, and worked through a hypothesis. I tried to think like my mom would have. She had read it and got concerned that her student had done something, so she'd gone to Josephine first. There was no name on the essay, though, so my mom had been piecing things together, maybe through the process of elimination. If she'd scored all the other essays in the class and made her typical photocopies, she would have known which student the essay with no name belonged to. Assuming it was Jasmine's, she would have met with her first to talk about it. If that hadn't gone well, she would have met with Jasmine's mother. She'd been taking the cooking classes, so she already had a relationship of sorts with Jackie. Knowing my mom, she wouldn't have wanted to talk to Jackie at Well Done, with other people around. It was a private matter. So she'd gone over to Maple Street, expressed her concern about Jasmine, and given Jackie the essay.

Then what? It seemed logical that Jasmine had reacted to the news of a half sister, but what then? What had she done? I racked my brain, trying to piece things together.

Before I could make sense of anything, my cell phone rang.

"Hi, Mrs. Branford," I answered after I saw her name pop up on the screen.

"Interesting things going on over here on Maple Street, my dear," she said, skipping the greeting. "As always."

"Like what?"

"Jasmine is holed up in her mother's

house, and Nanette and Buck Masterson are pounding on the door there."

I thought of my mother's English lessons, her teaching about rising action and resolution and, most of all, turning points. This was it. It was all coming together. I could feel it. The climax of the story! Without a second thought, I grabbed my stuff, waved to Olaya, and raced to my car.

"I'm on my way," I said to Mrs. Branford before I ended the call.

I made it to Maple Street in record time and parked down the street, a few houses from Jackie Makers's Tudor. I was afraid whatever was going on would be resolved by the time I arrived, but I needn't have worried. The Mastersons were right where Penny Branford had said they were, standing on the front porch, arms folded, sour expressions on their faces. Mrs. Branford waved at me from her front porch. I quickly crossed the street to meet her.

"How long has the standoff been going on?"

She frowned, the lines of her face deepening the farther her lips were pulled down. "At least thirty minutes. Maybe a smidgen more."

"What do they want with Jasmine?"

"I wish I knew, dear."

I was done being subtle. I knew Jasmine had something to with this entire situation. Whatever Nanette and Buck Masterson's game was didn't concern me. I had bigger fish to fry. I slung my purse over my shoulder and marched across the street, determination coursing through me.

"Out on bail?" I asked Buck, shouldering between the two of them and raising my fist to the door.

"What the —" Buck tried to edge in front of me, but I blocked him.

"Jasmine? It's Ivy Culpepper."

I didn't really expect her to open the door to me, but that was what she did. It was just a crack, and suddenly an arm shot out, grabbed my wrist, and pulled me in. I felt like Alice slipping through the looking glass. From behind me, Buck and Nanette tried to push their way in, but I was barely through the door when Jasmine slammed it shut and turned the dead bolt.

"What do they want?" I asked, practically out of breath, but feeling kind of tough.

She threw up her hands. "Hell if I know. They did this to my mom, too. Harassed her until she could hardly take it anymore."

The pounding started on the door again, so she dragged me away from the entryway and into the kitchen.

"What did they do to your mom?"

She opened her mouth, ready to say something, but then she seemed to think better of it and closed her lips tight. The pounding started again, but this time it came from the other side of the house. "God, what is wrong with them?" Jasmine cursed under her breath. "Leave me alone!" she yelled.

"We just need to talk, Jasmine. Come on. Let us in!" Buck yelled and their pounding grew stronger and more persistent.

Jasmine's nostrils flared, and she yanked at the short strands of her black hair. Finally, she marched to a door off the kitchen, flung it open, and disappeared into the darkness. A few seconds later, there was a clicking sound, and then I heard the automatic garage door kick into gear. The chain rattled, and I wondered if the whole thing might collapse, but it managed to open all the way. A triangle of light came in through the slightly ajar door. I opened it a little more to spy on Jasmine and the Mastersons.

They were behind the white Toyota Camry parked in the garage, but I could see the top of Jasmine's head, Nanette Masterson's brightly dyed red hair, and Buck Masterson's stringy hair. Buck was wagging his finger at Jasmine, while Nanette nodded vehemently. Jasmine shook her head just as intensely, saying something I couldn't hear.

It was all extremely suspicious, but I had no idea what it was about. I edged into the garage and stood next to the hood of the car. I crouched down slightly. I didn't want to broadcast my presence for fear they'd stop their heated argument. My hand rested in a small dent on the cool metal of the car. I craned my neck to listen, but before I could hear anything, Jasmine threw up her hands, turned around, and stormed back into the house.

Buck Masterson looked at me with his dark, beady eyes but made no move to actually set foot inside the garage. Instead, I left the safety of the car and walked out of the garage.

"What was that about?" I asked, cutting to the chase.

His lips twisted in a muted sneer. "God Almighty, she's stubborn, just like her mother was."

Nanette scoffed. "That's not the word I'd use."

I swung my attention to her. "What word *would* you use?"

"I could name several. *Vindictive. Vengeful. Vile.*" She had a corner on words beginning with the letter *V.*

"Jackie? She seemed nice enough to me," I said.

"You didn't know her like we did," Nanette said.

I didn't know her at all, I thought, but I didn't say so.

Buck blew an exasperated raspberry. "She didn't have anything against *you.* She wanted to destroy me."

"Right. With the letters and pictures," I said, more snarkily than I'd planned, but he deserved it.

"Us," Nanette corrected again. "We could have destroyed her, you know. If she hadn't died, we'd have crushed her." The anger oozing from Nanette was palpable.

"Crushed her?"

"Destroyed. Ruined. Ended."

"Why was there such bad blood between you?"

"Some people think they're so much better than you."

"Why did Jackie think that?"

"Because she was messed up in the head," Buck snarled. "Let he who is without sin cast the first stone. Right? She thought . . . Well, I don't know what she thought, but let me tell you, she wasn't an innocent."

"But what did she *do*?"

Buck flapped his hand and turned on his heel. "I'm done. Ask Jasmine, why don't you?"

I looked over my shoulder, back toward the door to the kitchen. "I will —" I started to say, but as I turned back around, I stopped. All I could see were the backs of Buck and Nanette Masterson as they walked down the driveway and turned onto the sidewalk.

Back inside the house, I searched everywhere, but Jasmine was gone. The Mastersons must have completely spooked her with their accusations about her mother. I didn't know Jackie Makers, but I had gotten to know Olaya Solis over the past few weeks, and I found it hard to believe she could so dramatically misjudge a person. Mrs. Branford had thought Jackie was a good person, too.

If I trusted my gut, which I did, then something wasn't adding up. Renee Ranson and the Mastersons had to be missing something.

But what was it?

I hated leaving the house unlocked, but I had no choice. I turned the dead bolt on the front door and then went out the back. It was my first good look at the backyard. Whatever her faults might have been, Jackie

Makers had had a knack for landscaping. Or she'd paid someone well. There was a flagstone patio right off the kitchen. A redwood trellis climbing with bright fuchsia bougainvillea shaded the area. A stone path crossed a small grassy area and led to raised flower beds and a small greenhouse tucked in a back corner. The blooming flowers created a kaleidoscope of color everywhere I looked.

"Beautiful," I murmured, taking a moment to look around. The beds were free flowing and looked like those in an English cottage garden. I was no expert, but I recognized lavender, sage, phlox, and purple coneflowers. Butterflies fluttered about and rested on the blooms.

My cell phone rang. I grabbed for it, the sound loud and intrusive in the peacefulness of the garden.

"Hey, Ivy." It was Emmaline. "We know the cause of death for Jackie Makers."

"You said it was poison." They'd suspected that almost from the beginning.

"I mean specifically. It's called ricin. Administered through cupcakes she had in her kitchen."

I remembered the pink bakery box, but there hadn't been an identifying sticker on the box or a business noted on it.

"It's odorless and tasteless, and it can be concocted at home, in any ordinary kitchen, from castor beans."

My throat turned dry. "So someone really planned this."

"Looks like it. It affects the immune system and can take days before it actually kills, but it will. The cupcakes in Jackie's kitchen were infused with ricin."

I went cold. "So she ate a cupcake, and it was just coincidence that she died at Yeast of Eden?" I asked, half to myself.

"Looks that way," Emmaline said before we ended the call.

The peacefulness of the yard suddenly felt stifling. Reluctantly, I veered to the right, followed the flagstone pavers to the side gate, and let myself out. I went across the street to Mrs. Branford's house, filled Mrs. Branford in on what Emmaline had told me, then drove back home to walk Agatha and shower.

And to process.

I was at a standstill. In my gut, I didn't believe Jackie Makers could have run over Renee Ranson or my mom, because that didn't answer the question of who had killed Jackie herself. But if it wasn't her, then who had?

Before I knew it, it was time to head back

to Yeast of Eden. As I walked into the lobby, I noticed the fresh glass vases and sprigs of fresh flowers on the bistro tables; the fiesta Mexican garlands draped in the windows, each intricate, lacy rectangle in a different primary color; the sparkling floor; and the crystal clear display cases filled with the scattered crumbs of the day's bread. I breathed in and instantly relaxed. This was like home away from home. I'd come to love the bread shop.

I walked through the front and into the *cocina*. Everyone else was already there. Everyone except Nanette, that is. I wasn't surprised. I couldn't imagine her showing up after the combative confrontation at Jackie's house.

I waved to Mrs. Branford.

"Long time, no see, my dear," she said, her snowy hair perfect, as usual, her lips rimmed with a bright pink lipstick. On anyone else, that color would have been too much; on Penelope Branford, with her fuchsia velour sweat suit and bright white sneakers, the lipstick was perfect.

The chalkboard had today's baking plan: Gruyère and black pepper popovers. I'd never actually had a popover, but if the illustration, with its muffin-shaped base and the billowy, full top, looked anything like it would taste, I knew it would become a favorite.

"You don't usually make popovers for the bread shop, do you?" I asked Olaya as I tied on my ruffled apron.

"Popovers are a quick delight but are best when they are served warm. So no, I do not carry them normally. Cold popovers, not so good."

"Terrible, in fact," Consuelo commented.

We got right to work, mixing the eggs and milk, then whisking in the flour mixture in three separate stages. Olaya had given us each a popover pan.

"It is special for popovers," she said, pointing to the six individual nonstick popover cups. "The air can circulate around each cup, forcing the batter up, up, up until it pops over the top of the pan. Now, the trick is to fill to nearly the top. None of this 'fill it halfway' stuff."

She demonstrated at her own station, filling each of her six prepared cups to within a quarter inch of the top with the heavily peppered, thin batter. "Take the cubes of Gruyère and plop them in the center." She fanned her hand across her pan like a game show host. "That is all. Now we bake."

While the popovers were in the high-heat oven, we washed our dirtied dishes. The women chattered on about life after college, baking successes and failures, and the spring weather at the beach.

"Tourists are coming," Consuelo said. "We get more and more each year. Does nobody stay home anymore?"

"I need the tourists," Olaya said. "They make my business."

After a few minutes, the conversation turned to Jackie Makers. "The police, they have found nothing about Jackie's murder?" Martina asked her sister.

Olaya shook her head. "Not that I know of."

I looked at the three sisters, and my thoughts turned to my first conversation with Emmaline after Jackie's death. She'd said they were all suspects. They all knew how to cook and could have easily given Jackie a box of ricin-infused cupcakes. I dismissed the idea the very next second. The truth was, I was no closer to knowing the truth and anyone could have killed both Jackie and my mom.

The bell in the lobby tinkled, and Olaya disappeared for a moment, then returned a moment later. "Ladies, you must excuse me for a few minutes. I have business to discuss." She turned and waited as a young man pushed a wheelchair into the kitchen. In the wheelchair was Renee Ranson.

CHAPTER THIRTY-ONE

Several things happened all at once.

Olaya introduced Renee as the owner of Divine Cuisine. "I'll be providing bread for Divine Cuisine's catering jobs," she said.

As I thought about what a small world it was and how strange it was that only this morning I'd met with Renee Ranson and heard about her theory that Jackie was behind her injuries, I saw Renee's face contort. She was staring at the women in our Yeast of Eden baking class, an inexplicable expression on her face.

"Becky?" she said.

At the same moment, the young man behind the wheelchair said, "Becks! What are you doing here?"

Becky . . . Ranson? The talented daughter who was good with numbers?

I whipped my head around to see Sally and Jolie both staring at Becky, who'd gone completely pale.

"I'm, um, taking a baking class."

"Why?" the young man asked. "You don't need a class."

"Tía Olaya!" The back door to the kitchen slammed open, and Jasmine burst in. She dropped her purse, so her eyes were on the floor in front of her. When she looked up, she froze, staring at the group of people in the kitchen. Slowly, she scanned the faces, growing paler and paler with each passing second.

Becky stared at Jasmine, made a choking sound, and took a step backward. She looked as if she'd been caught with her hand in the cookie jar, which I didn't understand. Her mom ran a catering business, not a bakery. There was no conflict here, so I couldn't understand her reaction.

Until suddenly I did.

The images around me became fixed in my mind like a tableau. My brain processed everything I knew at lightning speed. My mom, the teacher, the essay she'd found and then presumably given to Jackie. The one written by Jasmine. I thought about what Renee Ranson had told me just this morning. Jackie had been the one to hit her with her car. She'd been filled with guilt, showing up at the hospital, asking after Renee's well-being, wanting to make amends. But it wasn't because *she'd* been the one to hit her.

Renee had said she'd seen a blur of white. My mind went to the white car housed in Jackie's garage. The one with the dent in front. The one Olaya had told me belonged to Jasmine. The hit-and-run vehicle.

Jasmine had hit Renee Ranson. That had to be why Jackie had felt guilty and why she'd tried to help Renee. She'd been protecting her daughter, but also trying to make things right . . . in her own way.

Had the Mastersons figured it out?

When I looked at Jasmine now, I knew I was right. Her face seemed to crumple into complete guilt and misery when she looked at Renee Ranson. All at once, my body went cold. My mom had figured it out, and she'd died because of it.

I surged forward toward the girl. "You." Needles pricked under my skin. "You did this?" I pointed to Renee, but then I wheeled back around and put my hand over my mouth, trying to hold in the bubbling emotions. "You killed my mom?"

Jasmine reached for the wall, trying to grab hold and keep herself upright, but she couldn't. She slid down, fell onto her knees. Her sobs were painful and tortured, like a wounded animal's. "I couldn't . . . I didn't know. . . ." She moaned. "I'm sorry."

"You're sorry?" I felt my face turn hot, imagined the rage climbing from my broken heart to my brain. Somewhere in the back recesses of my mind, I heard Olaya's voice, but I couldn't make out what she was saying. I heard the word *now. Now. Now. Now.* Over and over again, it echoed in my mind. "You killed my mother, and you're sorry?"

In my peripheral vision, I saw Jolie move toward me. Felt her arm slip around my shoulder. "Shhh." She tried to soothe me, but it was too late for that. I shrugged free.

"Why? Why would you kill her? She wanted to help you!"

Jasmine's howls had reduced her to a puddle on the floor. If I hadn't been so hurt, so stunned, so overwhelmed by my grief, I might have felt sorry for the wreck she'd become. But I didn't. Anger bubbled inside of me like a volcano on the verge of erupting.

"I'm sorry," she said again, but this time it was directed to Renee Ranson. Becky gasped, stumbling back against her baking station. "I didn't mean to. I — I was so . . . my mom had —" She looked at Jolie, and I knew what she was trying to say.

I spoke for her. "You found out about Jolie —"

She nodded.

"What does that have to do with me?" Renee's voice held its own degree of confusion. Of shock.

"I . . . nothing," Jasmine managed to say. "I was so mad. I wanted her to pay, so I was going to *help* you. It was a mistake. It was an accident. Please believe me. I never meant to hurt you."

Renee let out a cruel laugh. "Help me? You ruined my life."

Jasmine broke down again, half nodding, half shaking her head. "I —" She sobbed. "Know."

Renee wasn't about to let Jasmine sink into her own self-preserving grief. "And Anna Culpepper, she figured it out, so you mowed her down just like you did me? Figured it worked once, might work again, right?"

Jasmine dipped her chin in a fractured nod. "I wasn't thinking."

Olaya had moved next to me, pale and stunned. "And Jackie? Did you kill your mother, too?"

"No." We all turned to see Mrs. Branford with her cane outstretched like a weapon. "She didn't kill her mother. This one did."

Becky, with her brown hair falling around her pale face, her eyes wide and scared, tried to shrink back. She turned and clutched the stainless-steel counter. Her gaze found her mother. "You said it was Jackie Makers," she said, pointing at Renee. "Every day you said how she ruined your life. How she'd done this to you."

Renee let out a leaden cry. "You . . . ?"

Jolie, Sally, and the Solis sisters stood dumbstruck. I felt my legs go rubbery. I couldn't keep myself upright. Couldn't make sense of what was happening. What had happened. How Jackie's indiscretion so many years ago had ended up impacting so many lives. As Jasmine had said in her essay, it was the butterfly effect.

My gaze found Jasmine again, and rage filled me. "You took my mother." Tears streamed down my face. "You did this."

I somehow stiffened my body and tried to move forward. I didn't know what I was going to do, but I wanted to touch her, to hurt her, to make her pay. But just as I started to propel myself forward, out of my mind, an arm snaked around my shoulder, stronger this time, holding me back.

"Ivy, it won't change anything." Miguel's voice in my ear was like a lifeline. My body trembled with six months of grief, but he held on to me, grounding me, holding me back. "I'm here, Ivy. I'm not letting you go," he said.

"But she killed —"

"It won't change anything," he said again, and in that instant, I knew he was right. My mother was gone. And nothing I did could bring her back. Like I'd wished for Renee, I had to let go of my anger and move forward. I had to accept what had happened and make the choice to live my life.

Suddenly Emmaline was flanking me on the other side. She directed her officers to detain both Jasmine and Becky. Mrs. Branford finally lowered her cane, her arm shaking with the effort of having held it up for so long.

"You figured out the truth," Em whispered, squeezing my hand. "Like I said, you missed your calling, Ivy."

I managed a small smile through my tears. I had figured out the truth. It was the only thing I could hang on to at the moment, but it was enough.

CHAPTER THIRTY-TWO

Two months later, I parked my mother's pearl-white Fiat on Maple Street. "It belongs to you," my dad had said, handing me the keys, a few days ago. "She would have wanted that. And so do I."

Now Agatha and I stood in front of 615 Maple Street, the brick Tudor I'd fallen in love with the first moment I'd laid eyes on it. The house I'd just bought. Every detail was emblazoned in my mind, from the tall pine tree to the right of the front door, to the dark brick facade, to the steeply gabled green roof and the tall chimney.

Penny Branford swung her cane as she walked across the street, spritely as ever. "Hello, neighbors!"

Her snowy curls looked freshly done, and her Nike sneakers were brand new. This pair was sparkling white. *To match her hair,* I thought with a grin. Today she wore a coral velour sweat suit. I hoped I could be half the woman she was when I was eighty-five, with a fraction of the energy. She was a force to be reckoned with, and I was proud to call her my friend.

I stooped to give her a hug. "Can you believe it?"

We stood side by side in front of Jackie Makers's former home.

"Actually, I can. You were meant for this street. For this house," Mrs. Branford said.

"Meant for? I don't know about that. I definitely love the house, though."

"Meant for, most definitely. I believe in fate, Ivy Culpepper. Your mother's death brought you back to Santa Sofia. It was a tragedy, to be sure, but it also brought you to me, and to Olaya," she said, adding the last part a little reluctantly. "And that is our good fortune. This is where you're supposed to be. Of that, I'm sure."

When I thought about everything that had happened, I still couldn't believe that I'd been the one to realize that my mother had unwittingly wandered into a situation that had cost her her life. I missed her so much, I could almost taste the sorrow, but knowing why she died and bringing her killer to justice went a long way toward making me feel like I'd let her rest in peace. She was still with me, and always would be, and like my mother, I knew I'd always try to do my best to help the people around me.

Mrs. Branford linked her arm with mine and tugged me forward. "Ready?"

I smiled. "Ready." We walked up the front pathway to the porch. A little table, the top a mosaic made from broken glass and tiles, sat in one corner. On it was the beautiful Galileo thermometer from the glass shop on the pier. The blue glass bubble inside was at the top, and the yellow-filled one hovered slightly below it. A little note was tucked under the base. I slipped it out and smiled.

There's a bottomless bowl of queso for you at Baptista's. But stay balanced, like Galileo. Eat your veggies, too.

Miguel

The front door opened. Olaya Solis stood there, a tray of *pan dulce* in her hands. "*Bienvenida,* Ivy. Welcome home."

GRUYÈRE AND BLACK PEPPER POPOVERS

This recipe was inspired by Jodi Elliott, a former co-owner and chef of Foreign & Domestic Food and Drink and the owner of Bribery Bakery, both in Austin, Texas.

Butter for greasing the popover pans or muffin tins
2 cups whole milk
4 large eggs
1 1/2 teaspoons salt
1/2 teaspoon freshly ground black pepper
2 cups all-purpose flour
Nonstick cooking spray
3/4 cup Gruyère cheese (5 ounces), cut into small cubes, plus grated Gruyère cheese for garnishing (optional)

1. Place the oven rack in the bottom third of the oven and preheat the oven to 450°F.
2. Prepare the popover pans or muffin

tins (with enough wells to make 16 popovers) by placing a dot of butter in the bottom of each of the 16 wells. Heat the pans or tins in the oven while you make the popover batter.

3. Warm the milk in a small saucepan over medium heat. It should be hot, but do not bring it to a boil. Remove from the heat.

4. In a large bowl, whisk the eggs with the salt and black pepper until smooth. Stir in the reserved warm milk.

5. Add the flour to the egg mixture and combine. The batter should have the consistency of cream. A few lumps are okay!

6. Remove the popover pans or muffin tins from the oven. Spray the 16 wells generously with nonstick cooking spray. Pour about 1/3 cup of the batter into each well. Place several cubes of cheese on top of the batter in each well.

7. Reduce the oven temperature to 350°F. Bake the popovers until the tops puff up and are golden brown, about 40 minutes. Remember not to open the oven door while bak-

ing. You don't want the popovers to collapse!

8. Remove the popovers from the oven and turn them onto a wire cooling rack right away to preserve their crispy edges. Using a sharp knife, pierce the base of each popover to release the steam. Sprinkle grated Gruyère over the finished popovers, if desired, and serve immediately.

Makes 16 popovers

CONCHAS

CONCHAS DOUGH
3 teaspoons active dry yeast
1/2 cup warm water
1/2 cup lukewarm milk
1/3 cup granulated sugar
1/3 cup unsalted butter, softened
1 egg
1 teaspoon salt
3 1/2–4 cups all-purpose flour
Nonstick cooking spray for greasing the cookie sheet

CINNAMON AND VANILLA TOPPING
1/3 cup granulated sugar
1/4 cup salted butter
1/2 cup all-purpose flour
1 1/2 teaspoons ground cinnamon
1/2 teaspoon vanilla extract

1. Prepare the *conchas* dough by dissolving the yeast in the warm water

in a large bowl. Add the milk, sugar, butter, egg, and salt. Next, stir in 2 cups of the flour and mix until smooth. Add more flour, a little at a time, until the dough is easy to handle and forms a ball.

2. Turn the dough out onto a lightly floured surface and knead it until it is smooth and elastic, about 5 minutes.

3. Place the dough in a large greased bowl, and then turn it so that it is greased side up. Cover the bowl, place it in a warm place, and let the dough rise until it has doubled in size, about 1 1/2 hours. You'll know the dough is ready if an indentation remains after you press on it.

4. While the *conchas* dough is rising, prepare the topping. Beat together the sugar and butter in a medium bowl until light and fluffy. Stir in the flour and mix until a dough with the consistency of a thick paste forms.

5. Divide the topping dough into 2 equal portions. Mix the cinnamon into the first portion and the vanilla extract into the second portion. Divide each portion of topping

dough into 6 equal pieces, and then pat each piece into a 3-inch circle. Set the circles aside.

6. Next, grease a cookie sheet with nonstick cooking spray. Punch the *conchas* dough down and divide it into 12 equal pieces. Shape the pieces into balls and place the balls on the prepared cookie sheet.

7. Place 1 topping circle on each ball of *conchas* dough. Shape the circle so that it fits over the ball. Make about 5 cuts across each topping circle to create a shell pattern.

8. Cover the dough balls and let them rise until doubled, about 40 minutes. When 15 minutes of rising remain, preheat the oven to 375°F.

9. Bake the *conchas* for 20 minutes, or until lightly browned.

Makes 12 *conchas*

ABOUT THE AUTHOR

The indefatigable **Winnie Archer** is a middle school teacher by day and a writer by night. Born in a beach town in California, she now lives in an inspiring century-old house in North Texas and loves being surrounded by real-life history. She fantasizes about spending summers writing in quaint, cozy locales, has a love/hate relationship with both yoga and chocolate, adores pumpkin spice lattes, is devoted to her five kids and husband, and can't believe she's lucky enough to be living the life of her dreams. Visit her online at WinnieArcher .com.

The employees of Thorndike Press hope you have enjoyed this Large Print book. All our Thorndike, Wheeler, and Kennebec Large Print titles are designed for easy reading, and all our books are made to last. Other Thorndike Press Large Print books are available at your library, through selected bookstores, or directly from us.

For information about titles, please call:
(800) 223-1244

or visit our website at:
gale.com/thorndike

To share your comments, please write:
Publisher
Thorndike Press
10 Water St., Suite 310
Waterville, ME 04901